Abortion, Society, and the Law

ABORTION, SOCIETY, AND THE LAW

EDITED BY
DAVID F. WALBERT
&
J. DOUGLAS BUTLER

THE PRESS OF
CASE WESTERN RESERVE UNIVERSITY
CLEVELAND & LONDON
1973

Library of Congress Cataloging in Publication Data
Walbert, David F.   comp.
    Abortion, society, and the law.
    Includes bibliographical references.
    CONTENTS: George, B. J. The evolving law of abortion. —
Guttmacher, A. F. The genesis of liberalized abortion in New York:
a personal insight. — Callahan, D. Abortion: some ethical issues.
[etc.]
    1. Abortion — United States — Addresses, essays, lectures. I.
Butler, John Douglas, 1942-   joint comp. II. Title. [DNLM:
1. Abortion, Induced. 2. Ethics, Medical. 3. Forensic medicine. 4.
Religion and medicine. HQ 767 W151a 1973]
HQ767.5.U5W34   301   72-12288
ISBN 0-8295-0250-5

Contents

FOREWORD

ROBERT E. HALL, M. D.

IN 1966, THE EDITORS OF THE *Western Reserve Law Review* commissioned a series of essays on the subject of abortion. These essays first appeared in a special issue of the *Law Review* (Volume 17, No. 2) and were subsequently published by the Press of Case Western Reserve University under the title *Abortion and the Law* (1967). This volume constituted the first major legal review of the abortion subject.

The editors of the *Case Western Reserve Law Review* for 1971-72 invited contributors to submit essays for publication in another special issue of the *Law Review* (Volume 23, No. 4). The six *Law Review* essays are supplemented in this volume by others, two of which initially appeared in *Abortion and the Law*. The *Case Western Reserve Law Review* deserves great credit for its initiative in making the original report and for its perception of the need for bringing the book up to date. Much has happened in the field of abortion during the past five years. I would like to sketch this progress and outline the present status of abortion in this country.

It was in 1967, the year in which *Abortion and the Law* was published, that the first three new abortion laws were enacted.[1] Colorado led the way with a statute permitting abortions for protecting the mental and physical health of the mother and preventing risk of fetal deformity, and in cases of rape and incest, as recommended by the American Law Institute (ALI) in 1959. This law set no time limit in pregnancy, required review by a three-man committee, and did not stipulate that the applicant must live in the state. North Carolina was next to pass an ALI law, which also set no pregnancy time limit and required approval by three consultants; it included a 4-month residency requirement. Then came a California law, with a 20-week time limit, a requirement for two- and three-man committees before and after the 12th week respectively, and exclusion of the fetal-deformity part of the ALI proposal.

There is obviously considerable variation among these three reform laws. Regrettably, the same lack of uniformity exists among the 9 other ALI laws enacted later — 2 in 1968, 5 in 1969, and 2 in 1970 — as well as the 4 repeal laws passed in 1970. All 16 require that abortions be performed only by physicians, but here the similarity stops. Only 12 limit the site of performing abortions to hospitals. Ten permit abortions for the reasons outlined by the ALI, California excluding fetal deformity and Oregon allowing consideration of "the mother's total environment, actual or reasonably foreseeable." Four limit abortions to the stage of fetal viability or the first 20 weeks of pregnancy (which are virtually synonymous), one to 150 days, one to 4 lunar months, one to 24 weeks, and one to 26 weeks; 8 states place no time limit on abortion, and 4 permit abortions after their time limit for the preservation of maternal life. All 12 of the reform laws require approval of the abortion by other physicians, ranging from one consultant or an undefined "review authority" to three consultants and three-member boards. Seven of the 12 reform laws and 3 of the 4 repeal laws establish residency requirements.

Numerous other variations exist, in both the laws themselves and their implementation by the medical profession. Some of these differences have no significant effect, but others do. In California, for example, the law was at first interpreted much more liberally in San Francisco than in Los Angeles. In New York, although the law was regulated more stringently by the New York City Board of Health than by the State Board of Health, most of the state's abortions are still performed in the city. In Washington, D.C., an unreformed law was declared constitutional but at the same time interpreted so broadly by the United States Supreme Court that the abortion rate there is now one of the highest in the nation. Some areas with unreformed and unchallenged abortion laws have continued to limit the performance of abortions to those permitted by a strict interpretation of the law; others have recognized the conflict between social and legislative progress by interpreting their old laws more liberally. And some of the states with newly changed laws have failed to translate de jure reform into de facto practice.

The actual need for abortions in this country probably amounts to about 20 percent of the pregnancies. Because of local inconsistencies, this ratio has actually been achieved in five areas: the District of Columbia, under an old law, California and Oregon under reform laws, and New York and Hawaii under repeal laws. Rates approaching 20 percent are found in Alaska, Kansas, Maryland, New Mexico, and Washington. And, inexplicably, the rate in Massachusetts, under its 1845 law, is higher than that in five of the states with reform laws (Arkansas, Georgia, North Carolina, South Carolina, and Virginia). In fact, most of the abortions on women from these reform states are performed in other states.

The statistical results of all this confusion are encouraging, for legal abortions are now being performed at the rate of 500,000 a year, up from 10,000 in 1967. Almost half of the 500,000 are done in New York City, and almost 100,000 in California. Broken down by states or by economic status or by race, however, the results are far from satisfactory. In California, for example, the ratio of abortions to births is about 1 in 4, whereas in Arkansas, with an almost identical reform law, the ratio is about 1 in 200. The well-to-do Midwesterner can come to New York, but the poor cannot. And the southern black woman still cannot get a legal abortion, despite reform, in 7 of 14 southern states. In other words, abortion reform has indeed progressed rapidly in the past 5 years, but it has now reached an awkward transitional phase still fraught with inequities.

This situation has been made even more difficult by the fact that the reform movement has momentarily stalled, at least on the legislative front. In 1971, for the first time since 1967, no new abortion laws were passed. Reform measures were considered but rejected by 26 legislatures. This was largely because the lack of a residency requirement in New York's law allows at least the well-to-do from other states to travel there. Also, the legislators are sitting back, waiting for a decision from the courts. Efforts have been made to repeal the reform laws in California, Colorado, North Carolina, and New York, but to no avail. The Colorado bill lost by one vote, and the New York bill was actually passed before being vetoed by Governor Rockefeller. In most states, Catholic organizations have fought vigorously to prevent reform and even to tighten the laws already in existence (including an effort to outlaw all abortions in Pennsylvania).

There is no doubt that the solution to this chaos must come from the courts, just as it has in the civil rights area. There is no chance that all 50 states will act. And with President Nixon opposed to reform and Congress apathetic, there is little chance of federal action. When *Abortion and the Law* was first published, there were no court cases testing the constitutionality of abortion laws. Now there are dozens. They argue that such laws are unconstitutionally vague; that they deprive women of their rights to due process, to marital privacy, and to the control of their reproductive lives; that they constitute cruel and unusual punishment; that they reflect undue influence of the church on the state; that they discriminate against the poor; and that they prevent the physician from practicing medicine in accordance with modern standards.

Many of these cases have already been decided by the lower courts, and most are on appeal. The appeals from Georgia and Texas have been heard by the Supreme Court; the court's decision will be found in the appendix of this volume. Certain other related issues must also be clarified judicially; these include the right of minors to have abortions without parental permission and of wives without their husbands' consent, the constitutionality of residency and hospital requirements, the eligibility of women undergoing abortions for Medicaid benefits, and the certification of commercial referral agencies.

In the courts, as in the legislatures, Catholic opposition is much in evidence. Usually this takes the form of defending the old laws in the courts and opposing new laws in the capitols. In New York a Catholic lawyer — maintaining, incredibly, that his religion had nothing to do with his action — went so far as to have himself appointed guardian of the city's unborn fetuses and sought an injunction against the municipal hospital's implementation of the state law. I find it even more incredible that the religion of the presiding judges in these cases is usually reflected in their decisions.

The present situation cannot be allowed to continue. A woman's eligibility for abortion cannot be allowed to depend on where she happens to live or how much money she has. Doctors, hospitals, and referral agencies cannot be allowed to take advantage of a local monopoly in abortions. And the views of a religious minority cannot be allowed to determine public policy. Soon, abortion will have to be recognized as the constitutional prerogative of all American women. Then, at last, our children can be educated about sex, taught to practice contraception, and permitted to have abortions — without fear or shame — if their contraceptive efforts fail.

I am grateful to the Case Western Law Review and the University Press for allowing me to present this brief chronicle. In the articles that follow, some of this material is expanded, and much more is added by some of the true experts in this field. I am confident that this volume constitutes a thorough and scholarly review of this vitally important subject and will remain a valuable source of information for years to come.

NOTE

1. In 1966 Mississippi broadened its law to permit abortions for rape, in addition to the preservation of maternal life. But this change does not seem sufficiently significant to warrant including Mississippi among the reform states.

EDITORS' PREFACE

In 1967, before the movement to liberalize abortion laws had achieved many tangible results, the Press of Western Reserve University published *Abortion and the Law*. That book has provided valuable information to many people over the past six years, and it stands as one of the best and most thorough collections on abortion. Today, particularly because of the increase in abortions which will follow the Supreme Court's recent decisions, the public's interest in abortion is greater than it has ever been, and there is a definite need for new information. The Press of Case Western Reserve University is publishing *Abortion, Society, and the Law*, its second book on abortion, to satisfy the need of lawyers, legislators, doctors, and many others for a current and comprehensive treatise.

When the Supreme Court declared the Texas and Georgia abortion laws unconstitutional, it opened the way for dramatic liberalization of the laws in nearly every state. During the first trimester of pregnancy, the Constitution now requires that the abortion decision rest with the patient and her doctor, free from government interference. During the second trimester, a state can regulate abortion procedures only to protect the woman's health. And during the third trimester, the state can flatly prohibit all abortions, except those necessary to preserve the woman's health.

The opinions of the Supreme Court are unusually definitive, but they still leave many questions unanswered and the content of future abortion laws is far from certain. The role of fathers in the abortion decision and the rights of minors, for example, may be more difficult to resolve than the questions decided in the Texas and

Georgia cases. Moreover, entirely new problems are continually emerging, problems that were unforseeable or too remote to warrant attention a few years ago. Abortion counselling and referral services, for example, now pose practical, ethical, and legal problems that were of little consequence until recently.

From the medical point of view, the problems of the doctor are as perplexing as ever, and in most states doctors will be dealing with abortion problems with increasing frequency. The traditional questions, like the patient's mental and physical well-being, will become more important by sheer force of numbers.

Beyond these traditional medical questions lie provocative new ones. For example, the possibility that fetal tissue may be a medically valuable byproduct of abortions raises a host of sensitive problems.[1] And the development of new drugs may completely transform the abortion issue. A woman may soon be capable of chemically inducing any menstrual period that is a few days late, which would allow her convenient control over her menstrual cycle. But at the same time, unbeknown even to herself, monthly regulation of this sort may also abort an embryo.[2]

Abortion, Society, and the Law is intended to cover the broadest range of abortion issues, from the traditional ones to the ones that are just now on the horizon. The law-oriented essays are especially timely since every state will be reevaluating its abortion policies from the point of view that the right to an abortion is fundamental, the position vindicated by the Supreme Court. B. James George, Jr., provides a summary of the statutory and decisional law of abortion, and his essay will be very useful as the states reconsider their laws. Harriet Pilpel and Ruth Zuckerman discuss the legal obstacles that restrict the availability of abortions for minors. Gerald Messerman describes the legal problems encountered by abortion counselling services and referral agencies, and he explains arguments that may overcome the present restrictions on these services.

Alan Guttmacher relates his many experiences in the movement for abortion reform and explains the origins of his liberal attitudes. He discusses the New York experience with its repeal law, and he concludes with a summary of the medical advances relating to abortion inducement. Richard Schwartz provides a comprehensive analysis of the psychiatric implications of allowing abortion on request.

He contends that the potential improvement in the nation's overall mental health is, by itself, adequate justification for abortion on request. Stephen Fleck discusses the role of the psychiatrist in the field of abortion, largely from an historical perspective. Kenneth Niswander describes the indications for therapeutic abortion and the legal abortion practices as they existed in the United States prior to the rulings of the Supreme Court. The subject of M. Neil Macintyre's essay is genetic counselling and clinical cytogenetics, topics too often slighted in discussions of abortion.

Finally, three well-known writers discuss religious and philosophical aspects of abortion. Daniel Callahan evaluates some of the common arguments in the abortion debate. Rabbi Jakobovits presents Jewish views on abortion, and Congressman Drinan discusses abortion from a Catholic viewpoint.

David F. Walbert
April, 1973

NOTES

1. Two uses for fetal tissue are reported in TIME, Feb. 28, 1972, p. 54. The first is the transplantation of the thymus gland from an aborted fetus to a child born without a thymus. Since the thymus must come from a 14- to 20-week-old fetus, one might wonder if a doctor would encourage his patient to delay her abortion. The other is the use of fetal tissue to make vaccine.
2. See Guttmacher, *The Genesis of Liberalized Abortion in New York: A Personal Insight*, in this volume.

Abortion, Society, and the Law

THE EVOLVING
LAW OF ABORTION

B. JAMES GEORGE, JR.

LAWS REGULATING SEXUAL BEHAVIOR have no peers when it comes to stirring up intense emotional reactions; when the element of life itself combines with human sexuality, as it does only in the context of abortion, the intensity of emotional disagreement and conflict is compounded. In the short span of years since 1966, the starting date of a definite trend toward liberalization of abortion laws, proponents of liberalized abortion have gained significant ground on both the legislative and judicial fronts. Despite these successes, the battle over abortion law reform or revision remains intense. And this battle is likely to continue, because there is fundamental and probably irreconcilable disagreement over the primacy of personal and social interests and the extent to which these interests are to be effectuated through the law.

I. CONFLICTING INTERESTS AFFECTED BY ABORTION LEGISLATION

Any discussion of abortion necessarily revolves around four different foci: the fetus itself, the pregnant woman, the family into which the expected child will be born, and the surrounding community. As to the first of these, the fetus, there is clearly a semantic problem in that the choice from among an array of terms — conceptus, zygote, embryo, fertilized ovum, fetus, and prenate infant — is probably more an index to the thinking of the speaker than it is a scientifically accurate choice of terms.[1] Whatever the term selected, concern with the fetus typically reflects two contradictory schools of thought. According to one of these schools, there is inviolate life in being from the time of fertilization of the ovum.

3

The strongest adherence to this view, of course, is found within the Roman Catholic faith, which condemns abortion under all circumstances,[2] although there is also strong Protestant support for the idea.[3] The second view is that the possible fate of the fetus, if it were to go to term, should be taken into account. If the child would be born deformed, mentally defective, or otherwise incapable of living a normal life, or if it would be born into a highly detrimental environment which could not be reasonably compensated for,[4] it is preferable that its incipient life be nipped in the bud. This premise is likely to be an incidental argument to advocacy of liberalized abortion based on social necessity.[5] Adoption of the first view of fetal life means rejection of all abortion, or any abortion unnecessary to save the life of the mother;[6] to adopt the second is usually to favor abortion in at least some greater range of situations.

The second focus is the pregnant woman.[7] Most of the propositions advanced on this point are basically favorable to her obtaining an abortion. The only exception is the contention that intercourse which produces pregnancy is licit only if done within marriage and for procreation,[8] and that an unwanted pregnancy is not only unfortunate, but the fulfillment of Divine mandate. Therefore, the woman must carry the child to term, whatever the consequences. This exception aside, most statements of policy are sympathetically inclined in favor of the pregnant woman, although not all of these necessarily favor according her a free choice in the matter of abortion.[9] The most obvious point of concern is for the life of the woman — because there are medical indications that she may not survive a pregnancy,[10] because she may attempt suicide if she cannot obtain an abortion,[11] or because she may submit to the hazards of an illegal abortion at the hands of an untrained physician if she is denied the facilities of a reputable hospital or clinic.[12] A further point of emphasis is the concern for the pregnant woman's physical and mental health.[13] All of these factors, of course, tend to support the rationale in favor of a liberalization of abortion laws. But it should be noted that one area of concern, the mental health of the woman, is also emphasized in the contrary assertion that an abortion works irreparable psychological harm to the woman.[14]

A third focus is the family unit of which the pregnant woman is a part and into which the new baby will be born. Some stress concern for the freedom of the sexual partners to decide whether and when they will have children.[15] Others emphasize the economic well-being of the whole family, which may be adversely affected if the same resources must be stretched to care for another member, or concentrate on the mother's care of the living siblings who might be detrimentally affected by yet another addition to the family unit.[16] A person who emphasizes these factors is almost certain to favor liberal abortion, particularly if approved and administered through medical channels.[17]

The final focus is on the needs of the community. Any of the concerns already listed can of course be restated in terms of social interests (e.g., protection of the life of the fetus or the mother, protection of the health of the mother, or protection of the viable family unit). But with the community dimension, there are at least two additional concerns. One is the factor of population control. Abortion is clearly one means of birth control, albeit a much less satisfactory method than mechanical or chemical means of contraception.[18] But it is only in Japan that population control appears to be the primary basis for statutes authorizing medical abortion on socio-economic grounds,[19] which is a result of the traditional Japanese belief that contraceptives are not used by proper married couples.[20] As contraception becomes more generally accepted among younger couples, particularly those who set up nuclear family units in urban centers,[21] the population-control function of abortion in Japan will probably decline to about the same level as in Western countries.[22]

Some writers suggest there may be an impermissible exercise of state power inherent in any legal use of abortion as a means of population control,[23] or that there may be too serious a decline in population to permit the state to survive.[24] In general, however, population control is only incidental to the practice of abortion and is not a primary objective;[25] thus, abortion poses no serious threat either to population or to personal liberties. The second social factor frequently advanced in support of relaxed abortion laws is the freedom of the medical profession to handle the abortion problem as it would any other medical problem — free from arbitrary legal controls.[26]

These, then, while not necessarily all, are the principal policy interests which are affected by and affect the coverage of abortion statutes and underlie the developing body of constitutional precedent. As will be shown,[27] in most jurisdictions before 1967, abortions were permitted only to save the life of the pregnant woman. Many still consider this to be the maximum relaxation of a prohibition against abortion that a legal and social system can tolerate. For certain others, even this exception is intolerable; they believe there should be absolute prohibition of all abortions, whatever the circumstances.[28] For many individuals in law, medicine, and society in general, however, the traditional law is entirely too strict and must be liberalized in those jurisdictions that have not yet revised their statutes.[29]

The author of this article stands with the latter group, which of course dictates in large measure the form and content of what follows. Briefly stated, his premises are these: women cannot be deterred from having sexual relations (nor their partners motivated to join them in abstinence) by the fear that they will have to carry a fetus to term if they become pregnant, any more than they will be deterred by being denied contraceptives or anaesthesia during childbirth.[30] If they intend to have sexual relations, they will have them despite legal controls or unpleasant but remote physical consequences. To put the matter another way, proscribing abortion does not promote celibacy; nor does liberalizing abortion promote promiscuity. Among those women, married and unmarried, who become pregnant, a certain number will wish to be aborted. Those with money and connections will either find a compliant practitioner who will terminate the pregnancy safely (though not cheaply), or purchase a ticket to a jurisdiction in which an abortion can be performed openly. For those without the means or connections necessary to obtain an abortion in that way, the choice is less satisfactory. The mother may have to carry the fetus to term; if so, it may not be born into a satisfactory home or may not be adoptable. She may seek out an unqualified butcher, or she may have to try to induce an abortion herself. Either alternative poses an abnormally high statistical possibility of serious bodily injury, sterility, or death.

Though the community may encourage exhaustion of all other alternatives before allowing abortion, it should facilitate performance of abortions in aseptic clinics rather than in motels or filthy tenement rooms if it is in fact concerned with the life and health of women who do not want to continue their pregnancies to term. The logical thrust of these concerns is to authorize the performance of abortions by qualified practitioners on medical grounds without any controls other than those found in the law of medical malpractice.

This, however, does not go beyond the freedom desired by those doctors who want to practice medicine unfettered by special criminal statutes. There is an ever-increasing pressure from advocates of women's rights for complete freedom on the part of each woman to determine the condition of her own body.[31] Probably there is no way intellectually or emotionally to resolve the conflict between this position and that which accords an absolute primacy to the rights of the zygote-embryo-fetus to life.[32] Moreover, a recognition of the right to the absolute control of one's own body creates the problem of the degree to which doctors and hospitals, whether public[33] or private,[34] must accommodate and make effective the woman's desires despite their own unwillingness to do so. That such conflicts are beginning to confront the courts and legislatures is indication in itself that the claim to personal freedom for each woman has made considerable headway in American law.

With this jurisprudential discussion as a background, this article will turn now to a consideration of the legal regulation of abortion practices in the United States. Because our system of laws has only recently crossed a watershed between restrictive legislation and more permissive legal controls, the article will examine the legal coverage through 1966 and then consider the subsequent legislative and judicial developments.

II. LEGAL REGULATION OF ABORTION PRACTICES BEFORE 1967

A. *Criminal Statutes*

1. *Statutes Penalizing Abortion* — Criminal statutes outlawing abortion are of relatively recent vintage,[35] and there is so little common law authority covering abortion that it should play no significant role in evaluating the legality of abortion.[36] The statutes may be roughly classified as those which prohibit all abortions and those which permit some abortions under carefully limited circumstances.

The statutes in 4 states — Louisiana,[37] Massachusetts,[38] New Jersey,[39] and Pennsylvania[40] — provide no specific exceptions to the general prohibition against abortion.   In Massachusetts, however, the Supreme Judicial Court, by judicial construction, has added a limitation in favor of a physician who acts in the honest belief that the operation is necessary to save the woman from great peril to her life or health, if his judgment corresponds "with the average judgment of the doctors in the community in which he practices."[41] In New Jersey the state supreme court apparently agreed that a doctor could act to save the life of the mother, although it did not agree that he could act merely to protect her health.[42]   In New Hampshire the statute prohibiting attempted abortion[43] provides no exception, although the section penalizing an actual abortion[44] does justify acts necessary to preserve the mother's life.   In all the other states, the legislatures have specifically provided for certain instances in which abortions may be legally performed.[45]   In 44 states[46] and the District of Columbia,[47] an abortion is permissible if it is necessary to save the life of the mother.

Even before the onset of reform legislation, a few states provided for abortion other than that necessary to preserve the woman's life. Seven states have permitted abortions to preserve the life of the unborn child,[48] a qualification that probably has no functional effect other than to make it clear that induced labor is not a violation of the criminal law.   Since a fetus has little chance of survival if it is born before the seventh month of gestation, and since most medically justified abortions are performed within the first trimester of pregnancy, this qualification has little impact on the abortion problem as such, and serves only to remove any hypothetical bar to generally legitimate obstetrical practice. A handful of jurisdictions before 1967 granted an even broader license to perform abortions necessary to prevent serious and permanent bodily injury[49] or to protect the health of the mother.[50] Florida and Massachusetts accomplished the same thing by judicial decision.[51]   This permits a more normal medical determination to be made than is the case when the law requires proof of a necessity to preserve the pregnant woman's life.

Under all these statutes, a number of difficult legal problems have arisen over how the statutory exceptions should be administered.[52]

One problem has to do with the matter of who is to be permitted to perform an abortion to save the pregnant woman's life or preserve her health. Fourteen states[53] appear to permit anyone to perform the operation; the rest of the states have required that the abortion be done by a physician or surgeon. The Missouri statute seems to favor an unlicensed person. There, an abortion is unlawful unless necessary to preserve the woman's life or that of her unborn child. However, if the person who performs an abortion "is not a duly licensed physician," the abortion is lawful if its performance "has been advised by a duly licensed physician to be necessary for such a purpose."[54] Thus, while a licensed physician is held to a standard of "objective necessity" for abortions he performs, an unlicensed person is apparently justified in acting upon the advice of a licensed physician, whether or not the abortion is objectively necessary. This theoretically protects, for example, the office nurse; but whether she should be protected is a matter on which opinions may well differ.

A second point of difference turns on whether necessity is to be determined on an objective, or strict liability, basis or whether the important issue is the good faith belief that justifying medical grounds exist. Many statutes support in form an interpretation that necessity is an objective element of the crime,[55] although three of them have been interpreted to include a defense of good faith belief of necessity, despite their strict wording to the contrary.[56] The harshness of these statutes is also modified to a degree if the burden is on the state to prove the want of medical necessity.[57] In 3 states and the District of Columbia,[58] however, statutes make it clear that it is the motivation and not the objective necessity which constitutes the basis for the exception from coverage. It is appropriate to mention here that several of the statutes enacted in 1967 and later use the terminology of "reasonable belief."[59] This is an effort to reach a compromise position between strict liability and subjective criminality, but what it achieves is criminality based on negligence,[60] a standard of culpability that appears inappropriate in the context of abortion.[61]

The common law requirement that the child be quick before there could be a criminal abortion[62] has disappeared from the statutory law,[63] which most commonly refers merely to "pregnancy"

— 29 states utilize this approach.[64]   Five other states[65] specify that
quickening does not matter, usually through the phrase "whether
quick or not."   Still another legislative cure for the interpretive
problem has been accomplished through the employment of "attempt" provisions, which will be discussed below.[66]

Time of duration of pregnancy, however, has reappeared as an
important factor in several of the recently revised statutes.   Three
states[67] specifically limit the period of abortions to the period of
nonviability, and 6 others[68] place limits in terms of the weeks or
days of pregnancy within which, other than in emergency situations,
the operation must be performed.   Under several of the older statutes, the fact of quickening or the passage of a specified portion of
the gestation period also governs the severity of the punishment.[69]

Another set of legal problems arises when, despite efforts to abort
the woman, no miscarriage occurs.   This may happen either when
the abortion operation is incompetently performed or when the
woman is not in fact pregnant.   Thirty-four states and the District
of Columbia eliminate the first problem by penalizing the use of instruments, the administration of drugs, or the use of any other means
intended to produce an abortion;[70] Texas has a special attempt statute.[71]   If the woman is not pregnant, however, it might be argued
that the crime was "impossible" to attempt.[72]   Several states eliminate this as a defense by covering the doing of the prohibited
acts to "any woman,"[73] to a woman "whether pregnant or not,"[74]
or to a woman believed by the defendant to be pregnant.[75]   Several
decisions support the idea that, under statutes like these, the victim
need not be pregnant.[76]   In 2 states, however, punishment varies
according to whether or not a miscarriage is actually produced.[77]

2. *Statutes Prohibiting Killing an Unborn Quick Child* — Six
states make it a separate offense wilfully to kill an unborn quick
child under circumstances in which, if the mother and not the fetus
had been killed, it would have been murder.[78]   The aim of these
statutes is not entirely clear from either the language or the interpreting cases, but their target is probably the person who intends to
cause a pregnant woman to miscarry without her consent and who
uses physical violence against her body in an attempt to achieve that
purpose.   In legal concept, these laws clearly accord independent
personality to the fetus,[79] for the killing of the fetus under these

circumstances is called manslaughter, and the sections themselves are usually found with other homicide provisions.

3. *Statutes Penalizing Death of the Pregnant Woman Resulting from Abortion* — If a pregnant woman dies as the result of an abortion, there should be little difficulty in establishing either: (1) second-degree murder, based upon either felony murder in the context of commission of a felony not enumerated in the first-degree murder statute, the intentional infliction of great bodily injury, or the performance of an act with known dangerous consequences; or (2) manslaughter, based on gross criminal negligence.[80] Several states, however, meet the problem directly in the context of the abortion statutes by providing for increased punishment for abortion if the woman dies as a result of the abortion,[81] or by characterizing the death as either murder[82] or manslaughter.[83]

4. *Statutes Penalizing the Woman Who Seeks an Abortion* — In the absence of a specific statute, a woman who seeks or submits to an abortion is usually not considered to be an accomplice to the abortion.[84] Rhode Island[85] and Vermont[86] preserve this doctrine by statute, and the Reporter's Comment to the Louisiana statute[87] indicates there is no intent to change the earlier Louisiana case law to the same effect. In several states, however, the legislatures have decreed that the woman commits a criminal act by soliciting or submitting to an abortion.[88] These statutes appear to have two significant legal effects, and probably one practical result as well. First, they may be accompanied by statutes requiring the woman's testimony to be corroborated,[89] or are held by judicial construction to require corroboration.[90] Second, the fact that the woman is deemed to have committed a criminal act means that she may claim privilege when she is summoned to testify for the state.[91] However, because of the importance in many instances of the woman's testimony in establishing the abortionist's guilt, legislatures have had to provide either that the privilege against self-incrimination does not apply[92] or that immunity against prosecution is conferred upon the woman when she testifies for the state.[93] This brings the matter around full circle, to where it would be if the woman were not considered a criminal in the first place.[94] In addition to these two legal problems created by criminal sanctions against the woman, there may be some slight practical advantage to the prosecution in being able to coerce

cooperation from the woman by threatening to prosecute her if she does not cooperate, while promising her immunity from prosecution if she does cooperate.

5. *Statutes Penalizing Activity Which Facilitates Performance of Abortions* — A medical doctor who performs an abortion utilizes instruments which are part of the regular equipment of any gynecologist or obstetrician.[95] It is not realistic to try to control traffic in these instruments, and in any case, the very nature of the channels which supply equipment to physicians and hospitals makes it unlikely that a layman could casually purchase it. But self-induced abortion is a major medical problem,[96] and the devices or chemical substances used for "do-it-yourself" abortion are sufficiently identified and devoid of legitimate modern uses that some effort at controlling them can be made. In any event, legislatures have fairly consistently tried to regulate their availability.

The advertising of abortifacients is penalized in 23 states. In 19 of those jurisdictions there is a special statute covering the abortifacient either alone or in the context of medicines preventing conception, curing venereal disease, and the like,[97] while in some jurisdictions this sort of advertising is prohibited in the context of obscenity regulation.[98] Whether these statutes are in fact invoked at the local level is uncertain; there is a dearth of appellate opinion construing them.[99] But if the state liberalizes its abortion laws to permit unrestricted medical abortions, efforts to interfere with advertising about the availability of abortions may be voided on constitutional grounds.[100]

State legislatures also frequently seek to regulate the actual traffic in abortifacients by prohibiting their manufacture,[101] distribution,[102] furnishing,[103] sale or keeping or exposing for sale,[104] giving away,[105] or lending.[106] Two states require that all sales be on registerable prescriptions.[107] Oregon penalizes one who furnishes a place knowing that abortions, other than those performed as therapeutic under the medical licensing statutes,[108] are to be performed there.[109] These statutes have produced no appellate litigation, but their fate may well be that of the federal statutes which prohibit mailing, importing, and transporting various kinds of "obscene" matter, including articles for "producing abortion."[110] The limited case law interpreting these sections in the context of traffic in abortifacients[111] suggests that so long as the substance sold or transported has a legitimate medical or commercial use, it will not in fact be effectively covered by the legislation.

B. *Administrative Sanctions*

Criminal penalties are blunt instruments with which to regulate human conduct. More efficient control can often be effected through the state power to grant and revoke special licenses to engage in a business or profession, or by imposing administrative fines or penalties. For example, many aspects of prostitution are controlled primarily in this way.[112] In the context of abortion, however, only licensed medical personnel and hospitals are subject to control through administrative action; a layman or a person with medical training whose license to practice has been revoked can be reached only through criminal prosecution. This does not mean, however, that licensing statutes and license revocation proceedings are unimportant in the context of abortion control. The claim that an abortion is justified because it is necessary to preserve the life, or the life or health, of the pregnant woman on whom it is performed is either limited in law to or asserted in fact by licensed medical personnel. Loss of a license to practice is such a fearsome thing to a professional person that medical licensing and license-revocation standards and procedures must be considered as prime controls on the availability of therapeutic abortions.

The overwhelming majority of jurisdictions authorize revocation of a medical doctor's license when he has committed or participated in the commission of a criminal abortion.[113] (Two states provide for revocation of the license in the criminal provision itself.[114]) In most of these states the reference is to "criminal abortion" or "unlawful abortion," which seems to mean that the administration of the criminal law determines the administration of the medical licensing law. But in a growing number of states, as the concept of therapeutic abortion is established as part of legitimate medical practice, the regulation of which is in turn covered in the licensing provisions, the criminal code provisions serve the residual function of reaching those who either are not medical practitioners or are medical practitioners who do not comply with the provisions affecting them.[115]

Performance of a criminal abortion is not mentioned as a ground for revocation of a license in the laws of the remaining jurisdictions. However, in these states there is statutory authorization for revocation based on conviction of a felony[116] or unprofessional conduct in general.[117] Since abortion has been denominated a form of unprofessional conduct,[118] it is clear that there is no state in which a proven criminal abortionist can continue to practice without rendering his license subject to revocation. Many of the statutes cited above also include practitioners of the healing arts other than medical doctors. Some jurisdictions, however, have enacted special statutes covering osteopaths,[119] nurses,[120] midwives,[121] and other practitioners specially regulated by law.[122]

Most revocation proceedings are carried on as a purely administrative matter and are subject to review as are administrative proceedings in general. Reviewing decisions usually examine only whether the administrative agency stayed within the proper limits of discretion in determining that charges were properly laid and substantiated and that disciplinary penalties were properly assessed.[123] There are, however, two questionable aspects of the use of license revocation procedures against professional persons who are alleged to have committed abortions. It has been held that license-revocation proceedings may be begun even though the statute of limitations has run on a criminal prosecution[124] or the defendant has been acquitted in an earlier criminal prosecution based on the same act.[125] Although as a general matter agencies which regulate professions should be able to remove the unfit from practice regardless of what may happen in specific criminal prosecutions or civil actions against them, it is doubtful that a properly performed abortion creates any medical problem as such or reflects adversely in any way on the level of professional skill of the person who performs it. Therefore, to revive an outlawed transaction or to proceed despite an acquittal looks as if the state is seeking again to exact retribution, rather than to protect the public against an inept medical practitioner. If the former is the case, it would seem close to or within the United States Supreme Court holding incorporating the doctrine of collateral estoppel into the constitutional concept of double jeopardy;[126] furthermore, there are decisions holding that revocation of a license is a penalty which is outlawed by a statute conferring immunity in return for incriminating testimony.[127]

Even more critical constitutional problems are raised if the disciplining authority insists on proceeding before pending or potential criminal charges are disposed of.[128] The United States Supreme Court made it clear in *Spevak v. Klein* that a professional license cannot be revoked or suspended merely on the ground that the person under investigation interposed a valid claim of privilege against self-incrimination.[129] Therefore, if the licensing agency bases any part of its action on the claim of privilege, it denies due process to the respondent. Moreover, an insistence on carrying through with the matter may result in an impairment of any criminal prosecution that has been or may be brought. If incriminating statements are in fact elicited from one who seeks to avoid loss of license or employment by cooperating with the investigating agency, those statements cannot be used by the state without impairing the respondent-defendant's privilege against self-incrimination.[130] Although there is post-*Spevack* authority that disciplinary proceedings do not always have to be stayed until the courts have disposed of all possible criminal charges,[131] it would be far safer from the point of view of both prosecutor and licensing agency if revocation proceedings were suspended at least until the trial court stages of the criminal prosecution are completed.

C. *Civil Responsibility*

On occasion the question has arisen whether a woman on whom an abortion has been performed, or her representative if she is dead as a result of the operation, can bring a civil action to recover damages. If a court were disposed to deny recovery, it might invoke the traditional concept that one cannot recover for injuries arising from activities in which he voluntarily engaged (*volenti non fit injuria*), especially if they are, by their nature, "highly offensive and injurious to society."[132] If, on the other hand, it were predisposed toward permitting recovery, a court might hold that the state is wronged, and therefore permit the civil recovery in indirect enforcement of the state's policies,[133] or that consent to an abortion is not consent to bungled aftercare.[134]

As one might expect, the cases are not in agreement, although something of a consistent pattern develops if one ascertains: (1) whether the action is against the doctor himself or the male friend of the woman plaintiff who both made her pregnant and put her in contact with the abortionist; (2) whether the woman is alive or dead; and (3) whether death, if it occurred, stemmed from the abortion itself or can be attributed to a failure to provide adequate aftercare when the woman was in a position of peril in which emergency treatment by the physician might have been expected. It seems unlikely that a woman will be permitted to maintain an action against someone who cooperated with her in making contact with the abortionist who performed the bungled operation.[135] This holding appears fair enough, for in fact the woman and her sexual partner were in trouble together and equally motivated to have the abortion performed. There is, therefore, no good legal or practical reason why he, rather than she, should bear the economic burden of the aftermath of the abortion (at least as long as joint tortfeasors in general cannot distribute losses among themselves) or why courts should lend their aid in support of a subsequent falling-out between the couple.

When the action is by the woman against the doctor, there is a split of authority over whether a suit may be maintained. Some decisions deny the possibility of an intervivos action no matter how careless the doctor may have been;[136] but some other courts have permitted the woman to recover,[137] at least to the extent of the injuries actually suffered.[138]

If the woman has died from the abortion operation itself (as in a case in which an embolism results from the insertion of instruments into the uterus) or because of complications arising afterwards (like septicemia), it is possible that her survivors may commence a wrongful death action, chiefly against the doctor. Only two cases have refused to permit the action under these circumstances;[139] the remaining decisions permit recovery.[140] In these latter cases it is evident that if the courts can point to willful or negligent failure to provide adequate medical aftercare for the aborted woman whom the defendant doctor knows to be in need of qualified medical attention, they find it easier to justify a recovery of damages than they do if they must base recovery on the fact of the abortion itself. This showing of subsequent neglect can probably be made in many instances and is something the plaintiff's attorney should bear in mind as he presents his medical evidence.

Although some reservations have been expressed about permitting civil recovery based on a bungled abortion under any circumstances whatever,[141] there seems to be no special reason to treat this situation any differently than any other malpractice situation.[142] If a doctor fails to provide the sort of aftercare expected of him according to generally accepted medical standards, he ought to be liable in damages whether or not the original operation or technique is legally an abortion. Holdings in line with the majority position not only promote higher standards of medical care in general, but also serve to support the rapidly accelerating trend to place control over therapeutic abortions principally in the hands of the medical profession itself. It is to a consideration of this trend that we now turn our attention.

III. THE ACCELERATING TREND TOWARD LEGALIZED THERAPEUTIC ABORTION

A. *Checklist of Preliminary Considerations for a Legislature*

Most of the changes in the law of abortion since 1966 have been accomplished through legislative action, although there is a recent trend evident on the part of some courts to intervene on constitutional grounds. The article will examine both trends in this section. But at the outset, certain problems will be discussed that a legislature should consider in the event it is preparing a revised abortion statute, however broad or narrow it ultimately decides such a statute should be.

1. *Burden of Proving Justification or Non-Justification* — Lawyers know that more cases are won or lost because of the placement of burdens of proof and persuasion than on the basis of the propriety or impropriety of the substantive law underlying the litigation. An astute legislator who opposes expansion of therapeutic abortion can achieve a considerable restriction on what otherwise seems, on its face, to be a much-expanded authorization for medically supervised abortion by simply placing the burden of establishing medical justification on the doctor who performs the abortion. The fear of having to defend criminal charges can be a powerful deterrent to a professional person. On the other hand, if the prosecutor has to attack the medical judgment of a doctor, particularly one who performs an abortion in a hospital or public clinic under the supervision of his peers on a special committee, and sustain that attack in court subject to a burden of proving non-compliance with

law beyond a reasonable doubt, it is unlikely that he will proceed at all. As at least circumstantial evidence of this, under restrictive abortion statutes doctors have written openly in medical journals about abortions performed by them that were hospital-approved but probably not within the proper scope of the test of necessity to preserve the life of the mother;[143] yet no prosecutions were brought. This may suggest only that prosecutors do not read medical journals, but it may also suggest that elected prosecutors by and large are not anxious to lock horns with the organized medical profession.

From the point of view of traditional statutory construction, whether the burden of disproving or proving medical justification under the particular statute lies with the prosecution or the defendant depends upon whether that element is considered an exception to the statute or a proviso. Sometimes the statute itself is specific, either relieving the prosecution of any necessity to disprove justification[144] or characterizing the issue as an affirmative defense.[145] In the absence of a specific legislative indication, the matter is left to judicial interpretation. The overwhelming weight of authority places the burden on the state to plead and prove the want of medical justification,[146] provided the defendant is shown to be a licensed medical practitioner.[147]

Does a legislature today have the option to reject the weight of judicial opinion and place the burden of medical justification on the doctor defendant? It is doubtful that it does. In *United States v. Vuitch*,[148] the Supreme Court examined the question of whether the federal courts in the District of Columbia had construed the abortion statute there properly when they placed the burden of proving medical justification on the defendant. Exercising its power to construe District of Columbia legislation on other than constitutional grounds, it held that the lower courts had not properly interpreted the statute. Although not, therefore, a constitutional precedent, the Court's opinion contains language that should be given close attention by legislative drafters. The Court stated: "Certainly a statute that outlawed only a limited category of abortions but 'presumed' guilt whenever the mere fact of abortion was established, would at the very least present serious constitutional problems under this Court's previous decisions interpreting the Fifth Amendment . . . ."[149] The burden of pleading, proof, and persuasion of non-justification, therefore, should be clearly on the state whenever a licensed medical practitioner is the defendant.

One may, of course, ask whether at a minimum a doctor-defendant ought not bring forward the hospital records showing compliance with board or committee review procedures, a common feature in revised abortion statutes,[150] since perhaps that information is more readily available to the doctor than to the prosecutor; presumptions based on procedural convenience have been sustained as valid.[151] The answer probably is that the prosecutor should have little difficulty in identifying the hospital or hospitals in which the doctor is permitted to practice or perform surgery, and he has adequate subpoena powers or available discovery procedure to obtain the needed records. Admittedly, in a metropolitan area this may be a burden, but the police investigation should reveal where the abortion apparently was performed. If it was not done in a hospital, the doctor has failed to comply with a statutory condition in most of the states with revised abortion laws;[152] if it was done in a hospital, investigation of records need take place only there. Therefore, although it may be convenient for the prosecutor to have the burden of bringing forth evidence placed on the medical practitioner, that convenience is clearly outweighed by the danger of constitutional attack under *Vuitch*.

2. *Corroboration* — Mention has already been made of the problems in law enforcement that arise if the woman on whom an unlawful abortion is performed is denominated a criminal, particularly if corroboration of her testimony against the abortionist is required.[153] The need in many instances to have her available to testify as the principal witness against the abortionist far outweighs any deterrent effect in the abstract that denominating her conduct as criminal may have. Therefore, criminality should be eliminated as to the woman herself, thus converting abortion into a species of "victimless crime."[154]

3. *Placement of Revised Provisions* — Abortion probably has been the only aspect of medical practice regulated by criminal statute. As a result, lawyers preparing drafts of revised legislation have tended to work within the context of a criminal code rather than with statutes regulating the medical profession; the Model Penal Code is the prototype of this approach.[155] With the advantage of a

decade's hindsight, this legislative approach to the problem appears undesirable.

For one reason, much of the weight behind the drive for liberalized abortion laws has come from those segments of the medical profession that wish abortion to be simply a matter of normal medical practice unfettered by special legal regulations. If this approach is accepted by a legislature, then the most appropriate setting for the new legislation is the body of rules regulating the practice of medicine in general. This placement is likely to promote an *in pari materia* construction of the new law with other aspects of medical licensure, rather than with the crimes of homicide and assault that have been the statutory "companions" of traditional abortion statutes.

As a second reason, if changes in newly devised screening and approval procedures become necessary in light of experience under the revised statute, it is far easier to make changes in the context of licensure laws than in a criminal code. Indeed, it may be possible in time to leave the matter essentially as one of administrative law with relatively few details of therapeutic abortion practice spelled out by statute. Accordingly, medical proponents of liberalized abortion should make every effort to have legislation introduced as amendments to licensing laws, with conforming amendments in the criminal code only if absolutely necessary.

4. *Definitions of Terms* — If enacted, the Model Penal Code provisions would authorize termination of pregnancy on any of three grounds: (1) that continuance of the pregnancy would gravely impair the physical or mental health of the mother; (2) that the child would be born with a grave physical or mental defect; and (3) that the pregnancy resulted from rape, incest, or felonious intercourse, defined to include illicit intercourse with a girl below the age of sixteen. Each term, of course, raises a need for interpretation as cases arise under new legislation patterned on the Model Penal Code. But some disputes are resolved relatively easily — for example, definitions of rape and incest, which can be drawn from specific criminal statutes. Other terms are essentially undefinable screening words like "gravely." Falling between these is another interpretation problem, which has to do with the scope of the term "health" if that word alone is used. The *Vuitch* decision[156] holds that an attack on the term as vague and indefinite can be obviated

if it is construed to include both physical and mental health considerations. *Vuitch* no doubt will provide the standard for interpreting the word, but as a matter of legislative drafting technique it is preferable to include the specific qualifiers to cut down somewhat the potential scope of litigation under the new statute.

5. *Requirement of Consent* — A legislature may need to grapple with the issue of consent to therapeutic abortion. One might question whether, from the point of view of traditional criminal law theory, any special mention need be made of the matter. Nonconsensual abortions are as rare as nonconsensual appendectomies. Indeed, written consents or waivers for surgery are apparently obtained as standard hospital practice, the fact that the patient has sought treatment and enters the hospital voluntarily constitutes consent by conduct to nonnegligent treatment that ensues, and if a rare instance of coerced abortion should arise in which the defendant doctor operates with knowledge of the coercion, a standard felonious assault statute is all that is needed.[157] Nevertheless, revised abortion legislation usually contains a reference to consent, which suggests that some attention ought to be paid to the matter.

The requirement of a written consent from the woman may accomplish the same thing as a request or application,[158] being nothing more than a means of triggering the committee or board action that is a prerequisite to lawful performance of the operation. It is clear from the context in other statutes, however, that a consent is viewed as a condition precedent to the invocation of the statute by the performing physician.[159] From the standpoint of the latter, this is an undesirable detail to be written into a statute bearing criminal penalties, in that there is at least a possibility that want of a signed consent in the hospital records might be asserted as a failure to comply with the statute, rendering the doctor criminally responsible. If the legislative desire is to make clear that the woman must take the initiative in obtaining her own abortion, the "request" or "application" approach is by far preferable.

Unless a legislature is prepared to say that a woman has absolute control over her own body, it must deal with the question of involvement of her husband if she is married, or her parent or guardian if she is a minor or incompetent. Some of the new statutes require consent by the spouse, whatever the woman's age,[160] at least if the couple lives together.[161] Others require the husband's consent only if the woman is a minor as defined in the statute.[162] Consent by a parent or guardian is required if the woman is an unmarried minor or an incompetent.[163]

Should a legislature attempt to settle this problem specifically in the revised abortion statute, or should it be left to judicial decision, as it is in related matters like voluntary sterilization? Certainly so far as the husband is concerned there are ample family law analogies in matters like the use of contraceptives, artificial insemination by a donor, and sterlization[164] to enable a court to resolve the issue should it arise between spouses who have fallen out with one another.

But what of parental consent for unmarried minors? This is certainly an aspect of liberalized abortion in which emotional feelings will run high. Staffs of university student health services or clinics serving street people will no doubt confirm the frequency with which young girls living away from home seek aid in terminating pregnancies, as well as the difficulty or impossibility of obtaining parental consent to performance of an abortion. Though the risk of civil suit is slight as a practical matter, doctors may be reluctant to terminate a pregnancy, particularly with the long tradition of criminal sanctions against performance of abortions not necessary to preserve the pregnant woman's life. Clearly, this area of law needs clarification.

A few of the new statutes try to meet the problem at least partially, either by limiting the requirement of parental consent to those under 18 or 19 (rather than the traditional age of 21),[165] or by providing that the consent of only one parent is necessary if the unmarried minor lives away from home.[166] As in the instance of spousal consent, however, it may be better to solve the basic problem of pregnant minors in a broader setting. A recent illustration of that approach is *Ballard v. Anderson*,[167] a mandamus action against a therapeutic abortion committee to require it to consider an application by an unmarried pregnant minor for an abortion; the committee had refused to consider the request because no parental consent was tendered. Relying on a general civil code provision governing medical contracts by minors,[168] the court held that an abortion was "surgical care related to" pregnancy under the applicable pregnancy care statute, so that any pregnant minor would be deemed emancipated for purposes of therapeutic abortion procedures. While the quite specific provisions of the civil code were no doubt of help to the *Ballard* majority, the combination of a liberalized abortion statute and pressures toward elimination of common law property-oriented aspects of parent-child relationships is probably sufficient to enable other courts to do the same thing without the benefit of such a statute. Silence in the therapeutic abortion statute on the matter of parental consent would help rather than hinder that judicial approach.

In an Orwellian world, it may be only a short step from permitting consent to therapeutic abortion to a withholding of benefits unless consent is given. Such a shift of emphasis came about fairly rapidly in the matter of contraception. Until *Griswold v. Connecticut*[169] the principal question was whether the state could prohibit the sale and use of contraceptives, but now the major issue seems to be whether public agencies can make available contraceptive information and devices, or condition welfare grants on their use. Although the matter may be more covert than not, one may rationally entertain more than a slight suspicion that some legislators have voted for therapeutic abortion in the hope that the number of ADC cases may decrease. It is conceivable, therefore, that local welfare agencies might not only give information about the availability of abortions to pregnant welfare mothers, but might also suggest a diminution or termination of benefits if an abortion is not obtained. To forestall this possibility, four of the recent statutes specifically prohibit the use of a refusal to submit to an abortion as grounds for the loss of privileges or immunities, and they also state that submission to an abortion or giving consent to one cannot be made a condition precedent to the receipt of any "public benefit."[170]

B. *Coverage of the New Legislation*

1. *Grounds for Therapeutic Abortion* — A survey of the statutes enacted since 1966 reveals how substantial the influence of the Model Penal Code[171] has been, particularly in terms of the grounds stated to authorize abortions. The first is the necessity of the abortion to prevent impairment of the physical or mental health of the woman.[172] Thirteen statutes now recognize this factor as a basis for

a lawful abortion,[173] as does the recently enacted English statute.[174] The chief point of vulnerability in these statutes is the use of qualifiers like "substantial," "serious," "permanent," and "grave." The legislative purpose obviously is to discourage overly liberal use of medical grounds to justify therapeutic abortions. However, several recent decisions cast doubt on whether necessity to preserve life or health is sufficiently precise to pass constitutional muster.[175] If the qualifications should be ruled unconstitutionally vague, the result would be unrestricted abortion on medical grounds.[176]

A second ground for abortion — recognized in 12 states[177] and England[178] — permits termination of pregnancy on eugenic grounds if the fetus, if born, would be seriously handicapped mentally or physically. Although there are no decisions as yet on the constitutionality of the qualifiers, determinations of vagueness as far as the pregnant woman's health is concerned[179] probably will affect this ground as well, thus accelerating a trend toward abortion on request.

A third ground, based on humanitarian considerations, permits a victim of rape[180] or incest[181] to have her pregnancy terminated. Because the legal content of rape and incest is well established through statutory definitions and precedent, it is unlikely that any constitutional basis can be validly asserted to strike down this portion of a revised abortion statute.

These three grounds together do not exhaust the possibilities of liberalization, since each imposes legislative restrictions on the freedom of the pregnant woman to seek, and a medical practitioner to perform, an abortion. Four states have now eliminated from their statutes any substantive qualifications whatever on medically performed abortions;[182] the only controls are in terms of qualifications of the person performing the abortion, the place where the abortion is performed, and the duration of the pregnancy at the time of its termination. The English Abortion Act of 1967 reaches about the same result by permitting a medical practitioner to consider the pregnant woman's actual or reasonably foreseeable environment in determining whether she faces injury to her physical or mental health, as well as whether the risk to existing children is greater if an additional child is born.[183] Until the day when all references to abortion as such are eliminated from the criminal statutes, this seems to be the maximum relaxation that can be anticipated in the United States.

2. *Length of Pregnancy* — Mention has been made earlier[184] of the relevance of the length of pregnancy to the lawfulness of therapeutic abortions. To the extent that such a limitation is imposed by statute, it constitutes an arbitrary limitation on medical practice. Since the four most liberal states in terms of substantive grounds[185] impose time limitations, doctors in some instances may be barred from performing abortions that are necessary to the good physical or mental health, but not necessarily the life, of the pregnant woman. If so, this invites constitutional attack on equal protection grounds.[186]

3. *Residency Requirements* — As legislatures decide to expand the permissible scope of abortion, a commonly shared fear is that the state will become an abortion haven for residents of other states with restrictive laws. Therefore, many of the new laws contain requirements of residency within the state for specified periods before an application for a therapeutic abortion may be made.[187] The language used places the burden on the woman to reveal, and not on the doctor or board to ascertain the truth of her claim of residency; only the Georgia and Virginia statutes specifically attach perjury consequences to her declaration of residency.

These residency requirements appear vulnerable to attack on the basis that they infringe the freedom of citizens to travel from one state to another.[188] One three-judge federal district court has already voided this aspect of the revised North Carolina statute.[189] If the constitutional premise invoked in that case is endorsed by the Supreme Court, an additional legal limitation on the practice of medicine in this area will have been removed.

4. *Preliminary Approval by Medical Peers* — Even before the abortion law revision movement began, a number of states required[190] or permitted as an alternative to the operating physician's own belief the advice of two other independent physicians.[191] The recent statutes generally require preliminary consultation with or approval by medical colleagues before an abortion can be performed. This approval may be in the form of a certification by medical practitioners other than the practitioner who wishes to terminate pregnancy; the certifying practitioners cannot be relatives of or associated in medi-

cal practice with the physician on the case.[192]   Others require a more elaborate procedure involving a hospital review board or authority.[193]   Two states combine these two systems.[194]   Because a certain amount of time is required to process the necessary requests, certifications, and approvals, several of the statutes make an exception for emergency situations, with the necessary certification to follow in a very brief time after the abortion is performed.[195]

5. *Special Approval in Rape and Incest Cases* — The inclusion in some states of rape or incest as a basis for abortion on humanitarian grounds was discussed earlier.[196]   Most of these statutes require some form of substantiation of the claim because the usual medical grounds do not necessarily underlie the performance of these abortions.   Occasionally, all that is required is some form of complaint or affidavit on the part of the victim.[197]   It is more common, however, to require some sort of approval or certification by a prosecuting agency as a condition precedent.[198]   The California procedure is the most elaborate.[199]   The hospital medical staff committee reports the rape and forwards the applicant's affidavit to the district attorney.   If he indicates probable cause or makes no indication within 5 days, the committee may approve the abortion.   If within this period he indicates a lack of belief of probable cause, the applicant may petition a superior court for a review of that decision, and the matter must be heard within one week.   A finding of probable cause by the superior court will then clear the way for further committee action.[200]

6. *Persons Authorized to Perform Abortions* — Because the underlying purpose of the reformed abortion statutes is to see that abortions are performed by qualified practitioners on medical grounds, all the new statutes require that the pregnancy be terminated by a medical practitioner licensed in the particular state.[201] This requirement poses two potential problems of interpretation. One concerns the status of those who assist in the procedures.   (Or, as techniques like aspiration become increasingly simple, so that a registered nurse or medical paraprofessional might safely perform them, the concern is with who actually performs the abortion under the general direction of a medical practitioner.)   If medical skill and the patient's safety are the paramount considerations, it seems unnecessary to require that only licensed physicians perform abor-

tions. A second problem concerns a staff physician of a state hospital who is not yet qualified to practice medicine in the state but is nonetheless hired to perform general medical duties. There might be a technical question whether he is "licensed by the state" within the meaning of the abortion statutes. These questions, while hardly earth-shaking, suggest that it is probably a better legislative drafting technique to leave the matter of professional qualifications to administrative regulation.

7. *Place of Performance of Abortions* — Those statutes that limit the grounds for abortion to health, eugenic, or humanitarian grounds almost always restrict the performance of abortions to hospitals.[202] However, once the qualifications or conditions are wholly or largely eliminated, so that the determination to terminate a pregnancy is made by the woman and her doctor, the way is likely to be opened to the performance of abortions in clinics outside of licensed or accredited hospitals. This is the case in 3 states[203] and Great Britain.[204] If state law permits a state-level agency to authorize performance of abortions outside a hospital, a local governmental unit lacks the power to impose its own requirement that only the facilities of an accredited hospital be used.[205]

8. *Required Records and Reports* — When statutory conditions precedent to the performance of hospital abortions are created, it usually follows that various reports and records are required. Sometimes all that must be filed are the applications or certificates, to be retained in permanent hospital files.[206] In some states, however, reports of therapeutic abortions performed or refused are to be filed by the hospital with a state agency within a stated period.[207] These statutes generally require that the identity of the women applying for or receiving abortions be kept strictly confidential.[208]

9. *Freedom of Conscience Exemptions* — Many doctors, nurses, and hospital employees have strong religious or moral scruples against abortion, and many private hospitals, particularly church-related ones, will not tolerate the performance of abortions on their premises. As legal controls on medical abortion are reduced or eliminated, the question arises whether these individuals or hospitals can refrain from participation. To maintain freedom of conscience, most of the statutes state specifically that no individual need participate in abortions, no (private) hospital need permit abortions, and

no civil liability, disciplinary action, or recriminatory action can flow from such a refusal.[209]   But this same freedom to opt out of the system may not pertain to public hospitals,[210] and even private hospitals may be barred from adopting restrictions on abortion eligibility more severe than those imposed by state law.[211]   It is clear that the delicate balancing of the interests of private practitioners and hospitals, women who desire abortions, and the governmental apparatus in promoting relatively free medical abortion, still remains to be achieved through the judicial process.[212]

C.   The Judicial Frontier: Constitutional Attacks on Abortion Legislation

Even before the surge of revised abortion legislation, a wide array of attacks was made on traditional abortion legislation; new statutes have, if anything, accelerated the resort to federal courts for relief against application of abortion statutes to medical practitioners, pregnant women, and even unpregnant women.[213]   While the United States Supreme Court may soon take a position on some of the issues being currently litigated, chiefly before three-judge federal district courts,[214] one may well expect a large amount of litigation over the next few years.   Therefore, it seems appropriate to survey briefly the principal legal points to be resolved.

1.   *Standing to Litigate* — In each federal case, attacks are made on the standing of the plaintiffs to bring the action.   There is general agreement that medical practitioners have standing even though they may not be able to obtain concrete relief in a particular case because the duration of the litigation will render termination of pregnancy impossible.[215]   The fact that invocation of a state's laws will affect the doctor's professional activities is enough to confer standing.   Naturally, if a doctor has been convicted of abortion and has exhausted his state remedies, federal habeas corpus will lie.[216]

A pregnant woman, whether married or unmarried, also has standing to attack the statute under which an abortion has been denied to her,[217] and expiration of a statutory period of eligibility while the litigation progresses does not render the action moot as to her.[218]   If she proceeds to obtain an unlawful abortion within the state or goes somewhere else where she can obtain a lawful abortion, however, she will lose her standing to sue.[219] Women not pregnant at the time the action is commenced are not permitted to maintain a class action on the basis that they might become pregnant in the future and be denied an abortion upon request.[220] The position is not entirely clear as to psychiatrists, nurses, social workers, or ministers who may counsel pregnant women. Some decisions have given them the same standing as physicians,[221] but others have refused them permission to proceed.[222]

The recent decisions of the United States Supreme Court limiting the power of federal courts to issue declaratory judgments and injunctions against present or future application of state laws in alleged violation of the federal Constitution[223] must also be taken into account in the area of abortion legislation. A district court may avoid the necessity to decide the matter by finding no imminent irreparable injury under *Younger* and dismissing the action.[224] If it does not do so, it may still be required to by a higher court.[225] Nonetheless, two recent decisions assert the power of a district court to rule a state statute unconstitutional, even though no emergency existed warranting the issuance of an injunction against its future invocation by state officials.[226] This, too, is an area of federal procedure calling for clarification.

2. *Grounds for Attack: Vagueness* — Legislation that uses language too general to give any concrete indication of the acts it is intended to control is constitutionally defective.[227] This theory has proven to be fairly successful in recent attacks on state abortion legislation,[228] although there is some contrary authority.[229] The Supreme Court consideration of the concept in *Vuitch*[230] certainly suggests that the vagueness theory has to be taken into account in the setting of abortion legislation.

3. *Grounds for Attack: Equal Protection* — The 14th amendment equal protection clause can be violated either through the use of arbitrary legislative classifications[231] or by placing indigents at a procedural disadvantage in comparison to those with greater financial means.[232] Attacks on both grounds have been advanced, contending either that denial of abortions to some pregnant women but not to others constitutes an arbitrary and unreasonable legislative classification or that insistence on hospital certification and review procedures works in fact to the detriment of the indigent.

Thus far, however, neither ground has gained judicial acceptance;[233] courts desiring to void state abortion statutes seem to prefer vagueness or right of privacy grounds over equal protection arguments.

4. *Grounds for Attack: Right of Privacy* — The Supreme Court's holding in *Griswold v. Connecticut*[234] that a right of individual privacy exists under the ninth amendment clearly offers a great potential for attacks on restrictive abortion legislation on the part of women who want to control their own bodies and medical practitioners who want to practice medicine without arbitrary restriction.[235] Although some decisions refuse to recognize the application of the concept to abortion laws,[236] a growing number of holdings finds this the most acceptable constitutional basis for striking down restrictions on medical abortion.[237] The cases recently deliberated by the Supreme Court should produce a clear ruling on the applicability of ninth amendment considerations to abortion statutes.

5. *Grounds for Attack: Rights of Fetus* — The preceding three grounds of attack are those utilized by proponents of free medical abortion. Obviously, a great many doctors and laymen wish to outlaw all abortions or all but those necessary to preserve the life of the mother. When legislatures have broadened the scope of lawful abortion, attacks against the new statutes have been founded primarily on ninth amendment grounds, but this time in terms of the claimed right of a fetus to develop to term and to be born. The attack typically relies on an analogy to those decisions that have permitted recovery after birth by the infant and his parents for prenatal injuries.[238]

Because of the novelty of the expanded abortion statutes in this country, there is no clear body of precedent on which to rely; the new statutes themselves usually avoid language suggesting any fetal right to life.[239] Therefore, the issue, when raised, is essentially one of first impression for the judiciary. Probably because the prevailing federal judicial attitude is hostile to restrictions on medical abortion practice, and because some state benches appear to share that attitude, the assertion of a fetal right to life has been thus far uniformly rejected.[240] The analogy of the prenatal injury cases is disposed of by pointing out that no cause of action arises unless the fetus is born alive, and that the recovery is primarily for the benefit of the parents.[241]

IV. CONCLUSION

Now that 18 states have expanded the scope of lawful medical abortion, some of them quite radically, it can be expected that the "bandwagon" effect will be increasingly felt. Indeed, within a very few years, it may be that only those states with a heavy representation of adherents to conservative religious tenets will fail to respond to the pressures of example. Moreover, unless the United States Supreme Court puts an end to it, either through a restricted interpretation of the scope of ninth amendment personal privacy in the abortion context or by a requirement of federal abstention under *Younger v. Harris*,[242] it is very likely that federal and state courts will strike down statutes restricting abortions to those necessary to preserve the pregnant woman's life; perhaps even the Model Penal Code list will prove vulnerable. As other legislative restrictions, such as residency requirements and limits on duration of pregnancy at the time of termination, also fall on constitutional grounds, the legal system will come close to recognizing abortion as an unfettered medical procedure to be agreed upon by the pregnant woman and her attending physician.

But one additional limitation will have to be removed if such a result is to occur — the requirement that medical abortions be performed in hospitals subject to hospital committee review. Most doctors are wary of or even hostile toward abortion, no doubt primarily because they view themselves as preservers of life. Abortion creates, although perhaps to a lesser degree than the related problem of euthanasia, a real cognitive dissonance between the physician's desire to preserve life and his awareness that by performing or approving an abortion he is terminating life. If he practices in a field of medicine in which he sees the hardships that refusal to perform an abortion works on the pregnant patient, he probably arrives by stages at a satisfactory accommodation between his abstract image of himself as a healer and preserver of life and his feelings as to what the best interests of his patients require. The strongest advocates of liberalized abortion certainly are specialists in gynecology, obstetrics, and psychiatry who interrelate with pregnant women as persons and not as a nonspecific class. But in most hospitals, the administrators and specialists in other medical fields who view abortion with distaste, and abortionists as pariahs of the profession,[243] will control the review committees and thus render therapeutic abortion unavailable to a great many patients.

Therefore, it is necessary as quickly as possible to permit the performance of medical abortions in public and private clinics away from hospitals, so that women of all income groups can obtain inexpensive abortions if they wish. In such a setting, relevant counselling, which may in fact cause women contemplating abortions to change their minds, also can be made available. Until statutory restrictions on clinical abortion practice are removed or voided, legislatures may expand the substantive grounds for abortion and courts may void those that remain, without in fact overcoming the injustices and hardships inherent in the traditional law of abortion.

NOTES

1. On other semantic aspects of the abortion debate, see Hardin, *Semantic Aspects of Abortion*, 24 ETC.: A REVIEW OF GENERAL SEMANTICS 263 (1967).

2. Canon 2350, § 1. *See* 8 C. BACHOFEN, COMMENTARY ON CANON LAW 397-402 (1931); 3 T. BOUSCAREN, CANON LAW DIGEST 669-70 (1954); 2 S. WOYWOOD, PRACTICAL COMMENTARY ON THE CODE OF CANON LAW 625 (C. Smith rev. 1962). Also important is the Papal Encyclical of Pius XI, CASTI CONUBII (ON CHRISTIAN MARRIAGE) (Dec. 31, 1930), particularly the part reprinted in ASSOCIATION OF AMERICAN LAW SCHOOLS, SELECTED ESSAYS ON FAMILY LAW 132, 149-51 (1950). For recent examples of essays based on the traditional Roman Catholic view, see Brown, *Recent Statutes and the Crime of Abortion*, 16 LOY. L. REV. 275 (1970); Granfield, *Law and Morals*, CRIMINOLOGICA, Feb. 1967, at 11. Adherence to an unconditional opposition to abortion, however, is not common to all authors writing from a Roman Catholic background. *Cf.* Giannella, *The Difficult Quest for a Truly Humane Abortion Law*, 13 VILL. L. REV. 257 (1967-68).

3. *E.g.*, D. BONHOEFFER, ETHICS 130-31 (N. Smith trans. 1955); H. THIELICKE, THE ETHICS OF SEX 226-47 (J. Doberstein trans. 1964); Ramsey, *The Ethics of a Cottage Industry in an Age of Community and Research Medicine*, 284 NEW ENGLAND J. OF MED. 700, 701-03 (1971).

4. Dahlberg, *Abortion*, in SEXUAL BEHAVIOR AND THE LAW 379, 389 (R. Slovenko ed. 1965).

5. *Cf.* Samuels, *Termination of Pregnancy: A Lawyer Considers the Arguments*, 7 MEDICINE, SCI. & L. 10, 12-13 (1967); Hardin, *Abortion — or Compulsory Pregnancy?*, 30 J. MARRIAGE & THE FAMILY 246, 247 (1968).

6. H. THIELICKE, *supra* note 3. *But cf.* Giannella, *supra* note 2, at 301-02.
7. *See* Thomson, *A Defense of Abortion*, 1 PHILOSOPHY & PUB. AFFAIRS 47 (1971). *Cf.* Comment, *The Right to Privacy: Does it Allow a Woman the Right to Determine Whether to Bear Children?*, 20 AM. U. L. REV. 136 (1970); Note, *Isolating the Male Bias Against Reform of Abortion Legislation*, 10 SANTA CLARA LAWYER 301 (1970).
8. For an interpretation of Saint Augustine's view of sexual relations not too far from this, see D. BROMLEY, CATHOLICS AND BIRTH CONTROL 9-15 (1965).
9. *E.g.*, Comment, *supra* note 7.
10. With advances in medical knowledge, there are probably fewer instances today than formerly in which the pregnant woman is unlikely to survive. *See* Mahoney, *Therapeutic Abortion — The Psychiatric Indication — A Double-Edged Sword?*, 72 DICK. L. REV. 270, 278-80 (1968); Guttmacher, *Abortion Laws Make Hypocrites of Us All*, 4 NEW MEDICAL MATERIA 56 (1962); Hall, *Therapeutic Abortion, Sterilization, and Contraception*, 91 AM. J. OBSTETRICS & GYNECOLOGY 518, 522 (1965); Russell, *Therapeutic Abortions in California in 1950*, 60 W. J. SURGERY, OBSTETRICS, & GYNECOLOGY 497, 500 (1952). The hypothetical cases used as the survey reported in Packer & Gampell, *Therapeutic Abortion: A Problem in Law and Medicine*, 11 STAN. L. REV. 417, 431-44 (1959), include several in which the life of the mother might well be shortened were the pregnancy carried to term. As to one experience under a system of relatively unrestricted medical abortions, see Ottosson, *Legal Abortion in Sweden: Thirty Years' Experience*, 3 J. BIOSOC. SCI. 173, 180-81 (1971). The matter of the relative mortality rates of therapeutic abortion and childbirth also figured in the California Supreme Court's interpretation of that state's pre-1967 abortion statute. People v. Belous, 71 Cal. 2d 954, 969-74, 458 P.2d 194, 203-06, 80 Cal. Rptr. 354, 363-66 (1969).
11. This is not a particularly high statistical possibility. *See, e.g.*, Bolter, *The Psychiatrist's Role in Therapeutic Abortion: The Unwitting Accomplice*, 119 AM. J. PSYCH. 312 (1962); Mahoney, *supra* note 10, at 286-91; Rosenberg & Silver, *Suicide, Psychiatrists and Therapeutic Abortion*, 102 CALIF. MED. 407 (1965); Walter, *Psychologic and Emotional Consequences of Elective Abortion*, 36 OBSTETRICS & GYNECOLOGY 482 (1970). For the Swedish experience, see Ottosson *supra* note 10, at 181-85, 187. For a methodology in ascertaining the psychic potential of permitting or refusing a therapeutic abortion, see Butler, *Psychiatric Indications for Therapeutic Abortion*, 63 SO. MED. J. 647 (1970).
12. Calderone, *Illegal Abortion as a Public Health Problem*, 50 AM. J. PUB. HEALTH 948 (1960); Culiner, *Some Medical Aspects of Abortion*, 10 J. FORENSIC MEDICINE 9, 12 (1963). For an equal protec-

tion use of this consideration, see City of New York v. Wyman, 66 Misc. 2d 402, 420-22, 321 N.Y.S.2d 695, 713-15 (Sup. Ct.), *aff'd on other grounds*, 37 App. Div. 2d 700, 322 N.Y.S.2d 957 (1971). *See* text accompanying notes 234-36 *infra*.

13. In addition to the sources cited in notes 10-11 *supra*, see Kummer, *Post-Abortion Psychiatric Illness — A Myth?*, 119 AM. J. PSYCH. 980 (1963); Moore & Randall, *Trends in Therapeutic Abortion: A Review of 137 Cases*, 63 AM. J. OBSTETRICS & GYNECOLOGY 28, 38-40 (1952).

14. *E.g.*, Mahoney, *supra* note 10. The Kinsey study does not particularly bear this out. P. GEBHARD, W. POMEROY, C. MARTIN & C. CHRISTENSON, PREGNANCY, BIRTH AND ABORTION 208-11 (1958).

15. "Is it not time . . . that we matured sufficiently as a people to assert once and for all that the sexual purposes of human beings and their reproductive consequences are not the business of the state, but rather free decisions to be made by husband and wife?" Rabbi Israel Margolies, *quoted in* Hall, *Thalidomide and Our Abortion Laws*, 6 COLUM. U. FORUM 10, 13 (1963). *See also* J. FLETCHER, MORALS AND MEDICINE 92-99 (Beacon Press ed. 1960); Thomson, *supra* note 7.

16. Only Japan appears to embody this specifically in its statute. Article 3(5) of the Eugenic Protection Law of 1948, (*Yūseihogohō*, Law No. 156, of 1948, ROPPO ZENSHO 2108 [1971 ed.]) permits an abortion "if there are several children and the mother's health will be seriously impaired if she again delivers." Article 14 permits a doctor empowered by a district medical association to terminate a pregnancy in his discretion, and with the consent of both husband and wife, for several reasons, including the likelihood of substantial injury to the mother's health for either physical or economic reasons if the pregnancy continues to term (author's translation and paraphrase). Some Scandinavian laws go almost this far. Clemmesen, *State of Legal Abortion in Denmark*, 112 AM. J. PSYCH. 662 (1956); Klintskog, *Survey of Legislation on Legal Abortion in Europe and North America*, 21 MEDICO-LEGAL J. 79 (1953). On changing societal attitudes as a result of relatively unrestricted medical abortions, see Ottosson, *supra* note 10, at 190-91. The recent English statute, The Abortion Act of 1967, c. 87, § 1(2), also permits a medical practitioner to take account of "the pregnant woman's actual or reasonably foreseeable environment" in deciding whether under section 1(1)(a) there is a risk of "injury to the physical or mental health of the pregnant woman or any existing children of her family, greater than if the pregnancy were terminated." *See* Simms, *Abortion Law Reform: How the Controversy Changed*, 1970 CRIM. L. REV. 567, 568-71. *Cf.* ORE. REV. STAT. § 435.415(2) (1971) permitting consideration of actual or reasonably foreseeable total environment in considering whether pregnancy poses a substantial risk to the woman's physical or mental health.

17. *E.g.*, Schwartz, *The Abortion Laws: A Severe Case of Resistance to Change*, 67 OHIO ST. MED. J. 33 (1971); Margolis & Overstreet, *Legal Abortion Without Hospitalization*, 36 OBSTETRICS & GYNECOLOGY 479 (1970).

18. There is of course the problem, as yet generally ignored, of distinguishing abortion from some forms of contraception, a problem that might be particularly troubling if the so-called "morning-after pill" is perfected and marketed. *See* Hardin, *The History and Future of Birth Control*, 10 PERSPECTIVES IN BIOLOGY & MEDICINE 1 (1966); Note, *Criminal Law — Abortion — The "Morning-After Pill" and Other Pre-Implantation Birth-Control Methods and the Law*, 46 ORE. L. REV. 211 (1967). *Compare* COLO. REV. STAT. § 40-6-101(1) (1969) *and* N.M. STAT. ANN. § 40A-5-1(A) (1969), which define pregnancy as "the implantation of an embryo in the uterus," *with* KAN. STAT. ANN. § 21-3407(3) (1969), which defines pregnancy as "that condition of a female from the date of conception to the birth of her child."

19. *But see* Roemer, *Abortion Law Reform and Repeal: Legislative and Judicial Developments*, 61 AM. J. PUB. HEALTH 500, 505-06 (1971), indicating similar trends in several Pacific Basin Countries.

20. *See* R. BEARDSLEY, J. HALL & R. WARD, VILLAGE JAPAN 335-36 (1959).

21. R. DORE, CITY LIFE IN JAPAN 205 n.196 (1958).

22. *But cf.* Roemer, *supra* note 19.

23. *See* H. THIELICKE, *supra* note 3, at 215-25.

24. This factor may account for the rescission of the law permitting easy abortion in Russia. *See* G. WILLIAMS, THE SANCTITY OF LIFE AND THE CRIMINAL LAW 219-20, 224 (1957). This rescission in turn, however, is reported to have been modified. P. GEBHARD, *supra* note 14, at 218. So was a similar change in Bulgarian law. Roemer, *supra* note 19, at 504.

25. Sulloway, *The Legal and Political Aspects of Population Control in the United States*, 25 LAW & CONTEMP. PROB. 593, 597-98 (1960); Tietze, *The Current Status of Fertility Control*, 25 LAW & CONTEMP. PROB. 426, 442-44 (1960). *See also* the sources cited *supra* note 18.

26. *Cf.* Hall, *The Medico-Legal Aspects of Abortion*, CRIMINOLOGICA, Feb. 1967, at 7; Hall, *Therapeutic Abortion, Sterilization, and Contraception*, 91 AM. J. OBSTETRICS & GYNECOLOGY 518, 522 (1965); Leavy & Kummer, *Criminal Abortion: Human Hardship and Unyielding Laws*, 35 S. CAL. L. REV. 123, 138-39 (1962). *See also* note 17 *supra*.

27. *See* text accompanying notes 37-47 *infra*.

28. *Cf.* Quay, *Justifiable Abortion — Medical and Legal Foundations*, 49 GEO. L.J. 173, 233-35 (1960); Note, *A New Approach to Old Crimes: The Model Penal Code*, 39 NOTRE DAME LAWYER 310, 313-14 (1964).

29. *See* text accompanying notes 170-83 *infra*.

30. These are some of the propositions advanced by strict opponents of re-

form. *Cf.* G. Williams, *supra* note 24, at 61-63. *See also* Sturop, *Abortion in Denmark*, Criminologica, Feb. 1967, at 29, 33-34, noting no increase in "immorality" after liberalization of abortion laws in Denmark and Sweden.

31. *See* note 7 *supra*. *See also* Clark, *Religion, Morality, and Abortion: A Constitutional Appraisal*, 2 Loy. L.A.L. Rev. 1, 8 (1969).

32. Wertheimer, *Understanding the Abortion Argument*, 1 Philosophy & Pub. Affairs 67 (1971).

33. *Cf.* Doe v. General Hospital, 434 F.2d 427 (D.C. Cir. 1970). *See also* note 210 *infra*.

34. See the statutory exemption of individual doctors and private hospitals in the recent statutes cited in note 209 *infra*.

35. G. Williams, *supra* note 24, at 152-56; Quay, *supra* note 28, at 231-38.

36. Most common law cases reach only conduct that causes a miscarriage of a pregnant woman after the fetus has quickened. R. Perkins, Criminal Law 140 (1969). This rules out most abortions, for abortions generally must be performed within the first trimester of pregnancy to minimize the danger to the pregnant woman. *See* text accompanying notes 185-87 *infra* for the legislative handling of this problem in the new statutes.

37. La. Rev. Stat. § 14:87 (Supp. 1972). The only intent required is the intent to procure premature delivery of the embryo or fetus. There is internal inconsistency in Louisiana statutory law, however, in that the statement of causes for revocation of a medical license includes: "Procuring, aiding or abetting in procuring an abortion unless done for the relief of a woman whose life appears in peril after due consultation with another licensed physician . . . ." La. Rev. Stat. § 37.1285 (1964). If both are considered *in pari materia*, then Louisiana law is in accord with the majority of states as listed in note 46 *infra*.

38. Mass. Gen. Laws Ann. ch. 272, § 19 (1968).

39. N. J. Rev. Stat. § 2A:87-1 (1969). The statute reads "without lawful justification," but nothing in the license revocation statute provides any clue as to what may be lawful justification. N.J. Rev. Stat. § 45:9-16 (1963). *Cf.* cases cited in note 42 *infra*.

40. Pa. Stat. Ann. tit. 18, § 4719 (1963). *See also* Trout, *Therapeutic Abortion Laws Need Therapy*, 37 Temp. L.Q. 172, 184-86 (1964), for a discussion of the Pennsylvania abortion law.

41. Commonwealth v. Brunelle, 341 Mass. 675, 677, 171 N.E.2d 850, 852 (1961).

42. State v. Brandenburg, 137 N.J.L. 124, 58 A.2d 709 (1948). *But see* Raleigh Fitkin-Paul Morgan Memorial Hospital v. Anderson, 42 N.J. 421, 201 A.2d 537, *cert. denied*, 377 U.S. 985 (1964) (court could order blood transfusions for a pregnant woman who resisted the procedure on religious grounds).

43. N.H. Rev. Stat. Ann. § 585:12 (1955) (attempts to procure miscarriage).

44. *Id.* § 585.13 ("unless by reason of some malformation or of difficult or protracted labor, it shall have been necessary, to preserve the life of the woman . . . .").

45. This includes all the jurisdictions discussed in text accompanying notes 142-241 *infra* that have liberalized their statutes after 1966.

46. Ala. Code tit. 14, § 9 (1959); Ariz. Rev. Stat. Ann. § 13-211 (1956); Ark. Stat. Ann. § 41-304 (Supp. 1969); Cal. Health & Safety Code § 25951 (Supp. 1971); Colo. Rev. Stat. Ann. § 40-6-101(3)(a) (1971); Conn. Gen. Stat. Ann. § 53-29 (1958) (held unconstitutional in Abele v. Markle, ___ F. Supp. ___ (D. Conn. April 18, 1972)); Del. Code Ann. tit. 24, § 1790(a)(1) (Supp. 1970); Fla. Sess. Laws ch. 72-196 (West 1972) (the earlier statutes, Fla. Stat. Ann. §§ 782.10, 797.01 (1965) were held unconstitutional in State v. Barquet, 10 Crim. L. Rep. 2431 (Fla. 1972); Ga. Code Ann. § 26-1202(a)(1) (1970) (held partially unconstitutional in Doe v. Bolton, 319 F. Supp. 1048 (N.D. Ga. 1970) (per curiam), *jurisdiction postponed*, 402 U.S. 941 (1971) (No. 971, 1970; renumbered No. 70-40, 1971 Term)); Idaho Code Ann. § 18-1506 (Supp. 1971); Ill. Ann. Stat. ch. 38, § 23-1 (Smith-Hurd 1970) (held unconstitutional in Doe v. Scott, 321 F. Supp. 1385 (N.D. Ill. 1971), *appeals docketed sub. noms.* Hanrahan v. Doe and Heffernen v. Doe, 39 U.S.L.W. 3438 (U.S. Mar. 29, 1971) (Nos. 1522, 1523, 1970 Term; renumbered Nos. 70-105, 70-106, 1971 Term)); Ind. Ann. Stat. § 10-105 (1956); Iowa Code Ann. § 701.1 (1950); Kan. Stat. Ann. § 21-3407 (1969) (Supp. 1970); Ky. Rev. Stat. § 436.020 (1969); Me. Rev. Stat. Ann. ch. 17, § 51 (1964); Md. Ann. Code art. 43, § 137(a)(1) (1971); Mich. Comp. Laws Ann. § 750.14 (1968); Minn. Stat. Ann. § 617.18 (1963); Miss. Code Ann. § 2223 (Supp. 1971); Mo. Ann. Stat. § 559.100 (1953); Mont. Rev. Codes Ann. § 94.401 (1969); Neb. Rev. Stat. §§ 28-404, -405 (1965); Nev. Rev. Stat. § 201.120 (1967); N.H. Rev. Stat. Ann. § 585.13 (1955) (abortion of quick child); N.M. Stat. Ann. § 40A-5-1 to -3 (Supp. 1971); N.Y. Penal Law §§ 125.05, 125.40-.55 (McKinney Supp. 1971); N.C. Gen. Stat. § 14-45.1 (Supp. 1971); N.D. Cent. Code § 12-25-01 (1960); Ohio Rev. Code § 2901.16 (Page 1953); Okla. Stat. Ann. tit. 21, § 861 (Supp. 1971); Ore. Rev. Stat. § 435.415 (1971); R.I. Gen. Laws Ann. § 11-3-1 (1969); S.C. Code Ann. § 16-87 (Supp. 1971); S.D. Code § 22-17-1 (1967); Tenn. Code Ann. §§ 39-301 to -302 (1955); Tex. Pen. Code Ann. art. 1191 (1961) (held unconstitutional in Roe v. Wade, 314 F. Supp. 1217 (N.D. Tex. 1970) (per curiam), *jurisdiction postponed*, 402 U.S. 941 (1971) (No. 808, 1970 Term; renumbered 70-18, 1971 Term); Utah Code Ann. § 76-2-1 (1953);

VA. CODE ANN. § 18.1-62.1 (c)(1)(i) (Supp. 1971); VT. STAT. ANN. tit. 13, § 101 (1958); WASH. REV. CODE § 9.02.010 (1961) (*but see* note 67 *infra*); W. VA. CODE ANN. § 61-2-8 (1966); WIS. STAT. ANN. § 940.04 (1958); WYO. STAT. ANN. § 6-77 (1959).

47. D.C. CODE ANN. § 22-201 (1967).

48. Connecticut, Minnesota, Missouri, Nevada, New York (but not under the Revised Penal Law in force since 1967), South Carolina (now repealed), and Washington (*but see* note 67 *infra*). The statutes still in force are cited in note 46 *supra*.

49. Both Colorado and New Mexico have since expanded the area of permissible medical abortions beyond this phraseology. COLO. REV. STAT. ANN. § 40-6-101(3)(a) (1971); N.M. STAT. ANN. § 40A-5-1 (Supp. 1971).

50. ALA. CODE tit. 14, § 9 (1959); D.C. CODE ANN. § 22-201 (1967).

51. *See, e.g.,* Walsingham v. State, 250 So. 2d 857 (Fla. 1971) (construing the then current statute which excepted abortions necessary to preserve the woman's life as meaning "physical and mental health"); Commonwealth v. Brunelle, 341 Mass. 675, 171 N.E.2d 850 (1961).

52. Several still continue to be live issues even under the liberalized statutes discussed in text accompanying notes 142-241 *infra*.

53. Alabama (*but see* the license revocation statute, ALA. CODE tit. 46, § 270 (1959)), Arizona, Connecticut, Idaho, Indiana, Iowa, Kentucky, Maine, Michigan, Minnesota, Montana, Nebraska, Nevada, North Dakota, Ohio, Oklahoma, Rhode Island, South Dakota, Tennessee, Texas, Utah, Vermont, West Virginia and Wyoming. These statutes are cited in note 46 *supra*. All 18 states with recently revised legislation were originally in this group also.

54. MO. ANN. STAT. § 559.100 (1953).

55. Alabama, Arizona, Connecticut, Idaho, Illinois, Indiana, Iowa, Kentucky, Maine (good faith belief no defense, State v. Rudman, 126 Me. 177, 136 A. 817 (1927)), Michigan, Minnesota, Missouri (*but see* text accompanying note 54 *supra*), Montana, Nevada, North Dakota (good faith belief no defense, State v. Shortridge, 54 N.D. 779, 211 N.W. 336 (1926)), Oklahoma, Rhode Island, South Dakota, Utah, Vermont and Wyoming. These statutes are cited in note 46 *supra*. The revised laws in Alaska, California, Delaware, Maryland, New York, North Carolina, Oregon, South Carolina and Washington, all formerly in this group, place the problem in a different perspective. *See* text accompanying notes 59 & 143-52 *infra*.

56. Steed v. State, 27 Ala. App. 263, 170 So. 489 (1936) (*semble*: a woman who consents to an abortion is an accomplice, unless she does so under an honest belief that the abortion is necessary to save her own life). Honnard v. People, 77 Ill. 481 (1875); State v. Dunklebarger, 206 Iowa 971, 221 N.W. 592 (1928).

57. *See* text accompanying notes 149-50 *infra*.

58. TENN. CODE ANN. § 39-301 (1955); TEX. PEN. CODE art. 1191
(1961) (held unconstitutional in Roe v. Wade, 314 F. Supp. 1217
(N.D. Tex. 1970) (per curiam), *jurisdiction postponed*, 402 U.S. 941
(1971) (No. 808, 1970 Term; renumbered 70-18, 1971 Term)); W.
VA. CODE ANN. § 61-2-8 (1966); D.C. CODE ANN. § 22-201 (1967).
59. ARK. STAT. ANN. § 41-304 (Supp. 1969) ("reasonably establish");
FLA. SESS. LAWS 72-196 (West 1972) ("reasonable degree of medical
certainty"); GA. CODE ANN. § 26-1201 (1971) ("best clinical judgment"; approval of other physicians required); N.Y. PENAL LAW §
125.05 (McKinney 1967) (only as to the original life of the mother
exception; 1970 addition to the same section of abortion for any reason
within first 24 weeks of pregnancy is not so qualified); N.C. GEN.
STAT. § 14-45.1 (1967), *as amended* (Supp. 1971) ("reasonably establish"; approval of other doctors required); ORE. REV. STAT. §§
435.415-.425 (1971) ("reasonable grounds"; approval of medical
board required); S.C. CODE ANN. § 16-87 (Supp. 1971) ("can be
reasonably established"; certification of other doctors required). In
the other reform states (Alaska, California, Colorado, Delaware, Florida, Hawaii, Kansas, Maryland, Mississippi, New Mexico, Virginia,
Washington), the matter is handled solely on the basis of individual
medical judgment or board or committee approval in advance. *See*
text accompanying notes 190-95 *infra*.
60. *Cf.* MODEL PENAL CODE § 202(2)(d) (Proposed Official Draft 1962).
61. Malpractice, if involved, can best be dealt with in the setting of revocation or suspension of the right to practice medicine. *See* text accompanying notes 112-22 *infra*. If death results from a grossly mis-
managed operation, it can be brought within manslaughter or dealt
with in a personal injury action. *See* text accompanying notes 132-42
infra.
62. Note, *Abortion Reform: History, Status, and Prognosis*, 21 CASE W.
RES. L. REV. 521, 526-27 (1970).
63. An abortion statute, however, may be voided on one of the constitutional grounds being advanced with increasing frequency. *See* notes
227-37 *infra* & accompanying text. Should this happen in any state
that has not by statute abolished criminal common law, the common
law will be revived. *See* State v. Barquet, 10 Crim. L. Rptr. 2431
(Fla. 1972).
64. ALA. CODE, tit. 14, § 9 (1959); ARIZ. REV. STAT. ANN. § 13-202
(1956); COLO. REV. STAT. ANN. § 40-6-101(1) (1969); DEL. CODE
ANN. tit. 24, § 1790 (Supp. 1971); FLA. SESS. LAWS ch. 72-196
(West 1972); GA. CODE ANN. § 26-1202 (1971); IDAHO CODE
ANN. § 18-1505 (Supp. App. 1971); ILL. ANN. STAT. ch. 38, § 23-1
(1970); IND. ANN. STAT. § 10-105 (1956); KAN. STAT. ANN. ch.
21, art. 3407 (1) (Supp. 1971); KY. REV. STAT. ANN. tit. 40, §
436.020 (1969) ("at any time during the period of gestation"); LA.

REV. STAT. ANN. § 14:87 (Supp. 1971) (reference to "a pregnant female" has recently been revised to read "a female"); MICH. COMP. LAWS ANN. § 750.14 (1968); MISS. CODE ANN. § 750.14 (1968); MISS. CODE ANN. § 2223 (Supp. 1971); MONT. REV. CODES ANN. § 94-401 (1969); NEB. REV. STAT. § 28-405 (1965); NEV. REV. STAT. § 201.120 (1967); N.J. STAT. ANN. § 2A:87-1 (1969); N.M. STAT. ANN. § 40A-5-3 (Supp. 1971); N.C. GEN. STAT. § 14-45 (1969); N.D. CENT. CODE § 12-25-01 (1960); OKLA. STAT. ANN. ch. 32, § 861 (Supp. 1971) (reference to "any pregnant woman" was deleted in 1961 and revised to read "any woman"); S.C. CODE ANN. § 16-83 (1962) ("any woman with child"); S.D. COMP. LAWS ANN. § 22-17-1 (1967); TENN. CODE ANN. § 39-301 (1955); TEX. PEN. CODE ANN. art. 1191 (1961); UTAH CODE ANN. § 76-2-1 (1953); WYO. STAT. ANN. § 6-77 (1959).

65. ARK. STAT. ANN. § 41-301 (1948); KY. REV. STAT. § 436.020(2) (1969); ME. REV. STAT. ANN. tit. 17 § 51 (1965); TENN. CODE ANN. § 39-301 (1955).

66. See text accompanying notes 70-76 infra.

67. ALASKA STAT. § 11.15.060 (1970); HAWAII REV. STAT. tit. 25, § 453-16(b) (Supp. 1971); WASH. REV. CODE § 9.02.070 (Supp. 1970) ("woman not quick with child and not more than four lunar months after conception"). Since the 1970 Washington therapeutic abortion provisions were added without a repealer of section 9.02.010, an abortion at any time during pregnancy to preserve the life of the woman or her unborn child is apparently valid. Neither of the other two above statutes indicates any exception, which is perhaps an invitation to an attack based on an unreasonable classification in violation of the 14th amendment equal protection clause.

68. CAL. HEALTH & SAFETY CODE § 25953 (West Supp. 1972) (20 weeks); COLO. REV. STAT. ANN. § 40-6-101(3)(a) (1971) (16 weeks, rape and incest cases only); DEL. CODE ANN. tit. 24, § 1790(b)(1) (Supp. 1971) (20 weeks, unless necessary to preserve woman's life or fetus is dead); N.Y. PENAL LAW § 125.05 (McKinney Supp. 1971) (24 weeks unless necessary to preserve woman's life); ORE. REV. STAT. §§ 435.425(1), 435.445 (1971) (150 days, unless life of woman is in imminent danger); WASH. REV. CODE § 9.02.070 (Supp. 1970) (4 lunar months; see note 67 supra). ARK. STAT. ANN. § 41-306 (Supp. 1969) has a four month residency requirement unless there is an emergency endangering the woman's life, which may be intended to have a similar functional effect.

69. N.H. REV. STAT. ANN. § 585.13 (1955); N.Y. PENAL LAW § 125.45 (McKinney 1967); N.D. CENT. CODE § 12-25-02 (1960); PA. STAT. ANN. tit. 18, § 4719 (1963); WIS. STAT. ANN. § 940.04 (1958).

70. D.C. CODE ANN. § 22-201 (1967); ALA. CODE tit. 14, § 9 (1959); ARIZ. REV. STAT. § 13-211 (1956); ARK. STAT. ANN. § 41-303

(Supp. 1969); Cal. Penal Code § 274 (West 1968); Conn. Gen. Stat. Ann. § 53-29 (1960); Del. Code Ann. tit. 24, § 1790 (Supp. 1971) ("termination or attempt at termination"); Ga. Code Ann. § 26-1201 (1971); Idaho Code Ann. § 18-1505 (Supp. App. 1971); Ill. Ann. Stat. ch. 38, § 23-1 (1970); Ind. Ann. Stat. § 10-105 (1956); Iowa Code Ann. § 701.1 (1950); Ky. Rev. Stat. Ann. tit. 40, § 436.020 (1969); La. Rev. Stat. Ann. § 14.87 (Supp. 1972); Me. Rev. Stat. Ann. tit. 17, § 51 (1964); Mass. Gen. Laws Ann. ch. 272, § 19 (1970); Mich. Comp. Laws Ann. § 750.14 (1968); Mo. Ann. Stat. § 559.100 (1953); Mont. Rev. Codes Ann. § 94-401 (1969); Neb. Rev. Stat. § 28-405 (1965); Nev. Rev. Stat. § 201.120 (1967); N.H. Rev. Stat. Ann. § 585.12 (1955) ("attempt" catchline); N.J. Stat. Ann. § 2A:87-1 (1969); N.Y. Penal Law § 125.05(2) (McKinney 1967); N.C. Gen. Stat. § 14-45 (1969); N.D. Cent. Code § 12-25-01 (1960); Ohio Rev. Code Ann. § 2901.16 (Page 1953); S.C. Code Ann. § 16-83 (1962); S.D. Comp. Laws § 22-17-1 (1967); Tenn. Code Ann. § 39-302 (1955) ("attempt" catchline); Utah Code Ann. § 76-2-1 (1953); Va. Code Ann. § 18.1-62 (Supp. 1971); Wash. Rev. Code Ann. § 9.02.010 (1961); Wyo. Stat. Ann. § 6-77 (1959). The new Alaska statute (Alas. Stat. § 11.14.060 (1970)) is ambiguous, in that it refers to "an operation or procedure to terminate the pregnancy of a non-viable fetus [sic]."

71. Tex. Pen. Code art. 1193 (1961) ("provided it be shown that such means were calculated to produce that result . . . .").

72. See R. Perkins, Criminal Law 566-72 (1969). Cf. Dupuy v. State, 204 Tenn. 624, 325 S.W.2d 238 (1959).

73. Ten states use this language: D.C. Code Ann. § 22-201 (1967); Cal. Penal Code § 274 (West 1968); Iowa Code Ann. § 701.1 (1950); La. Rev. Stat. § 14.87 (Supp. 1971); Mass. Gen. Laws Ann. ch. 272, § 19 (1970); Ohio Rev. Code Ann. § 2901.16 (Page 1954); Pa. Stat. Ann. tit. 18, § 4719 (1963); Va. Code Ann. § 18.1-62 (Supp. 1971); Wash. Rev. Code Ann. § 9.02.010 (1961); W. Va. Code Ann. § 61-2-8 (1966). There is some internal inconsistency in the Virginia and West Virginia statutes which speak of "intent to destroy her unborn child." Cf. the Alaska terminology cited in note 70 supra. The woman was pregnant in the reported cases of Anderson v. Commonwealth, 190 Va. 665, 58 S.E.2d 72 (1950), and Coffman v. Commonwealth, 188 Va. 553, 50 S.E.2d 431 (1948), but the exact question apparently has not been presented for decision. Colo. Rev. Stat. Ann. § 40-6-103 (1971) penalizes a pretended termination of a real or apparent pregnancy other than by justified medical termination or birth.

74. Ill. Ann. Stat. ch. 38, § 23-1 (1970) ("It shall not be necessary in order to commit abortion that such woman be pregnant . . . ."); Mo.

ANN. STAT. § 559.100 (1953); N.Y. PENAL LAW § 125.05(2) (Mc-Kinney 1967).

75. IND. ANN. STAT. § 10-105 (1956) ("whom he supposes to be pregnant"); KY. REV. STAT. ANN. tit. 40, § 436.020(1) (1969) ("has reason to believe pregnant"); R.I. GEN. LAWS ANN. § 11-3-1 (1970) ("woman supposed by such person to be pregnant"); VT. STAT. ANN. tit. 13, § 101 (1958) ("woman supposed by such person to be pregnant"); WYO. STAT. ANN. § 6-77 (1959) ("whom he supposes to be pregnant").

76. See, e.g., People v. Kutz, 187 Cal. App. 2d 431, 435, 9 Cal. Rptr. 626, 629 (1960); Urga v. State, 155 So. 2d 719, 723 (Fla. App. 1963), cert. denied, 379 U.S. 829 (1964); People v. Marra, 27 Mich. App. 1, 5, 183 N.W.2d 418, 419 (1970); reh. denied, 183 N.W. 2d 418 (1971); Wyatt v. State, 77 Nev. 490, 503, 367 P.2d 104, 111 (1961), reh. denied, 367 P.2d 104 (1962). Cf. Williams v. State, 218 Tenn. 359, 365-6, 403 S.W.2d 319, 322-23 (1966) (no defense that substances and instruments would not produce miscarriage).

77. KY. REV. STAT. ANN. tit. 40, § 436.020 (1969); ME. REV. STAT. ANN. tit. 17, § 51 (1964).

78. ARK. STAT. ANN. § 41-2223 (1964); FLA. STAT. ANN. § 782.09 (1965); MICH. COMP. LAWS ANN. § 750.322 (1968); MISS. CODE ANN. § 2222 (1957); N.D. CENT. CODE ANN. § 12-25-03 (1960) (semble); OKLA. STAT. ANN. tit. 21, § 713 (1958).

79. Cf. note 237 infra & accompanying text, where the matter of civil damages for prenatal injuries is discussed.

80. Wechsler & Michael, A Rationale of the Law of Homicide, 37 COLUM. L. REV. 701, 702-23 (1937).

81. COLO. REV. STAT. ANN. §§ 40-6-102(2), 40-6-103(2) (1971); FLA. SESS. LAWS ch. 72-196 (West 1972); MASS. GEN. LAWS ANN. ch. 272 § 19 (1970); N.J. STAT. ANN. § 2A:87-1 (1969); N.M. STAT. ANN. § 40A-5-3 (Supp. 1971); R.I. GEN. LAWS ANN. § 11-3-1 (1970); S.C. CODE ANN. § 16-82 (1962); VT. STAT. ANN. tit. 13, § 101 (1958) (held unconstitutional in Beecham v. Leahy, _ _ _ Vt. _ _ _, 287 A.2d 836 (1972)).

82. D.C. CODE ANN. § 22-201 (1967) (second degree murder); KY. REV. STAT. ANN. tit. 40, § 435.040 (1969) ("murder or voluntary manslaughter as the facts may justify"); N.H. REV. STAT. ANN. § 585.14 (1955) (second degree murder); TEX. PEN. CODE ANN. art. 1194 (1961); W. VA. CODE ANN. § 61-2-8 (1966).

83. MICH. COMP. LAWS ANN. § 750.14 (1968); MO. ANN. STAT. § 559.100 (1953); N.Y. PENAL LAW § 125.20(3) (McKinney 1967) (manslaughter in the first degree); N.D. CENT. CODE ANN. § 12-25-02 (1960) (manslaughter in the first degree).

84. See, e.g., Heath v. State, 249 Ark. 217, 219, 459 S.W.2d 420, 422 (1970) (no corroboration of her testimony required); Commonwealth v. Follensbee, 155 Mass. 274, 277, 29 N.E. 471, 471 (1892); In re

Vickers, 371 Mich. 114, 118-9, 123 N.W.2d 253, 254-5 (1963) (woman cannot claim self-incrimination); *In re* Vince, 2 N.J. 443, 450, 67 A.2d 141, 144 (1949) (no self-incrimination unless the fetus has quickened, in which case the offense is against the fetus and not the mother); State v. Shaft, 166 N.C. 407, 409, 81 S.E. 932, 933 (1914); Smartt v. State, 112 Tenn. 539, 554, 80 S.W. 586, 589 (1904); Willingham v. State, 33 Tex. Crim. 98, 99, 25 S.W. 424, 424 (1894). *See also* Committee Notes to GA. CODE ANN. ch. 26-12 (1971). *Contra,* Steed v. State, 27 Ala. App. 263, 263, 170 So. 489, 489 (1936); State v. McCoy, 52 Ohio St. 157, 160, 39 N.E. 316, 316 (1894). In Iowa, although a woman cannot be an accomplice to her own criminal abortion, she may be adjudged guilty of conspiracy if she consents to the operation. State v. Crofford, 133 Iowa 478, 480, 110 N.W. 921, 922 (1907). In that case the victim was not charged (she had died as a result of the abortion), but the theory was used to make her statements admissible as a declaration in promotion of the common enterprise. The Pennsylvania Supreme Court has said that the woman cannot be guilty of conspiracy because she is the victim. Snyder Appeal, 398 Pa. 237, 246, 157 A.2d 207, 212 (1960).

85. R.I. GEN. LAWS ANN. § 11-3-1 (1970).
86. VT. STAT. ANN. *tit.* 13, § 101 (1958) (held unconstitutional in Beecham v. Leahy, ___ Vt. ___, 287 A.2d 836 (1972)).
87. LA. REV. STAT. ANN. § 14:87 (1951).
88. ARIZ. REV. STAT. ANN. § 13-212 (1956); CAL. PENAL CODE § 275 (1968); CONN. GEN. STAT. ANN. § 53-30 (1960); IDAHO CODE ANN. § 18-1506 (Supp. 1971); IND. ANN. STAT. § 10-106 (1956); MINN. STAT. ANN. § 617.19 (1963); N.Y. PENAL LAW §§ 125.50, 125.55 (1967); N.D. CENT. CODE § 12-25-04 (1960); OKLA. STAT. ANN. tit. 21, § 862 (1958); S.C. CODE ANN. § 16-84 (1962); S.D. COMP. LAWS ANN. § 22-17-2 (1967) (*but see* State v. Burlingame, 47 S.D. 332, 198 N.W. 824 (1924), which held that the woman was not an accomplice under the abortion statute, section 22-17-1); UTAH CODE ANN. § 76-2-2 (1953) (*but see* State v. Cragun, 85 Utah 149, 38 P.2d 1071 (1934), in which it was held that this statute did not make her an accomplice under the primary abortion statute, section 76-2-1); WASH. REV. CODE ANN. § 9.02.020 (1961); WIS. STAT. ANN. § 940.04 (1958); WYO. STAT. ANN. § 6-78 (1957).
89. *E.g.,* CAL. PENAL CODE § 1108 (1970); IDAHO CODE ANN. § 19-2115 (1948); MONT. REV. CODE ANN. § 94-7216 (1947); N.D. CENT. CODE § 12-25-07 (1960); S.C. CODE ANN. §§ 16-82, 16-83 (1962).
90. People v. Peyser, 380 Ill. 404, 44 N.E.2d 58 (1942); State v. McCoy, 52 Ohio St. 157, 39 N.E. 316 (1894).
91. *See* Snyder Appeal (Commonwealth v. Fisher), 398 Pa. 237, 157 A.2d 207 (1960).
92. MINN. STAT. ANN. § 617.21 (1964); WASH. REV. CODE ANN. §

9.02.040 (1961). Whatever the validity of these statutes under state constitutional law, they clearly conflict with the self-incrimination concept engrafted on the 14th amendment due process clause by Malloy v. Hogan, 378 U.S. 1 (1964), and Murphy v. Waterfront Comm'n, 378 U.S. 52 (1964).

93. Nev. Rev. Stat. § 201.140 (1967); N.J. Rev. Stat. § 2A:87-2 (1969); Ohio Rev. Code Ann. § 2901.17 (Page 1953); S.C. Code Ann. § 16-85 (1962).

94. See, e.g., Petition of Vickers, 371 Mich. 114, 123 N.W.2d 253 (1963); In re Vince, 2 N.J. 443, 67 A.2d 141 (1949).

95. J. Bates & E. Zawadski, Criminal Abortion 38-39 (1964).

96. Id. at 85-91.

97. Ariz. Rev. Stat. Ann. § 13-213 (1956); Cal. Bus. & Prof. Code § 601 (Supp. 1971); Conn. Gen. Stat. Ann. § 53-31 (1958); Del. Code Ann. tit. 11, § 302 (1953); Fla. Stat. Ann. § 797.02 (1965); Idaho Code Ann. § 18-1507 (Supp. 1971); Ill. Ann. Stat. ch. 38, § 23-3 (Smith-Hurd 1970); Ind. Ann. Stat. § 10-2806 (1956); La. Rev. Stat. Code § 14:88 (1951); Mass. Gen. Laws Ann. ch. 272, § 20 (1970); Mich. Comp. Laws Ann. § 750.34 (1968); Mo. Ann. Stat. § 563.300 (Supp. 1971); Pa. Stat. Ann. tit. 18, § 4525 (1963); R.I. Gen. Laws Ann. § 11-3-4 (1969); S.D. Comp. Laws Ann. § 34-15-1 (1967); Vt. Stat. Ann. tit. 13, § 104 (1959); Va. Code Ann. § 18.1-63 (1960); Wis. Stat. Ann. 143.075 (1963); Wyo. Stat. Ann. § 6-105 (Supp. 1971). The following states have recently repealed their statutes: Me. Rev. Stat. Ann. ch. 17, § 53 (1964) (repealed 1967); Md. Ann. Code art. 27, § 3 (1957) (repealed 1968).

98. See, e.g., Colo. Rev. Stat. Ann. § 40-9-17 (1963); Miss. Code Ann. § 2289 (Supp. 1971).

99. The author has found only two cases, People v. McKean, 76 Cal. App. 114, 243 P. 898 (Dist. Ct. App. 1925); Commonwealth v. Hartford, 193 Mass. 464, 79 N.E. 784 (1907). See also Shapiro v. Board of Regents, 22 App. Div. 2d 243, 254 N.Y.S.2d 906 (1964), a license suspension case that appears to stress the physician's misrepresentation or fraud rather than his offer to procure an abortion.

100. See Mitchell Family Planning Inc. v. City of Royal Oak, 335 F. Supp. 738 (E.D. Mich. 1972), striking down an ordinance invoked against a private organization because it advertised its name and telephone numbers through which abortion information might be obtained. Note that Michigan retains a strict abortion statute, note 46 supra, exempting only operations to preserve the life of the pregnant woman. Nevertheless, the advertisement was held to be within first amendment protection because there was nothing to indicate that an unlawful abortion would be performed as the result of a call to a telephone number listed on a billboard.

101. Mass. Gen. Laws Ann. ch. 272, § 21 (1968) (this section has been held unconstitutional. *See* note 111 *infra* for discussion of the *Eisenstadt* case); Minn. Stat. Ann. § 617.20 (1964); Nev. Rev. Stat. § 201.130 (1967); N.Y. Penal Law § 125.60 (1967); Wash. Rev. Code Ann. § 9.02.030 (1956).

102. Colo. Rev. Stat. Ann. § 40-6-105 (1971); Ill. Ann. Stat. ch. 38, § 23-2 (Smith-Hurd 1970) (other than to a licensed physician); La. Rev. Stat. Ann. § 14:88 (1964); Md. Ann. Code art. 43, § 149G(a)(1) (1968).

103. Tex. Pen. Code Ann. art. 1192 (1961). This statute was recently held unconstitutional in Roe v. Wade, 314 F. Supp. 1217 (N.D. Tex. 1970) (per curiam), *jurisdiction postponed*, 402 U.S. 941 (1971) (No. 808, 1970 Term, renumbered 70-18, 1971 Term) (violation of right of privacy).

104. Colo. Rev. Stat. Ann. § 40-6-105 (1971); Del. Code Ann. tit. 24, § 1792(1) (1969); Ill. Ann. Stat. ch. 38, § 23-2 (Smith-Hurd 1970); Iowa Code Ann. § 205.1 (1969) (other than on prescription); Md. Ann. Code art. 43, § 139(a)(1) (1971); Mass. Gen. Laws Ann. ch. 272, § 21 (1968) (see note 111 *infra*); Mich. Comp. Laws Ann. § 750.15 (1968) (except on prescription); Minn. Stat. Ann. § 617.20 (1964); Miss. Code Ann. § 2289 (Supp. 1971); Mo. Ann. Stat. § 563.300 (Supp. 1971); Nev. Rev. Stat. § 201.130 (1967); R.I. Gen. Laws Ann. § 11-3-4 (1969); Vt. Stat. Ann. tit. 13, § 104 (1958); Wash. Rev. Code Ann. § 9.02.030 (1961).

105. Colo. Rev. Stat. Ann. § 40-9-17 (1963) (obscenity statute); Del. Code Ann. tit. 24, § 1792(1) (1969); Iowa Code Ann. § 205.1 (1969); Mass. Gen. Laws Ann. ch. 272, § 21 (1968) (*see* note 111 *infra*); Minn. Stat. Ann. § 617.20 (1964); Miss. Code Ann. § 2289 (Supp. 1971) (obscenity statute); Mo. Ann. Stat. § 63.300 (1967); Nev. Rev. Stat. § 201.130 (1967); Vt. Stat. Ann. tit. 13, § 104 (1958); Wash. Rev. Code Ann. § 9.02.030 (1961).

106. Colo. Rev. Stat. Ann. § 40-9-17 (1963) (obscenity statute); Mass. Gen. Laws Ann. ch. 272, § 21 (1968) (*see* note 111 infra); Miss. Code Ann. § 2289 (Supp. 1971) (obscenity statute).

107. Colo. Rev. Stat. Ann. § 66-3-66 (1963). Mich. Comp. Laws Ann. § 750.15 (1968).

108. Ore. Rev. Stat. §§ 435.405-.495 (1971).

109. *Id.* § 465.110.

110. 18 U.S.C. §§ 1461, 1462 (1970).

111. Youngs Rubber Corp. v. C.I. Lee & Co., 45 F.2d 103 (2d Cir. 1930) (dictum). *See also* Eisenstadt v. Baird, 40 U.S.L.W. 4303 (U.S. Mar. 22, 1972), where the Court held unconstitutional Mass. Gen. Laws Ann. ch. 272, §§ 19, 21, 21A (1968). Specificaly the *Eisenstadt* Court voided the conviction of a birth control advocate under the Massachusetts statute which prohibited distribution of contraceptive ma-

terials to unmarried persons except for the prevention of disease. This dissimilar treatment of married and unmarried persons violated the equal protection clause of the 14th amendment.

112. George, *Legal, Medical and Psychiatric Considerations in the Control of Prostitution,* 60 MICH. L. REV. 717, 736-43 (1962).

113. ALA. CODE tit. 46, § 270 (Supp. 1969); ALASKA STAT. §§ 08.64.330, 380 (1962); ARIZ. REV. STAT. ANN. §§ 32-1401, 32-1451 (Supp. 1971); ARK. STAT. ANN. § 72-613 (Supp. 1969); CAL. BUS. & PROF. CODE §§ 2360, 2361, 2377 (Supp. 1971); COLO. REV. STAT. ANN. § 91-1-17 (1963); DEL. CODE ANN. tit. 24, § 1741 (Supp. 1970); FLA. STAT. ANN. § 458.12 (1965); GA. CODE ANN. § 84-916 (1970); HAWAII REV. STAT. § 453.8(1) (Supp. 1971); IDAHO CODE ANN. § 54-1810 (Supp. 1971); IOWA CODE ANN. §§ 147.55, 147.56 (1949); KY. REV. STAT. ANN. § 311.595 (1963); LA. REV. STAT. ANN. § 37:1285 (1964); MD. ANN. CODE art. 43 § 130(h) (1971); MICH. COMP. LAWS ANN. § 338.53 (1967); MINN. STAT. ANN. § 147.02 (1970); MISS. CODE ANN. §§ 8893, 8893.1 (Supp. 1971); NEB. REV. STAT. §§ 71-147, -148 (1966); NEV. REV. STAT. §§ 630.030, 630.300 (1969); N.J. REV. STAT. § 45:9-16 (1963); N.M. STAT. ANN. § 67-5-9 (Supp. 1971); N.C. GEN. STAT. § 90-14 (Supp. 1971); N.D. CENT. CODE § 43-17-31 (1960); OKLA. STAT. ANN. tit. 59, § 509 (1963); ORE. REV. STAT. § 677.190 (1971); PA. STAT. ANN. tit. 63, § 410 (1968); R.I. GEN. LAWS ANN. § 5-37-4 (Supp. 1971); S.D. COMP. LAWS ANN. §§ 36-4-29, 36-4-30 (1967); TENN. CODE ANN. §§ 63-618, 63-619 (1955); TEX. REV. CIV. STAT. ANN. arts. 4505, 4506 (1960); UTAH CODE ANN. § 58-12-18 (1963); VT. STAT. ANN. tit. 26, § 1398 (1967); VA. CODE ANN. §§ 54-316, -317 (1967); WASH. REV. CODE ANN. §§ 18.71.120, .140, 18.72.030 (1959); WIS. STAT. ANN. § 448.18 (Supp. 1957); WYO. STAT. ANN. § 33-340 (1957).

114. MISS. CODE ANN. § 2223(3) (Supp. 1971); MO. ANN. STAT. § 559.100 (1959).

115. ALASKA STAT. § 11.15.060 (1970), § 08.64.105 (Supp. 1971); CAL. HEALTH & SAFETY CODE §§ 25950-54 (Supp. 1971); DEL. CODE ANN. tit. 24, § 1790 (Supp. 1970); HAWAII REV. STAT. § 453-16 MD. ANN. CODE art. 43, § 137(a) (1971); ORE. REV. STAT. §§ 435.405-.495 (1969). The Alabama and Louisiana statutes (*see* notes 46, 113 *supra*) have the licensure sections in terms broader than the criminal code provisions, which could create a problem of construction as to which controls. *See* note 37 *supra*.

116. D.C. CODE ANN. § 2-131 (1961); CONN. GEN. STAT. ANN. § 20-45 (1969); IND. ANN. STAT. § 63-1306 (1962); ME. REV. STAT. ANN. ch. 32, § 3203 (1964), *as amended* (Supp. 1972); N.H. REV. STAT. ANN. § 329:17 (1966); OHIO REV. CODE § 4731.22 (Page 1953), *as amended* (Supp. 1970); S.C. CODE ANN. § 56-1368 (Supp. 1971)

(conviction of "illegal practice" as also included; this may well include abortion).

117. MASS. GEN. LAWS ANN. ch. 112, § 61 (1965); MONT. REV. CODES ANN. § 66-1037 (2d Replacement vol. 1970). This phrase is also included in the various statutes cited notes 113, 116 *supra.*

118. Lawrence v. Bd. of Registration, 239 Mass. 424, 132 N.E. 174 (1921); State *ex rel.* Sorenson v. Lake, 121 Neb. 331, 236 N.W. 762 (1931). *Cf.* Moormeister v. Dept. of Registrations, 76 Utah 146, 288 P. 900 (1930).

119. ARIZ. REV. STAT. ANN. § 32-1854 (Supp. 1971-72); ORE. REV. STAT. § 681.140 (Supp. 1967-68).

120. ARIZ. REV. STAT. ANN. § 32-1663 (Supp. 1971-72). ILL. ANN. STAT. ch. 91, § 35.46 (Smith-Hurd Supp. 1972); CAL. BUS. & PROF. CODE § 2761 (West 1962) (Nursing); *id.* § 2878 (vocational nursing).

121. COLO. REV. STAT. ANN. § 91-4-6 (1963); GA. CODE ANN. § 88-1405 (Rev. 1971); ILL. ANN. STAT. ch. 91, § 16a (Smith-Hurd Supp. 1972).

122. FLA. STAT. ANN. § 462.14 (1965) (naturopath), § 460.13 (Supp. 1971-72) (chiropractor); NEV. REV. STAT. tit. 54, § 634.010 (1967) (chiropractor); N.Y. EDUC. LAW § 6514 (1953) (physiotherapist); ORE. REV. STAT. § 684.100 (Supp. 1971) (chiropractor); *id.* § 685.110 (naturopath).

123. *See, e.g.,* Application of Jones, 4 App. Div. 2d 994, 168 N.Y.S.2d 42 (1957).

124. Blumberg v. State Bd. of Medical Examiners, 96 N.J.L. 331, 115 A. 439 (Sup. Ct. 1922).

125. State v. Lewis, 164 Wis. 353, 159 N.W. 746 (1916); FLA. OP. ATT'Y GEN. 505, 509 (1962).

126. Ashe v. Swenson, 397 U.S. 436 (1970).

127. Florida State Bd. of Architecture v. Seymour, 62 So. 2d 1 (Fla. 1952) (architect's license); Malouf v. Gully, 187 Miss. 331, 192 So. 2d 2 (1939) (liquor license).

128. *See, e.g.,* Florida State Bd. of Medical Examiners v. James, 158 So. 2d 574 (Fla. App. 1964).

129. Spevack v. Klein, 385 U.S. 511 (1967). On the related matter of discharge or discipline of public employees who claim privilege, see Uniformed Sanitation Men Ass'n, Inc. v. Comm'r of Sanitation, 392 U.S. 280 (1968); Gardner v. Broderick, 392 U.S. 273 (1968).

130. Garrity v. New Jersey, 385 U.S. 493 (1967). The Court noted that "[t]he choice given petitioners was either to forfeit their jobs or incriminate themselves. The option to lose their means of livelihood or to pay the penalty of self-incrimination is the antithesis of free choice to speak out or to remain silent." *Id.* at 497.

131. DeVita v. Sills, 422 F.2d 1172 (3d Cir. 1970) (no requirement to defer disciplinary hearings against attorney-judge until all criminal

charges disposed of). The court relied on United States v. Kordel, 397 U.S. 1 (1970), holding that interrogatory practice under FED. R. CIV. P. 33 in a civil forfeiture proceeding against a corporation need not be suspended until pending criminal charges are disposed of, although there are several important factors on which the two situations may be distinguished. The corporate status of the defendant and the availability of needed evidence through testimony not incriminating to the one responding to interrogatories are two such grounds.

132. Martin v. Morris, 163 Tenn. 186, 188, 42 S.W.2d 207, 208 (1931).
133. Milliken v. Heddesheimer, 110 Ohio St. 381, 388-89, 144 N.E. 264, 267 (1924).
134. *See* note 140 *infra* & cases cited therein.
135. Sayadoff v. Warda, 125 Cal. App. 2d 626, 271 P.2d 140 (1954); Goldnamer v. O'Brien, 98 Ky. 569, 33 S.W. 831 (1896); Bowlan v. Lunsford, 176 Okla. 115, 54 P.2d 666 (1936).
136. Nash v. Meyer, 54 Idaho 283, 31 P.2d 273 (1934); Martin v. Morris, 163 Tenn. 186, 42 S.W.2d 207 (1931).
137. Richey v. Darling, 183 Kan. 642, 331 P.2d 281 (1958); Henrie v. Griffith, 395 P.2d 809 (Okla. 1964).
138. Lembo v. Donnell, 117 Me. 143, 103 A. 11 (1918); Miller v. Bayer, 94 Wis. 123, 68 N.W. 869 (1896).
139. Szadiwicz v. Cantor, 257 Mass. 518, 154 N.E. 251 (1926) (no indication in the report that the defendant was in fact a doctor; the negligence consisted of using "non-sterile instruments"); Miller v. Bennett, 190 Va. 162, 56 S.E.2d 217 (1949).
140. Wolcott v. Gaines, 225 Ga. 373, 169 S.E.2d 165 (1969); Martin v. Hardesty, 91 Ind. App. 239, 163 N.E. 610 (1928); True v. Older, 227 Minn. 154, 34 N.W.2d 700 (1948); Milliken v. Heddesheimer, 110 Ohio St. 381, 144 N.E. 264 (1924); Andrews v. Coulter, 163 Wash. 429, 1 P.2d 320 (1931) (only for negligent aftercare, not for the abortion itself).
141. Note, *Legal and Social Control of Abortion*, 40 KY. L.J. 410, 414-15 (1952).
142. *Cf.* B. SHARTEL & M. PLANT, THE LAW OF MEDICAL PRACTICE §§ 1-17, -18 (1959). *See also* GA. CODE ANN. § 26-1202 (d) (Rev. 1971) (no wrongful death action for death of fetus if abortion performed under therapeutic abortion act).
143. *E.g.*, Henker, *Abortion and Sterilization From Psychiatric and Medico-Legal Viewpoints*, 57 J. ARK. MED. SOC'Y 368 (1961); May, *Therapeutic Abortion in North Carolina*, 23 N.C. MED. J. 547 (1962); Moore & Randall, *Trends in Therapeutic Abortion in California in 1950*, 60 W. J. OF SURGERY, OBSTETRICS & GYNECOLOGY 497 (1952).
144. MICH. COMP. LAWS ANN. § 750.14 (1968).
145. ARK. STAT. ANN. § 41-304 (Supp. 1969) (doctor must "reasonably establish" statutory grounds); ILL. ANN. STAT. ch. 38, § 23-1(b)

(Smith-Hurd 1967); N.C. GEN. STAT. § 14-45.1 (Supp. 1969) (doctor must "reasonably establish" grounds); ORE. REV. STAT. § 435.425 (1968) ("rebuttable presumption" arises from noncompliance). *Cf.* S.C. CODE § 16-87 (Supp. 1971) (when it can be reasonably established).

146. People v. Gallardo, 41 Cal. 2d 57, 257 P.2d 29 (1953); State v. Lee, 69 Conn. 186, 37 A.75 (1897); State v. Brown, 26 Del. 499, 85 A. 797 (1912); State v. Riley, 256 A.2d 273 (Del. Super. Ct. 1969); Holloway v. State, 90 Ga. App. 86, 82, S.E.2d 235 (1954); State v. Dunkelbarger, 206 Iowa 971, 221 N.W. 592 (1928); Commonwealth v. Stone, 300 Mass. 160, 14 N.E.2d 158 (1938); Ladnier v. State, 155 Miss. 348, 124 So. 432 (1929); State v. DeGroat, 259 Mo. 364, 168 S.W. 702 (1914); People v. Harrison, 40 Misc. 2d 601, 243 N.Y.S.2d 432 (Sup. Ct. 1963); Moody v. State, 17 Ohio St. 110 (1866); State v. Elliott, 206 Ore. 82, 289 P.2d 1075 (1955); State v. St. Angelo, 72 R.I. 412, 52 A.2d 513 (1947); State v. Wells, 35 Utah 400, 100 P. 681 (1909); State v. Montifiore, 95 Vt. 508, 116 A. 77 (1922); State v. Bates, 52 Wash. 2d 207, 324 P.2d 810 (1958). *Contra,* Fitch v. People, 45 Colo. 298, 100 P. 1132 (1909). The Connecticut, Oregon, and Washington decisions hold, however, that the state meets its burden by proving that the woman was healthy immediately before the abortion was performed.

147. State v. Abodeely, 179 N.W.2d 347 (Iowa 1970); State v. Hawkins, 255 Ore. 39, 463 P.2d 858 (1970). If before or during trial the fact appears that the defendant is indeed a licensed medical practitioner within the class defined in the abortion statute, then presumably the burden will rest on the prosecution under the decisions in note 146 *supra.*

148. 402 U.S. 62 (1971).

149. *Id.* at 70. *See also* Corkey v. Edwards, 322 F. Supp. 1248 (W.D.N.C. 1971), *appeal docketed,* 40 U.S.L.W. 3098-99 (U.S. Sept. 14, 1971) (No. 92), holding that despite statutory language (*see* note 145 *supra*), the burden to show nonjustification is on the prosecution.

150. *See* text accompanying notes 190-95 *infra. See also* ORE. REV. STAT. § 435.425(3) (1968) (rebuttable presumption arises, from a failure to follow certification requirements, that termination of pregnancy was unjustified).

151. *See* C. MCCORMICK, LAW OF EVIDENCE 157 (1954).

152. *See* text accompanying notes 202-05 *infra.*

153. *See* text accompanying notes 88-94 *supra.*

154. *Cf.* E. SCHUR, CRIMES WITHOUT VICTIMS 169 (1965); Johnson, *Rethinking the Abortion Problem: A Sociological Critique,* CRIMINOLOGICA, Feb. 1967, at 20, 22-23.

155. MODEL PENAL CODE § 230.3 (Proposed Official Draft 1962).

156. United States v. Vuitch, 402 U.S. 62, 71-73 (1971).

157. *Cf.* State v. Bass, 255 N.C. 42, 120 S.E.2d 580 (1961) (mayhem conviction sustained against physician who amputated fingers of one intending to make a fraudulent insurance claim).

158. CAL. HEALTH & SAFETY CODE § 25952(a); COLO. REV. STAT. ANN. § 40-6-101(3) (1971); GA. CODE ANN. § 26-1202(b)(1), (6) (Rev. 1971); MD. ANN. CODE art. 43, § 137(C) (1968) (requests for authorization); N.M. STAT. ANN. § 40A-5-1(C) (Supp. 1971).

159. ARK. STAT. ANN. § 41-305 (Supp. 1969); N.Y. PENAL LAW § 125.05(3) (1967); N.C. GEN. STAT. § 14-45.1 (Supp. 1969); ORE. REV. STAT. § 435.435 (1969); S.C. CODE ANN. § 16-87 Supp. 1970); VA. CODE ANN. § 18.1-62.1(e) (Supp. 1971); WASH. REV. CODE § 9.02.070 (Supp. 1971).

160. Colorado, South Carolina (unless emergency endangering life), and Washington. The statutes are cited notes 158-59 *supra.*

161. This is the case in Oregon and Virginia. *See* statutes cited in note 159 *supra.* The provision in the Virginia statute only applies if the abortion is to be performed on eugenic grounds because the child will likely be born with an irremediable and incapacitating mental or physical defect.

162. *See, e.g.*, the Arkansas, Colorado, North Carolina, South Carolina, and Virginia statutes cited in notes 158-59 *supra.*

163. ALASKA STAT. § 11.15.060(a)(3) (1970); DEL. CODE ANN. tit. 24, § 1790(b)(3) (1969). *See also* the New Mexico, North Carolina, Oregon, South Carolina, Virginia, and Washington statutes cited in notes 158-59 *supra.*

164. *Cf.* H. CLARK, LAW OF DOMESTIC RELATIONS 157, 329, 337, 346 (1968); 1 W. NELSON, DIVORCE AND ANNULMENT § 4.08 (2d ed. 1945); Wadlington, *Artificial Insemination: The Dangers of a Poorly Kept Secret*, 64 NW. U.L. REV. 777, 785-93 (1970); Note, *Elective Sterilization*, 113 U. PA. L. REV. 415, 437-39 (1965).

165. *See* the Alaska, Delaware, New Mexico, Virginia and Washington statutes cited in notes 158-59, 163 *supra.*

166. DEL. CODE ANN. tit. 24, § 1790(b)(3) (1969).

167. 4 Cal. 3d 873, 484 P.2d 1345, 95 Cal. Rptr. 1 (1971).

168. Section 34.5 provides that:
> Notwithstanding any other provision of the law, an unmarried, pregnant minor may give consent to the furnishing of hospital, medical and surgical care related to her pregnancy, and such consent shall not be subject to disaffirmance because of minority. The consent of the parent or parents of an unmarried, pregnant minor shall not be necessary in order to authorize hospital, medical and surgical care related to her pregnancy. CAL. CIV. CODE § 34.5 (1954).

169. 381 U.S. 479 (1965). *See also* Eisenstadt v. Baird, 40 U.S.L.W. 4303 (U.S. Mar. 22, 1972).

170. ARK. STAT. ANN. § 41-310(C) (Supp. 1969); DEL. CODE ANN. tit. 24, § 1791(c) (Supp. 1971); MD. ANN. CODE art. 43, § 138(c) (1971); ORE. REV. STAT. § 435.435(3) (1971).

171. *See* text accompanying note 156 *supra*.

172. *Id*.

173. ARK. STAT. ANN. § 41-304 (Supp. 1969) ("substantial risk" that pregnancy will "threaten the life or gravely impair the health"); CAL. HEALTH & SAFETY CODE § 25951(c)(1) (West Supp. 1972) ("substantial risk" to "physical or mental health"); *id*. § 25954 (mental health equated to civil commitment standards); COLO. REV. STAT. ANN. § 40-6-101(3)(a) (1971) ("serious permanent impairment of the physical . . . or . . . mental health of the woman"); DEL. CODE ANN. tit. 24, § 1790(a)(1) (Supp. 1971) ("likely to result in the death of the mother"); *id*. § 1790(a)(4) ("substantial risk of permanent injury to the physical or mental health of the mother"); FLA. SESS. LAWS ch. 72-196 (West 1972); GA. CODE ANN. § 26-1202(a) (1) (1971) (endanger the mother's life or "seriously and permanently injure her health"); KAN. STAT. ANN. § 21-3407(2) (Supp. 1971) ("substantial risk" of impairing physical or mental health); MD. ANN. CODE art. 43, § 137(a)(2) (1971) ("substantial risk" of grave impairment of physical or mental health); N.M. STAT. ANN. § 40A-5-1(C)(1) (Supp. 1971) (death or "grave impairment of the physical or mental health of the woman"); N.C. GEN. STAT. § 14-45.1 (Supp. 1971) ("substantial risk" that pregnancy will "threaten the life or gravely impair the health"); ORE. REV. STAT. § 435.415(1)(a) (1971) ("substantial risk" that pregnancy will "greatly impair the physical or mental health"); *id*. § 435-415 (2) (mother's total environment may be taken into account in determining whether there is "substantial risk"); S.C. CODE ANN. § 16-87(1) (Supp. 1971) ("substantial risk" that pregnancy will "threaten the life or gravely impair the mental or physical health of the woman"); VA. CODE ANN. § 18.1-62.1(c)(1) (i) (Supp. 1971) ("substantially impair the mental or physical health of the woman").

174. Abortion Act of 1967, ch. 86, § 1(1)(a) ("risk to the life of . . . or . . . injury to the physical or mental health of the pregnant woman").

175. Doe v. Bolton, 319 F. Supp. 1048 (N.D. Ga. 1970), *jurisdiction postponed*, 402 U.S. 941 (1971) (invalidating even the liberalized Georgia statute); Roe v. Wade, 314 F. Supp. 1217 (N.D. Tex. 1970), *jurisdiction postponed*, 402 U.S. 941 (1971); State v. Barquet, 10 Crim. L. Rep. 2431 (Fla. 1972); People v. Belous, 71 Cal. 2d 954, 458 P.2d 194, 80 Cal. Rptr. 354 (1969).

176. *See* notes 182-83 *infra* & accompanying text.

177. ARK. STAT. ANN. § 41-304 (Supp. 1969) ("substantial risk" of "grave physical or mental defect"); COLO. REV. STAT. ANN. 40-6-101(3)(a) (1971) ("grave and permanent physical deformity or mental retarda-

tion"); DEL. CODE ANN. tit. 24, § 1790(a)(2) (Supp. 1971) ("substantial risk" of "grave and permanent physical deformity or mental retardation"); FLA. SESS. LAWS ch. 72-196 (West 1972); GA. CODE ANN. § 26-1202(a)(2) (1971) ("likely born with a grave, permanent, and irremediable mental or physical defect"); KAN. STAT. ANN. § 21-3407(2) (Supp. 1971) ("substantial risk" of "physical or mental defect"); MD. ANN. CODE art. 43, § 137 (a)(3) (1971) ("substantial risk" of "grave and permanent physical deformity or mental retardation"); N.M. STAT. ANN. § 40A-5-1(C)(2) (Supp. 1971) ("child probably will have a grave physical or mental defect"); N.C. GEN. STAT. § 14-45.1 (Supp. 1971) ("substantial risk" of "grave physical or mental defect"); ORE. REV. STAT. § 435.415(1)(b) (1971) ("reasonable grounds for believing serious physical or mental defect"); S.C. CODE ANN. § 16-87(2) (Supp. 1971) ("substantial risk" of "grave physical or mental defect"); VA. CODE ANN. § 18.1-62.1(c)(1)(ii) (Supp. 1971) ("substantial medical likelihood" of "irremediable and incapacitating mental or physical defect").

178. Abortion Act of 1967, ch. 87, § 1(1)(b) ("substantial risk" of "such physical or mental abnormalities as to be seriously handicapped"). Similar legislation is found in Singapore (Singapore Abortion Act, 1969) and South Australia. See Roemer, *supra* note 19.

179. See note 175 *supra.*

180. ARK. STAT. ANN. § 41-304 (Supp. 1969) (rape); CAL. HEALTH & SAFETY CODE §§ 75951(c)(2), 25952 (West Supp. 1972) (rape); COLO. REV. STAT. ANN. § 40-6-101(3)(b) (1971) (forcible and statutory rape); DEL. CODE ANN. tit. 24, § 1790(a)(3)(B) (Supp. 1971) ("rape committed as a result of force or bodily harm, or threat of force or bodily harm"); FLA. SESS. LAWS ch. 72-196 (West 1972); GA. CODE ANN. § 26-1202(a)(3) (1971) (forcible or statutory rape); KAN. STAT. ANN. § 21-3407(2) (Supp. 1971) ("rape . . . or other felonious intercourse"); *id.* § 21-3407(4) (intercourse with girl under 16 is felonious); MD. ANN. CODE art. 43, § 137(a)(4) (1971) (rape through force or bodily harm, or threat of force or bodily harm); MISS. CODE ANN. § 2223(1)(b) (Supp. 1971) (rape); N.M. STAT. ANN. § 40A-5-1(C)(3) (Supp. 1971) (forcible or statutory rape); N.C. GEN. STAT. § 14-45.1 (Supp. 1971) (rape); ORE. REV. STAT. § 435.415(1)(c) (1971) (felonious intercourse); S.C. CODE ANN. § 16-87(3) (Supp. 1971) (rape); VA. CODE ANN. § 18.1-62.1(c)(2) (Supp. 1971). Whether the unadorned term "rape" applies both to forcible and statutory rape can be determined only by reference to the rape provision elsewhere in the criminal code of the particular state.

181. ARK. STAT. ANN. § 41-304 (Supp. 1969); CAL. HEALTH & SAFETY CODE §§ 25951(c)(2), 25952 (West Supp. 1972); COLO. REV. STAT. ANN. § 40-6-101(3)(a) (1971); DEL. CODE ANN. tit. 24, § 1790 (a)(3)(A) (Supp. 1971); FLA. SESS. LAWS ch. 72-196 (West 1972);

KAN. STAT. ANN. § 21-3407(2) (Supp. 1971); N.M. STAT. ANN. § 40A-5-1(C)(4) (Supp. 1971); N.C. GEN. STAT. § 14-45.1 (Supp. 1971); ORE. REV. STAT. § 435.415(1)(c) (1971) (felonious intercourse); S.C. CODE ANN. § 16-87(3) (Supp. 1971); VA. CODE ANN. § 18.1-62.1(c)(2) (Supp. 1971).

182. ALASKA STAT. § 11.15.060 (1971); HAWAII REV. LAWS § 453.16 (Supp. 1971); N.Y. PENAL LAW § 125.05(3)(b) (McKinney Supp. 171); WASH. REV. CODE § 9.02.070 (Supp. 1971).

183. Abortion Act of 1967, ch. 87, §§ 1(1)(a), (2).

184. See text accompanying notes 62-69 supra.

185. See note 182 supra.

186. See notes 175 supra, 233 infra.

187. ALASKA STAT. § 11.15.060(a) (4) (1971) ("domiciled or physically present" 30 days before abortion); ARK. STAT. ANN. § 41-306 (Supp. 1969) (resident at least 4 months, unless emergency endangering woman's life); DEL. CODE ANN. tit. 24, § 1793(a) (Supp. 1971) (resident at least 120 days); GA. CODE ANN. § 26-1202(b)(1) (1971) (bona fide legal resident); HAWAII REV. LAWS § 435-16(a)(3) (Supp. 1971) (domiciled in state or physically present at least 90 days immediately before abortion); N.C. GEN. STAT. § 14-45.1 (Supp. 1971) (resident at least 30 days immediately before operation); ORE. REV. STAT. § 435.415(1) (1971) (Oregon resident); S.C. CODE ANN. § 16-87 (Supp. 1971) (continuously in state for 90 days immediately preceding operation); VA. CODE ANN. § 18.1-62.1(a) (Supp. 1971) (resident 120 days immediately preceding termination of pregnancy); WASH. REV. CODE § 9.02.070(b) (Supp. 1971) (resident at least 90 days prior to date of termination). Section 3 of the English Abortion Act of 1967 imposes no residency requirement, but makes provision for visiting forces and dependents.

188. Cf. Lopez v. Wyman, 329 F. Supp. 483 (W.D.N.Y. 1971), aff'd, 40 U.S.L.W. 3351 (U.S. Jan. 24, 1972); Shapiro v. Thompson, 394 U.S. 618 (1968).

189. Corkey v. Edwards, 322 F. Supp. 1248, 1254-55 (W.D.N.C. 1971), appeal filed, 40 U.S.L.W. 3098 (U.S. July 17, 1971) (No. 71-94).

190. LA. REV. STAT. § 37:1285(6) (1964); MISS. CODE ANN. § 2223(2) (Supp. 1971).

191. FLA. STAT. ANN. § 782.10 (1965), repealed, FLA. SESS. LAWS ch. 72-196 (West 1972); NEB. REV. STAT. § 28-404 (1964); N.H. REV. STAT. ANN. § 585:13 (1955); OHIO REV. CODE ANN. § 2901.16 (Page 1953); WIS. STAT. § 940.04(5)(b) (1958). MO. REV. STAT. § 559.100 (1949) provides for advice by one duly licensed physician if the abortion is performed by one not a duly licensed physician. See note 54 supra & accompanying text.

192. ARK. STAT. ANN. § 41-308 (Supp. 1969) (three doctors, one of whom may be the attending physician); DEL. CODE ANN. tit. 24, § 1790(a),

(b)(2) (Supp. 1971) (two doctors, one of whom may be the attending physician; certification is to hospital review authority; *see* note 193 *infra* & accompanying text); GA. CODE ANN. § 26-1202(b)(3) (1971) (two additional physicians certify necessity; medical staff committee then reviews under *id.* § 26-1202(b)(5); *see* note 193 *infra* & accompanying text); KAN. STAT. ANN. § 21-3407(2)(a) (Supp. 1971) (three licensed doctors, one of whom may be the attending physician, certify necessity to hospital); N.C. GEN. STAT. § 1-45.1 (Supp. 1971) (two doctors certify necessity to hospital); ORE. REV. STAT. § 435.425 (1971) (two physicians certify necessity to hospital); S.C. CODE ANN. § 16-87 (Supp. 1971) (three doctors, one of whom is the attending physician, certify circumstances of necessity to hospital). The English Abortion Act of 1967, ch. 7, § 1(1), requires the good faith opinion of two medical practitioners.

193. CAL. HEALTH & SAFETY CODE § 25951(b) (West Supp. 1972) (medical staff committee operating within standards promulgated by Joint Commission on Accreditation of Hospitals; if no more than three members, unanimous approval required); *id.* § 25953 (committee must have at least two members, or at least three if termination is to be after 13th week); COLO. REV. STAT. ANN. §§ 40-6-101(3), -(4) (1971) (hospital board of three licensed staff physicians of hospital where abortion to be performed, who meet regularly or on call to review requests); DEL. CODE ANN. tit. 24, § 1790(b)(2) (Supp. 1971) (hospital abortion review authority); GA. CODE ANN. § 26-1202 (b)(5) (1971) (hospital medical staff committee operating under standards of Joint Commission on Accreditation of Hospitals; majority vote of committee of at least three members, with attending physician's vote not counted); MD. ANN. CODE art. 43, § 137(b)(2) (1971) (hospital abortion review committee); N.M. STAT. ANN. § 40A-5-1(C)-(D) (Supp. 1971) (special hospital committee of two licensed physicians or appointed alternates, on medical staff of hospital where abortion to be performed); VA. CODE ANN. § 18.1-62.1(d) (Supp. 1971) (hospital abortion review board of hospital where abortion to take place; written consent by majority); *id.* § 18.1-62.2 (Supp. 1971) (board to consist of at least three physicians, one of whom is a specialist in obstetrics or gynecology; such a board required before hospital can perform abortions). The matter is left to administrative regulations by ALASKA STAT. § 08.64.105 (Supp. 1971).

194. DEL. CODE ANN. tit. 24, § 1790(b)(2) (Supp. 1971); GA. CODE ANN. § 26-1202(b)(5) (1971). The Georgia and Kansas screening procedures were held unconstitutional in part in Doe v. Bolton, 319 F. Supp. 1048 (N.D. Ga. 1970) and Poe v. Menghini, 11 CRIM. L. RPTR. 2021 (D. Kan. 1972). The *Bolton* case also denies the right of an individual hospital to develop its own restrictive standards to circumvent the holding.

195. ARK. STAT. ANN. §§ 41-306, -309 (Supp. 1969) (emergency to save life; three physicians must certify abortion within 24 hours afterwards); KAN. STAT. ANN. § 21-3407(2)(b) (Supp. 1971) (emergency to preserve life of mother); N.C. GEN. STAT. § 14-45.1 (Supp. 1971) (emergency; certification within 24 hours afterwards); ORE. REV. STAT. § 435.445 (1971) (emergency to save life and compliance with certification procedures not possible; report within 48 hours to appropriate hospital committee or State Board of Health); S.C. CODE ANN. § 16-87 (Supp. 1971) (emergency; certification within 24 hours afterwards); VA. CODE ANN. § 18.1-62.3 (Supp. 1971) (emergency to save life; usual consent by mother required); WASH. REV. CODE § 9.02.070 (Supp. 1971) (in emergency may perform abortion outside hospital or approved medical facility; no prior approval required under statute). The English Abortion Act of 1967, ch. 87, § 1(4), creates an emergency exception where necessary to save the life or prevent grave permanent injury to the physical or mental health of the pregnant woman.

196. *See* text accompanying notes 180, 181 *supra.*

197. ARK. STAT. ANN. § 41-304 (Supp. 1969) (rape must be reported to prosecutor within 7 days); GA. CODE ANN. § 26-1202(b)(6) (Rev. 1971) (applicant must present certified copy of report to any law enforcement officer or agency; N.M. STAT. ANN. § 40A-5-1(C)(3) (Supp. 1971) (woman submits affidavit indicating rape has been or will be reported to an appropriate law enforcement official); N.C. GEN. STAT. § 14-45.1 (Supp. 1971) (report to law enforcement agency or court official within 7 days after rape); S.C. CODE § 16-87(3) (Supp. 1971) (report within 7 days of rape or 60 days after incest); VA. CODE ANN. § 18.1-62.1(c), (e) (Supp. 1971) (report to law enforcement agency or prosecutor within 7 days of rape or as soon as possible if kidnapped or abducted; incest affidavit must identify male).

198. CAL. HEALTH & SAFETY CODE § 25952 (Supp. 1971) (district attorney informs committee that there is probable cause to believe that offense was committed); COLO. REV. STAT. ANN. § 40-6-101 (3)(b) (1971) (prosecutor informs committee over signature that there was probable cause to believe offense was committed); DEL. CODE ANN. tit. 24, § 1790(a)(3)(B) (1970) (attorney general certifies in writing that there was probable cause; this is unnecessary if proceeding within 48 hours after rape); GA. CODE ANN. § 26-1202(b)(6) (Rev. 1971) (after report, prosecutor of jurisdiction certifies on best information probable cause to believe rape occurred); MD. ANN. CODE art. 43, § 137(a)(4) (1971) (state's attorney informs hospital abortion review committee, in writing over signature, belief of probable cause); ORE. REV. STAT. § 435.425 (1969) (*semble*: certificate by woman sent to district attorney of county in which hospital is located); S..C CODE § 16-87(3) (Supp. 1971) (warrant must issue for offender; chief law

enforcement officer of county in which hospital located certifies reasonable cause to believe offense committed). This requirement of the Georgia statute was held unconstitutional in Doe v. Bolton, 319 F. Supp. 1048 (N.D. Ga. 1970) (per curiam), *jurisdiction postponed*, 402 U.S. 941 (1971) (No. 971, 1970 Term; renumbered No. 70-40, 1971 Term).

199. *See* Leavy & Charles, *California's New Therapeutic Abortion Act: An Analysis and Guide to Medical and Legal Procedure*, 15 U.C.L.A.L. REV. 1, 9, 12-22 (1967).

200. Evidence at the hearing is inadmissible in any proceeding other than a perjury prosecution, although a witness called at the special hearing may appear as a witness in other proceedings. The burden of proof is by a preponderance of the evidence.

201. ARK. STAT. ANN. § 41-304 (Supp. 1969); CAL. HEALTH & SAFETY CODE § 25951 (Supp. 1971); COLO. REV. STAT. ANN. § 40-6-101(3) (1971); DEL. CODE ANN. tit. 24, § 1790(a) (Supp. 1970); FLA. SESS. LAWS ch. 72-196 (West 1972); GA. CODE ANN. § 26-1202(a) (Rev. 1971); HAWAII REV. STAT. § 453-16(a)(1) (Supp. 1971); KAN. GEN. STAT. ANN. § 21-3407(2) (Supp. 1970); MD. ANN. CODE art. 43, § 137(a) (1971); MISS. CODE ANN. § 2223(1) (Supp. 1971); N.M. STAT. ANN. § 40A-5-1(c) (Supp. 1971); N.Y. PENAL LAW § 125.05(3) (Supp. 1971); N.C. GEN. STAT. § 14-45. 1 (Supp. 1971); ORE. REV. STAT. §§ 435.405(3), 435.415(3) (1971); S.C. CODE § 16-87 (Supp. 1971); VA. CODE ANN. § 18-1-62.1 (Supp. 1971); WASH. REV. CODE § 9.02.060 (Supp. 1971). The English Abortion Act of 1967, ch. 87, §§ 1(1), 2(1)(b), contemplates abortion by registered medical practitioners.

202. ARK. STAT. ANN. § 41-307 (Supp. 1969) (hospital licensed by state board and accredited by Joint Commission on Accreditation of Hospitals); CAL. HEALTH & SAFETY CODE § 25951(a) (Supp. 1971) (hospital accredited by Joint Commission); COLO. REV. STAT. ANN. § 40-6-101(2) (1971) (hospital accredited by state board); DEL. CODE ANN. tit. 24, § 1790(a) (1970) (hospital accredited by "nationally recognized medical or hospital accreditation authority"); FLA. SESS. LAWS ch. 72-196 (West 1972); GA. CODE ANN. § 26-1202(b) (4) (Rev. 1971) (hospital licensed by state board and accredited by Joint Commission); HAWAII REV. STAT. § 453-16(a)(2) (Supp. 1971) (hospital licensed by state department or operated by Federal Government or agency); KAN. GEN. STAT. ANN. § 21-3407(2)(a) (Supp. 1971) (accreditation requirement in Poe v. Menghini, 11 CRIM. L. RPTR. 2021 (D. Kan. 1972); MD. ANN. CODE art. 43, § 137(a) (1971) (hospital accredited by Joint Commission and licensed by state board); N.M. STAT. ANN. § 40A-5-1(B), (C) (Supp. 1971) (accredited hospital licensed by state department); N.C. GEN. STAT. § 14-45.1 (Supp. 1971) (hospital licensed by state commission); ORE.

REV. STAT. §§ 435.405(2), 435.415(3) (1971) (hospital licensed under licensing statutes, excluding nursing and convalescent homes); S.C. CODE ANN. § 16-87 (Supp. 1971) (hospital licensed by state board); VA. CODE ANN. § 18.1-62.1(b) (Supp. 1971) (hospital accredited by Joint Commission and state department); WASH. REV. CODE § 9.02.070(c) (Supp. 1971) (hospital accredited by Joint Commission or medical facility approved by state board); WIS. STAT. ANN. § 940.04 (5)(c) (1958) (requirement of a licensed maternity hospital except in an emergency; grounds are limited to preservation of the life of the mother).

203. ALASKA STAT. § 11.15.060(a)(2) (1970) (hospital or other facility approved by state department, or hospital operated by Federal Government); WASH. REV. CODE § 9.02.070(c) (Supp. 1971) (accredited hospital or medical facility certified by state board and meeting standards set by the board). The New York statute, N.Y. PENAL LAW § 125.05(3) (Supp. 1971), is silent as to place, and permits termination of pregnancy for any reason within 24 weeks.

204. The English Abortion Act of 1967, ch. 87, § 1(3) permits performance of abortions in a hospital or place approved by the Minister of Health or Secretary of State, with emergency exception in section 1(4).

205. Robin v. Village of Hempstead, ___ N.Y.2d ___ (1972). *See also* the lower court opinion, 66 Misc. 2d 482, 321 N.Y.S.2d 20 (Sup. Ct. 1971).

206. ARK. STAT. ANN. §§ 41-308, -309 (Supp. 1969); COLO. REV. STAT. ANN. § 40-6-101(4) (1971); N.M. STAT. ANN. § 40A-5-1(D) (1971); VA. CODE ANN. § 18.1-62.1 (Supp. 1971). This requirement may be coupled with reporting requirements. *E.g.*, GA. CODE ANN. § 26-1202(b)(7) (Rev. 1971); MD. ANN. CODE art. 43, § 137(c) (1971); ORE. REV. STAT. §§ 435.425(1), 435.435(2) (1971).

207. DEL. CODE ANN. tit. 24, § 1790(c) (1970); FLA. SESS. LAWS ch. 72-196 (West 1972); GA. CODE ANN. § 26-1202(b)(8), (9) (Rev. 1971); MD. ANN. CODE art. 43, § 137(c) (1971); S.C. CODE § 16-88 (Supp. 1971) (report by physician on standard form within 7 days after abortion). ORE. REV. STAT. § 435.495 (1971), leaves the matter to administrative regulation, which is also the approach in the English Abortion Act of 1967.

208. *See* Lefkowitz v. Woman's Pavilion Inc., 66 Misc. 2d 743, 321 N.Y.S.2d 963 (Sup. Ct. 1971), holding that the attorney general investigating alleged fraudulent practices in an abortion referral clinic had no right to the names of individual clients; only fiscal information need be supplied.

209. ALASKA STAT. § 11.15.060(a)(4) (1970); ARK. STAT. ANN. § 41-310(a), (b) (Supp. 1969); COLO. REV. STAT. ANN. § 40-6-104 (1971); DEL. CODE ANN. § 1791(a), (b) (1970); FLA. SESS. LAWS ch. 72-196 (West 1972); GA. CODE ANN. § 26-1202(e) (Rev. 1971)

(but individual staff member must file written statement of moral or religious objections if he is to be exempted from participation); HAWAII REV. STAT. § 453-16(d) (Supp. 1971); MD. ANN. CODE art. 43, § 138(a), (b) (1971); N.M. STAT. ANN. § 40A-5-2 (Supp. 1971); ORE. REV. STAT. §§ 435.475(1), 435.485 (1971); S.C. CODE § 16-89 (Supp. 1971) (private physician or hospital); VA. CODE ANN. § 18.1-62.2 (Supp. 1971); WASH. REV. CODE § 9.02.080 (Supp. 1971). *Cf.* Stewart v. Long Island College Hospital, 35 App. Div. 2d 531, 313 N.Y.S.2d 502 (1970) (no action lies on behalf of parents and child born with defects caused by rubella of mother, based on refusal of hospital committee to approve abortion in 1968, before liberalization).

210. *See* the Oregon and South Carolina statutes cited in note 2 *supra*; *cf.* Doe v. General Hospital, 313 F. Supp. 1170 (D.D.C. 1970) (public hospital must consider an indigent's application for a therapeutic abortion). Under a broad national health services program, a duty can be placed on every medical practitioner to perform abortions to save life or prevent grave permanent injury to physical or mental health; in other cases a recognition of conscientious objection exists, but the burden of proof is on the practitioner claiming reliance. English Abortion Act of 1967, ch. 87, § 4.

211. Doe v. Bolton, 319 F. Supp. 1048 (N.D. Ga. 1970) (per curiam), *jurisdiction postponed*, 402 U.S. 941 (1971) (No. 971, 1970 Term; renumbered No. 70-40, 1971 Term).

212. *See* the equal protection litigation discussed in the text accompanying notes 231-33 *infra*.

213. *See generally* Baude, *Constitutional Reflections on Abortion Reform*, 4 J. LAW REFORM 1 (1970); Lucas, *Federal Constitutional Limitations on the Enforcement and Administration of State Abortion Statutes*, 46 N.C.L. REV. 730 (1968); Comment, *Abortion Laws: A Constitutional Right to Abortion*, 49 N.C.L. REV. 487 (1971).

214. *See* 28 U.S.C. § 2281 (1970).

215. Crossen v. Breckenridge, 446 F.2d 833 (6th Cir. 1971); Y.W.C.A. v. Kugler, 10 Crim. L. Rptr. 2469 (D.N.J. Feb. 29, 1972) (violative of right to privacy); Doe v. Dunbar, 320 F. Supp. 1297 (D. Colo. 1970); Doe v. Bolton, 319 F. Supp. 1048 (N.D. Ga. 1970) (per curiam), *jurisdiction postponed*, 402 U.S. 941 (1971) (No. 971, 1970 Term; renumbered No. 70-40, 1971 Term); Ballard v. Anderson, 4 Cal. 3d 873, 484 P.2d 1345, 95 Cal. Rptr. 1 (1971) (mandamus against hospital committee).

216. United States *ex rel.* Zelker, 445 F.2d 451 (2d Cir. 1971).

217. Crossen v. Breckenridge, 446 F.2d 833 (6th Cir. 1971); Doe v. Dunbar, 320 F. Supp. 1297 (D. Colo. 1970); Doe v. Bolton, 319 F. Supp. 1048 (N.D. Ga. 1970) (per curiam), *jurisdiction postponed*, 402 U.S.

941 (1971) (No. 971, 1970 Term; renumbered No. 70-40, 1971 Term); Doe v. Scott, 321 F. Supp. 1385 (N.D. Ill. 1970), *appeals docketed sub. noms.* Hanrahan v. Doe and Heffernan v. Doe, 39 U.S.L.W. 3438 (U.S. Mar. 29, 1971), (Nos. 1522, 1523, 1970 Term; renumbered Nos. 70-105, 70-106, 1970 Term) (pregnant 16-year-old rape victim has standing to intervene in litigation).

218. Ballard v. Anderson, 4 Cal. 3d 873, 484 P.2d 1345, 95 Cal. Rptr. 1 (1971).

219. Y.W.C.A. v. Kugler, 10 Crim. L. Rptr. 2469 (D.N.J. Feb. 29, 1972); Doe v. Dunbar, 320 F. Supp. 1297 (D. Colo. 1970); Doe v. Bolton, 319 F. Supp. 1048 (N.D. Ga. 1970) (per curiam), *jurisdiction postponed*, 402 U.S. 941 (1971) (No. 971, 1970 Term; renumbered No. 70-40, 1971 Term).

220. Crossen v. Breckenridge, 446 F.2d 833 (6th Cir. 1971); Y.W.C.A. v. Kugler, 10 Crim. L. Rptr. 2469 (D.N.J. Feb. 29, 1972).

221. Doe v. Bolton, 319 F. Supp. 1048 (N.D. Ga. 1970) (per curiam), *jurisdiction postponed*, 402 U.S. 941 (1971) (No. 971, 1970 Term; renumbered No. 70-40, 1971 Term). *Cf.* Crossen v. Breckenridge, 446 F.2d 833 (6th Cir. 1971) (case remanded to district court to consider whether minister giving abortion counselling had standing).

222. Doe v. Dunbar, 320 F. Supp. 1297 (D. Colo. 1970) (psychiatrist not performing abortions).

223. Younger v. Harris, 401 U.S. 37 (1971); Samuels v. Mackell, 401 U.S. 66 (1971).

224. Planned Parenthood Ass'n v. Nelson, 327 F. Supp. 1290 (D. Ariz. 1971). Similar holdings were encountered even before *Younger.* *E.g.*, Doe v. Randall, 314 F. Supp. 32 (D. Minn. 1970), *aff'd*, 402 U.S. 967 (1971).

225. McCann v. Babbitz, 402 U.S. 903 (1971), remanding for reconsideration an injunction against a specific prosecution issued in Babbitz v. McCann, 320 F. Supp. 219 (E.D. Wis. 1970). *See also* Babbitz v. McCann, 310 F. Supp. 293 (E.D. Wis. 1970), denying plaintiff the injunctive relief sought.

226. Poe v. Menghini, 11 Crim. L. Rptr. 2021 (D. Kan., 1972); Y.W.C.A. v. Kugler, 10 Crim. L. Rptr. 2469 (D.N.J. Feb. 29, 1972).

227. Papachristou v. Jacksonville, 40 U.S.L.W. 4216 (U.S. Feb. 24, 1972); Cohen v. California, 403 U.S. 15 (1971); Coates v. Cincinnati, 402 U.S. 611 (1971); Palmer v. Euclid, 402 U.S. 544 (1971).

228. Y.W.C.A. v. Kugler, 10 Crim. L. Rptr. 2469 (D.N.J. Feb. 29, 1972); Doe v. Wade, 314 F. Supp. 1217 (N.D. Tex. 1970) (per curiam), *jurisdiction postponed*, 402 U.S. 941 (1971) (No. 808, 1970 Term, renumbered 70-18, 1971 Term) (violation of right of privacy); People v. Belous, 71 Cal. 2d 954, 458 P.2d 194, 80 Cal. Rptr. 354 (1969); State v. Barquet, 10 Crim. L. Rptr. 2433 (Fla. 1972).

229. Steinberg v. Brown, 321 F. Supp. 741 (N.D. Ohio 1970); Babbitz v. McCann, 310 F. Supp. 293 (E.D. Wis. 1970); State v. Abodeely, 179 N.W.2d 347 (Iowa 1970), *cert. denied*, 402 U.S. 936 (1971).

230. United States v. Vuitch, 402 U.S. 62, 71-73 (1971).

231. *E.g.*, Humphrey v. Cady, 40 U.S.L.W. 4324 (U.S. March 22, 1972).

232. *E.g.*, Mayer v. Chicago, 404 U.S. 189 (1972).

233. Steinberg v. Brown, 321 F. Supp. 741 (N.D. Ohio 1970); Doe v. Bolton, 319 F. Supp. 1048 (N.D. Ga. 1970) (per curiam) *jurisdiction postponed*, 402 U.S. 941 (1971) (No. 971, 1970 Term; renumbered No. 70-40, 1971 Term); State v. Abodeely, 179 N.W.2d 347 (Iowa 1970), *cert. denied*, 402 U.S. 936 (1971). A New York supreme court holding finding an equal protection denial in a New York City Department of Social Services ruling that medicaid payments were unavailable unless an abortion was "medically indicated," City of New York v. Wyman, 66 Misc. 2d 402, 321 N.Y.S.2d 695 (Sup. Ct. 1971), was supplanted by an appellate division holding to the same end based on conflict of the city policy with state-level policies. City of New York v. Wyman, 37 App. Div. 2d 700, 322 N.Y.S.2d 957 (1971).

234. 381 U.S. 479 (1965). *See also* Eisenstadt v. Baird, 40 U.S.L.W. 4303 (U.S. March 22, 1972) (birth control devices to unmarried persons); Stanley v. Georgia, 394 U.S. 557 (1969) (private possession of pornographic material). *But see* United States v. Thirty-Seven Photographs, 402 U.S. 363 (1971) (such material subject to seizure in transit where intended for commercial use); United States v. Reidel, 402 U.S. 351 (1971) (same).

235. *See generally* Note, *Unenumerated Rights — Substantive Due Process, the Ninth Amendment and John Stuart Mill*, 1971 WIS. L. REV. 922, 928-32; Note, *The Right to Privacy: Does It Allow a Woman the Right to Determine Whether to Bear Children?*, 20 AM. U.L. REV. 136 (1970).

236. Corkey v. Edwards, 322 F. Supp. 1248 (W.D.N.C. 1971), *appeal docketed*, 40 U.S.L.W. 3098 (U.S. July 17, 1971) (No. 71-92); Steinberg v. Brown, 321 F. Supp. 741 (N.D. Ohio 1970) (also rejecting a cruel and unusual punishment argument); Rosen v. Louisiana State Bd. of Medical Examiners, 318 F. Supp. 1217 (E.D. La. 1970), *appeal docketed*, 39 U.S.L.W. 3247 (U.S. Nov. 27, 1970) (No. 1010, 1970 Term; renumbered No. 70-42, 1971 Term); State v. Shirley, 256 La. 665, 237 So.2d 676 (1970).

237. Y.M.C.A. v. Kugler, 10 Crim. L. Rptr. 2469 (D.N.J. Feb. 29, 1972) (in early stages of pregnancy); Doe v. Scott, 321 F. Supp. 1385 (N.D. Ill.), *appeals docketed sub noms.* Hanrahan v. Doe *and* Heffernen v. Doe, 39 U.S.L.W. 3438 (U.S. Mar. 29, 1971) (Nos. 1522, 1523, 1970 Term; renumbered Nos. 70-105, 70-106, 1971 Term); Roe v. Wade, 314 F. Supp. 1217 (N.D. Tex. 1970) (per curiam), *jurisdic-*

tion postponed, 402 U.S. 941 (1971) (No. 808, 1970 Term; renumbered 70-18, 1971 Term); Babbitz v. McCann, 310 F. Supp. 293 (E.D. Wis.), *permanent injunction granted*, 320 F.2d 219 (E.D. Wis. 1970), *vacated and remanded*, 402 U.S. 903 (1971), *noted in* 46 WASH. L. REV. 565 (1971), 48 J. URBAN L. 969 (1971) and 4 GA. L. REV. 907 (1970); People v. Belous, 71 Cal. 2d 954, 458 P.2d 194, 80 Cal. Rptr. 354 (1969), *noted in* 8 DUQUESNE L. REV. 439 (1970); State v. Munson, (S.D. 7th Jud. Cir. Ct., April 7, 1970) (decision is printed in full in 15 S.D.L. REV. 332 (1970)).

238. A few decisions permit recovery by survivors of a still-born infant if there was prenatal negligence. *E.g.*, O'Neill v. Morse, 385 Mich. 130, 188 N.W.2d 785 (1971); Verkennes v. Corniea, 229 Minn. 365, 38 N.W.2d 838 (1949). However, many more states do not. *E.g.*, McKillip v. Zimmerman, 191 N.W.2d 706 (Iowa 1971); Endresz v. Friedberg, 24 N.Y.2d 478, 248 N.E.2d 901, 301 N.Y.S.2d 65 (1969); Gay v. Thompson, 266 N.C. 394, 146 S.E.2d 425 (1966). If the child is born alive, a greater number of decisions recognize the right to recover for birth defects caused by prenatal negligent injury. *E.g.*, Fallaw v. Hobbs, 113 Ga. App. 181, 147 S.E.2d 517 (1966); Daley v. Meier, 3 Ill. App.2d 218, 178 N.E.2d 691 (1961) (even though not yet viable at time of accident); Bennett v. Hymers, 101 N.H. 483, 147 A.2d 108 (1958); Shousha v. Matthews Drivurself Service, Inc., 210 Tenn. 384, 358 S.W.2d 471 (1962).

239. An exception is GA. CODE ANN. § 26-1202(c), (d) (1969), which gives the local prosecutor or anyone who would be a relative of the child, if born, the power to seek a declaratory judgment as to whether the projected abortion would "violate any constitutional or other legal rights of the fetus"; the attending doctor and the woman are the respondents. The matter must be heard expeditiously and the court may enjoin the projected abortion. However, if the statute is complied with, then section 26-1202(d) rules out any wrongful death claim. A three-judge federal district court has ruled this portion of the statute unconstitutional, apparently because the mother's right is paramount. Doe v. Bolton, 319 F. Supp. 1048 (N.D. Ga. 1970) (per curiam), *jurisdiction postponed*, 402 U.S. 941 (1971) (No. 971, 1970 Term; renumbered No. 70-40, 1971 Term).

240. Y.W.C.A. v. Kugler, 10 Crim. L. Rptr. 2469 (D.N.J. Feb. 29, 1972); People v. Belous, 71 Cal. 2d 954, 458 P.2d 194, 80 Cal. Rptr. 354 (1969); Byrn v. New York City Health & Hospitals Corp. 38 App. Div. 2d 316, 329 N.Y.S.2d 722 (1972), *aff'd*, N.Y. Times, July 8, 1972, at 1, col. 2. *Byrn* is an interesting case in that a state supreme court justice appointed a law professor guardian ad litem for all unborn fetuses in the city, and then granted a preliminary injunction against the performance of all abortions not necessary to preserve the life of the mother. The upper courts vacated the order because it

found the New York penal law constitutional, infringing no rights of fetus to life.

241. *Cf.* Stewart v. Long Island College Hospital, 35 App. Div. 2d 531, 313 N.Y.S.2d 502 (1970), disallowing an action for damages by a child born with birth defects caused by rubella, and its parents, against the hospital and therapeutic abortion committee members who had refused to authorize an abortion under the 1967 version of the statute; the refusal occurred in 1968, two years before liberalization of the statute.

242. *See* text accompanying notes 223-26 *supra.*

243. Compare this situation to the status dilemma of marginal lawyers as described in J. CARLIN, LAWYERS ON THEIR OWN 173-84 (1962).

THE GENESIS
OF LIBERALIZED ABORTION
IN NEW YORK:
A PERSONAL INSIGHT

ALAN F. GUTTMACHER, M. D.

I. PRELUDE TO LIBERALIZED ABORTION STATUTES

SINCE MY DEBUT as an Aesculapian antedates those of other physician contributors to this volume, I thought it valuable to relate medical practices and attitudes toward induced abortion a half century ago and to analyze the genesis, direction, and magnitude of the change in those attitudes and practices and its reflection in the legal position on abortion.

I was taught obstetrics at The Johns Hopkins Medical School by Dr. J. Whitridge Williams, one of the great medical figures of the 1920's. He was forceful, confident and didactic. To him, and therefore to us, induced abortion was either therapeutic or "criminal." He told us therapeutic abortion was performed to save the life of the pregnant woman and that the primary threats involved dysfunction by three organs: the heart, the lung, and the kidney. To these hazards he begrudgingly added toxic vomiting of pregnancy. I say "begrudgingly" because I remember full well the drastic treatment meted out to hyperemetic gravidae: isolation, submammary infusions, rectal clyses, and feeding by stomach tube. To resort to therapeutic abortion in these cases was admission of medical failure. No medical sanction was then given to abortion on socio-economic or psychological grounds.

The experiences I encountered during my residency from 1925 to 1929 made me question the wisdom of such a restrictive medical policy. In a short period I witnessed three deaths from illegal abortions: a 16-year-old with a multiperforated uterus, a mother of four who died of sepsis rejecting another child, and a patient in early menopause who fatally misinterpreted amenorrhea. My skepticism of the wisdom of existing abortion laws was further reinforced by an incident involving Dr. Williams. A social worker came to me seeking abortion services for a 12-year-old black child who had been impregnated by her father. Dr. Williams was a court of one to validate abortion requests, so I sought his permission to perform the operation. He was sympathetic but reminded me that Maryland prohibited abortion except where necessary to preserve the life of the mother,[1] and he did not believe that continuation of pregnancy in this case would endanger the girl's life. When I brought up the social injustice of compelling a child to bear her father's bastard, Dr. Williams compromised, saying that if I could obtain a letter from the district attorney granting special permission to The Johns Hopkins Hospital, then I could perform the abortion.[2] I failed to get this permission and delivered the baby 7 months later. At about the same time, one of the residents at a neighboring hospital showed me a child, the daughter of an army colonel, who had been hysterotomized to eliminate pregnancy conceived through "rape." Experiences such as this made me question the possibilities for social injustice and disparate treatment, ever present under a restrictive policy which gave one man the sole power to determine the validity and permissibility of abortion services.

Such a restrictive policy could only lead to reliance on those who would go outside the law to provide the desired services. Indeed, during the same period there were two competent physician-abortionists in Baltimore who practiced for many years relatively unmolested by the police. They were so well known that an inquiry addressed to either a traffic policeman or a salesgirl would have elicited their names with equal ease. They were not partners, but close collaborators, occasionally preparing death certificates for each other. One, while attending a public national meeting in Washington, rose to defend the service provided by illegal medical abortionists who had been defamed by a speaker. He stated openly that there had been but 4 deaths in the 7000 abortions with which he had been associated. This was before the first use of antibiotics, "salting out," and other precautionary procedures. Finally, years later when a complaint was filed, the district attorney was compelled to take official cognizance of the existence of one of the two abortionists. At the trial, the abortionist offered to produce, in his defense, a list of 300 reputable physicians who had referred cases to him. I assume my name was among them.

On one occasion, the nestor of American gynecologists, Dr. Robert L. Dickinson, called me from New York requesting that I arrange a meeting in Baltimore with Dr. T. We lunched at a hotel, and Dr. T produced a roster of his patients, duration of pregnancy, parity, city of residence, fees, source of referral, etc. On another occasion Dr. T met with a few of the senior medical faculty of Johns Hopkins to disclose his technique. To minimize infection, he had invented a boilable rubber perineal shield with a rubber sleeve that fitted into the vagina and through which he worked. His technique was to pack one inch gauze strips into the cervix and lower uterine segment the night before he was to evacuate the conceptus. After 12 hours of packing, the cervix was wide open, and he was able to empty the uterus with an ovum forceps, followed by curettage without anesthesia. In advanced pregnancies he inserted intra-uterine bougies, held in place by a vaginal pack until strong contractions commenced, which not infrequently took several days.

These early medical experiences with the unavailability of abortions in reputable hospitals and the incidence of illegal abortions convinced me that permitting abortion only "to preserve the life of the mother"[3] was undesirable and unenforceable. I thus sought changes which would both curb the morbidity and mortality of illegal abortion and eliminate the ethnic and social discrimination which was inherent to all induced abortions, whether legal or illegal.

I found in my hospital contacts that obstetricians and gynecologists were the most conservative medical group in regard to abortion. Internists and psychiatrists were constantly berating us for our low incidence of legal pregnancy terminations. Indeed, there had developed a feeling of prideful accomplishment among the obs-gyn staff if one's hospital had a low therapeutic abortion rate and a feeling of disgrace if the rate was relatively high compared to similar institutions. I shared this viewpoint, no doubt swayed by the writings and addresses of obstetrical leaders such as Drs. George Kosmak and Samuel Cosgrove. My sentiment was that as long as the law was as restrictive as it was, doctors should not breach it, but work to change the law — a position which I forthrightly espoused in the classroom.   Despite the fact that it was not a radical notion, this position had few adherents.   Members of the medical profession were content to leave things as they were; they would frequently perform a therapeutic abortion for a favored patient because of her important social position, or at least refer her to a safe, illegal medical operator.   But acceptance of generally available legal abortion was still far in the future.   In the early 1930's, I was invited to present a paper on abortion reform before the New Jersey Obstetrical and Gynecological Society.   One participant, Dr. Cosgrove, tore into me like a tank.   I can still recall my discomfiture and frustration at the unyielding establishment.

Until 1940, the decision to permit or to deny therapeutic abortion in the individual case was made solely by the chief of the obstetrical service.   The physician handling the case presented the patient's history, physical examination, and laboratory findings to the chief who, in turn, made an immediate decision.   Through personal observations, I learned that it was impossible to predict how the chief would decide, for such decisions seemed to turn on his mood and on the latest article he had read on the subject.

It was in recognition of the inadequacies of such a procedure that, when I became Chief of Obstetrics at Baltimore's Sinai Hospital in 1942, I decided to have a staff committee of five make decisions about abortion.[4]   This committee consisted of representatives from medicine, surgery, pediatrics, psychiatry, and obstetrics, with the obstetrician as chairman.   As far as I knew, such a plan had never been tried, although I have since learned that it had been in force in a few other hospitals.   The abortion committee system functioned well.   Among other things it added medical expertise in special areas beyond obstetrics.   Moreover, greater consistency was attained through adherence to guidelines adopted in cases with similar factual patterns.   I do not believe that the committee system significantly affected the hospital's incidence of legal abortion, but at least all applicants were treated on an equal basis.

When I became Director of Obstetrics and Gynecology at the Mount Sinai Hospital in New York in 1952, I learned that the Department of Gynecology (there had been no department of obstetrics previous to my arrival) had performed 30 abortions in the previous 6 months. I was told that if a private patient was denied abortion in another institution, she frequently sought abortion at Mount Sinai because of its well-known, relatively liberal policy. I recall resenting this reputation. Forthwith we introduced the committee system, the results of which have been reported in three publications.[5] The committee met each Wednesday afternoon if any case was to be heard. Forty-eight hours prior to that meeting, the staff obstetrician who wished to carry out an abortion would have provided each member a summary of the case together with recommendations from consultants, if any had examined the patient. The staff obstetrician and frequently a consultant from a medical discipline germane to the problem (for example, a cardiologist for a cardiac case or a neurologist for the mother who had borne a child with muscular dystrophy) presented their findings or views. The committee always voted in executive session, and a unanimous vote was required to authorize abortion. This requirement was not as forbidding as it sounds, for in almost every instance the other members of the committee would agree with the opinion of the member within whose discipline the problem lay.

Statistics on the number of abortions performed at Mount Sinai and at other New York hospitals over generally contemporaneous time periods are illuminating. At Mount Sinai Hospital, 207 therapeutic abortions were performed between 1953 and 1960, yielding an incidence of 5.7 abortions per 1000 live births. Partly because of my efforts to eliminate discrimination, the rate was 6.3 per 1000 live births on the private service and 4.6 per 1000 births on the ward service.[6] One commentator, in reporting figures from another large New York voluntary hospital for the years 1951 to 1954, showed an incidence of 8.1 abortions per 1000 live births on the private service and a rate of 2.4 on the ward service.[7] Statistics were also available for two New York municipal hospitals: Metropolitan Hospital (1959-61) and Kings County Hospital (1958-60). In the former the abortion incidence was 0.077 per 1000 live births, and in the latter the incidence was 0.37 per 1000 live births.[8] Gold published a study of abortion incidence for all New York hospitals for the period 1960-62.[9] The incidence in proprietary institutions was shown to be 3.9 per 1000 live births; and in the voluntary hospitals the incidence was 2.4 on the private services and 0.7 on the ward services. Municipal hospitals showed a rate of 0.1 per 1000 live births. There was also a marked ethnic differential: the ratio of therapeutic abortions per 1000 live births was 2.6 for whites, 0.5 for Negroes, and 0.1 for Puerto Ricans.

Not only was there great disparity in the incidence rates among various hospitals but, in addition, the abortion policies and rules established by hospitals were confusingly different. Mount Sinai, for example, validated abortion for well-documented rubella (German measles), whereas Columbia-Presbyterian did not. Mount Sinai did not permit abortion for rape, whereas St. Johns in Brooklyn did. The marked differences among hospitals in regard to incidence and standards as well as patient discrimination — discrimination between ward and private patients and between ethnic groups — served to aggravate my dissatisfaction with the status quo and led to my desire for the enactment of a new law.

The question was, what should be the content of an ideal law? Because my twin brother, the late Dr. Manfred Guttmacher, a forensic psychiatrist, was a member of the American Law Institute (ALI), which was then engaged in writing a revised penal code, I was present on a Sunday afternoon in December, 1959 when Mr. Herbert Wechsler (Professor of Law at Columbia) unveiled his model abortion statute now called the ALI bill.[10] The recommended statute provided that a doctor would be permitted to perform an abortion: (1) if continuation of pregnancy "would gravely impair the physical or mental health of the mother"; (2) if the doctor believed "that the child would be born with grave physical or mental defects"; or (3) if the pregnancy resulted from rape or incest.[11]

When Professor Wechsler had finished presenting his suggested statute, an elderly gentleman sitting at the large, felt-covered table inaudibly mumbled some comment. Mr. Wechsler said, "What did you say, Judge Hand?" The eminent federal jurist, Learned Hand said, "It is a rotten law." Mr. Wechsler asked why, and Judge Hand responded, "It's too damned conservative." How right he was. Yet most of those present, including myself, disagreed with him. The Wechsler abortion bill was passed by the Institute as part of the total revised penal code revealed to the public in 1962. Many, including myself, hailed it as the answer to the legal problems surrounding abortion, which had always been the doctors' dilemma.

Even though the ALI Code had not yet been adopted by any state, its mere promulgation opened the medical profession's eyes to the preservation of health as being a justification for abortion. The most difficult health hazard to document (but equally difficult to refute) was significant trauma to the psychic stability of the pregnant individual. "Psychiatric" indications for abortion rapidly increased in importance. Tietze's figures demonstrate that in 1963 psychiatric indications accounted for 0.57 legal abortions per 1000 live births in the United States; in 1965 the rate was 0.76 per 1000, and in 1967 it was 1.50 per 1000.[12] The increasing frequency of psychiatric justifications for abortion caused concern for many. Because the psychiatric indications were so ill-defined and pliable, it was feared that they might become an upperclass ticket for legal abortion, thus increasing discrmination and doing little to lower the morbidity and mortality rates in the population at large. In 1967, Colorado, California, and North Carolina,[13] and in 1968, Maryland and Georgia,[14] all modified their respective statutes, using the ALI bill as the prototype. Between 1967 and 1968 the incidence of legal abortions in the United States increased from 2.59 to 5.19 per 1000 live births, and abortions for psychiatric indications increased from 1.50 to 3.61 per 1000 live births.[15]

In December, 1968, I was appointed to Governor Rockefeller's 11-member commission which had been formed to examine the abortion statute of New York State and to make recommendations for change. When the Governor convened the commission, he said, "I am not asking whether New York's abortion law should be changed, I am asking how it should be changed." The commission was made up of a minister, a priest, a rabbi, 3 professors of law, 3 physicians, a poetess, and the president of a large Black woman's organization. There were 4 Catholics, 4 Protestants, and 3 Jews. The commission met every 2 weeks for more than 3 months. It was apparent that 3 members wanted no change in the old law despite the Governor's charge, 2 wished abortion removed entirely from the criminal code, and 6 advocated the enactment of the ALI model with further liberalization: the majority report — approved 8 to 3 — added legal abortion on request for any mother of four children. My proposal of adding a clause to permit abortion on request for any woman 40 years or older was voted down — this was April, 1969.

The more I studied early results from the 5 states which had been the first to liberalize their laws, the more I began to espouse the opinion that abortion statutes should be entirely removed from the criminal code. The number of legal abortions being undertaken under the new liberalized laws, when contrasted with the figures for the previously undertaken illegal abortions, were far too low. In 1968, for example, California reported only about 5000 abortions under the new law.[16] It is true that this number has steadily increased to a present rate of over 100,000 per year, but that increase stems in large part from an increase in the number of abortions legitimized on psychiatric grounds: over 90 percent of current abortions are performed on that ground.[17] In actuality it places the psychiatrist in the untenable situation of being an authority in socio-economics. I examined the situation personally in Colorado and discovered that two Denver hospitals were doing vitually all of the pregnancy interruptions and these were being performed primarily on the private sector. This clearly implied that the state-imposed requirement of two psychiatric consultations was causing an effective discrimination against ward patients: private consultations were so expensive as to be available only to the wealthier patients, and psychiatric appointments in public facilities were booked solid for 3 months — far beyond the time limitation on obtaining an abortion. From these experiences, I reluctantly concluded that abortion on request — necessitating removal of "abortion" from the penal codes — was the only way to truly democratize legal abortion and to sufficiently increase the numbers performed so as to decrease the incidence of illegal abortions. I came to this conclusion in 1969, 47 years after abortion first came to my medical attention when I was a third-year medical student. Abortion on request, a position which I now support after having been converted by years of medical practice and observation, was soon to have its trial in New York, the state in which I reside. This gave me the opportunity to observe firsthand how effectively it would function. The three criteria to be used for evaluation were straightforward. Did abortion on request save lives? Did it minimize socioethnic discrimination? Did it reduce the incidence of illegal abortion?

II. THE NEW YORK SITUATION

On April 10, 1970, the New York State Legislature amended the State Penal Code, permitting licensed physicians to provide abortion services for any consenting woman less than 24 weeks pregnant.[18] The law specifies no restrictions on place of residence, age, marital status, or consent of spouse, if married, and it makes no restrictions as to the type of facility where abortions might be performed. After 142 years of one of the most restrictive abortion statutes — allowing abortions only when necessary to preserve the life of the mother — New York suddenly had the most liberal abortion law in the world.

The New York State Legislature in 1969 had flatly rejected the bill produced by the Governor's Commission — basically the ALI model plus permissible abortion on request for any woman with four or more children. Those of us in favor of reform hoped in 1970 that we could somehow put through a modified ALI bill. We knew of the "radical" bill sponsored by Constance Cook, an upstate legislator, but had no hope for its passage. Much to everyone's surprise, however, it passed the House by a modest majority. When it came before the Senate there was a tie vote and an expectation that the speaker would break the tie with his negative vote since he was a strong opponent of abortion reform. However, a senator from an upstate Catholic county broke the tie by changing his negative vote to an affirmative one. The bill was to become law July 1, less than 3 months later.

The medical community was in a state of shock, not from opposition, but from total surprise. There were dire prophecies that all existing medical facilities would be dangerously overtaxed by a nationwide demand for abortion.[19] But the New York City Department of Health began to ready the facilities of the 15 municipal hospitals, and the mayor appropriated an extra 3 million dollars to fund the new abortion service. In recognition of the financial potential, several proprietary hospitals were converted into abortoria. The voluntary hospitals agreed to do their part and some arranged to perform abortions on both an inpatient and an outpatient basis. Some physicians began to prepare their private offices for abortions, and others advocated free-standing clinics with built-in safety factors, such as blood available for transfusion, cardiac arrest equipment, quick access to a back-up hospital, counselling before and after the operation, and performance of abortion only by specialists in obstetrics and gynecology.

When July 1 arrived, the City Board of Health had not yet established its own standards for abortion services, and it did not do so until September 17. On that day the New York City Board of Health issued regulations outlawing private office abortions within New York City.[20] They agreed that abortions could be performed in accredited hospitals and their outpatient departments. Also permitted were abortions in licensed free-standing abortion clinics which could meet certain enunciated standards regarding factors such as the size of the operating room, the availability of resuscitating equipment, and the availability of blood; furthermore, abortion of a pregnancy beyond 12 weeks could not be performed in such a free-standing clinic.

A. *Incidence Figures*

The New York City statistics on abortion have been accurately recorded and reported,[21] but abortion statistics for the state outside of New York City are fragmentary. During the first 18 months of the new law (July 1, 1970 to December 31, 1971) 278,122 legal abortions were performed in New York City in 15 municipal, 52 voluntary, 37 proprietary hospitals, and 18 free-standing clinics.[22] It is estimated that another 78,000 were performed in the rest of the state.[23] From the reports on the first 15 months of the abortions performed in New York City, it was found that 68,391 were performed on residents (35.5 percent) and 127,129 on nonresidents (64.5 percent).[24] During the first 12 months 8 states supplied the most out-of-state patients: New Jersey, 11,849; Ohio, 7,403; Michigan, 7,296; Illinois, 7,163; Pennsylvania, 6,660; Florida, 5,255; Massachusetts, 5,107; and Connecticut, 3,729.[25] A few even came from Alaska, Hawaii, and Washington.[26] Although these latter states have abortion laws almost as liberal as New York's,[27] the influx of these nonresidents is probably attributable to the fact that New York permits abortion in pregnancies of longer duration.

When the law was proposed, there was no concerted effort by any medical group to extend the permissible abortion period to its present maximum of 24 weeks following conception. That provision appears to have been inserted by legislators who drew up the statute. Tietze and Lewit have shown that the period of gestation at which abortion is performed is inversely associated with the woman's age at the time of abortion — the younger the woman, the more advanced her pregnancy, and the older the woman, the earlier she seeks abortion.[28] In their study, carried out on a different population sample than the New York City studies, the abortions performed in the second trimester accounted for 49 percent of all abortions performed on girls 14 years or less, and 20 percent of all abortions performed on women over 30. They also found an ethnic difference — 36 percent of the blacks had abortions after 12 weeks while only 23 percent of the whites waited that long.[29] Modifying social factors such as availability of services may have played a role in the latter instance.

B. *Abortions of New York City Residents per 1000 Births*

Comparing the number of women of reproductive age (between the ages of 15 and 44) residing within the city of New York with the number of abortions performed on New York City residents during the first year of the new statute, Tietze has computed an annual legal abortion rate of 37 per 1000 women of reproductive age.[30] Applying this rate to the 43.8 million females between the ages of 15 and 44 in the United States,[31] he projects a possible figure of 1,640,000 annual legal abortions if all 50 states had abortion regulations and practices similar to New York City.[32] Using the reduction in live births in New York City during the first 9 months of 1971, compared to the 1970 rate, Tietze concludes that if the whole country followed the pattern of New York City, there would be 330,000 fewer live births annually, resulting in a reduction in the crude birth rate of 1.6 points per 1000 population. Using the reduction in New York City births, one may roughly calculate that 3 in 4 of the legal abortions performed replaced illegal abortions. One in 4 prevented the birth of a child which was unwanted in early pregnancy but under the old law would have been born nevertheless. On the basis of the fact that there was a 14 percent decline in out-of-wedlock births compared to a 7 percent decline for births within marriage, Tietze calculates that almost two-fifths of the eliminated unwanted conceptions is represented by a decline of out-of-wedlock births.[33]

C. Effect on Maternal Mortality

The effect of the new abortion statute on maternal mortality and ethnic discrimination in abortion practices is revealed in a paper presented by Harris at the recent meeting of the American Public Health Association.[34] The paper compares the maternal deaths in New York City for the first 8 months in 1969, 1970, and 1971 and provides the following figures, here presented in tabular form:

	Number of Maternal Deaths		Ratio per 10,000 Live Births		Percentage of Maternal Deaths Due to Abortion
	Total	Due to Abortion	Total	Due to Abortion	
Jan.-Aug. 1969	49	17	5.1	1.8	34.7
Jan.-Aug. 1970	54	19	5.5	1.9	35.2
Jan.-Aug. 1971	18	5	2.0	0.6	27.8

The figures thus indicate that New York City in 1971 experienced the lowest maternal mortality rate on its record. This abrupt improvement in the maternal mortality rate is explained in part by the displacement of unsafe criminal abortion by safe, legal procedures. There were 9 deaths from criminal abortions during the first 18 months of the new law in New York City, but only 2 of these occurred in the third 6-month period.[35] If this low rate is maintained, there would be 4 in the second 12-month period of the new law.

The most extraordinary feature of the statistics presented is not the decline in total abortion deaths, but the dramatic decline of approximately 60 percent in maternal mortality unassociated with abortion. One contributory factor is that 6 percent of the abortions performed on New York City residents involved children aged 17 or less, and 10 percent involved women over 35 years of age — the two age groups with the highest obstetric death rates.[36] If the trend in greatly reduced obstetric mortality is sustained in subsequent years, the contribution of "abortion on demand" in reducing nonabortion obstetric deaths would merit more extensive analysis.

D. Third Six-Month

According to information provided to the *New York Times* by Mr. Gordon Chase, Health Services Administrator for New York City, the third 6-month period of the new law (July to December, 1971) showed interesting changes.[37]   In the total 18-month period, 278,122 legal abortions were performed in New York City.   But figures showed a decline in legal abortions *during* the third 6-month period: from 57,090 abortions in the third quarter of 1971 to 52,282 in the final quarter.   The decline was felt most in municipal, voluntary, and proprietary hospitals, while there was an increase in the number of patients served by free-standing clinics.   "Almost half of all abortions in the city during the period July-December 1971 were performed in clinics — up from about one-third during the first year of the law."[38]   Finally, according to Mr. Chase, the death rate dropped from 4.7 per 100,000 abortions during the first year to a rate of 3.7 in the third 6-month period.   But since 2 out of 3 abortions were performed on nonresidents, who may remain only a few hours, it is possible, despite serious efforts of the New York City Health Department to search out such deaths, that the latest rate of 3.7 deaths per 100,000 abortions is an understatement.

E. Effect on Illegal Abortion

There is no satisfactory way to determine the effect legal abortion on demand has on illegal abortion.   There are suggestive data, however.   One is the decline in total abortion deaths, and another is the decrease in hospital admissions for "spontaneous" and incomplete abortions.   In 10 municipal hospitals taken together, incomplete and spontaneous abortions averaged 480 per month from July to December 1970, 350 per month from January to June 1971, and 199 per month from July to December 1971.[39]   It is impossible to document a trend by the observations of one illegal medical abortionist of the effect of the new law on his own practice.   Still, a most popular illegal physician abortionist complained to me 5 months after the new law had gone into effect that he had not seen a patient in the preceding 2 weeks.

F. *Effect on Ethnic Discrimination*

As was noted earlier in this discussion, Gold documented the social and ethnic discrimination of legal abortion as practiced in New York City in 1962.[40] Removal of abortion from the criminal code and the exemplary efforts of the municipal hospital system to implement the new liberal policy seem to have largely eliminated discrimination. In his report of the first 12 months,[41] Harris states that 42.8 percent of the abortions performed on the city's residents involved nonwhites, while only 31 percent of all live births involved nonwhites; 10.2 percent of those aborted were Puerto Rican, but they accounted for 18 percent of the births; whites formed 47 percent of those aborted and gave birth to 51 percent of the babies. The ratio of legal abortions to live births among New York City residents for nonwhites is 60:100; for whites, 40:100, and for Puerto Ricans 30:100.

III. ABORTION PROCEDURES

A. *New Developments in the Field of Abortion*

Two new developments in the field of abortion may have important impact on the expanding liberalization of abortion availability: high-dosage, post-coital estrogens (the "morning-after pill") and the prostaglandins.

1. *High Dosage Estrogens* — Implantation, a highly complex and sensitive physiological process, can be disrupted and inhibited by interference from a variety of environmental conditions.[42] As early as 1926, it had been demonstrated that injection of an estrogen in rodents shortly after successful mating would prevent nidation. In 1967, Morris and Van Wagener gave estrogens to 35 monkeys following artificial insemination, and instead of attaining an anticipated 50 percent pregnancy rate none became pregnant.[43] Estrogen was then prescribed for humans, at a dosage of 50 mg of diethylstilbestrol per day for 5 days beginning within 3 days of the unprotected coitus. Other estrogens are in trial: 2.5 mg of ethinylestradiol taken orally twice a day for 5 days; and 20 mg of pre-

marin introduced intravenously every other day for 3 doses. Published and unpublished results are encouraging, although final evaluation is not yet completed. Kuchera from the University of Michigan Health Service reports that her subjects avoided conception in each of 1,000 cases treated with post-coital stilbestrol.[44] And in a personal communication from Yale, I was told there was only one pregnancy in 1,500 patients on similar treatments. According to Tietze,[45] each isolated unprotected coitus scattered over the full intermenstrual month yields a 2 to 4 percent likelihood of pregnancy. The Michigan report states that 80 percent of the women with regular menses were exposed to impregnation in midcycle, and their expectation of pregnancy should have been more than 2 to 4 percent.[46] Massey reports prevention of all but 4 pregnancies (1.6 percent) in 247 rape cases treated with stilbestrol immediately after the crime.[47]

Like any new medical treatment, possible harmful side-effects have not yet been completely ruled out in the use of stilbestrol. Herbst reports the development of adenocarcinoma of the vagina in eight young women born between 1946 and 1951, and in 7 cases their mothers had been given diethylstilbestrol to *prevent* spontaneous abortion beginning in the first trimester and continuing through most of the pregnancy.[48] Since then, Greenwald has documented 5 additional cases.[49] There is, however, little similarity between the use of post-coital stilbestrol to prevent pregnancy and later post-conceptional stilbestrol applications to prevent spontaneous abortion. In the former method a relatively high dose is given acutely over a short period, and in the latter treatment a smaller amount is introduced over a lengthy period, the total dose being at least 15 times as great. Then, too, the time of administration is different: in one, before the zygote is even a blastocyst; in the other, after the Mullerian ducts are laid down. Nevertheless, should stilbestrol ever be adopted as a primary means of preventing nidation, the possibility of harmful side-effects occuring in the offspring is a problem to be faced: it makes one question whether it would not be prudent to terminate pregnancy by induced abortion should post-coital stilbestrol ever fail in preventing nidation.

2. *Prostaglandins* — In 1930, Kurzrok and Lieb, while carrying out experiments on artificial insemination, observed that if se-

men was introduced directly into the uterine cavity, the uterus would react with violent contractions and cramps. They then excised strips of uterine muscle at Cesarean section and suspended them in a water bath. The addition of semen to the bath stimulated vigorous contractions.[50] Five years later Von Euler investigated the reaction and concluded that the active principle was an acidic lipid, present in seminal vesicle extracts, which he called prostaglandin.[51] In a sense, the label is a misnomer, since the compounds are in much higher concentration in seminal vesicle fluid than in prostatic fluid. Subsequent studies have shown that there are at least 14 different prostaglandins in various body tissues including uterine endometrium. There was an extreme shortage of the drug until 1965 when the group at the Karolinska Institute succeeded in producing pure prostaglandins biosynthetically by incubating one of six fatty acid precursors with sheep seminal vesicle glands. Recently, prostaglandins have been produced by total synthesis, and it is anticipated that they will soon be readily available at low cost.[52]

The two prostaglandins which act upon the female reproductive tract are E_2 and F_{2a}, the letter and subscript number having reference to chemical structure. Karim, Professor of Pharamacology at Makerere University in Uganda, began clinical studies with these two compounds in the mid-1960's. At first, they were administered in an intravenous drip to initiate term labor in cases in which the fetus had died in utero; later, they were successfully used to induce term labor in patients bearing a live fetus. Being successful in his work with term pregnancies, Karim next turned his attention to the induction of abortion.[53] Recently, in a paper before the New York Academy of Sciences, Karim reported on 200 therapeutic abortions; 150 induced by means of an intravenous drip of E_2, with only 5 failures, and 50 induced by using F_{2a} with only 6 failures.

Other workers have not been able to report the same degree of success, especially in pregnancies beyond 8 weeks.[54] It is uncertain whether the difference in results may be due to a difference in the definition of a successful result or some technical difference in administration. Side-effects, in the form of nausea, vomiting, and diarrhea, are very common with the intravenous drip administration. In order to use a lesser amount of prostaglandin and thus reduce side-effects, the Karolinska group introduced prostaglandin directly into the uterine cavity through a polyethylene catheter inserted through the cervix and left in place between the fetal membranes and uterine wall. They report complete or partial expulsion of the conceptus in 12 cases with pregnancies of 5 to 13 weeks, using one-tenth the usual intravenous dose.[55]

In an attempt to reduce side-effects, Karim is working with analogues of E_2 and F_{2a} and is also seeking methods other than i.v. for administering the natural prostaglandins. He is using oral capsules, lactose intravaginal tablets, and vaginal suppositories which melt at body temperature.[56] There are three different times at which the prostaglandins may be given to control conception: (1) when pregnancy is firmly implanted, in which case a visible abortus will be expelled; (2) when a woman is 2 to 7 days overdue on her period, in which case the delayed menses will be brought on; and (3) once a month on a late cycle day, thus acting as a contraceptive agent.

Many clinical investigations of the possible use of E_2 and F_{2a} as abortifacients are being conducted worldwide. The attempt to bring on delayed menses is being carried out at Makerere in Uganda, and monthly application as a contraceptive is being studied by investigators at the Karolinska Institute and Makerere University. Karim reported the successful treatment of 11 of 12 patients who had menstrual delays of 2 to 7 days by intravaginal insertion in the posterior fornix of either 40 mg of E_2 or 100 mg of F_{2a} in two divided doses four hours apart. Of the 12 women, 8 initially had positive pregnancy tests. In 10 cases, menstrual-like uterine bleeding started within 1 to 6 hours after the intravaginal insertion of the second lactose tablet. In the remaining 2 cases, no bleeding occurred on the first day. A third prostaglandin tablet inserted the next day induced bleeding in one. The other did not bleed and had a positive pregnancy test 1 week later.[57] In Sweden, monthly dosages of prostaglandins are being administered to a group of women at the time of their expected menses; no other contraceptive is used. The compounds are inducing menses, and none of the women has become pregnant during the first 6 months of the study.[58]

It is generally agreed that E_2 and F_{2a} exert their oxytocic effect directly on uterine muscle cells. F_{2a} may also be a luteolysin, regulating the secretion of progesterone by the corpus luteum through an effect on local blood flow. F_{2a}, a venoconstrictor, is present in significant amounts in secretory endometria and may play an important role in the physiology of normal menstruation.[59]

The prostaglandins are exciting drugs, but it is too early to assess their full impact. If abortion could be induced by self-insertion of a vaginal suppository, or if menses could be harmlessly and infallibly produced once monthly either premenstrually or after a period is briefly delayed, the fields of contraception and abortion would be significantly altered.

B. Traditional Abortion Techniques

1. *Aspiration versus D & C* — Surgical induction of abortion in pregnancies less than 12 weeks in duration can be accomplished either by suction aspiration or by dilatation and curettage (D & C). Since both techniques are discussed elsewhere in this volume,[60] it is not necessary to do so here. I want to point out, however, that aspiration termination is rapidly replacing curettage in New York City, for it has been found simpler, quicker, associated with less blood loss, and more susceptible to performance under local, paracervical anesthesia. The trend in the preference for aspiration over D & C is graphically recorded in a recent release by the Health Services Administration of New York City.[61] From July 1 to December 31, 1970, the first 6 months of experience under the new law, 58.5 percent of the 31,507 early pregnancy terminations in New York City were done by aspiration. During the most recent 3-month period reported (July 1 to September 30, 1971), however, 84.4 percent of 44,658 early terminations were accomplished by aspiration.

2. *Hysterotomy and "Salting Out"* — The two techniques commonly used in the United States for terminating pregnancies which have gone beyond 12 weeks are hysterotomy, a miniature abdominal Cesarean section, and "salting out," a procedure entailing the replacement of 200 cc of amniotic fluid by 200 cc of a 20 percent saline solution which kills the fetus and initiates uterine contractions causing spontaneous abortion. "Salting out" has almost replaced hysterotomy in New York City, except in cases in which sterilization by tubal ligation is planned concomitantly. Of 12,452 late pregnancy terminations performed during the first half year of

the new law, 5.7 percent were done by hysterotomy, while in the third quarter of 1971, only 3.5 percent of 11,157 late cases were so terminated.[62] The significant advantage of "salting out" over hysterotomy is that it leaves the uterus unscarred for future childbearing.

The use of intra-amniotic hypertonic solutions was first described by Aburel of Rumania in 1934.[63] He used a 33 percent saline solution to induce labor in cases of lethal fetal malformations, deaths in utero, and for patients needing therapeutic abortions. The technique was used in Japan beginning in 1948, but discarded because of a high maternal morbidity and mortality. Beginning in the early 1960's, the use of hypertonic saline to induce late abortion or labor in cases of a dead fetus was introduced into Scandinavian, British, and United States obstetrics.[64]

Kerenyi has detailed the standard technique which has evolved over 10 years of use at the Mount Sinai Hospital, reporting on 50 consecutive cases treated on an outpatient basis.[65] No premedication is used, and the abdomen and pubic areas are not shaved. The site for puncture is determined by bimanual palpation, selecting the uterine area which feels most cystic and is clearest of fetal parts. The skin is sprayed with iodine and the operative area sterilely draped. A skin wheal is raised, and the abdominal wall is infiltrated with 5 cc of 2 percent zylocaine. An 18-gauge, 3¼ inch disposable spinal needle with obturator in position is inserted into the amniotic cavity. In the occasional case in which free flow of clear amniotic fluid is not obtained, a teflon catheter is inserted through the needle. If free flow does not then occur, the procedure is postponed and repeated in several days. Approximately 220 cc of amniotic fluid is withdrawn and replaced by an equal amount of 23 percent saline, which is infused by the drip technique. Patients are queried about headache, dizziness, and tingling sensation in the lips, tongue, or the needle site. During the course of introducing the saline, the bottle is lowered several times to check for a clear backflow. When the infusion is complete, the obturator is replaced before the needle is withdrawn. Manual pressure on a gauze pad is exerted by the patient for 5 minutes to prevent even a few drops of saline from leaking into the peritoneal cavity. The patient is discharged from the outpatient department and told to return after contractions commence. If no contractions occur within 36 hours, she is admitted and given an intravenous infusion of oxytocin in lactated Ringer's solution.

In the cases of 50 patients treated as out-patients, the time lapse from the initial saline instillation to the completion of abortion averaged 35.2 hours. This can be compared to 36.5 hours for 200 treated as hospital inpatients. In each group the latent period averaged more than 30 hours, and the period between the onset of contractions and the expulsion of the conceptus averaged about 5 hours.

While an oxytocin drip is not used routinely in conjunction with hypertonic saline instillation, it may be necessitated by medical complications. The most common complication in the Mount Sinai series of cases was retention of the placenta which occurred in 11.2 percent of the reported cases. Most of the placentas were expelled spontaneously if a concentrated intravenous drip of oxytocin (50-100 international units per 500 cc) was used. Other complications were bloody tap or loss of free flow of fluid, both necessitating postponement and later repetition of amniocentesis in 6.4 percent of the cases; prolonged latent period in 6.8 percent of the cases; postpartum fever in 4.0 percent of the cases; failure to accomplish amniocentesis in 4.0 percent of the cases; and premature rupture of membranes in 3.2 percent of the cases. Hypotension or agitation and acute abdominal pain were noted in 2.8 and 1.6 percent of the cases, respectively.[66] No live-born fetuses were delivered in the series, and in 15 carefully monitored cases the fetal heart usually disappeared in less than 1 hour, though one was detectable for 2 hours.

Mackenzie and his coworkers have shown that duration of gestation affects the likelihood of successful amniocentesis. When the uterus was 12-15 weeks in size, 50 percent of the treatments succeeded; when the uterus was 16-18 weeks in size, 95 percent succeeded, and after 19 weeks, 100 percent of the treatments succeeded.[67]

A survey of the literature reveals three potential serious complications: perforation of the intestines; infection of the uterine contents; and accidental intravascular or intraperitoneal injection of hypertonic saline. The third complication may trigger a pulmonary reaction or lead to permanent brain damage or death: when serum sodium exceeds 170 mEq/liter, there is likelihood of irreversible brain damage.[68] In attempts to eliminate the danger of natremia, efforts have been made to find a substance which will cause abortion if substituted for 200 cc of amniotic fluid, but which is relatively free of danger if inadvertently injected intravascularly or intraperitoneally. The British have focused their experimentation on urea, since it can be given intravenously even when there is present any one of several potentially harmful physical conditions, including cerebral edema and glaucoma. Craft and Musa report 30 successful inductions of mid-trimester abortion using intra-amniotic urea.[69]

IV. Conclusion

In a field as vast as abortion, one has to select those facets of the topic for discussion for which training and experience have equipped him. I chose three: the first, a very personal discussion of the evolution of an attitude and my conversion from a conservative to a liberal position; the second, observation at firsthand of how well an extremely liberal statute functions; and the third, a survey of newer abortion techniques.

This volume will not be the end of the story; it is simply a chapter. Attitudes and practices toward the control of conception are in a highly fluid state. The newest concept is "menstrual regulation." Perhaps at some time in the near future a woman one week overdue in her menses may choose to have aspiration of the uterine contents, or possibly the insertion of an intravaginal prostaglandin suppository. No pregnancy test will be done, and neither physician nor patient will ever know whether an early pregnancy was evacuated or a tardy period brought on.

It can be expected that during the remainder of the 1970's, abortion procedures and laws will continue to present an intense example of the rapidity of socio-medical-legal change.

NOTES

1. *Cf.* MD. ANN. CODE art. 43, § 137(a) (1971). The present statute is patterned after the Model Penal Code. *See* note 10 *infra* & accompanying text.
2. Presently, California follows a similar procedure in cases of incest. CAL. HEALTH & SAFETY CODE § 25952 (West Supp. 1971) (permitting abortion where the district attorney is satisfied that there is

probable cause to believe that the pregnancy resulted from rape or incest and this validation is transmitted to the Committee of the Medical Staff).

3. *See, e.g.,* TENN. CODE ANN. § 39-301 (1955), which currently restricts abortions to such cases of necessity.

4. The committee method of decisions regarding abortions is prevalent and is codified in many states. CAL. HEALTH & SAFETY CODE § 25951(b) (West Supp. 1971), for example, requires the consent of an approved hospital committee before an abortion can be performed. The statute requires that the committee be composed of not less than three licensed physicians and requires that the decision to permit an abortion be unanimous.

5. Guttmacher, *Therapeutic Abortion: The Doctor's Dilemma*, 21 J. MT. SINAI HOSPITAL 111 (1954); Guttmacher, *Therapeutic Abortion in a Large General Hospital*, 37 SURGICAL CLINICS OF NORTH AMERICA 459 (April, 1957); Guttmacher, *The Legal and Moral Status of Therapeutic Abortion*, in PROGRESS IN GYNECOLOGY IV 279 (J. Meigs & S. Sturgis eds. 1963).

6. Guttmacher, *The Legal and Moral Status of Therapeutic Abortion*, in PROGRESS IN GYNECOLOGY IV 289 (J. Meigs & S. Sturgis eds. 1963).

7. C. McLANE, ABORTION IN THE UNITED STATES (Calderone ed. 1958).

8. Guttmacher, *supra* note 6.

9. Gold, Erhardt, Jacobziner, & Nelson, *Therapeutic Abortions in New York City: A 20 Year Review*, 55 AM. J. OF PUBLIC HEALTH 964 (1965).

10. MODEL PENAL CODE § 230.3(2) (Proposed Official Draft, 1962).

11. *Id.*

12. Tietze, *United States: Therapeutic Abortions, 1963 to 1968*, 59 STUDIES IN FAMILY PLANNING 5 (1970). Tietze's figures were based on hospitals reporting to The Professional Activities Survey in Ann Arbor, Michigan.

13. *See* COLO. REV. STAT. ANN. § 40-6-101(3)(a) (1971); CAL. HEALTH & SAFETY CODE § 25951 (West Supp. 1971); N.C. GEN. STAT. § 14-45.1 (Supp. 1971).

14. *See* MD. ANN. CODE art. 43, § 137(a) (1971); GA. CODE ANN. § 26-1202 (1971). *See also* GA. CODE ANN. § 26-9925a(a) (1971) (worded identically to section 26-1202) (a prefatory note preceding section 26-9921a indicates that there is some doubt as to which statute is in effect).

15. Tietze, *supra* note 12, at 7.

16. California's Therapeutic Abortion Act became operative November 8, 1967. During the first calendar year under the new law, legal abortions reported from the entire state were 5,030. *See* Overstreet, *California's Abortion Law — A Second Look*, in ABORTION AND THE UNWANTED CHILD 16 (C. Reiterman ed. 1971).

17. *See* Bureau of Maternal and Child Health, 4th Annual Report on the Implementation of the California Therapeutic Abortion Act (1971).
18. N.Y. Penal Law § 125.05(3) (McKinney Supp. 1971).
19. *See, e.g.,* Hall, *Widening Frontiers of Legalized Abortion,* 12 Medical World News 44 (1971).
20. Health Service Administrative Regulations art. 42 (1970).
21. Pakter & Nelson, *The First Nine Months,* 3 Family Planning Perspectives 4 (1971); *New York State Study* (a joint publication of the New York City Health Department and Planned Parenthood-World Population).
22. Figures obtained from the Health Service Administration of the City of New York.
23. *Id.*
24. N.Y. Times, Feb. 20, 1972, § L*, at 41, col. 4.
25. News release prepared by Gordon Chase, Administrator of the Health Service Administration of the City of New York, Feb. 20, 1972.
26. *Id.*
27. *See* Alaska Stat. § 11.15.060 (1970); Hawaii Rev. Laws § 453.16 (Supp. 1971); Wash. Rev. Code § 9.02.060 (Supp. 1971).
28. Tietze & Lewit, *Early Medical Complications of Legal Abortion: Highlights of the Joint Program for the Study of Abortion.*
29. *Id.*
30. Tietze, The Potential Impact of Legal Abortion on Population Growth in the United States (prepared for the President's Commission on Population Growth and the American Future) (unpublished).
31. U.S. Dep't of Commerce, Bureau of the Census, Statistical Abstract of the United States, 1971, at 23.
32. Tietze, *supra* note 30.
33. *Id.*
34. Harris, O'Hare, Pakter, & Nelson, Legal Abortion 1970-71, The New York City Experience, Oct. 12, 1971 (unpublished paper presented to the A.P.H.A. convention in Minneapolis, Minn., 1971).
35. News release prepared by Gordon Chase, *supra* note 25.
36. Harris, *supra* note 34.
37. N.Y. Times, Feb. 20, 1972, § L*, at 41, cols. 1-6.
38. *Id.* at col. 4.
39. Figures obtained from the Health Service Administration of the City of New York.
40. *See* Gold, *supra* note 9.
41. Harris, *supra* note 34.
42. In the laboratory, implantation has been shown to suffer from interference caused by a number of experimental techniques: stress reactions brought about by overcrowding in a rat population; stress caused by placing a recently mated mouse in a cage significantly larger than its home cage; and exposure of the recently mated mouse either to a

strange male or to a cage soiled by the urine of a strange male. *See* A. Rosenblatt, *Social-Environmental Factors Affecting Reproduction & Offspring in Infrahuman Mammals*, in CHILDBEARING — ITS SOCIAL AND PSYCHOLOGICAL ASPECTS 256 (S. Richardson & A. Guttmacher eds. 1967).

43. J. MORRIS & G. VAN WAGENER, PROCEEDINGS OF THE EIGHTH INTERNATIONAL CONFERENCE OF THE INTERNATIONAL PLANNED PARENTHOOD FEDERATION (1967).

44. Kuchera, *Post-Coital Contraception with Diethyl-Stilbestrol*, 218 J. AM. MED. ASS'N 562 (1971).

45. Tietze, *Probability of Pregnancy Resulting from a Single Unprotected Coitus*, 11 FERTILITY & STERILITY 485 (1960).

46. *See* Kuchera, *supra* note 44.

47. Massey, Garcia, & Emich, *Management of Sexually Assaulted Females*, 38 OBSTETRICS & GYNECOLOGY 29 (1971). Of the four reported cases of pregnancy, three should not properly be considered therapeutic failures: one was "raped" on the 29th day of the menstrual cycle and admitted other occasional unprotected coital exposures during the same month, and two cases discontinued therapy after only a few tablets.

48. Herbst, Ulfelder, & Poskanzer, *Adenocarcinoma of the Vagina*, 284 NEW ENGLAND J. OF MED. 878 (1971).

49. Greenwald, Barlow, Nasca & Burnett, *Vaginal Cancer After Maternal Treatment with Synthetic Estrogen*, 285 NEW ENGLAND J. OF MED. 390 (1971).

50. Kurzrok & Lieb, *Biochemical Studies of Human Semen. II The Action of Semen on the Human Uterus*, 28 PROCEEDINGS OF THE SOCIETY FOR EXPERIMENTAL BIOLOGY AND MEDICINE 268 (1930).

51. Van Euler, *On the Specific Vaso-dilating and Plain Muscle Stimulating Substances from Accessory Genital Glands in Man and Certain Animals (Prostaglandin and Vesiglandin)*, 88 J. OF PHYSIOLOGY 213 (1936).

52. Anderson & Speroff, *Prostaglandins and Abortion*, 14 CLINICAL OBSTETRICS & GYNECOLOGY 245 (1971).

53. Karim & Filshie, *Use of Prostaglandin E_2 for Therapeutic Abortion*, 3 BRITISH MED. J. 198 (1970); Karim & Filshie, *Therapeutic Abortion Using Prostaglandin F_{2a}* 1 LANCET 157 (1970).

54. Bygdeman & Wiquist, *Early Abortion in the Human*, in ANNALS, NEW YORK ACADEMY SCIENCE (in press); Anderson & Speroff, *supra* note 52.

55. Wiquist & Bygdeman, *Therapeutic Abortion by Local Administration of Prostaglandin*, 2 LANCET 716 (1970).

56. Personal conversation with S. Karim.

57. Karim, *Once-a-month Vaginal Administration of Prostaglandins E_3 and F_{2a} for Fertility Control*, 3 CONTRACEPTION 173 (1971).

58. Anderson & Speroff, *supra* note 52.

59. *See id.*

60. Niswander, *Abortion Practices in the United States: A Medical Viewpoint*, pp. 241-74, in this volume.

61. News release prepared by Gordon Chase, *supra* note 25.

62. *Id.*

63. *See* discussion in Berkowitz, *Electrolyte Changes and Serious Complications After Hypertonic Saline Instillation*, 14 CLINICAL OBSTETRICS & GYNECOLOGY 166 (1971).

64. It was introduced on my service at New York's Mt. Sinai Hospital in 1961. *See* Jaffin, Kerenyi, & Wood, *Termination of Missed Abortion by the Induction of Labor in Mid-trimester Pregnancy*, 84 AM. J. OBSTETRICS & GYNECOLOGY 602 (1962).

65. Kerenyi, *Outpatient Intra-Amniotic Injection of Hypertonic Saline*, 14 CLINICAL OBSTETRICS & GYNECOLOGY 124 (1971).

66. *Id.*

67. MacKenzie, Roufa & Tovell, *Mid-trimester Abortion: Clinical Experience with Amniocentesis and Hypertonic Instillation in 400 Patients*, 14 CLINICAL OBSTETRICS & GYNECOLOGY 107 (1971).

68. *See* Berkowitz, *supra* note 63.

69. Craft & Musa, *Induction of Mid-trimester Therapeutic Abortion by Intra-Amniotic Urea and Intravenous Oxytocin*, 2 LANCET 1058 (1971).

ABORTION: SOME ETHICAL ISSUES

DANIEL CALLAHAN

I. Introduction

ABORTION IS A PECULIARLY passionate topic, largely because many people invest their positions with a symbolic weight that transcends immediate social and legal issues. The most obvious examples of this tendency can be found in some segments of the women's liberation movement, on the one hand, and in some factions of those opposed to abortion, on the other. For each the way society solves the abortion problem will be taken to show just what its deepest values are. And those values have implications that extend far beyond abortion.

The Women's Liberation movement sees abortion as the most significant liberation of all, from the body and from male domination. The most effective solution to unwanted pregnancy, it removes the final block to full control of reproduction. Unless reproduction can be fully controlled, women will remain in bondage not only to their sexuality but, even more, to those legions of male chauvinists who use female sexuality to their own domineering ends.

By contrast, many of those opposed to abortion see the issue as indicating the kind of respect society will show the most defenseless beings in our midst. If the life of a defenseless fetus is not respected, then there is good reason to believe that the most fundamental of all human rights — the right to life — will have been subverted at its core. The test of the humane society is not the respect it pays to the strongest and most articulate, but that which it accords to the weakest and least articulate.

Of course, these arguments and the symbolic weight they carry simply bypass one another. The opposition seems so fundamental, and the starting premises so different, that any meaningful debate — the kind that leads to give-and-take, concession and adaptation — is ruled out from the start. Moreover, the very charges each side hurls at the other are of a psychologically intolerable nature. No vigorous proponents of abortion are likely to admit, either privately or publicly, that they sanction "murder"; nor are opponents of abortion likely to admit that they sanction the suppression of women. I am using the word "admit" here in a serious sense which implies that one is willing to ponder seriously the possibility that the worst things said about oneself are true. Given that possibility, there remain only two choices: change one's views and confess the errors of one's old ways or violently and aggressively deny the charges.

There is, of course, a third possibility: concede that there may be a grain of truth in what one's opponent says and then undertake the development of a position that tries to meet and integrate the objection in some new position. But this may be the most distasteful solution of all for most people, since it entails a long, drawn-out wrestling with oneself. Abortion is a painful issue, and for just that reason people seem impelled to proceed in all haste to the comfort of "Here I stand," which ends the self-wrestling.

My comments here are not drawn from any hard evidence. They are meant only as reflections on years of trying to discuss abortion in a reasonably calm, rational way, both in public and private. My own professional training is in philosophy, a discipline which (to the despair of many nonphilosophers) places a heavy premium on precision of argument, careful distinctions, developed justifications of ethical positions, methodological elegance, and a cool, temperate mode of discourse. These traits have, to be sure, led to more than one accusation that philosophers are prone to fiddle while the city is burning; and there is probably some truth in this. Nonetheless, I think these traits are still somewhat useful, especially when discussing a topic like abortion, which many take as an invitation to express their unbridled feelings and convictions. Worse still, the politics of abortion seems to pay handsome dividends for such a stance. It can, and has, pushed many an abortion reform bill through reluctant legislatures, just as it has, in different hands, killed many a bill. When argument fails, what better tactic is there than to bring out the fetus-in-a-bottle ("See what you are doing to innocent life!") or the raped mongoloid mother of ten with the drunken husband ("See what you are doing to her!")?

In discussing the quality and weight of ethical arguments here, I hope to achieve the most minimal kind of goal — simply to make plausible the radical notion that there remain some unresolved questions, some hazy areas, and some further points to be thought about. Before proceeding, let me state something for the record about my "position." (Experience has taught me the painful lesson that abortion politicians of either persuasion usually care not at all about one's arguments, but only about one's final "position.") My position is that abortion should be legally available on request up to the twelfth week of pregnancy; that abortion is morally justifiable under a variety of circumstances, but should always be undertaken reluctantly and with a strong sense of tragedy; and that the humane society would be one in which women were neither coerced to go through with pregnancies they do not want nor coerced by social, economic, or psychological circumstances into abortion. I cannot accept the position of those who would deny all respect to the fetus. Nor can I accept the position of those who hold that the right to life of the fetus is sufficient in all cases to override the right of women to choose an abortion. On the contrary, I accord the right of women to control their procreation a high status, as a crucial ingredient of the sanctity or dignity of life.

I will not try to defend or fully explain this position here. My intent is, resolutely, to talk about what seem to me good and bad arguments. But I want to note, no less resolutely, that it is perfectly possible for those with bad arguments to come nevertheless to good conclusions. This happens all the time, even if it is a process which does some violence to logic. (Or, as is more likely the case, people begin with good intuitions and then defend them with bad reasons.) Let me begin by laying out what seem to me bad or at least incomplete arguments. For convenience, I shall set them out as propositions, most of which should be readily recognizable to anyone even faintly acquainted with the abortion literature.

II.   NINE INADEQUATE ARGUMENTS

 A.   *Abortion is a religious or philosophical issue, best left*
to the private conscience rather than to public legislation.

This argument rarely makes much sense. If it means that for some churches and some religious believers their positions are the direct result of religious teachings, this hardly entails the conclusion that the issue is thus intrinsically religious. One might as well say that the Vietnamese war is a religious issue, not subject to legislation because there are some churches which declare that war immoral on religious grounds. Religious groups have taken religious stands on many social issues, including war, race, poverty, population, and ecology, without exempting those problems from public legislation or turning them into "theology."

Nor is it enough to argue "sociologically" that religion plays a large role in what people feel and think about abortion, and that, somehow, this shows the religious issue to be paramount. If that were the case (and the sociological facts are, in any event, more complicated), then everyone, regardless of position, is implicated; for virtually everyone can be identified (if only culturally) with one or another religious heritage. Why is it, however, that the person who comes out of a religious heritage (*e.g.*, Roman Catholicism) that condemns abortion is said to be acting on "religious" grounds, while a person from a heritage which does not condemn abortion is not (particularly when the latter tradition has *theological* reasons for not condemning abortion, as with some branches of Judaism and Protestantism)?

The claim that abortion is not a religious but a "philosophical" issue is surely true. But, then, every serious social question is philosophical. What is justice? What is freedom? Those questions arise all the time, and they are philosophical (and legal) in nature. The answers to them shape legislation in a very decisive way. It is inconsistent to argue that the right of the fetus is exclusively a philosophical problem, to be left to individual conscience, while the right of women is a matter to be protected or implemented legislatively. If it is legitimate to legislate on the latter (which it is), then it should be equally legitimate to legislate on the former.

B. *To remove restrictive abortion laws from the books passes no judgment on the substantive ethical issues; it merely allows individuals to make up their own minds.*

That an absence of legislation allows freedom of individual choice is undoubtedly true. But it would be highly surprising if a social decision to remove restrictive laws did not reflect a significant shift in public moral thinking about the issue at hand. Civil libertarians, for instance, would be outraged if it were proposed to repeal all legislation designed to protect the civil rights of blacks on the ground that this would maximize individual freedom of choice: they would accurately discern any such trend as both moral and constitutional regression.

In the instance of abortion, a public decision to leave the question up to individuals reflects at least three premises of a highly philosophical sort: (1) that private abortion decisions have few if any social implications or consequences; (2) that there are no normative standards whatever for determining the rights of fetuses, except the standard that individuals are free to use or create any standard they see fit; and (3) that changes in law have no effect one way or another on individual moral judgments. My point here is not to judge these premises (though obviously much could be said about them), but only to point out that each involves a philosophical judgment and has philosophical implications. A decision to remove abortion laws from the books is no more ethically neutral than a decision to put such laws on the books or keep them there.

C. *Any liberalization of abortion laws, or a repeal of such laws, will lead in the long run to a disrespect for all human life.*

This is a fundamental premise of those opposed to abortion. There is no evidence to support such a judgment, however, and evidence rather than speculation is what is required.

In the first place, it is exceedingly difficult to correlate abortion attitudes throughout the world with any trend toward disrespect for nonfetal life. On the contrary, insofar as liberal abortion laws are designed to promote free choice for women, there is a prima facie case that their intent is to enhance respect for the lives of women.

Secondly, there is no evidence to support a "domino theory" of the kind which predicts a quick move from liberalization of abortion laws to the killing of the defective, the elderly, and the undesirable. This has certainly not happened in Japan or the eastern European countries, which have had liberal abortion laws for a number of years.

Finally, since most of those who support liberal abortion laws either do not believe that fetal life is human life or do not believe that it is life which has reached a stage requiring social protection, it is unfair to accuse them of harboring attitudes which inevitably lead to atrocities against all forms of human life. This kind of judgment reflects more the moral logic of the group leveling such charges than the moral principles of those at whom the charge is leveled.

D. *Scientific evidence, particularly modern genetics, has shown beyond a shadow of a doubt that human life begins at conception, or at least at the time of implantation.*

Scientific evidence does not, as such, tell us when human life begins. The concept "human" is essentially philosophical, requiring both a philosophical and an ethical judgment. Even if it could be shown that human life begins at conception, that finding would not entail the further moral judgment that life at that stage ethically merits full protection. When human life begins and when human life, once begun, merits or requires full respect are two different questions.

It is, I think, reasonable to contend that human life begins at conception. But this is as much a philosophical and ethical position as it is scientific. At the same time, however, it is capricious to ignore all scientific evidence. As any elementary textbook in genetics shows, the fusion of sperm and egg marks a decisive first step in the life of any individual. It is only in abortion arguments that one hears vague protestations that life is just one great continuum, with no decisive, significant changes from one stage or condition to another. But if it is bad science to talk that way, it is equally bad science to say that science dictates in some normative manner when human life begins.

E. *The fetus is nothing more than "tissue" or a "blob of
protoplasm" or a "blueprint."*

Definitions of this kind can only be called self-serving. This is
not the way a fetus is defined in any dictionary or any embryological text. All life is tissue and protoplasm; that fact alone tells us
nothing whatever. Would it be acceptable for a student in a college biology course to define "fetus" with a one-word term "tissue"
or "protoplasm"?

It is no less unscientific to call an embryo or a fetus a mere
"blueprint." Blueprints of buildings are not ordinarily mixed into
the mortar; they remain in the hands of the architects. Moreover,
once a building has been constructed, the blueprint can be thrown
away, and the building will continue to stand. The genetic blueprint operates in an entirely different way: it exerts a directly causal action in morphological development; as an intrinsic part of the
physiological structure, it can at no point be thrown away or taken
out.

F. *All abortions are selfish, ego-centered actions.*

This reflects a strain of thought which runs very deep among
those violently opposed to abortion. But the argument manages to
ignore the decisions of those who choose abortion out of a sense of
responsibility to their living children. It also manages to beg the
question of whether individuals have some rights to determine what
is in their own welfare, and to choose in favor of themselves some of
the time.

Most broadly, this contention typifies the widespread tendency
on all sides of the abortion debate to indulge in amateur psycholo-
gizing and *ad hominem* argumentation. Those opposed to abortion
are adept at reducing all proabortion arguments to their psychological ingredients: homicidal impulses, selfishness, the baneful effects of a decadent culture, genocidal aspirations, a hatred of children, and the like. Those favorable to abortion are no mean masters
of the art themselves: since it is well known that all opposed to
abortion are dogma-ridden, male chauvinists (or females brainwashed by male chauvinists), insensitive to the quality of life, sa-

dists and/or fascists. In short, don't listen to anyone's arguments; it is more profitable to hunt out hidden pathologies. And don't credit anyone with a mistake in reasoning, too small and human a flaw for propaganda purposes, when it is far more emotively effective to convict them of general crimes against humanity.

G. *Abortions are "therapeutic," and abortion
decisions are "medical" decisions.*

Abortion is not notably therapeutic for the fetus — an observation I presume will elicit little disagreement. Even in the instance of a fetus with a grave defect, abortion is not therapeutic. It may be merciful and it may be wise, but, unless I am mistaken, the medical profession does not classify procedures with a 100 percent mortality rate as therapeutic.

Perhaps, then, abortion is therapeutic for the woman who receives it. That it is beneficial to her in some ways seems undeniable; she is relieved of an unwanted social, economic, or psychological burden. But is it proper to employ language which has a very concrete meaning in medicine — the correction or amelioration of a physical or psychological defect — in a case where there is usually no physical pathology at all? Except in the now-rare instances of a direct threat to a woman's life, an abortion cures no known disease and relieves no medically classifiable illness.

Thomas Szasz has been an especially eloquent spokesman for two positions. The first is that abortion should be available on request in the name of individual freedom. The second is that essentially nonmedical decisions should not be dressed in the mantle of "medical" language simply because they require medical technology for their execution. "To be sure," he has written, "the procedure is surgical; but this makes abortion no more a medical problem than the use of the electric chair makes capital punishment a problem of electrical engineering."[1]

Szasz's point seems undeniable, yet it is still common to hear abortion spoken of as a medical problem, which should be worked out between the woman and her physician. Even if that is the proper way to handle abortion, that does not make it a medical solution. The reason for this obfuscation is not far to be sought, and Szasz has stressed it as a constant theme in a number of his writings: the predilection in our society to translate value judgments into medical terms, giving them the aura of settled "scientific" judgments and the socially impregnable status of medical legitimation.

H. *In a just society there would be no abortion problem, since there the social and economic pressures that drive women to abortion would not exist.*

This proposition is usually part of a broader political argument which sees abortion as no more than a symptom of unjust, repressive societies. To concentrate on abortion as a response to poverty, poor housing, puritanical attitudes toward illegitimacy, and racism is a cheap and evasive solution. It achieves no more than reinforcement of unjust political and social structures and institutions.

Up to a point there is some merit in this kind of argument, and that is why I believe that (as in the Scandinavian and eastern European countries) abortion should be handled in a context of full maternal and child-care welfare programs. A woman who wishes to have a child but is not socially and economically free to do so is not a free woman. Her freedom is only superficially enhanced by allowing her, in that kind of repressive context, to choose abortion as a way out. She is not even being given half the loaf of freedom, which requires the existence of a full range of viable options.

At the same time, however, there are some serious limitations to the notion that abortion is nothing but a symptom of an unjust society. It utterly ignores the fact, common enough in affluent countries, that large numbers of women choose abortion because they have decided they want no children at all, or at least no more children than they already have. They are acting not out of social or economic coercion but out of a positive desire to shape and live a life of their own choosing, not dominated by unexpected pregnancies and unwanted children. In addition, it neglects the reality of contraceptive failure, which can and does occur independently of economic and social conditions (though it may of course be influenced by them). Short of the perfect contraceptive perfectly used, some portion of women, against their intentions, will become pregnant.

I. *Abortion is exclusively a women's issue, to be decided by women.*

The underpinning of this argument seems to consist of three assumptions. First, that there is no role for male judgment, intervention, or interference because it is women who get pregnant and who have to live with the pregnancies. Second, that abortion laws are repressive because they have been established by male legislators. And, third, that the fetus is a part of a woman's body and is thus exclusively subject to her judgments and desires.

While I am fully prepared to agree that approval of a male, whether husband and/or father, should not be a legal condition for a woman to receive an abortion, this should not be construed to mean that nothing is owed, in justice, to the male. Even ignoring the well-known fact that women do not get pregnant by themselves, a few other considerations remain. At the least, there is an injustice in giving males no rights prior to birth but then imposing upon them a full range of obligations after birth. If the obligations toward a child are mutual after birth, why should there not be a corresponding parity of rights prior to birth? I have not seen a satisfactory answer to that question. Moreover, if — to accept the feminist premise — women have been forced to carry through unwanted pregnancies because of male domination, the sexist shoe is put on the other foot if all the rights involved in having a child are ceded exclusively to women. One injustice is corrected at the expense of creating another, and sexism is still triumphant.

That legislatures are dominated by males is an obvious fact. That the history of abortion legislation would have been different had there been legislative equality or even a female majority, however, has not been demonstrated. Indeed, it has been a consistent survey finding that women are less willing than men to approve permissive abortion laws. There have of course been attempts to explain these rather awkward findings, since they are inconsistent on their face with claims that resistance to abortion is a male phenomenon. These efforts usually take the form of speculations designed to show that the resistant women were culturally brainwashed into adopting repressive male attitudes. This is a plausible theory, but one for which there unfortunately is no evidence whatever. And, apart from these speculations, there is no evidence that the thinking of women on abortion must, of biological and experiential necessity, be utterly different from that of men. But that is exactly the premise necessary if the contention is to be sustained that an exclusively female domination of abortion legislation would produce a different result from either a male domination or legislative equality.

In this context it should be mentioned that child-bearing and child-rearing have consequences for everyone in a society, both men and women. To imply that women alone should have all the rights, even though the consequences involve the lives of both sexes, is an unfair conclusion. Or are we to overthrow, as the price of abortion reform, the long-honored principle that all of those who will have to bear the consequences of decisions have a right to be consulted? I find that price too high. Yet, since I agree that abortion decisions should not legally require the consent of husband and/or father — for I see no way to include such a requirement in the law without opening the way for a further abuse of women — I am left with the (perhaps pious) hope that there will be some recognition that problems of justice toward the male are real (however new!) and that an ethical resolution will be found.

Finally, a quick word about the contention that a fetus is "part" of a woman's body. That a fetus is *in* a woman's body is an evident biological datum. That it is thereby a *part* of her body, in much the same way that her heart, arm, liver, or leg is part of her body, is biologically false. The separate genetic constitution of the fetus, its rate of growth and development, and its separate organ system clearly distinguish the body of the fetus from the body of the mother.

Some clarity would be brought to the language of the abortion debate if this distinction were admitted. It could still be argued that, because the fetus is in the mother's body, she should have full rights in determining its fate. But that argument is different from likening the fetus to any other part of a woman's body and then transposing the rules concerning the exercise of rights over one's body. Here is a clear instance where, in order to find a constitutional precedent for women's right to control procreation, violence is often done to some elementary facts of biology.

III. SOME VALID CONCLUSIONS

I have tried to show, using nine different propositions, that some bad, or at least incompletely developed, arguments are too much in currency to be allowed to go by default. Would the abortion debate be significantly altered if these arguments were no longer used by the contending sides? This is a moot question, as there seems to be little likelihood that they will cease being employed. They are too powerful to be set aside, for both good and bad reasons — the good being that they are able to elicit responses which build upon some pervasive feelings about abortion, feelings which are decisive in shaping thought and behavior, even if they are poorly articulated.

The great strength of the general movement for abortion on request (apart from the questionable validity of particular arguments brought to bear in support of it) is that it perceives and seeks to correct two elementary realities, one social and the other biological. The social reality is that women have not had the freedom to make their own choice in a matter critical to their development as persons. Society, through the medium of male domination, has forced its choice upon them. The biological reality is that it is women who become pregnant and bear children; nature gave them no choice. Unless they are given a means to control the biological facts — and abortion is one very effective means — they will be dominated by them.

Without such control, which must be total if it is to have any decisive meaning, women are fated to accept Freud's principle that "anatomy is destiny." That kind of rigid biological determinism is increasingly unacceptable, not only to women in the case of procreation, but to most human beings confronted with the involuntary rigidities of nature. The deepest philosophical issue beneath the abortion question is the extent to which, in the name of freely chosen ends, biological realities can be manipulated, controlled, and set aside. This is a very old problem, and the trend toward abortion on request reflects the most recent tendency in modern thought — namely, the attempt to subordinate biology to reason, to bring it under control, to master it. It remains to be seen whether procreation can be so easily mastered. That question may take centuries to resolve.

The great strength of the movement against abortion is that it seeks to protect one defenseless category of human or potentially human life; furthermore, it strives to resist the introduction into society of forms of value judgments that would discriminate among the worth of individual lives. In almost any other civil rights context, the cogency of this line of reasoning would be quickly respected. Indeed, it has been at the heart of efforts to correct racial injustices, to improve health care, to eradicate poverty, and to provide better care for the aged. The history of mankind has shown too many instances of systematic efforts to exclude certain races or classes of persons from the human community to allow us to view with equanimity the declaration that fetuses are "not human." Historically, the proposition that all human beings are equal, however "inchoate" they may be, is not conservative but radical. It is constantly threatened in theory and subverted in practice.

Although the contending sides in the abortion debate commonly ignore, or systematically deride, the essentially positive impulses lying behind their opponents' positions, the conflict is nonetheless best seen as the pitting of essentially valuable impulses against one another. The possibility of a society which did allow women the right and the freedom to control their own lives is a lofty goal. No less lofty is that of a society which, with no exceptions, treated all forms of human life as equally valuable. In the best of all possible worlds, it might be possible to reconcile these goals. In the real world, however, the first goal requires the right of abortion, and the second goal excludes that right. This, I believe, is a genuine and deep dilemma. That so few are willing to recognize the dilemma, or even to admit that any choice must be less than perfect, is the most disturbing element in the whole debate.

The bad reason why the arguments I have analyzed will endure is that they readily lend themselves to legal use. Nothing in our society has so muddied the ethical issues as its tendency to turn ethical problems into legal matters. The great prize, sought by all sides, is a favorable court decision. Toward that end, the best tactic is to find a way of bringing one's own ethical case under one or more constitutional protections or exclusions. If one can succeed in convincing the courts that abortion is a religious issue (which it is not), then there is a good chance that they will favor private choice and rule against legislation. The same tactic is evident in efforts to show that abortion decisions come under the constitutional protections afforded to "privacy" (which begs the question of the rights of the fetus), or, on the other side, to show that abortion violates the equal protection and due process requirements of the Constitution (which also begs the question of the rights of the fetus). Since the possibility of a legal victory is an irresistible goal, there seems to be no limit to the bad arguments which will be brought to bear to gain it.

NOTE

1. Szasz, *The Ethics of Abortion*, HUMANIST, Sept.-Oct. 1966, at 148.

JEWISH VIEWS
ON ABORTION

RABBI DR. IMMANUEL JAKOBOVITS

WITH THE STAGGERING RISE in the rate of abortions and with the motives for such operations now including the fear of abnormal births as well as birth control considerations, abortion has become the most widely debated medico-moral subject. (What was previously either a therapeutic measure for the safety of the mother or a plainly criminal act is now widely advocated as a means to prevent the birth of possibly defective children, to curb the sordid indignities and hazards imposed on women resorting to clandestine operators, to contain the population explosion, and simply to allow women the right to decide more freely whether or not they will bear children.) Under the mounting pressure of these new factors, a crushing responsibility is sought by, and is often conferred upon, medical practitioners. Many of them claim that, within some broad general guidelines, the decision whether or not legally to terminate a pregnancy should be left to their judgment.

In the Jewish view, this position cannot be upheld. The judgment that is required here, while it must be based on medical evidence, is clearly of a moral nature. (The decision on whether, and under what circumstances, it is right to destroy a germinating human life depends on the assessment and weighing of values, on determining the title to life in any given case. Such value judgments are entirely outside the province of medical science. No amount of training or experience in medicine can help in ascertaining the criteria necessary for reaching such capital verdicts, for making such life-and-death decisions. Such judgments pose essentially a moral, not a medical, problem. Hence they call for the judgment of moral, not medical, specialists.)

In demanding that they should have the right to determine or adjudicate the laws governing their practice, physicians are making an altogether unprecedented claim, one not advanced by any other profession. Lawyers do not argue that, because law is their specialty, the decision on what is legal should be left to their conscience. And teachers do not claim that, since they are professionals competent in education, the laws governing their work should be administered or defined at their discretion. Such claims are patently absurd, for they would demand jurisdiction on matters completely beyond their professional competence.

There is no more justice or logic in advancing similar claims for the medical profession. A physician, in performing an abortion or any other procedure involving moral considerations, such as artificial insemination or euthanasia, is merely a technical expert; he is no more qualified than any other layman to pronounce on the rights or legality of such acts, let alone to determine what these rights should be, relying merely on the whims or dictates of his conscience. The decision on whether a human life, once conceived, is to be or not to be, therefore, properly belongs to moral experts, or to legislatures guided by such experts.

I. Jewish Law

A. *The Claims of Judaism*

Every monotheistic religion embodies within its philosophy and legislation a system of ethics — a definition of moral values. None does so with greater precision and comprehensiveness than Judaism. It emphatically insists that the norms of moral conduct can be governed neither by the accepted notions of public opinion nor by the individual conscience. In the Jewish view, the human conscience is meant to enforce laws, not to make them. Right and wrong, good and evil, are absolute values which transcend the capricious variations of time, place, and environment, just as they defy definition by relation to human intuition or expediency. These values, Judaism teaches, derive their validity from the Divine revelation at Mount Sinai, as expounded and developed by sages faithful to, and authorized by, its writ.

B. *The Sources of Jewish Law*

For a definition of these values, one must look to the vast and complex corpus of Jewish law, the authentic expression of all Jewish religious and moral thought. The literary depositories of Jewish law extend over nearly 4,000 years, from the Bible and the Talmud, serving as the immutable basis of the main principles, to the great medieval codes and the voluminous rabbinical *responsa* writings recording practical verdicts founded on these principles, right up to the present day.

These sources, which will be detailed below, specify a very distinct attitude on all aspects of the abortion problem. They clearly indicate that Judaism, while it does not share the rigid stand of the Roman Catholic Church, which unconditionally proscribes any direct destruction of the fetus from the moment of conception, refuses to endorse the far more permissive views of many Protestant denominations. The traditional Jewish position is somewhere between these two extremes, recognizing only a grave hazard to the mother as a legitimate indication for therapeutic abortion.

1. *Abortion in the Bible* — The legislation of the Bible makes only one reference to our subject, and this is by implication:

> And if men strive together, and hurt a woman with child, so that her fruit depart, and yet no harm follow, he shall be surely fined, according as the woman's husband shall lay upon him; and he shall pay as the judges determine. But if any harm follow, then shalt thou give life for life. . . .[1]

(a) *The Jewish interpretation.* This crucial passage, by one of the most curious twists of literary fortunes, marks the parting of the ways between the Jewish and Christian rulings on abortion. According to the Jewish interpretation, if "no harm follow" the "hurt" to the woman resulting in the loss of her fruit refers to the survival of the woman following her miscarriage; in that case there is no capital guilt involved, and the attacker is merely liable to pay compensation for the loss of her fruit. "But if any harm follow," *i.e.*, if the woman is fatally injured, then the man responsible for her death has to "give life for life"; in that event the capital charge of murder exempts him from any monetary liability for the aborted fruit.[2]

This interpretation is also borne out by the rabbinical exegesis of the verse defining the law of murder, "He that smiteth *a man*, so that he dieth, shall surely be put to death . . . ,"[3] which the Rabbis construed to mean "a man, but not a fetus."[4]

These passages clearly indicate that the killing of an unborn child is not considered murder punishable by death in Jewish law.

(b) *The Christian interpretation.* The Christian tradition disputing this view goes back to a mistranslation in the *Septuagint.* There, the Hebrew for "no harm follow" was replaced by the Greek for "[her child be born] imperfectly formed."[5] This interpretation, distinguishing between an unformed and a formed fetus and branding the killing of the latter as murder, was accepted by Tertullian, who was ignorant of Hebrew, and by later church fathers. The distinction was subsequently embodied in canon law as well as in Justinian Law.[6] This position was further reinforced by the belief that the "animation" (entry of the soul) of a fetus occurred on the fortieth or eightieth day after conception for males and females respectively, an idea first expressed by Aristotle,[7] and by the doctrine, firmly enunciated by Saint Augustine and other early Christian authorities, that the unborn child was included among those condemned to eternal perdition if he died unbaptized.[8] Some even regarded the death or murder of an unborn child as a greater calamity than that of a baptized person.[9] Eventually the distinction between animate and inanimate fetuses was lost; and since 1588, the Catholic Church has considered as murder the killing of any human fruit from the moment of conception.[10]

This position is maintained to the present day.[11] It assumes that potential life, even in the earliest stages of gestation, enjoys the same value as any existing adult life. Hence, the Catholic Church never tolerates any direct abortion, even when, by allowing the pregnancy to continue, both mother and child will perish;[12] "better two deaths than one murder."[13]

2. *Abortion in the Talmud* — Jewish law assumes that the full title to life arises only at birth. Accordingly, the Talmud rules:

> If a woman is in hard travail [and her life cannot otherwise be saved], one cuts up the child within her womb and extracts it member by member, because her life comes before that of [the child]. But if the greater part [or the head] was delivered, one may not touch it, for one may not set aside one person's life for the sake of another.[14]

This ruling, sanctioning embryotomy to save the mother in her mortal conflict with her unborn child, is also the sole reference to abortion in the principal codes of Jewish law.[15] They add only the further argument that such a child, being in "pursuit" of the mother's life, may be destroyed as an "aggressor" following the general principle of self-defense.[16]

This formulation of the attitude toward abortion in the classic sources of Jewish law implies (1) that the only indication considered for abortion is a hazard to the mother's life and (2) that, otherwise, the destruction of an unborn child is a grave offense, although not murder.

3. *Abortion in Rabbinical Writings* — Some of these conclusions, and their ramifications, are more fully discussed in later rabbinical writings, notably the prolific *responsa* literature. Before some of these writings are detailed, it should be pointed out that criminal abortion, as distinct from therapeutic abortion, is scarcely mentioned in Jewish sources at all. This omission seems all the more glaring in view of the extraordinary attention given to the subject in Christian literature and other legislation in ancient, medieval, and modern times. Criminal abortion was, with few exceptions, simply nonexistent in Jewish society. Consequently, the legal and moral problems involved were rarely submitted to rabbinical judgment, and their consideration thus did not enter into the *responsa*, at least not until comparatively recent times.[17]

Elaborating on the law as defined in the Talmud and the codes, the *responsa* add several significant rulings. While very little is written on abortions following rape, several opinions are expressed on the legality of aborting a product of incest or adultery, both capital offenses in Biblical law. One eighteenth-century authority considered the case of an adulteress different insofar as her capital guilt would also forfeit the life of the fruit she carried.[18] But others maintained that there could be no distinction between a bastard and a legitimate fetus in this respect, and that any sanction to destroy such a product would open the floodgates to immorality and debauchery.[19] A later *responsum* also prohibited such an operation.[20]

Since the Talmud permits the sacrifice of the child to save the mother only prior to the emergence of its head or the greater part of its body from the birth canal,[21] a widely discussed question concerns the right to dismember the fetus even during the final stage of parturition if it is feared that otherwise both mother and child may die. As the danger to the mother usually is likely to occur before that stage is reached, this is mainly a hypothetical question, but it may be of some practical significance in the case of a breech-birth if the child's head cannot be extracted following the delivery of the rest of the body. Notwithstanding the rule that the child in principle assumes full and equal human rights once the major part is born, and that consequently one may not thereafter save one life (the mother's) at the cost of another (the child's), this particular case may be an exception because (1) the child is liable to die in any event, whether the operation is carried out or not, while the mother can be rescued at the expense of the child and (2) in the Jewish view the viability of a child is not fully established until it has passed the thirtieth day of its life, so that of the two lives here at stake the one is certain and established, while the other is still in some doubt. This slight inequality in value is too insignificant to warrant the deliberate sacrifice of the child for the sake of the mother if, without such sacrifice, the child would survive; but it is a sufficient factor to tip the scales in favor of the mother if the alternative is the eventual loss of both lives. Hence, with one exception,[22] rabbinical verdicts are inclined to countenance the intervention, provided the physician is confident of the success of the operation.[23]

4. *Deformed Children in Rabbinical Writings* — More recently the tragic problem of abortions indicated by suspected fetal defects has occupied considerable space in rabbinical writings. The recognition of this problem dates only from 1941, when an Australian medical journal first drew attention to the incidence of abnormalities resulting from rubella[24] in the mother during her early pregnancy. Since then, the legal, moral, and religious issues involved have been widely but still inconclusively debated in medical as well as nonmedical circles. They aroused much public controversy when it was established that the birth of thousands of deformed babies could be traced to drugs, notably thalidomide, taken by pregnant mothers and when many such mothers sought to have their pregnancies terminated for fear that they would deliver malformed children.

Most authorities of Jewish law are agreed that physical or mental abnormalities do not in themselves compromise the title to life, whether before or after birth. Cripples and idiots, however incapacitated, enjoy the same human rights (though not necessarily legal competence) as normal persons.[25] Human life being infinite in value, its sanctity is bound to be entirely unaffected by the absence of any or all mental faculties or by any bodily defects: any fraction of infinity still remains infinite. (But see the Postscript, below.)

5. *Monster Births in Rabbinical Writings* — The absolute inviolability of any human being, however deformed, was affirmed in the first *responsum* on the status of monster births. Early in the nineteenth century, a famous rabbinical scholar advised a questioner that it was forbidden to destroy a grotesquely misshapen child; he ruled that to kill, or even starve to death, any being born of a human mother was unlawful as homicide.[26] Indeed, in a somewhat less legal context, a twelfth-century moralistic work referred to a ruling against terminating the life of a child born with teeth and a tail like an animal, counseling instead the removal of these features.[27]

C. *Arguments against the Destruction of Defectives*

Based on these principles and precedents, the consensus of present-day rabbis is to condemn abortion, feticide, or infanticide to eliminate a crippled being, before or after birth, as an unconscionable attack on the sanctity of life. Further considerations leading to this conclusion include the arguments that, conversely, the saving of an unborn child's life justifies the violation of the Sabbath (permitted only when human life is at stake);[28] that such a child is not in "pursuit" of the mother, thus excluding an important condition for the right to perform a therapeutic abortion;[29] that the interruption of a pregnancy is not without hazards to the mother, particularly the danger of rendering her sterile and the increase in maternal mortality resulting from abortions, as attested by physicians;[30] and that the killing of an embryo, while technically not murder according to a "scriptural decree," nevertheless constitutes "an appurtenance of murder" because "in matters affecting human life we also consider that which is going to be [a human being] without any further action, following the laws of nature."[31]

These considerations would be valid even if it were known for certain that the expected child would be born deformed. The almost invariable doubts about such a contingency only strengthen the objections to abortion in these circumstances, especially in view of the Talmudic maxim that in matters of life and death the usual majority rule does not operate; any chance, however slim, that a life may be saved must always be given the benefit of the doubt.[32]

A similar attitude was adopted in a recent rabbinical article on the celebrated trial in Liege (Belgium) in which a mother and others were acquitted of guilt for the confessed killing of a thalidomide baby.[33] The author denounces abortion for such a purpose as well as the Liege verdict. "The sole legitimate grounds for killing a fetus are the urgent needs of the mother and her healing, whereas in these circumstances the mother's efforts to have the child aborted are based on self-love and plain egotism, wrapped in a cloak of compassion for this unfortunate creature, and this cannot be called a necessity for the mother at all."[34]

D. *Psychological Considerations*

On the other hand, Jewish law would consider a grave psychological hazard to the mother as no less weighty a reason for an abortion than a physical threat. On these grounds a seventeenth-century *responsum* permitted an abortion in a case where it was feared the mother would otherwise suffer an attack of hysteria imperiling her life.[35] If it is genuinely feared that a continued pregnancy and eventual birth under these conditions might have such debilitating effects on the mother as to present a danger to her own life or the life of another by suicidal or violent tendencies, however remote this danger may be, a therapeutic abortion may be indicated with the same justification as for other medical reasons. But this fear would have to be very real, attested to by the most competent psychiatric opinion, and based on previous experiences of mental imbalance.[36]

II. MORAL AND SOCIAL CONSIDERATIONS

The legalistic structure of these conclusions must be viewed in the context of Judaism's moral philosophy and against the background of contemporary social conditions.

A. The "Cruelty" of the Abortion Laws

It is essential at the outset, in order to arrive at an objective judgment, to disabuse one's mind of the often one-sided, if not grossly partisan, arguments in the popular (and sometimes medical) presentations of the issues involved. A hue and cry is raised about the "cruelty" of restrictive abortion laws. Harrowing scenes are depicted, in the most lurid colors, of girls and married women selling their honor and their fortunes, exposing themselves to mayhem and death at the hands of some greedy and ill-qualified abortionist in a dark, unhygienic back alley. Equally distressing are the accounts and pictures of pitifully deformed children born because our "antiquated" abortion laws did not permit us to forestall their and their parents' misfortune. And then there are, of course, always heart-strings of sympathy to be pulled by the sight of "unwanted" children taxing the patience and resources of parents already "burdened" with too large a brood.

There is, inevitably, some element of cruelty in most laws. To a person who has spent his last cent before the tax bill arrives, the income tax laws are unquestionably "cruel"; and to a man passionately in love with a married woman the adultery laws must appear "barbaric." Even more universally "harsh" are the military draft regulations which expose young men to acute danger and their families to great anguish and hardship.

B. Moral Standards in Society

All these "cruelties" are surely no valid reason for changing those laws. No civilized society could survive without laws which occasionally cause some suffering for individuals. Nor can any public moral standards be maintained without strictly enforced regulations calling for extreme restraints and sacrifices in some cases. If the criterion for the legitimacy of laws were the complete absence of "cruel" effects, we should abolish or drastically liberalize not only our abortion laws, but our statutes on marriage, narcotics, homosexuality, suicide, euthanasia, and numerous other matters, which inevitably result in personal anguish from time to time.

So far the reasoning here, which could be supported by any number of references to Jewish tradition, has merely sought to demolish the "cruelty" factor as an argument valid in itself to judge the justice or injustice of any law. It remains to be demonstrated that the restrictions on abortion are morally sound enough and sufficiently important to the public welfare to outweigh the consequential hardships in individual cases.

C. The Cost in Healthy Lives

What the fuming editorials and harrowing documentaries on the abortion problem do not show are pictures of radiant mothers fondling perfectly healthy children who would never have been alive if their parents had been permitted to resort to abortion in moments of despair. There are no statistics on the contributions to society of outstanding men and women who would never have been born had the abortion laws been more liberal. Nor is it known how many "unwanted" children eventually turn out to be the sunshine of their families.

A Jewish moralistic work of the twelfth century relates the following deeply significant story:

> A person constantly said that, having already a son and a daughter, he was anxious lest his wife become pregnant again. For he was not rich and asked how would he find sufficient sustenance. Said a sage to him: "When a child is born, the Holy One, blessed be He, provides the milk beforehand in the mother's breast; therefore, do not worry." But he did not accept the wise man's words, and he continued to fret. Then a son was born to him. After a while, the child became ill, and the father turned to the sage: "Pray for my son that he shall live." Exclaimed the sage: "To you applies the biblical verse: 'Suffer not thy mouth to bring thy flesh into guilt.' "[37]

Some children may be born unwanted, but there are few unwanted children aged five or ten years.

D. Abortion Statistics

Thus there are — even from the purely utilitarian viewpoint of "cruelty" *versus* "happiness" or "usefulness" — two sides to this problem, not just one, as is pretended by those agitating for reform. There are the admittedly tragic cases of maternal indignities and deaths as well as of congenital deformities resulting from restrictive abortion laws. But, on the other hand, there are the countless happy children and useful citizens whose births equally result from these laws. What is the ratio between these two categories?

If one considers that even with rigid laws there were well over one million abortions performed annually in the United States (most of them by reputable physicians), it stands to reason that the relaxation of these laws will raise the abortion rate by many millions. Even allowing for more widespread recourse to birth control, there can be little doubt that the American abortion rate will soar to at least two or three times its previous level (probably a gross understatement).

Out of the several million pregnancies that will probably be terminated every year, no more than 30,000[38] would have resulted in deformed births; the remaining 99 percent would have been healthy children had their mothers been allowed or forced to carry them to term. One can certainly ask if the extremely limited reduction in the number of malformed children and maternal mortality risks really justify the annual wholesale destruction of several million germinating, healthy lives, most of them potentially happy and useful citizens, especially in a country as underpopulated as America (compared to Europe, for instance, which commands far fewer natural resources).

E. *The Individual's Claim to Life*

These numerical facts alone make nonsense of the argument for more and easier abortions. But moral norms cannot be determined by numbers. In the Jewish view, "he who saves one life is as if he saved an entire world";[39] one human life is as precious as a million lives, for each is infinite in value. Hence, even if the ratio were reversed, and there was only a 1 percent chance that the child to be aborted would be normal, the consideration for that one child in favor of life would outweigh any counterindication for the other 99 percent.

But, in truth, such a counterindication, too, is founded on fallacious premises. Assuming one were 100 percent certain that a child would be born deformed, could this affect its claim to life? Any line to be drawn between normal and abnormal beings determining their right to live would have to be altogether arbitrary. Would a grave defect in one limb or in two limbs, or an anticipated sub-normal intelligence quotient of 75 or 50 make the capital difference between one who is entitled to live and one who is not? And if the absence of two limbs deprives a person of his claim to life, what about one who loses two limbs in an accident? By what moral reasoning can such a defect be a lesser cause for denying the right to live than a similar congenital abnormality? Surely life-and-death verdicts cannot be based on such tenuous distinctions.

F. *The Obligations of Society*

The birth of a physically or mentally maldeveloped child may be an immense tragedy in a family, just as a crippling accident or a lingering illness striking a family member later in life may be. But one cannot purchase the relief from such misfortunes at the cost of life itself. So long as the sanctity of life is recognized as inviolable, the cure to suffering cannot be abortion before birth, any more than murder (whether in the form of euthanasia or of suicide) after birth. The only legitimate relief in such cases is for society to assume the burdens which the individual family can no longer bear. Since society is the main beneficiary of restrictive public laws on abortion (or homicide), it must in turn also pay the price sometimes exacted by these laws in the isolated cases demanding such a price.

Just as the state holds itself responsible for the support of families bereaved by the death of soldiers fallen in the defense of their country, it ought to provide for incapacitated people born and kept alive in the defense of public moral standards. The community is morally bound to relieve affected families of any financial or emotional stress they cannot reasonably bear, either by accepting the complete care of defective children in public institutions, or by supplying medical and educational subsidies to ensure that such families do not suffer any unfair economic disadvantages from their misfortune.

G. *Illegitimate Children*

Similar considerations apply to children conceived by rape. The circumstances of such a conception can have little bearing on the child's title to life, and in the absence of any well-grounded challenge to this title there cannot be any moral justification for an abortion. Once again, the burden rests with society to relieve an

innocent mother (if she so desires) from the consequences of an un-
provoked assault upon her virtue if the assailant cannot be found and
forced to discharge this responsibility to his child.

In the case of pregnancies resulting from incestuous, adulterous,
or otherwise illegitimate relations (which the mother did not resist),
there are additional considerations militating against any sanction
of abortion. Jewish law not only puts an extreme penalty on incest
and adultery, but also imposes fearful disabilities on the products of
such unions. It brands these relations as capital crimes,[40] and it de-
bars Jewish children born under these conditions from marriage with
anyone except their like.[41]

1. *The Deterrent Effect* — Why exact such a price from innocent children for the sins of their parents? The answer is simple:
to serve as a powerful deterrent to such hideous crimes. The would-
be partners to any such illicit sexual relations are to be taught that
their momentary pleasure would be fraught with the most disastrous
consequences for any children they might conceive. Through this
knowledge they are to recoil from the very thought of incest or adultery with the same horror as they would from contemplating murder
as a means to enjoyment or personal benefit. Murder is comparatively rare in civilized society for the very reason that the dreadful
consequences have evoked this horror of the crime in the public conscience. Incest and adultery, in the Jewish view, are no lesser
crimes,[42] and they require the same horror as an effective deterrent.

2. *Parental Responsibility* — Why create this deterrent by visiting the sins of the parents on their innocent children? First, because
there is no other way to expose an offense committed in private and
usually beyond the chance of detection. But, above all, this responsibility of parents for the fate of their children is an inexorable
necessity in the generation of human life; it is dictated by the law of
nature no less than by the moral law. If a careless mother drops
her baby and thereby causes a permanent brain injury to the child,
or if a syphilitic father irresponsibly transmits his disease to his offspring before birth, or if parents are negligent in the education of
their children, all these children will innocently suffer and for the
rest of their lives expiate the sins of their parents. This is what must
be if parental responsibility is to be taken seriously. The fear that
such catastrophic consequences would ensue from a surrender to

temptation or from carelessness will help prevent the conception of grossly disadvantaged children or their physical or mental mutilation after birth.

H. *Public Standards versus Individual Aberration*

In line with this reasoning, Jewish law never condones the relaxation of public moral standards for the sake of saving recalcitrant individuals from even mortal offenses. A celebrated Jewish sage and philosopher of the fifteenth century, in connection with a question submitted to his judgment, averred that it was always wrong for a community to acquiesce in the slightest evil, however much it was hoped thereby to prevent far worse excesses by individuals. The problem he faced arose out of a suggestion that brothels for single people be tolerated as long as such publicly controlled institutions would reduce or eliminate the capital crime of marital faithlessness then rampant. His unequivocal answer was: It is surely far better that individuals should commit the worst offenses and expose themselves to the gravest penalties than publicly to promote the slightest compromise with the moral law.[43]

Strict abortion laws, ruling out the *post facto* "correction" of rash acts, compel people to think twice *before* they recklessly embark on illicit or irresponsible adventures liable to inflict lifelong suffering or infamy on their progeny. To eliminate the scourge of illegitimate children, more self-discipline to prevent their conception is required, not more freedom to destroy them in the womb.

The exercise of man's procreative faculties, making him (in the phrase of the Talmud) "a partner with God in creation," is man's greatest privilege and gravest responsibility. The rights and obligations implicit in the generation of human life must be evenly balanced if man is not to degenerate into an addict of lust and a moral parasite infesting the moral organism of society. Liberal abortion laws will upset that balance by facilitating sexual indulgences without insisting on corresponding responsibilities.

I. *Therapeutic Abortions*

This leaves only the concern for the mother's safety as a valid argument in favor of abortions. In the view of Judaism, all human rights, and their priorities, derive solely from their conferment upon man by his Creator. By this criterion, as defined in the Bible, the rights of the mother and her unborn child are distinctly unequal, since the capital guilt of murder takes effect only if the victim was a born and viable person. This recognition does not imply that the destruction of a fetus is not a very grave offense against the sanctity of human life, but only that it is not technically murder. Jewish law makes a similar distinction in regard to the killing of inviable adults. While the killing of a person who already suffered from a fatal injury (from other than natural causes) is not actionable as murder,[44] the killer is morally guilty of a mortal offense.[45]

This inequality, then, is weighty enough only to warrant the sacrifice of the unborn child if the pregnancy otherwise poses a threat to the mother's life. Indeed, the Jewish concern for the mother is so great that a gravid woman sentenced to death[46] must not be subjected to the ordeal of suspense to await the delivery of her child.[47] (Jewish sources brand any delay in the execution, once it is finally decreed, as "the perversion of justice" *par excellence*,[48] since the criminal is sentenced to die, not to suffer.)

Such a threat to the mother need not be either immediate or absolutely certain. Even a remote risk of life invokes all the life-saving concessions of Jewish law,[49] provided the fear of such a risk is genuine and confirmed by the most competent medical opinions. Hence, Jewish law would regard it as an indefensible desecration of human life to allow a mother to perish in order to save her unborn child.

IV. CONCLUSION

This review may be fittingly concluded with a reference to the very first Jewish statement on deliberate abortion. Commenting on the *Septuagint* version of the *Exodus* passage[50] quoted earlier, the Alexandrian-Jewish philosopher Philo, at the beginning of the Current Era, declared that the attacker must die if the fruit he caused to be lost was already "shaped and all the limbs had their proper qualities, for that which answers to this description is a human being . . . like a statue lying in a studio requiring nothing more than to be conveyed outside."[51] The legal conclusion of his statement, reflecting Hellenistic rather than Jewish influence, may vary from the letter of Jewish law; but his reasoning certainly echoes its spirit.

The analogy may be more meaningful than Philo could have intended or foreseen. A classic statue by a supreme master is no less priceless for having become defective, even with an arm or a leg missing. The destruction of such a treasure can be warranted only by the superior worth of preserving a living human being.

POSTSCRIPT

Since the composition of this article several years ago, the attitude of Jewish law to abortion has been further discussed in a number of rabbinical *responsa* and other writings—prompted partly, no doubt, by the greatly increased recourse to abortion due to the permissive legislation passed in recent years in America, England, and elsewhere. While the predominant view, as expressed in the latest rabbinical verdicts,[52] reaffirms the Jewish opposition to abortion except in cases involving some grave anticipated hazard to the mother (whether physical or psychological), a few considerably more lenient opinions have also been added. Notable among them are the rulings of the Head of the Jerusalem Rabbinical Court. He is inclined to sanction the operation on a Jewish mother even in the absence of any actual danger to her life, provided there is a serious medical indication for it, as well as in cases of a conception by rape or incest, or of a definite risk that the child may be born physically or mentally handicapped. But such abortions should be carried out preferably within the first forty days of the pregnancy or at least within the first three months.[53] Another recent *responsum* finds no reason to object to the destruction of a hydrocephalic fetus if the mother is unwilling to submit to a caesarian operation for the delivery of the child.[54]

But even these rather isolated opinions do not substantially modify the general Jewish view as given in a public statement issued by the Association of Orthodox Jewish Scientists of America in 1971:

> . . . We appeal to Jewish rabbinic and lay leadership to join us in an educational program, within our Jewish communities, designed to promulgate the Jewish attitudes toward abortion. Jewish law permits abortion only when a potentially lethal deterioration in the mother's health might ensue if pregnancy is allowed to proceed to term. Jewish law prohibits abortion when its sole justification is to prevent the birth of a physically deformed or mentally retarded child. Abortion "on demand" purely for the convenience

of the mother or even of society is strictly prohibited and morally repugnant. . . .[55]

NOTES

1. *Exodus* 21:22-23.
2. *Mekhilta* and Rashi. For a translation of these sources, see 3 LAUTERBACH, MEKHILTA 66-67 (1935); ROSENBAUM & SILBERMAN, PENTATEUCH AND RASHI'S COMMENTARY 112-13 (1930).
3. *Exodus* 21:12. (Emphasis added.)
4. *Mekhilta* and Rashi. For a translation of these sources, see 3 LAUTERBACH, *supra* note 2, at 32-33; ROSENBAUM & SILBERMAN, *supra* note 2, at 110-10a.
5. The mistranslation, also followed in the Samaritan and Karaite versions, is evidently based on reading "zurah" or "surah" (meaning "form") for "ason" (meaning "harm" or "accident"). *See* KAUFMANN, GEDENKSCHRIFT 186 (1900).
6. *See* WESTERMARCK, CHRISTIANITY AND MORALS 243 (1939).
7. ARISTOTLE, DE ANIM. HIST., vii. 3; *see* 1 CATHOLIC ENCYCLOPEDIA 46-48 (1907).
8. *See* 1 PLOSS & BARTELS, WOMAN 483 (1935); 2 CATHOLIC ENCYCLOPEDIA 266-67 (1907).
9. *See* 2 LECKY, HISTORY OF EUROPEAN MORALS 23-24 (3d ed. 1891).
10. *See* 1 PLOSS & BARTELS, *supra* note 8, at 484; BONNAR, THE CATHOLIC DOCTOR 78 (1948).
11. *See, e.g.,* CATHOLIC HOSPITAL ASSOCIATION OF THE UNITED STATES AND CANADA, ETHICAL AND RELIGIOUS DIRECTIVES FOR CATHOLIC HOSPITALS 4 (1949).
12. See BONNAR, *supra* note 10, at 84.
13. Tiberghien, *Principles et Conscience Morale*, CAHIERS LAENNAC, Oct. 1946, at 13.
14. TALMUD, TOHOROTH II *Oholoth* 7:6.
15. MAIMONIDES, HIL. ROTZE'ACH, 1:9; SHULCHAN ARUKH, *Choshen Mishpat* 425:2.
16. This is based on a discussion of the Mishnah, TALMUD, *Sanhedrin* 72b. *See generally* JAKOBOVITS, JEWISH MEDICAL ETHICS 184-91 (1962).
17. JAKOBOVITS, *supra* note 16, at 181.
18. EMDEN, RESPONSA SHE'ILATH YA'AVETZ, pt. 1, no. 43.
19. BACHARACH, RESPONSA CHAVATH YA'IR no. 31.
20. HALEVI, RESPONSA LECHEM HAPANIM, KUNTERES ACHARON, no. 19.
21. *See* text accompanying notes 14-16 *supra*.
22. SOPHER, RESPONSA MACHANEH CHAYIM *Choshen Mishpat*, pt. 2, no. 50. Some authorities left the question unresolved; see EGER, OHOLOTH 7:6; MEIR OF EISENSTADT, RESPONSA PANIM ME'IROTH, pt. 2. no. 8.

23. SCHICK, RESPONSA MAHARAM SHIK, *Yoreh De'ah* no. 155; HOFF-MANN, RESPONSA MELAMED LEHO'IL, *Yoreh De'ah* no. 69.
24. German measles. *See* Gregg, *Congenital Cataract Following German Measles in Mother,* 3 TRANSACTIONS OF THE OPHTHALMOLOGICAL SOC'Y OF AUSTRALIA 35-46 (1941); *see also* Swan, Tostevin, Mayo & Black, *Congenital Defects in Infants Following Infectious Diseases During Pregnancy,* 2 MEDICAL J. OF AUSTRALIA 201 (1943).
25. *See* MISHNAH BERURAH, BI'UR HALAKHAH, ON ORACH CHAYIM 329:4. An idiot can even sue for injuries inflicted on him. TALMUD, *Baba Kamma* 8:4. Again, the killing of even a dying person is culpable as murder. MAIMONIDES, HIL. ROTZE'ACH 2:7.
26. ELEZAR FLECKELES, RESPONSA TESHUVAH ME'AHAVAH, pt. 1, no. 53. *See* ZIMMELS, MAGICIANS, THEOLOGIANS AND DOCTORS 72 (1952).
27. SEPHER CHASIDIM no. 186 (Zitomir ed. 1879).
28. BACHARACH, *supra* note 19. But there is some rabbinical dispute on this opinion. JAKOBOVITS, *supra* note 16, at 279 n.38.
29. *See* text accompanying notes 14-16 *supra*.
30. UNTERMAN, 6 NO'AM (Jerusalem) 1 (1963). Unterman, Chief Rabbi of Israel, refers to medical evidence given him by Professor Asherman, Director of the Maternity Department of the Municipal Hadassah Hospital in Tel Aviv.
31. *Id.*
32. TALMUD, YOMA 84; SHULCHAN ARUKH, *Orach Chayim* 329:2.
33. ZWEIG, 7 NO'AM (Jerusalem) 36 (1964).
34. *Id.*
35. MITZRACHI, RESPONSA P'RI HA'ARETZ, *Yoreh De'ah* no. 21.
36. UNTERMAN, HATORAH VEHAMEDINAH 25, 29 (4th ser. 1952); FRIEDMAN, RESPONSA NETZER MATA'AI pt. 1, no. 8; FEINSTEIN, RESPONSA IGROTH MOSHEH *Orach Chayim* pt. 4, no. 88. These authorities permit the violation of the Sabbath for the sake of psychiatric patients.
37. SEPHER CHASIDIM, *supra* note 27, no. 520.
38. This is the number of defective births resulting from German measles anticipated for 1965 in the United States. To this number may have to be added anticipated abnormalities for other reasons, but from it would have to be subtracted the considerably larger number of cases in which affected mothers would not resort to abortion, either because of their opposition to abortion or because the condition is undetected during pregnancy. The total of abortions fully justified by actual (not suspected) fetal defects due to factors that could be recognized during pregnancy could thus scarcely exceed thirty thousand.
39. TALMUD, *Sanhedrin* 4:5. For this reason, Jewish law forbids the surrender of a single life even if any number of other lives may thereby be saved. MAIMONIDES, HIL. YESODEI HATORAH 5:5.
40. *Leviticus* 20:10-20.

41. *Deuteronomy* 23:3, and Jewish commentaries.
42. Compare the juxtaposition of murder and adultery in the Ten Commandments. *Exodus* 20:13.
43. ARAMA, AKEDATH YITZCHAK ch. 20, at 41(b) (ed. Frankfurt a/o 1785).
44. TALMUD, *Sanhedrin* 78a.
45. Maimonides acquits such a murderer only before "a human court." HIL. ROTZE'ACH 2:7-8.
46. In practice Jewish law virtually abolished capital punishment thousands of years ago, as it insisted on numerous conditions whose fulfillment was almost impossible (such as the presence of, and prior warning by, two eye-witnesses).
47. TALMUD, *Erakhin* 1:4; TALMUD, TOSAPHOTH, *Erakhin* 7a.
48. ETHICS OF THE FATHERS 5:8.
49. SHULCHAN ARUKH, *Orach Chayim* 329:2-4.
50. *See* text accompanying note 1 *supra.*
51. DE SPEC. LEGIBUS 3:108-10, 117-18; DE VIRTUT, 138. But in the latter two passages, Philo himself qualified his statement by calling only a person who killed a child already born "indubitably a murderer."
52. So, e.g., GROSSNAS, London Beth Din Publications, no. 21, Tishri 5732 (1971); HUBNER 28 HADAROM (New York), Tishri 5729 (1968) at 31. For further sources, see 2 ASYA (Jerusalem), Shevat 5731 (1971) at 39.
53. WALDENBERG, RESPONSA TZITZ ELIEZER, pt. 7, no. 41; and pt. 9, no. 51.
54. RABINOWITCH, 28 HADAROM, op. cit. note 52, at 19.
55. 12 INTERCOM (New York), no. 1 (March 1971), at 4.

THE INVIOLABILITY
OF THE RIGHT TO BE BORN

ROBERT F. DRINAN, S. J.

EVERY DISCUSSION OF ABORTION must, in the final analysis, begin and end with a definition of what one thinks of a human embryo or fetus. If one has, by the application of several principles, come to the conviction that a fetus, viable or not, can be extinguished for the benefit of its mother or its own welfare, rational debate on changing or "liberalizing" existing laws forbidding abortion is not really possible or necessary. For if a person argues from the premise that a human fetus may have its existence terminated for any valid reason, then the only point about which to argue is the validity of the reasons asserted to be sufficient to justify the voluntary extinction of a human fetus. These reasons can have only three sources: the welfare of the fetus, the health or happiness of the mother, or the overall future of the family.

It is unfortunate that debates and discussions over the advisability of changing the anti-abortion laws which now exist in every state have not infrequently tended to polarize the disputants into those who desire to make America's abortion laws more "humane" on the one side and Roman Catholics on the other. Such a distortion of the real issues involved in this matter comes about, in part, because Catholic moral theology and philosophy have retained, more than the teaching of most other religious denominations, the traditional, and until recently unchallenged, view that an abortion is the taking of the life of an unborn but nevertheless real human being.

When a Catholic jurist defends the moral viewpoint of his church, he almost inevitably deepens the distortion that anti-abortion laws in America would be easily modified or repealed but for the

123

existing or expected opposition of Catholics, acting individually and collectively. The impression may also be given that the Catholic jurist is seeking simply to translate the views of his religion into the civil law and, as is sometimes alleged, to impose them on others.

The facts and the real issues are a good deal different from the supposed or the asserted posture of the abortion question as it is being debated, on the one hand, by "liberals" who seek a more "humane" law and, on the other hand, by Catholic spokesmen. This is illustrated by a discussion of the following topics: the several issues which are *not* disputed by any of the parties in the discussion about abortion laws; the areas of agreement between all parties regarding the nature of the fetus; and the arguments on why Anglo-American law should continue its basic public policy of discouraging abortion by making it illegal, either by criminal or civil sanctions.

I. The Non-Issues

A. *Peril to the Mother's Life*

Every state in the union permits an abortion by authorized persons when such action is required to save the life of the mother. Although the morality of such laws is open to question, participants in the current controversy over the advisability of easing the nation's laws proscribing abortion cannot cite as relevant the contention that laws in America forbid physicians from performing an abortion when, otherwise, the life of the mother would be endangered. Furthermore, it is well known that by the employment of generally available medical techniques by competent obstetricians, the dilemma of choosing whether to save the life of the mother *or* the life of the child will seldom if ever arise.[1]

B. *Abortion Not a Substitute for Birth Control*

It is further agreed among all persons concerned with a just and fair law regulating abortion that if abortion is to be allowed by society, it is understood to be a remedy which should be available only in unusual cases and not as a substitute for the ordinary methods of birth control. Those who favor a relaxation of the law regarding abortion would, in other words, presumably endorse a program of private and public birth control clinics designed to assist women to take measures which would make an abortion unnecessary.

It should be noted in this connection that the available statistics on the financial and marital status of the women who seek an abortion in the United States are not at all satisfactory. It is simply not reliably known how many or what percentage of those seeking an abortion are unwed, poor, married, or financially secure. Consequently, it is not known to what extent the greater availability of contraceptive information and devices would diminish the need for abortion.

C. *Abortion of a Nonviable Fetus Only*

It is also beyond contention that the advocates of a liberalized abortion law would in general permit an abortion only of a nonviable fetus. This is the position of the Model Penal Code of the American Law Institute (ALI), where it is proposed that the life of a fetus not older than 26 weeks may be terminated if such action can be justified because of the physical or mental health of the mother. This, the most carefully drawn of all the proposals in this area, would, furthermore, justify the abortion of a nonviable embryo because of prenatal injuries to the fetus even if such injuries are not deemed to be detrimental to the mental or physical health of the mother.[2]

Glanville Williams, who is surely one of the most vigorous advocates of the abolition of all legal penalties for abortion, appears to feel that, since virtually no abortions are sought after a fetus is viable, a repeal of the sanctions for abortions of nonviable fetuses would almost solve the entire problem.[3]

D. *Abortion in Rape Cases*

The frequently cited, emotion-laden example of the need for an abortion by a woman who has been raped is also really not relevant to the discussion regarding the liberalization of America's abortion laws. No law in the United States prohibits a doctor from taking appropriate medical measures following a rape to prevent the possibility of a pregnancy. The canon law of the Catholic Church permits such measures on the ground that the rapist is an unjust aggressor and allows that the victim of such aggression may prevent the conception which might result from such conduct. This act of prevention is not abortion but, rather, the elimination of the possibility of conception.[4]

II. AREAS OF AGREEMENT REGARDING ABORTION AND THE NATURE OF THE FETUS

Both in public opinion and in the law of America, there is a profoundly based consensus that an embryo or a fetus has at least *some* rights. Sharp differences arise not over the nature and extent of the rights of the fetus but over the question of whether these rights may be totally subordinated to the rights of the mother whose body contains the fetus.

A. *Right to Inherit*

One right of the fetus that is clearly guaranteed by the law is its right to inherit *en ventre sa mere*.[5] The exercise of this right obviously depends on the live birth of the fetus; therefore, it is uncertain how much about the law's attitude toward the inviolability of the right of the fetus to survive is actually proven by the recognition, by Anglo-American law, of the right to inherit *en ventre sa mere*.

B. *Right to Compensation for Prenatal Injuries*

The fact that ever more frequently both statutory and decisional law recognize prenatal injuries[6] as the basis for compensation also has dubious probative value regarding the underlying convictions of the law with respect to the right of the fetus to survive. The development of the right of an infant to compensation for prenatal injuries does, however, at least prove that the law assumes that this right becomes inchoate or vested in a fetus even if the fetus had hardly been conceived when the injury occurred; every fetus is, therefore, *sui juris* or capable of possessing rights.

C. *Right to Be Born*

Even among the most vigorous proponents of the repeal of laws forbidding abortion, there appears to be consensus that a fetus has a right to be born[7] unless its extinction can be justified by at least one of the following reasons: its birth would be detrimental to itself, to its mother, or to the family into which it would be born. The fetus, in other words, cannot arbitrarily or capriciously be deprived of its right to be born.

D.   Right to Self-Abort

Another area of agreement in the controversy over the fairness of America's abortion laws seems to exist by virtue of the fact that the advocates of the repeal of these laws apparently would not subscribe to an arrangement by which the woman desiring an abortion could unilaterally and without the advice and consent of any other person terminate her pregnancy.   The American Law Institute's proposal, for example, requires the consent of two physicians.   Similarly, some proponents of liberalized abortion laws recommend the arrangement operating in Sweden by which a medical-lay commission makes the decision concerning the advisability of an abortion. This same feature appeared in a 1965 proposal made to the House of Delegates of the American Medical Association;[8] under a plan urged upon the governing board of the AMA, a physician would be permitted to terminate a pregnancy only if two licensed physicians, neither of whom would be performing the operation, have certified in writing the circumstances that justified the abortion.[9]

There has been little if any speculation by the proponents of liberalized abortion laws on the question of what the law should be when medical science discovers a drug which may be safely and effectively self-administered by a woman desiring to procure an abortion.   All discussion on the advisability of more liberal abortion laws has, up to the present, assumed that a woman is not able, or should not be permitted, to be the exclusive decision maker in the process of securing an abortion; an outside agency has been recommended, presumably because the state owes some duty to the unborn fetus, or at least some duty to protect a pregnant woman against the consequences of her own unilateral decision — a judgment which may be made in excessive haste or fear.   If any of the advocates of eased abortion laws would categorically recommend the free availability of abortifacient drugs (when they have become safe for self-administration), the underlying position of these proponents of easier abortion laws will become much clearer. If they see no problem in permitting a pregnant woman to abort herself without the advice or consent of any other human being, then the fetus is, in this view, simply a quantum of protoplasm with no rights or interests, which the mother may destroy for any reason deemed valid by herself alone. Without such a position, however, those who would defend existing legal penalties against abortion must argue against adversaries who presumably think that an unborn fetus has *some* rights which the state should protect and preserve. Furthermore, the absence of individuals or legal groups that would advocate that a pregnant woman has the complete and exclusive right to determine whether to have an abortion indicates that those who are dissatisfied with existing legislation forbidding abortion in certain circumstances have not really thought through the central problem — the nature of the nonviable fetus.

E. *Additional Points of Agreement*

Other areas of agreement, or partial agreement, exist between those with opposing positions with regard to legislation regulating the availability of abortion. Unfortunately, these areas have not emerged in public discussions of this question. The polarization of the contending parties on the basic moral issue probably has been the major reason why little if any consensus has developed on certain legal-moral aspects of the abortion question. One of those aspects, for example, is the question of whether a married woman should have the right to secure an abortion of a nonviable fetus without the advice and consent of her husband. One could devise persuasive arguments on either side of this issue. It must be admitted, however, that if the law is to continue to promote family solidarity, it is questionable whether the law should permit a wife to dispose of an unborn child of a marriage without the knowledge, advice, or consent of her husband — the father of the child unwanted by its mother.

III. WHY THE LAW SHOULD HAVE SANCTIONS AGAINST THE ABORTION OF A NONVIABLE FETUS

When one has conceded the principle that the life and rights of a nonviable fetus may be subordinated to the desires or rights of its mother or parents, one must then justify this hierarchy of rights by recourse to one or more of three reasons: the welfare of the fetus; the health or happiness of the mother; or the overall future of the family into which the unwanted child would be born. It may be helpful to analyze each of these reasons in the light of the justification for abortion drawn from it.

A. *Future Welfare of the Fetus*

One of the reasons regularly advanced to justify abortion is the damage or disability suffered by a fetus because of the sickness of the mother or because of some prenatal disease contracted by the fetus itself. The assumption here, of course, is that it is better to terminate the life of a future person if it is certain (or highly probable?) that he will be seriously deformed, physically or mentally. The proponents of this position do not seem to limit their advocacy of this measure to only those infants who would be forever pitiable, "subhuman" creatures incapable in any way of developing into a fully human person. The thrust of the argument of those who recommend the elimination of defective embryos reaches all future children whose development may have been harmed by the mother taking a drug like thalidomide, contracting German measles, or suffering any other of the known medical conditions which can adversely affect a fetus.[10]

No one can deny the laudable humanitarian intentions of those who seek, by the elimination of anti-abortion legislation, to prevent the birth of those persons who, because of serious prenatal injuries, cannot enjoy a normal life. At the same time, however, to concede that the life of the fetus, disabled through no fault of its own or of its mother, may be extinguished because it might not attain complete physical or intellectual development is to concede either that the nonviable fetus is really *not* the repository of any inviolable rights or that the strong and dominant members of society may extinguish or terminate the life of those individuals whose physical or mental development may, in the judgment of society, be so substantially arrested that they cannot attain a life worth living.

Clearly no advocate of easier abortion laws will concede the second of these alternatives. He will resist and reject any imputation that by permitting abortion he is by implication permitting infanticide, euthanasia, "mercy killing" or anything else in the "parade of the horribles" not unknown in the rhetoric of the defenders of existing laws forbidding abortion. But can one logically and realistically claim that a defective nonviable fetus may be destroyed without also conceding the validity of the principle that, at least in some extreme cases, the taking of a life by society may be justified by the convenience or greater overall happiness of the society which takes the life of an innocent but unwanted and troublesome person?

I submit that it is illogical and intellectually dishonest for anyone to advocate as morally permissible the destruction of a defective, nonviable fetus but to deny that this concession is not a fundamental compromise with what is surely one of the moral-legal absolutes of Anglo-American law — the principle that the life of an innocent human being may not be taken away simply because, in the judgment of society, nonlife for this particular individual would be better than life.

It is intellectually dishonest to maintain that a defective, nonviable fetus may be destroyed unless one is also prepared to admit that society has the right to decide that for certain individuals, who have contracted physical and/or mental disabilities, nonexistence is better than existence. The advocate of abortion who bases his position on the ground that this is best for the fetus would no doubt shrink from this extension of the principle by which he justifies abortion; he would retreat to the familiar ground that the nonviable fetus is not even *medically* a person and, hence, does not possess the same right to survive enjoyed by a human being who has lived outside the body of its mother. But does this distinction really make a difference? Is there any real moral or ethical difference between prenatal and postnatal life? And is it not possible that medical discoveries will show more and more that fetal life is different from postnatal life only in degree and not in kind? Furthermore, if medical science makes it possible for a fetus to be viable at a time much earlier than the present moment of viability, will the advocates of the abortion of the defective fetus eliminate the distinction that only the nonviable fetus may be aborted?

Abortion performed for the asserted future welfare and happiness of a defective fetus cannot be justified morally or ethically except by the use of a principle which, however attenuated, leads logically to the validation of the termination by society of the life of an innocent but unwanted person. If one does not shrink from that consequence, the discussion has to be extended to a much broader base. But, I submit, it is intellectual dishonesty for anyone to advocate the destruction of a defective nonviable fetus without being prepared to accept the far-reaching consequences of the principle which justifies the termination of prenatal life.

B. *Health or Happiness of the Mother*

1. *A Mother's Health* — As previously noted, all states permit a therapeutic abortion in order to save the life of the mother. Although there is no meaningful decisional law on this matter, it is clear that this policy allows a physician to make the indisputably moral judgment that the life of the mother is to be preferred over the life of her unborn child. It could be argued that, since the law permits physicians to act upon their own moral judgments when a mother's life is at stake, the law should logically permit physicians to make similar moral judgments when the mother's future health, rather than her survival, is in question. If this line of reasoning is correct, it may be that those who oppose the legalization of abortion must urge that the right of physicians to perform an abortion to save the life of a mother be either abrogated or logically extended to a granting of permission to perform an abortion in order to save the health of the mother. On the assumption which permeates the case of those seeking the legalization of abortion — that society should concentrate on the quality rather than the quantity, of life it preserves — there would seem to be no reason why a doctor should *not* be allowed to preserve the health of the mother by performing an abortion.

The medical hypothesis running through this line of argumentation is, of course, open to question. Assuming reasonably modern medical techniques, in how many instances is it likely that the birth of a child will permanently impair the *physical* health of a mother?

Some cases, of course, do exist where the continuation of a pregnancy may bring about a substantial risk, not to the mother's life, but to her future physical health. If there is an inherent right in basic justice for a mother in this situation to request an abortion — and this case is probably the most appealing and compelling reason for a justifiable abortion — how should the law regulate the exercise of this right? The various proposals for changes in America's law regulating abortions silently suggest that the mother's right not to have her health impaired is paramount in this instance and that the state has no duty to speak for, or to protect, the fetus. However appealing such a solution may appear, its implications and consequences need examination.

Every married couple possesses a moral and a legal right to privacy from any undue interference from the state. This right, emphasized by the United States Supreme Court in *Griswold v. Connecticut*,[11] involving the Connecticut birth control statute, should be as broad and as inclusive as is consistent with the good of society. The right to have, or not to have, children and to determine the number of such children are matters in which the state, by general agreement, should not interfere. The welfare of children born to any marriage, however, is, by equally general agreement, a matter of grave concern for the state. Recent controversies over the advisability of statutes designed to curb the physical abuse or the battering of children by mentally upset or emotionally disturbed parents indicate that society feels a deep responsibility to protect children even at the expense of restricting the right to privacy enjoyed by married couples.

For at least a century and a half, this same concern of society and the law for children too young to speak for themselves has been extended to the unborn child by Anglo-American law. The law has taken the position that a married couple may refrain from having children or may restrict the number of their children[12] but that a child, once conceived, has rights which its parents may not extinguish, even if the parents seek only to prevent a permanent impairment of the physical health of the mother.

Once again, the advocates of the right of a mother to an abortion, when confronted with the interest of the state in the child, born or unborn, will take refuge in the medically questionable and logically indefensible position that the unborn child is so different from a child after birth that the state has no right to interfere with a mother's desire to extinguish the life of her unborn child. It appears, however, that if Anglo-American law is to retreat from its present position of extending some, though not total, protection to the fetus, it must logically say that the right to marital privacy precludes state interference with an abortion or that the nonviable fetus is not yet sufficiently a human being to merit the protection of the law.

The advocates of the abolition of anti-abortion laws will no doubt urge, as one of the principal arguments, the right to marital privacy as that right is explained in the *Griswold* decision. I submit, however, that even the broadest dicta in *Griswold*, and even the most sweeping language in other judicial decisions on the right to marital privacy, do not justify the exclusion of the interest of the state *after* a child has been conceived but not yet delivered. It may be, of course, that courts in the future will extend the right of marital privacy to exclude state interference with an abortion decided upon by a couple. But such a decision would be entirely different from existing decisional law and would, at least logically, have to reject the underlying assumption of present laws forbidding abortion, which is, of course, that a nonviable fetus has an inherent and inviolable right to be born even if it is physically or mentally defective and even if its birth results in the impairment of the physical health of its mother.

2. *A Mother's Mental Health or Happiness* — The various proposals designed to liberalize America's abortion laws, including that of the American Law Institute (ALI), do not attempt to restrict the right to have an abortion to women who might otherwise have an impairment of their *physical* health. Those who would ease existing abortion laws recognize the fact that physical and mental health are so interdependent that it would be unrealistic to state that an abortion is allowable only for threatened damage to *either* the physical *or* mental health of the mother.

When the meaning and scope of mental health are evaluated, however, many problems arise. The legislative history of the section on abortion of the Model Penal Code of the ALI[13] suggests that the term "mental health" is not meant to be used in the proposed law in a narrow or technical sense but, rather, in a comprehensive way which would permit two physicians to authorize an abortion if in their judgment an operation of this nature would be best for the long-range happiness of the mother. Hence, the term "mental health" is not intended to be restricted to cases where there is a diagnosis that severe mental depression or some similar psychiatric phenomenon will follow childbirth.

Therefore, in view of the broad authorization which would result if the mental health of the mother became a norm for judging the advisability of abortions, it may be that the married and unmarried mother should be treated differently.

3. *Mental Health of Unwed Mothers* — There is not much scientifically compiled information available on the number and nature of unwed mothers in America. Even less is known about those unwed mothers who terminate their pregnancy by an abortion.[14] As a result, any writer moves into a sea of ambiguities when he attempts to analyze the factors involved in reaching a prudential judgment on the question of whether more relaxed abortion laws would promote the mental health of unwed mothers. Among the many factors which should be weighed in coming to a decision regarding the basic legal-moral policy which America should adopt with respect to the availability of abortion for unwed mothers are the following.

(a) *Promiscuity among single persons.* To what extent would more relaxed abortion laws promote promiscuity among single persons?

(b) *Adoption of children of unwed mothers.* Should law and society give greater consideration to childless couples (one out of ten) who seek an adoptable child? If so, should the nation's public policy tend to encourage unwed mothers *not* to destroy their unborn child but to arrange that the child be born and placed for adoption?

(c) *Guilt feelings of the unwed mother.* Who is to assess the nature and the consequences of the guilt which, according to reliable and virtually universal reports, comes to an unwed mother who resolves her problem by abortion? If accurate psychiatric testimony showed that the vast majority of unwed mothers who abort their child experience guilt that may have adverse consequences in their lives and their future marriages, would society be morally obliged to counsel unwed mothers about the likelihood of guilt before an easy method of abortion were made available to them? If, in other words, the mental health of the mother is to be the norm by which the advisability of an abortion is to be judged, then the assessment of the unwed mother's prospective mental health following an abortion must include the most careful and comprehensive evaluation of the impact which a feeling of guilt may have on her life.

(d) *"Happiness" of the unwed mother.* Since the term "mental health" in the Model Penal Code[15] actually translates into "happiness," how and by whom is this broad norm to be interpreted and applied, not merely to the present predicament of the unwed mother but, more importantly, to her entire future life?

Some may object to the relevance of some or all of these factors and urge that the desire of the unwed mother for an abortion should be controlling. As much as one must be sympathetic to this apparently simple solution to a most difficult problem, it should never be forgotten that in modern society the unwed mother is in a position of shame, humiliation, and anguish which is possibly worse than any other human predicament. One may feel that society's attitude of disdain towards the unwed mother is one of hypocrisy, but the fact remains that the pressures and problems confronted by an unwed mother are such that it is not likely that she will be in a position to make rational decisions substantially uninfluenced by fear or panic. Society, therefore, has a very special and unique duty to furnish the most careful counselling to unwed mothers before it allows them to employ a legally approved method of abortion.

The various proposals to modify or repeal anti-abortion laws in America do not distinguish between married and unmarried mothers with respect to the reasons and the procedures by which an abortion would be sanctioned. In view of the very different problems faced by unwed mothers, I submit that any new law regulating abortion should take these factors into consideration.

IV. THE WELFARE OF FAMILIES AND ABORTION

One of the recurring ideas in the literature recommending a liberalization of abortion laws is the concept that the coming of an unwanted child into a family may tend to disrupt the relationship of the husband and wife and destroy the unity and solidarity of the family. A persuasive article by an anonymous mother who secured the abortion of an unwanted child, published in the *Atlantic Monthly*, sets forth in a dramatic manner the argument that parents have a right and duty to plan their families, even to the extent of terminating an unplanned pregnancy.[16]

There is a growing consensus in America that couples should be assisted by private and public agencies in the planning of their families. Differences over the morality of various methods of birth control center on means rather than ends.

There is a serious question, however, whether there is a consensus which would support a public policy permitting a married mother to secure an abortion for an unplanned and unwanted pregnancy. Even to discuss such a question requires that one delve into the question of the origins or sources of public policy in America. Who or what groups, and for what reasons, should supply the guidelines for the shaping of the fundamental legal-moral policies underlying American law?

V. CONCLUSION

I submit that no logically defensible or rational change of a substantial nature can take place in America's abortion laws unless the proponents of less strict sanctions against abortion confront and resolve the issue underlying all the other issues: what or whose moral values should the law endorse and enforce?

America's laws against abortion derive in large part from the concept of the sacredness and the inviolability of every human being. This concept of the nonviolability of the human person clearly has many of its most profound roots in the Judeo-Christian religious tradition. That tradition, in fact, is probably the principal source of Anglo-American criminal law. Not all of the elements of that religious tradition are, of course, incorporated or embodied in the criminal laws of England and America; but the essence or the most fundamental principles of that tradition *are* an inherent part of Anglo-American criminal law. And any change of a substantial kind in America's abortion laws would be a notable departure from that body of Anglo-American law which regulates conduct deemed to constitute a crime against society.

No one can reasonably insist that *all* of the actions now penalized by law should remain as they are. On the other hand, no one, presumably, wishes to scuttle the entire fabric of Anglo-American criminal law. But, I submit, no one can take a position (allegedly between these two extremes) which advocates abortion without inevitably sanctioning a basic compromise of principle — a compromise which could undermine the very foundations of Anglo-American criminal jurisprudence.

The integrity, the untouchableness, the inviolability of every human life by any other human being has been the cardinal principle and the centerpiece of the legal institutions of the English-speaking world and, to a large extent, of every system of law devised by man. However convenient, convincing, or compelling the arguments in favor of abortion may be, the fact remains that the taking of a life, even though it is unborn, cuts out the very heart of the principle that *no one's* life, however unwanted and useless it may be, may be terminated in order to promote the health or happiness of another human being. If the advocates of legalized abortion desire to have an intellectually honest debate about the fundamental change they seek in the moral and legal standards of American life, they should not fall back on the error of fact that a fetus is not a human being. They should, rather, face the fact that they are stating that the rights of one or more human beings to health or happiness may in some circumstances become so important that they take precedence over the very right to exist of another human being.

The inescapable moral issues in the emerging struggle over the wisdom and fairness of America's abortion laws deserve to be discussed and dissected and eventually resolved. It will be a tragedy beyond description for America if the question of legislation on abortion is resolved on sentiment, utilitarianism, or expediency rather than on the basic ethical issue involved — the immorality of the destruction of any innocent human being carried out by other human beings for their own benefit.

NOTES

1. *See, e.g.,* Heffernan & Lynch, *What Is the Status of Therapeutic Abortion in Modified Obstetrics?,* 66 AM. J. OBSTETRICS & GYNECOLOGY 335-45 (1953).

2. For a discussion of some of the implications of the ALI proposals see Quay, *Justifiable Abortion — Medical and Legal Foundations,* 49 GEO. L.J. 173-256, 395-538 (1961).

3. WILLIAMS, THE SANCTITY OF LIFE AND THE CRIMINAL LAW 146-247, at 157-59 (1957).

4. Most manuals on Catholic moral theology touch on this subject. *See, e.g.,* MCHUGH, CALLAN & WAGNER, MORAL THEOLOGY (1930).

5. *See* ATKINSON, WILLS 75 (2d ed. 1953).
6. *See* PROSSER, LAW OF TORTS 354-57 (3d ed. 1964).
7. *See* Leavy and Kummer, *Criminal Abortion: Human Hardship and Unyielding Laws*, 35 SO. CAL. L. REV. 136-38 (1962).
8. Committee on Human Reproduction, American Medical Ass'n, A.P. Dispatch, N.Y. Times, Dec. 1, 1965, p. 1, col. 2.
9. See N. Y. Times, Nov. 29, 1965, p. 44, col. 6. See also N. Y. Times, Dec. 2, 1965, p. 24, col. 4, for an account of the vote by the AMA to defer action on a report of its Committee on Human Reproduction.
10. *See* ST. JOHN-STEVAS, THE RIGHT TO LIFE (1964).
11. 381 U.S. 479 (1965).
12. Only Massachusetts bans the use of contraceptives. See MASS. GEN. LAWS ANN. ch. 272, §§ 20, 21 (1956).
13. MODEL PENAL CODE § 230.3 (Proposed Official Draft 1962).
14. *See* GEBHARD, POMEROY, MARTIN & CHRISTENSON, PREGNANCY, BIRTH AND ABORTION (1958).
15. *See* text accompanying note 13 *supra.*
16. Atlantic Monthly, Aug. 1965, pp. 66-68.

ABORTION ON REQUEST: THE PSYCHIATRIC IMPLICATIONS

RICHARD A. SCHWARTZ, M. D.

I. INTRODUCTION

ALTHOUGH THE PRACTICE of abortion has been illegal in most states until recently, it has been an "open secret" that a woman can obtain a safe abortion in a licensed hospital if she can find a psychiatrist who will say she might commit suicide if her pregnancy is not terminated. Consequently, most practicing psychiatrists have often been consulted by pregnant women seeking abortions, which has provided the psychiatric profession with a unique opportunity to become familiar with the kinds of problems that lead women to the decision to abort and to observe women's emotional reactions before and after abortions. To the psychiatrist, then, abortion is not merely an abstract moral and legal question, but an intensely emotional experience concerning individual women and their families. Because of this direct personal experience, it is not surprising that psychiatrists — both individually through speeches and writings[1] and collectively through their professional organizations[2] — have been active participants in the public debate on abortion that has raged throughout the country for the past decade.

Generally, psychiatrists have occupied a liberal position in the debate, favoring repeal of the traditional, restrictive abortion laws. And this position is not limited to the leaders or a few vocal members, for the rank and file of the profession have tended to the liberal position as well.[3] There are a number of reasons why psychiatric opinion has been so heavily in favor of legalization of abortion. For one, it is a very convincing educational experience to talk with women who have become pregnant accidentally, who do not want a

139

child, and who are determined to have an abortion by one means or another. After several such interviews, one is hard pressed to maintain the view that the abortion decision should be made by anybody other than the pregnant woman. The decision is certainly much too personal and private to be decided by the state. Undoubtedly, another important factor is that only a minority of psychiatrists are members of those religions which voice most of the opposition to legalized abortion because of their belief that abortion is the taking of human life.[4]

In addition to these two general reasons for favoring legalization of abortion, there are four additional considerations of a more specifically psychiatric nature that have contributed to proabortion attitudes among psychiatrists. First, the existing practice of permitting so-called therapeutic abortions on psychiatric grounds for a small group of middle-class women is considered hypocritical and unjust. Secondly, follow-up studies have shown abortions to have few harmful psychiatric aftereffects. Thirdly, a social policy forbidding abortion and, in effect, forcing women to bear unwanted children is harmful to the mental health of many women, as well as the members of their families. And finally, unwanted children (the number of which could be minimized by liberalizing abortion laws) are likely to receive inadequate care during their early, formative years and, as a result, often become vulnerable to psychiatric disorders. This article will closely examine each of these four reasons while presenting its thesis that abortion laws should be liberalized.

II.   THERAPEUTIC ABORTIONS ON PSYCHIATRIC GROUNDS

Until 1967, when Colorado became the first of 16 states and the District of Columbia[5] to liberalize its abortion laws, virtually all states had laws which forbade abortion unless "necessary to preserve the woman's life."[6] As was commonly known, however, these restrictive laws did not deter large numbers of women from obtaining illegal abortions. Indeed, women have always obtained abortions and presumably always will, regardless of prohibitive laws. In addition to these illegal abortions, many upper middle-class women have been able to obtain so-called therapeutic abortions from their private gynecologists under ideal conditions and in some of the best hospitals in the United States. During the years 1963 through 1965, for example, there were an estimated 8000 therapeutic abortions performed each year, or 2 abortions per 1000 births.[7]

⟶ Since medical advances have made it possible for women with almost any kind of physical illness to survive pregnancy and child-birth, the only way that abortions can be legally justified as "necessary to preserve life" is on psychiatric grounds — i.e., if the patient is judged to be in danger of committing suicide. The practice of therapeutic, or more precisely psychiatric, abortions has always been controversial. First of all, it is impossible on any medical or scientific grounds to establish agreed-upon indications for psychiatric abortions. A woman who wants an abortion, and who knows that the only way she can obtain one is to persuade a psychiatrist that she will commit suicide, has a strong incentive to convince herself that she is deeply depressed, or at least to act depressed. In such situations, psychiatrists have no reliable way of judging the precise degree of suicidal risk.

Even if they could determine with exactitude the likelihood of suicide, psychiatrists would still be unable to decide whether a given woman "deserved" an abortion because of the vagueness of the requirement, "necessary to preserve the woman's life." There are no guidelines indicating whether the risk of suicide has to be 100, 50, or 1 percent in order for an abortion to be justified under the law. Nor is it clear whether the woman has to have a past history of suicidal tendencies or mental illness in order that the abortion be considered life-saving, or whether the woman has to be perfectly well adjusted and symptom-free prior to the onset of pregnancy. The laws offer no clarification of these points, which is one of the reasons why some courts have declared them to be unconstitutionally vague.[8]

In the absence of definite criteria for determining whether a given pregnancy is a threat to a woman's life, psychiatrists are obliged to fall back on purely subjective factors in making their decision. In deciding whether or not to approve a given abortion, psychiatrists have little more to guide them than their own personal opinions about whether abortions are good or bad for women, or for society as a whole. In practice, psychiatrists handle this predicament in one of four general ways.

One group refuses to have anything to do with abortion evaluations as a matter of principle. These psychiatrists feel that psychiatric abortions are hypocritical, that society should not pass laws forbidding abortion and then allow circumvention of the laws because a woman is emotionally upset and threatening suicide. Society, they believe, should decide whether or not to permit abortions, rather than evade this decision by delegating it to the psychiatrist, who is without special competence to determine the question.

This same group of psychiatrists also objects to the gross unfairness that results from the practice of psychiatric abortions, which favor the histrionic, the emotionally unstable, and the deceitful woman, permitting her to abort while denying abortion to women who are truthful and emotionally stable. Psychiatric abortions also favor the rich, who can afford private psychiatric fees, over the poor, who cannot. Although poor people have access to psychiatrists in public clinics, these clinics are dependent on public funds appropriated by elected officials and are usually unwilling to risk the disapproval of those officials by sanctioning abortions for their patients. In reality, whether a woman will be granted an abortion depends far less on the state of her health than upon the state of her pocketbook.

Many in this first group of psychiatrists further argue that those psychiatrists who participate in psychiatric abortions have a harmful social impact over the long term because they abate pressures that might lead to liberalization of the abortion laws. By enabling the most influential segment of the population to arrange for psychiatric abortions, psychiatrists remove whatever incentive this group might have to support reform of the laws. These psychiatrists are also concerned that the image of the psychiatric profession is tarnished by providing psychiatric "excuses" for rich women to evade the law.[9]

A second group of psychiatrists also refuses to participate in psychiatric abortions, but on moral or religious grounds. This group believes that abortion is morally wrong, or even murder, and argues that no psychiatric illness, however serious, can justify an abortion. In cases of women genuinely threatening suicide, these psychiatrists propose commitment to a psychiatric hospital, administration of antidepressant drugs, or electroshock treatment.[10]

A third group of psychiatrists, while agreeing that psychiatric abortions are hypocritical and unfair, believes that it would be unethical to refuse to consult with women who are emotionally upset and who request help. Although they may be reluctant or unenthusiastic, these psychiatrists will agree to consult with abortion-seeking women and will conscientiously try to determine if the degree of suicidal risk is substantial. If so, they will authorize the abortion.

The fourth group of psychiatrists strongly feels that most women who want abortions will benefit from them and should be permitted to obtain them. Moreover, they interpret their highest obligation as physicians, above all other considerations, to be the protection of their patients' health and well-being. In order to help women obtain abortions, this group is willing to authorize abortions in cases where they believe the risk of suicide is minimal or nonexistent because they consider that the slight deceit that is necessary is preferable to driving a desperate woman into the hands of a criminal abortionist or forcing her to bear an unwanted child. These psychiatrists, although acknowledging that their policies might help perpetuate unjust laws, believe it is even more beneficial to encourage the widespread practice of therapeutic abortions in order to help educate the public to the idea that abortions should be regarded as an accepted part of medical practice.

Thus, whether a patient is provided with an opportunity for a therapeutic abortion depends not only upon her pocketbook and whether she is living in an area where private psychiatrists are available, but also upon the philosophical point of view of the psychiatrist whom she happens to consult. If she sees one from the first or second group, she will be refused permission for a legal abortion. If she consults one from the third group, she has a fair chance of obtaining the requisite approval, and if she is lucky enough to happen upon one from the fourth group, she is virtually assured a safe hospital abortion.[11]

This situation pertains to those 26 states where abortion is prohibited "unless necessary to preserve the life of the woman."[12] Since 1967, the Model Penal Code[13] of the American Law Institute (ALI) has been adopted by 13 states[14] which now permit abortion to protect the woman's physical and mental health as well as her life. Most of these "reforms" have in many ways perpetuated the difficulties that existed previously. Because there are few medical illnesses that are genuinely made worse by pregnancy, most abortions are still granted on mental health grounds under the new laws. Also, a psychiatric abortion under new laws is a matter of whether the pregnancy will impair the woman's mental health, rather than of determining suicidal risk, and the standards for judging this question are even more nebulous than with respect to the older suicide standard. And, finally, all the inequities that existed under the previous laws have been perpetuated. The woman who cannot afford a private psychiatrist will still have difficulty in obtaining a therapeutic abortion via the public psychiatric clinics, and even the woman who can afford a private psychiatrist must still face the problem of finding one with the "right" philosophical persuasion.

Since 1970, when the New York law was amended[15] to permit abortion upon request, many of these problems have been solved at least in that state. New York State now allows a woman to obtain a safe, legal abortion for approximately 100 to 200 dollars. She no longer has to go through the humiliating charade of trying to convince psychiatrists that she is mentally ill or suicidal. And the psychiatrists in New York are no longer faced with the painful dilemma of deciding whether to allow themselves to be "used" by society to make decisions which properly should remain in the hands of the woman, her husband, and their physician. With the incidence of mental illness, alcoholism, and drug abuse on the rise, most psychiatrists believe that their time would be better spent caring for patients suffering with these more serious problems than by participating in the hypocritical, legally questionable, and ethically doubtful practice of certifying women for so-called therapeutic abortions.

III. ARE ABORTIONS EMOTIONALLY HARMFUL?

A question that is frequently raised by women contemplating abortion is, "How will this experience affect me emotionally?" It is a widespread belief in our culture that women suffer guilt reactions or depression following abortion, either immediately after the procedure or at a later point in life (particularly menopause). Dr. Galdston, among others, contends that:

> [I]f and when a so-called adult woman, a responsible female, seeks an abortion, unless the warrant for it is overwhelming — as say in the case of rape or incest — we are in effect confronted with a sick person and sick situation. Furthermore, and I want strongly to underscore this point, neither the given person nor the given situation is likely to be remedied by the abortion, *qua abortion*. It is of course true that both the person and the situation may be relieved and somewhat ameliorated by the abortion . . . but I would like to go on record that in numerous instances both the individual and the situation are actually aggravated rather than remedied by the abortion. Bad as the situation was initially it not infrequently becomes worse after the abortion has taken place. . . . Drawing upon my experience I would summate the major psychological effects in three terms: frustration, hostility, and guilt.[16]

Until recent years, psychiatric knowledge concerning the woman's psychological reaction was limited to clinical impressions derived from experience with patients seen in psychiatric practice. In the past 15 years, however, numerous systematic follow-up studies have been carried out in Europe and the United States. By and large, these studies strongly suggest that, contrary to folklore, serious psychiatric sequelae to abortion are relatively rare. Most women tolerate the procedure quite well from the emotional standpoint.

The table below summarizes the findings of 17 follow-up studies reported in the journals. At the outset, it should be noted that there are great differences in methodology and terminology among this group of studies. In the European studies, for example, it is often hard for the American psychiatrist to tell exactly what factors are being measured and by what criteria. Consequently, it is difficult to compare these studies with one another. But, despite these problems, the following conclusions can be made: First, psychiatric problems attributable to abortions were found to be rare, occurring in no more than 1 to 2 percent of the cases in 15 of the 17 studies.[17] Second, transient self-limited guilt or depression (the so-called "post-abortion hangover") lasting a few days or weeks may occur rather frequently.[18] Third, serious psychiatric reactions occur for the most part in two groups of patients: those who are pressured into abortion against their own judgment or against their religious or moral beliefs[19] and those who were mentally disturbed prior to

PSYCHOLOGICAL CONSEQUENCES OF ABORTION

AUTHOR(S)	COUNTRY	PERIOD WITHIN WHICH THE ABORTION TOOK PLACE	NUMBER OF WOMEN	PERCENTAGE OF WOMEN WITH PRE-EXISTING PSYCHIATRIC PROBLEMS	LENGTH OF FOLLOWUP	RESULTS
Ekbald[23]	Sweden	1949-50	479	58	22-50 months	65% — satisfied. 10% — abortion unpleasant, but no self-reproach. 14% — mild self-reproach. 11% — severe self-reproach (1% had impaired capacity to work).
Simon et al.[24]	United States	1955-64	46	65	2 months-10 years	44 women suffered no ill effects that could be directly traced to the abortion. 2 women suffered psychiatric illness subsequent to the abortion.
Peck & Marcus[25]	United States	Sept. 1962-Nov. 1964	50	76	3-6 months	79% — no adverse effects after abortion. 19% — mild, self-limited guilt or depressive reaction. 1 patient, a devoutly religious woman pressured into abortion by husband, had acute upset; but was relieved of symptoms after 3 psychiatric interviews.
Patt et al.[26]	United States	Feb. 1964-Feb. 1968	35	100	3 months-4 years	75% — improved. 11% — unchanged. 14% — worse (2 women related worse condition to abortion; the other 3 did not).

Levene & Rigney[27]	United States	1968-70	70	71	3-5 months	86% — no harmful effects. 14% — reported increased depression, but none attributed this to the abortion.
Jansson[28]	Sweden	1952-56	1773	unknown	4 years	1.9% — developed psychiatric illness requiring hospitalization. In half of these, the hospitalization was unrelated to the abortion.
Clark[29]	Great Britain	1961-64	120	unknown	unknown	90% — satisfied with outcome of abortion. 2½% — acquiescent. 2½% — dissatisfied. 5% — unknown.
Mehlan[30]	Germany	1949-50	243	unknown	unknown	90% — thought abortion was best solution. 10% — regretted decision to have abortion.

PSYCHOLOGICAL CONSEQUENCES OF ABORTION (cont.)

AUTHOR(S)	COUNTRY	PERIOD WITHIN WHICH THE ABORTION TOOK PLACE	NUMBER OF WOMEN	PERCENTAGE OF WOMEN WITH PRE-EXISTING PSYCHIATRIC PROBLEMS	LENGTH OF FOLLOWUP	RESULTS
Kolstad[31]	Norway	1940-53	135	unknown	3-16 years	82% — glad without reservation. 10% — satisfied but doubtful. 4% — not happy but knew abortion necessary. 4% — repentent.
Brekke[32]	Norway	1951-53	34	unknown	unknown	Only 2 women had even a slight transient reaction to abortion.
Ford et al.[33]	United States	1968-70	21	47	6 months	9 patients showed marked improvement in emotional status. 4 showed moderate improvement. 5 showed no change. 3 worse, but felt condition to be unrelated to abortion (all 3 had severe psychiatric problems predating the abortion).
Barnes et al.[34]	United States	Jan. 1968-June 1970	114	43	1 month-2½ years	In 2 cases, there was worsening of the psychiatric condition after abortion, but it was unclear whether this was related to the abortion.
Kretzschmar & Norris[35]	United States	1960-65	26	unknown	1-5 years	No psychiatric problems resulted from the abortions.
Gillis[36]	Great Britain	April 1968-Dec. 1968	31	unknown	1 year	No significant psychiatric problems.

Osofsky & Osofsky[37]	United States	1971	250	unknown	shortly after abortion	45% — very happy. 20% — moderately happy. 21% — neutral. 10% — moderately unhappy. 4% — very unhappy.
Malmfors[38]	Sweden	1948-50	84	12	approx. 2 years	46% — happy and satisfied with abortion. 12% — impaired mental health after abortion (since all had neurotic symptoms prior to abortion, not clear if impairment resulted from abortion).
Aren[39]	Sweden	1950-54	248	unknown	unknown	20% — dissatisfied with the abortion and said they would not go through with the experience again. 10% — severe guilt and associated psychiatric symptoms but not clear if these are related to the abortion.

the abortion.[20]   In this latter group, it is difficult to tell whether the psychiatric symptoms following the abortion were, in fact, the result of the abortion.[21]   Fourth, only two studies, both of which are relatively old, found a high incidence of serious psychiatric problems following abortion.   Both of these studies were performed in Sweden and found significant reactions in 10 to 12 percent of the cases.[22]

Admittedly, all of these studies together do not definitively settle the question of the psychiatric sequelae of abortion.   For one thing, most of them have a relatively short period of follow-up (in no instance did it exceed 10 years).   Therefore, the possibility that the women may develop depression later in life — at the time of menopause, for example — cannot be ruled out.

Another problem is that of experimenter bias.   Most people have strong views on abortion, and scientists are no exception.   There is no way to ensure that the investigators were completely objective in these studies and did not unconsciously overlook evidence of more serious postabortion problems than they reported.   Nor is there any way to eradicate bias that may have influenced their judgments as to whether symptoms were the result of the abortion or due to pre-existing psychiatric illness.   Until there are more studies in which systematic efforts are made to exclude experimental bias, these problems will remain.

Determining the presence or severity of psychiatric symptoms is highly subjective, and evaluating which of many influences in a person's life may be causing particular symptoms is often difficult.   Even if a woman with no history of psychiatric problems develops clear-cut depression after an abortion, it does not necessarily follow that the abortion per se was the cause of the symptoms.   The woman may be reacting to any number of related factors other than the abortion.   For example, she may be having marital problems, or, if single, she may be encountering rejection from her family for having become pregnant out of wedlock or be reacting to abandonment by a boy friend.

Further, some hospitals permit abortion only if the woman will agree to be sterilized.   In these cases, it may be the sterilization, with its connotations of mutilation and permanent loss of the ability to bear children, which is the cause of psychiatric symptoms.   In other situations — as in countries like Sweden, where motherhood is strongly encouraged by the government and where abortions are performed only where serious health problems exist — a woman must go through a long, humiliating series of consultations and convince a panel of doctors that there is something physically or mentally wrong with her in order to secure permission for an abortion. This experience can be degrading and dehumanizing and can contribute to the development of depressive symptoms even more than the abortion itself.

All of the studies reviewed concerned women who obtained legal abortions. It must be remembered that legal abortions are in many countries a small percentage of the total abortions. In the United States, for example, prior to the recent passage of reform laws, it had been estimated that approximately 1,000,000 women each year obtained illegal abortions.[40] The Institute for Sex Research studies found that between one-quarter and one-fifth of married women had obtained an abortion by the time they had reached age 45.[41] If abortions, especially the more traumatic illegal ones, were associated with a significant incidence of psychiatric illness, one would expect that abortion-related problems would be seen quite commonly in psychiatric practice. But, in fact, such problems are seen only rarely, which tends to support the findings of the follow-up studies. Doctor Kummer surveyed 32 practicing psychiatrists in California and found that 75 percent had never encountered any moderate or severe postabortion sequelae among their patients. Twenty-five percent encountered such sequelae only rarely, with the highest incidence being 6 cases in 15 years of practice.[42] Furthermore, the low risk of serious psychiatric problems following *abortion* must be contrasted with a relatively high frequency of psychosis following *childbirth*. There are some 4000 documented cases of post-partum psychosis requiring hospitalization in the United States each year, slightly less than 2 per 1000 deliveries.[43]

In summary, the weight of available evidence suggests that serious psychological harm to women following abortion is a relatively rare occurrence. Most psychiatrists believe that if a woman truly desires an abortion, if the abortion is not in conflict with her basic religious and moral beliefs, and if she is provided with emotional support by her family and physician at the time of the abortion, then the experience will be well tolerated psychologically. Although more follow-up studies would be a useful addition to our knowledge, most psychiatrists would oppose further delay in liberalization of the abortion laws for purposes of conducting more research. Enough investigations have been done to convince the profession that abortion, in the great majority of cases, is a safe procedure from a psychiatric standpoint.

IV. Do Unwanted Births Harm Women?

One of the most widespread myths of American life is that pregnancy invariably is, or at least should be, a beautiful and fulfilling event in the life of a woman. In reality, there are many circumstances in which an accidental pregnancy can be harmful for a woman and her entire family as well. The situations where this is most likely to occur are as follows.

A. *Unmarried Women*

For single women, or teenage girls, the birth of an illegitimate child can lead to loss of educational opportunities, diminished chances for a successful marriage, ostracism by family and friends, and welfare dependency. Of course, it becomes more important to deal with this problem as the frequency of illegitimate births continues to rise, and during the period of 1940-68, the percentage of births which were illegitimate rose from 3.5 to 9.7.[44] To compound the situation, it has been estimated that at least 90 percent of these illegitimate births were unwanted.[45]

Moreover, illegitimate *births* are only part of the much larger problem of illegitimate *pregnancy*, since women with illegitimate pregnancies often obtain illegal abortions. In many other instances, the problem is solved by hastily arranged and often forced marriages. A recent study conducted by the National Center for Health Statistics found that 19 percent of legitimate firstborn children in this country during the period 1964-66 were conceived out of wedlock,[46] and that 42 percent of the married women under age 20 had been married less than 8 months prior to the birth of their first child.[47]

These premature marriages have been shown to have a higher rate of divorce than marriages in which the bride was not pregnant at the altar. In one study, 4.9 percent of all sampled marriages ended in divorce, as compared with a divorce rate of 13 percent among couples who had had their first child within 9 months of marriage and 17 percent among couples whose first child was born within 6 months of marriage.[48]

It can be assumed that even when divorce does not occur, forced marriages between unwilling and incompatible partners are less likely to be mutually satisfying than those marriages where the couples made their decision freely. The awareness that one originally married because of love helps to sustain a couple through the difficult times that occur in virtually all marriages. By contrast, it is hard for two people to build a relationship of loyalty and commitment when they feel they were forced into marriage in the first place.

Some people naively believe that most of the problems associated with unwanted pregnancy among the unmarried can be adequately solved by arranging for the women to give up their babies for adoption. Although it is certainly true that there are many unfortunate, infertile couples who would welcome the opportunity to adopt a child, giving up one's baby after 9 months of pregnancy generally goes against the grain of human nature. The typical impulse for a woman is to want to keep her baby rather than to give it away to a complete stranger. Despite pressure from families and social workers, many women will quite understandably refuse to place their babies for adoption, regardless of the problems that will inevitably occur in trying to provide adequate care for the child. Still other women resort to illegal abortions rather than face the ordeal of giving up their babies for adoption.

B. *Physically Ill Women*

Many women who suffer from serious illness lack the energy and strength to care properly for a baby. In some instances, these women already have more children than they can cope with. A woman with severe multiple sclerosis or rheumatoid arthritis, for example, undergoes a severe hardship if she bears an unwanted child merely because she has accidentally become pregnant. And with some diseases, such as cancer, the patient's prognosis may show a life expectancy of only a few months or years. The abortion laws of most states would not allow a woman, even in this situation, to abort an accidental pregnancy.

C. *Mentally Ill Women*

Serious mental illness, including alcoholism and drug addiction, is characterized by extremely low tolerance for frustration and stress. When mental patients are exposed to more stress than they can handle, their symptoms — anxiety, depression, psychotic behavior, excessive use of drugs or alcohol, etc. — become even worse. An unwanted pregnancy can be a major stress even for a "normal" woman, but for mental patients, an unwanted pregnancy can be overwhelming and lead to exacerbation of her symptoms, suicidal tendencies, or complete psychotic breakdown.[49]

D. *Women with Severe Situational Problems*

Many women, although basically "normal" with respect to their emotional and mental stability, are burdened by personal problems or pressures which generate considerable nervous tension. The birth of an unwanted child in these circumstances can increase these pressures to an intolerable degree. Such situations would include women whose husbands are alcoholics or are physically ill, women who are unhappily married or in the process of divorce, and women who already have more children than they can adequately manage.

E. *Women in Poverty*

In many families, the size of the bread-winner's paycheck is inadequate to provide for the needs of a large family. If these couples can limit their number of children to one or two, the family can remain solvent. Limiting the family size can also help the family's financial situation by providing sufficient free time for the mother to hold a part-time or full-time job and augment the husband's earnings.

In poor families, several unwanted children can create severe economic hardship and can increase strains within the family to the breaking point. The family's income, which might have been adequate for a small family must now attempt to meet the housing, nutritional, clothing and recreational needs of several more people.

With a large number of children to care for, the mother is less likely to find time for gainful employment; and if she does take a job, it is at the cost of denying her children much-needed maternal care, guidance, and discipline. In circumstances such as these, it is quite common for the husband to desert the family. And women who have been deserted by their husbands and who are forced to try to raise a large family on welfare, frequently sink into a chronic state of apathy or depression or turn to drugs or alcohol for escape.[50]

F. *Elderly Mothers*

Many accidental pregnancies occur in women in their 40's who are entering menopause and who already have adult children. Having already devoted 20 or so years to raising their families, these women are often incapable of making the considerable emotional and psychological adjustment that would be required for them to initiate a second career of motherhood, devoting an additional 20 years to the care of children.

G. *Women Made Pregnant by Rape*

Even the most vehement opponents of abortion reform will admit that women made pregnant as a result of a criminal assault ought not to be forced to bear the offspring. Yet some opponents of abortion will argue that the occurrence of rape is not a satisfactory reason to change the abortion laws. They point out, quite correctly, that immediately following rape, a woman can undergo a surgical procedure (dilation and curettage of the uterus) which will, in most cases, prevent pregnancy from occurring. They also argue that many instances of rape are not bona fide, and that women frequently contribute to the assault by seductive behavior. They also contend that if rape were included as a justifiable ground for abortion, any woman could claim that she had been raped in order to get an abortion, thus allowing easy circumvention of the law's prohibitions.

In view of the traumatic nature of rape, however, these arguments seem very callous. Forcible rape is a common crime and one which is occurring with increasing frequency. According to

FBI reports, 37,000 rapes were reported in 1970, a 121 percent increase from 1960.[51]   Moreover, these statistics fail to reflect the true magnitude of the problem, because rape is one of the most underreported crimes.   Few women who have been raped wish to report this to the police, press charges against their assailants, or participate in a trial where they will be subjected to public embarrassment.

Because rape is such a terrifying and humiliating experience, it is unrealistic to expect a woman who has been raped to immediately seek proper medical attention against her natural impulse to suppress the incident.   Consequently, there is little practical merit to the argument that current medical procedures alone are adequate to deal with cases of rape, without a change in the laws as well.

Finally, there is no proof that a large percentage of rape victims are willing accomplices; to suggest this is to indicate little more than prejudice and contempt toward women.   In our present crime-ridden society, to deny women who have been forcibly and criminally impregnated an opportunity to terminate the pregnancy under safe medical conditions is, at the very least, inhumane.

H.   *Women Made Pregnant as the Result of Incest*

An incest-caused pregnancy is another case which most compassionate people concur should be a grounds for abortion.   The exact incidence of incest is not known, but psychiatrists are aware from their practices that incest is not extremely rare, as many people believe.   Clearly, an enlightened society should not insist that a 12- or 13-year-old child must bear the offspring of her deviate father.

I.   *Women Who Simply Do Not Desire Children*

Many women, both single and married, prefer careers to motherhood; still others may wish to delay motherhood until later in life in order to first pursue educational or career goals.   Such women justifiably regard it as an "extreme hardship" to be forced, because of an unwanted pregnancy, to abandon goals for which they have worked or planned throughout their lives.   And, finally, many women may simply prefer not to have children, regardless of any extrafamilial interests.   It is difficult to see why the state should compel these women to continue unwanted pregnancies.   The state's interest is minimal, whereas the impact on the women's personal lives is tremendous.

It has been shown that there are many situations and circumstances in which a woman may be unable to assume adequately the burdens and responsibilities of motherhood. Forcing her to bear an unwanted child in these situations can impose severe strain upon her mental and physical health and well-being. Until the time that foolproof contraceptive methods are invented and made readily available to all women, easy access to abortion is the only way that many thousands of women each year can be spared from bearing an unwanted child.[52] Making it possible for all women to choose the number and spacing of their children would greatly enhance the protection of the emotional health of American womanhood and, secondarily, would contribute substantially to the stability of the family unit as a social institution.

V. Abortion, the Unwanted Child, and the Prevention of Psychiatric Disorders

Psychiatrists generally agree that the single most important cause of mental disorders is inadequate parental care during the formative years. Children need generous amounts of affection, guidance, and discipline in order to develop into intellectually and emotionally mature adults. Children who feel rejected and unloved or who are given inconsistent or ineffective discipline have a much greater than average likelihood of developing serious psychiatric disorders, such as schizophrenia, alcoholism, drug addiction, mental retardation, or a psychopathic personality.[53] Raising a child successfully is a demanding and difficult task requiring love and dedication on the part of the parents for some 20 years.

It seems reasonable to assume that, all things being equal, the child who is wanted is far more likely to receive a high quality of parental care than one who is unwanted. Unmotivated parents who have the burdens of child-rearing thrust upon them because of accidental and unintentional pregnancy are less likely to raise a child as well as parents who have freely chosen to assume this responsibility. Most psychiatrists believe, therefore, that allowing the couple to decide the number and spacing of their children without compulsion by the state would decrease the percentage of unloved and inadequately reared children and, consequently, would decrease the incidence of psychiatric disorders.[54] The noted psychiatrist Karl Menninger has expressed this idea well:

> The reason that contraceptive knowledge and counsel seem to the psychiatrist to be essential is based not upon considerations of the welfare of the adult, but on the considerations of the welfare of the child. Nothing is more tragic, more fateful in its ultimate consequences, than the realization by a child that he was unwanted. . . . [P]lanned parenthood is an essential element in any program for increased mental health and for human peace and happiness. The unwanted child becomes the undesirable citizen, the willing cannon-fodder for wars of hate and prejudice.[55]

Admittedly the notion that unwanted children are more prone to develop psychiatric disorders, despite its common-sense appeal, has never been adequately tested scientifically because of intrinsic research problems. For example, the time interval required for follow-up studies of this kind (where the attitude of the parents at pregnancy is correlated with the subsequent life adjustment of the offspring) is 20 years or more. Few researchers are willing to commit themselves to a project spanning that length of time. Another problem is presented by the difficulties which attend the assessment of whether the mother or father "wanted" the child.[56]

The only pertinent investigation thus far was a 21-year follow-up study of 120 children born after their mothers had been refused therapeutic abortions. The investigators found that, compared with control subjects, the unwanted children had a higher incidence of many kinds of behavioral maladjustments; required more psychiatric care, were arrested more often for antisocial and criminal behavior and drunkenness, received welfare assistance more frequently, and failed to achieve as high a level of schooling as did the control group.[57] Similar studies are in progress at the present time, and it would be quite surprising if they produce significantly different results.

Further indirect confirmation of the assumption that unwanted children are more prone to mental illness is provided by recent research on the relationship of birth order to mental illness. Studies analyzing large groups of psychiatric patients with varying diagnoses show that the children in the last half of the birth order in families with four or more children were more likely to develop mental illness than children in the first half of the birth order.[58] In one of these studies, it was also shown that, compared to first-born patients, last-born patients were sicker and showed a lower degree of social competence and a higher incidence of bizarre and self-destructive behavior.[59] The most probable explanation for these findings is that later-born children in large families are more likely to be unwanted and hence are more likely to receive poorer parental care in childhood. Indeed, a recent survey has shown that only 11 percent of parents with two children said that their last-born child was unwanted, whereas the corresponding figures for parents with three, four, five, and six children were 28, 41, 45 and 47 percent, respectively.[60]

In the face of such a sparse body of research on the subject of the life outcome of the unwanted child, it can be asked whether it is scientifically defensible for mental health professionals to recommend the legalization of abortion on the grounds that doing so would lead to a reduction in the incidence of mental illness. An affirmative position on this question can be justified on the following grounds (each of which will be discussed at length in the next section). First, methods of curing or preventing psychiatric disorders — other than the preventive approach of improving family planning services — all have serious limitations. Second, the public health problem of mental illness is of such serious proportions that, in the absence of *proven* remedies, those measures judged to be *most likely to be effective* should be adopted as soon as possible. Third, the number of unwanted children born in the United States each year is substantial, so that a reduction in the incidence of such births can be expected to decrease the rate of mental illness. And, finally, legalization of abortion is the single most effective step that can be taken to reduce the incidence of unwanted births.

A. *Alternative Methods of Curing or Preventing Psychiatric Disorders*

If effective methods for the treatment of psychiatric disorders were available, all that would be needed to achieve a reduction in the number of psychiatrically disturbed people would be to establish adequate numbers of appropriately staffed treatment facilities. Unfortunately, modern psychiatric treatment methods, consisting mainly of group and individual psychotherapy and drugs, are most effective in relatively mild disorders, such as neuroses, depressions, and acute psychoses. These techniques are of limited benefit in the severe disabling disorders, such as chronic schizophrenia, severe alcoholism, drug addiction, and the psychopathic personality or chronic criminal offender. Individuals afflicted with severe disorders frequently lack motivation for treatment, or even insight into the fact that they are disturbed. If treatment accomplishes anything at all, it is slight palliation of the worst symptoms rather than a cure. Moreover, years of patient work by highly trained professionals are necessary to accomplish even modest goals. Because of the overwhelming difficulties, few mental health professionals seriously believe that a treatment-oriented strategy will significantly reduce the numbers of people afflicted with mental illness. The only realistic hope to control mental disorders is to take preventive measures.[61]

Unfortunately, the outlook for finding effective methods for preventing the occurrence of psychiatric disorders is little better than the outlook for curing them. Because the main cause of these disorders is inadequate parental care during the formative years of childhood, preventing mental illness would require either influencing parents to take better care of their children or providing supplementary or corrective child-rearing services to those children who are not being properly cared for at home. Both of these approaches, however, have major difficulties which make them extremely difficult to implement.

It would be desirable to educate or otherwise influence all parents to bring up their children properly, but there is, of course, no known way of accomplishing this goal. Most incompetent parents have multiple personal problems of their own which divert their energies from their parental responsibilities, were so poorly raised themselves that they failed to observe and learn how to be effective parents, or have manifest emotional disorders or subnormal intelligence. And our society lacks both the knowledge and the resources to alter any of these factors on a mass scale.

Even if we had a network of special parent education or counseling centers, and these facilities were capable of accomplishing their task, many of the parents who needed these services would fail to utilize them unless coerced. In order to select the inadequate parents for required counseling, it would first be necessary to determine which parents were failing in their responsibilities, which in turn would require a nationwide system of surveillance of home and family life. It is doubtful that the American public would tolerate such a massive invasion of privacy, even assuming that a relatively efficacious system could be made to work.

A seemingly more practical approach to preventing mental illness would be to provide supplementary or corrective child-rearing services for deprived or neglected children through institutions other than the family. The Head Start program[62] is a beginning effort in this direction. A 2-billion-dollar comprehensive child development program passed by Congress[63] but vetoed by President Nixon in 1971[64] was an even more ambitious attempt along these lines.

But on the basis of existing knowledge about child development, one has to be skeptical about whether these kinds of programs would accomplish what their proponents contend they will. A few hours a week of contact with a child care professional during the preschool years would have little impact upon the personality development of a child in comparison with the impact of the mother who is with the child much more time. In order for child care centers to have a substantial influence upon the personality, they would need to have access to the child at a very early age and for many hours each day. The staff-child ratio would have to be high, and efforts would have to be made to provide continuity so that the child could form a meaningful relationship with one or more workers. In effect, this would mean replacing the family as the principal child-rearing institution of our society by something similar to the kibbutz system in Israel, where child-rearing is a community, rather than a family, responsibility.[65] There is little likelihood, it would seem, that such a drastic change in our traditional family-centered way of life would be accepted by the American public in the foreseeable future.

Thus, one important reason for advocating improved methods of family planning as a means of preventing mental illness, despite the lack of *conclusive* proof that unwanted children are more prone to these disorders, is that few if any alternative methods promise to control mental illness.

B. *Psychiatric Disorders — A Major Public Health Problem*

If psychiatric disorders were a relatively minor social or public health problem, it would be sensible to delay the adoption of control measures pending further research. This research would increase the possibility that all remaining unanswered questions concerning the etiology of these disorders could first be resolved, which in turn would increase the likelihood that any programs adopted would prove effective. But the extent and severity of the mental illness pandemic makes such a leisurely approach unjustifiable.

Psychiatric disorders often lead to extreme suffering and anguish, not only for the persons affected but for their families and associates as well.[66] The children of schizophrenics, drug addicts, and alcoholics, for example, are particularly vulnerable to emotional trauma because of the constant turmoil to which they are exposed in the home.

Psychiatric disorders also impose enormous costs upon the general society in several ways. First, there are the costs of operating the nation's network of mental hospitals, clinics, and alcoholism and drug addiction facilities.[67] Second, there are the costs of operating that portion of the criminal justice system (police, courts, jails, and prisons) which is involved in dealing with the alcoholic,[68] the drug addict,[69] and the chronic criminal offender.[70] Third, because most of the severely disturbed and retarded[71] are unable to work, there is the cost of maintaining these persons and their families. Fourth, there are intangible costs, such as the diminished sense of safety in the community because of the rising rate of crimes of violence, many of which are committed by seriously disturbed individuals. As a corollary to the high crime rate, the survival of many of our free institutions is endangered. As public pressures mount for effective action against crime, police practices such as preventive detention and wire-tapping, hitherto considered alien to American traditions, seem likely to gain increasing public acceptance.

Considering these consequences, it is no surprise that mental illness is often termed the nation's number one health problem.[72] To combat mental disorders, some risks clearly seem warranted even if, after several more decades of research, it should turn out that some approach other than birth control might have been more effective in attacking this problem. Policy makers have an obligation to adopt those remedies that appear most likely to produce desired results on the basis of existing knowledge, rather than wait for some kind of definitive answers which may not be available for many years, if ever.

C. The Incidence of Unwanted Births

If the numbers of unwanted births in America were low, preventing their occurrence would obviously have little impact on the public health problem of mental illness. It would, under those circumstances, make little sense to press for improved techniques of family planning as a high-priority method for preventing mental illness.

Recent studies, however, have shown that the incidence of unwanted births is actually far higher than had been suspected previously. Based on interviews with 5600 married women during the period 1960-65, Professors Bumpass and Westoff of Princeton found that approximately 19 percent of the children born during that period were unwanted.[73] The Bumpass and Westoff study was limited to married women and therefore gave only a partial and overly optimistic view of the entire problem of unwanted pregnancies. When one further considers that approximately 9 percent of all births are illegitimate (339,000 in 1968) and that an estimated 90 percent of the illegitimate births are unwanted, a more complete picture of the problem materializes.[74] For example, in 1967 the total of unwanted *legitimate* births (19 percent of 3,203,000, or 608,500) and unwanted *illegitimate* births (90 percent of 318,000, or 286,000) was 894,000. In other words, 25 percent of all births were unwanted in that year. That close to 900,000 unwanted births are occurring each year in the United States clearly shows that our present system of family planning is falling far short of the goal of ensuring that all children born are wanted children.

D. *Is Abortion the Most Effective Way to Reduce Unwanted Births?*

Even if one accepts the idea that reducing the incidence of unwanted births deserves high priority as a method of preventing psychiatric disorders, one could still question whether legalization of abortion is the best way to accomplish that reduction. One might wonder, for example, whether the same objective could be reached by some other means, such as contraception.

Unfortunately, analysis of the current state of birth control technology suggests there is little likelihood that we can significantly reduce the incidence of unwanted births in the foreseeable future without legalizing abortion. Our present methods of contraception have three serious drawbacks which are quite difficult to overcome: technical imperfections, inadequate distribution, and human error.

1. *Technical Imperfections* — There is only one contraceptive method that is "fool-proof," the contraceptive pill.[75] The next most reliable method is the intrauterine device (IUD), which has a failure rate of approximately 2 to 3 percent per year (*i.e.,* for every 100 users, two to three will become pregnant each year).[76] This may seem like a high rate of reliability, but with 25 million fertile American women, there would be 250,000 accidental pregnancies annually, even if every woman used a 99 percent effective method.[77] Moreover, these high rates of reliability are misleading because all women will not be using either of these two high-reliability methods. Many women who begin using the pill stop because of its side-effects, while others refuse to use the pill because of the chance of dangerous side-effects. The same is true for the IUD where uterine bleeding and pain is a major factor in its removal.[78] Furthermore, the likelihood that 100 percent reliable and well-tolerated contraceptive methods will be developed in the near future appears remote.[79]

2. *Inadequate Distribution* — There are two large groups in our population who lack access to contraception: the poor and the unmarried young. Planned Parenthood-World Population has calculated that only 30 percent of the 5 million fertile, low-income women in the United States were served in 1971 by publicly or privately subsidized family planning programs.[80] And efforts to ex-

pand these programs are running into increasing difficulties because of opposition from a number of corners, including minority groups who contend that birth control programs are a form of genocide.[81]

There is strong opposition on the part of society at large to providing contraception to the unmarried young, despite evidence that a large percentage are sexually active. The public seems to believe that providing contraception to unmarried teenagers would lead to an increase in sexual promiscuity and to a weakening of the moral fabric of society. Since these beliefs are deep-rooted, there seems to be little reason to believe that they will change in the near future.

3. *Human Error* — The third problem with contraception is that its successful practice requires more foresight and self-discipline than many people possess. The very people who are least capable of raising children properly, the mentally retarded and emotionally unstable, are the same people least capable of successfully using contraception. Until methods of contraception can be developed which do not depend on foresight or self-discipline, this problem cannot be overcome.

Abortion has none of these shortcomings. Abortion is not 97 or 99 percent reliable, but 100 percent. Moreover, once it is legalized, abortion can be made readily available to the young[82] and the poor without encountering great political or societal opposition, as the experience in New York City has shown.[83] In the first 9 months after New York State's liberalized abortion law went into effect, 55 percent of the 31,382 New York City residents who obtained abortions were poor;[84] 34 percent of the abortions were performed in public hospitals;[85] and more than half of the patients were unmarried.[86]

Since abortion requires no foresight or self-discipline, legalization of abortion would make it possible for the most immature, emotionally unstable, or mentally retarded woman to achieve total control over her reproduction. The segment of the population least able to properly raise children would no longer have thrust upon them large and unwanted families.

If abortion were legalized, there could be a great reduction in the incidence of unwanted births. In the first 9 months after New York liberalized its abortion law, 447 abortions were performed for every 1000 live births in that city.[87]   If this ratio were projected to the United States as a whole, where 3,731,000 babies were born in 1970, this would lead to a national "abortion demand" of some 1,700,000 annually.[88]   Although many legal abortions terminate pregnancies that would have been aborted illegally before the laws were liberalized, Dr. Tietze has estimated that approximately 20 percent of the legal abortions performed in New York during the first 9 months under the new law ended pregnancies that otherwise would have become unwanted births.[89]   If we apply this 20 percent figure to the 1,700,000 legal abortions that would be expected in the United States if abortion were allowed upon request, the number of unwanted births that would be prevented would be 340,000 (20 percent of 1,700,000).   In other words, the present annual total of approximately 900,000 unwanted births occurring in the United States could be reduced by 38 percent merely by the single step of legalizing abortion nationwide.   This is a far greater reduction of unwanted births than could be achieved by any other single measure.

VI.   CONCLUSION

The proponents of legalization of abortion have, during the past decade, emphasized two principal arguments: first, that the denial of a woman's right to choose whether or not to bear a child is unjust and oppressive and, second, that the abortion laws force women to break the law and risk their lives at the hands of a criminal abortionist.   These two arguments have intense emotional appeal and serve as rallying cries for mass demonstrations and other forms of political action by pro-abortion groups.

Although both these arguments are certainly valid, other aspects of the abortion problem, particularly its social implications, have received inadequate attention.   The legalization of abortion would contribute greatly to alleviating many of our most serious social problems, especially overpopulation and poverty.   In this article, I have emphasized the anticipated impact of legalization of abortion on the social problem with which I am most familiar — mental illness and related behavioral disorders.   By bringing about a sharp reduction in the incidence of unwanted births, now estimated to be 25 percent of all births, legalizing abortion would contribute to the mental health and well-being of society in several ways.   Many thousands of women would be spared from severe hardship and suffering currently brought about by the birth of children under adverse circumstances. Opportunities for women to fulfill their educational and career aspirations would be significantly enhanced. And the proportion of children born who would receive adequate parental care during their formative years would increase, which in turn would decrease the number of children who would become mentally ill, alcoholic, mentally retarded, addicted to drugs, or criminals in later life.

If the potential social benefits to be derived from legalization of abortion, in terms of improvement of family life and mental health, are as substantial as I have suggested, one wonders why they have not been more widely recognized. Part of the reason may be that the idea of using abortion as a method of solving social problems runs contrary to many of our customary patterns of thought — it is "counter-intuitive." Abortion is a "negative" concept in most people's minds. It is associated with interference with, or destruction of, the basic natural processes of life, and it is also associated with the notion of irresponsibility (opponents of abortion argue that, if people conscientiously use contraception they would not need abortions). People intuitively look for "positive" rather than "negative" ideas for solving social problems. Thus, most proposals for improving the mental health of the population involve one form or another of service to people — educational programs, day care centers, mental health centers, rehabilitation programs for criminals, and the like. One naturally tends to assume that the larger these programs are and the more money they cost, the more "positive" they are and, therefore, the better the end result will be.

Legalization of abortion goes contrary to this whole set of assumptions, for it does not involve the institution of large-scale and expensive government service programs. Instead, all that is required is that society leave women alone to pursue their own personal wishes and desires. Instinctively we resist the idea that such a "negative" social policy could achieve major social benefits. Merely because we may not regard abortion per se as intrinsically noble or morally uplifting, we should not fail to recognize that legalization of abortion may well contribute substantially to the solution of many social problems. Although legalizing abortion is not a pan-

acea and will certainly not totally eliminate mental illness, it is difficult to think of any single measure that would do more to reduce
the incidence of serious psychiatric disorders.

NOTES

1. A selective list of articles and books representing the many compre-
hensive discussions of the abortion problem by psychiatrists includes:
ABORTION: CHANGING VIEWS AND PRACTICE (R. Sloane ed. 1970);
THERAPEUTIC ABORTION (H. Rosen ed. 1954); Aarons, *Therapeutic
Abortion and the Psychiatrist*, 124 AM. J. PSYCHIATRY 745 (1957);
Fleck, *Some Psychiatric Aspects of Abortion*, 151 J. NERVOUS & MEN-
TAL DISEASE 42 (1970); Kummer, *Post-Abortion Psychiatric Illness —
A Myth?*, 119 AM. J. PSYCHIATRY 980 (1963); Lebensohn, *Abortion,
Psychiatry, and the Quality of Life*, 128 AM. J. PSYCHIATRY 946
(1972); Levene & Rigney, *Law, Preventive Psychiatry, and Therapeu-
tic Abortion*, 151 J. NERVOUS & MENTAL DISEASE 51 (1970); Peck &
Marcus, *Psychiatric Sequelae of Therapeutic Interruption of Pregnancy*,
143 J. NERVOUS & MENTAL DISEASE 417 (1966); Rosen, *Psychiatric
Implications of Abortion: A Case Study in Social Hypocrisy*, 17 W.
RES. L. REV. 435 (1965); Schwartz, *Psychiatry and the Abortion Laws:
An Overview*, 9 COMPREHENSIVE PSYCHIATRY 99 (1968); Schwartz,
The Abortion Laws: A Severe Case of Resistance to Change, 67 OHIO
ST. MED. J. 33 (1971); Simon, Senturia & Rothman, *Psychiatric Ill-
ness Following Therapeutic Abortion*, 124 AM. J. PSYCHIATRY 59
(1967); Sloan, *The Unwanted Pregnancy*, 280 N. ENGLAND J. MED.
1206 (1969); White, *Induced Abortions: A Survey of Their Psychiatric
Implications, Complications, & Indications*, 24 TEXAS REP. OF BIOLOGY
& MED. 531 (1966).
2. The American Psychiatric Association, the official voice of organized
psychiatry, adopted the following resolution in 1969:
> A decision to perform an abortion should be regarded as strict-
> ly a medical decision and a medical responsibility. It should
> be removed entirely from the jurisdiction of criminal law.
> Criminal penalties should be reserved for persons who per-
> form abortions without medical license or qualification to do
> so. A medical decision to perform an abortion is based on the
> careful and informed judgments of the physician and the pa-
> tient. Among other factors to be considered in arriving at
> the decision is the motivation of the patient. Often psychiatric
> consultation can help clarify motivational problems and there-
> by contribute to the patient's welfare. Position Statement on
> Abortion, *reprinted in* 126 AM. J. PSYCHIATRY 1554
> (1970).

A similar policy statement was adopted in the same year by the Group for Advancement of Psychiatry, one of the largest and most prestigious psychiatric organizations. Their statement specifically said: "[W]e recommend that abortion when performed by a licensed physician be entirely removed from the domain of criminal law. We believe that a woman should have the right to abort or not, just as she has the right to marry or not." GROUP FOR THE ADVANCEMENT OF PSYCHIATRY, THE RIGHT TO ABORTION: A PSYCHIATRIC VIEW (Vol. 7, No. 75), 219 (1969).

3. The largest survey taken (2041 psychiatrists were contacted) to determine the views of psychiatrists on abortion showed overwhelming support for liberalized abortion laws. To the question, "Should abortion be available to any woman capable of giving legal consent upon her own request to a competent physician?" 79.5 percent answered in the affirmative (71.7 percent without qualification, and 7.8 percent with qualification). Compared with physicians in other specialties who were also surveyed, psychiatrists had the highest percentages favoring abortion on request. The percentage of all physicians favoring abortion on request was 62.8 percent (51.0 percent without qualification and 11.8 percent with qualification). MODERN MED., Nov. 3, 1969, at 19.

4. See Duffy, The Case Against Abortion: A Plea for the Unborn Child, 56 WOMEN L.J. 86 (1970); Abortion Legislation and the Establishment Clause, 15 CATHOLIC LAWYER 108, 114 (1969).

5. Prior to 1967 only three states amended their statutes to provide for abortion on additional grounds: Alabama in 1951, ALA. CODE tit. 14, § 9 (1959) (gravely impair physical health); New Hampshire in 1955, N.H. REV. STAT. ANN. § 585.13 (1955) (malformation of the fetus); Mississippi in 1966, MISS. CODE ANN. § 2223 (Supp. 1971) (pregnancy as a result of rape). The liberalizations since 1967 are: ARK. STAT. ANN. § 41-304 (Supp. 1969); ALASKA STAT. § 11.15.060 (1970); CAL. HEALTH & SAFETY CODE § 25951 (Supp. 1971); COLO. REV. STAT. ANN. § 40-6-101 (1971); DEL. CODE ANN. tit. 24, § 1790 (Supp. 1970); D.C. CODE ANN. § 22-201 (1967); GA. CODE ANN. § 26-1202 (Rev. 1971) [portion of statute allowing abortion only when necessary to preserve life or health held unconstitutional in Doe v. Bolton, 319 F. Supp. 1048 (N.D. Ga. 1970) (per curiam), jurisdiction postponed, 402 U.S. 941 (1971)]; HAWAII REV. LAWS § 453-16 (Supp. 1971); KAN. GEN. STAT. ANN. § 21-3407 (Supp. 1971) [Poe v. Menghini, 40 U.S.L.W. 2666 (D. Kan. Mar. 10, 1972) (requirement that all abortions be approved by three physicians and performed in an approved hospital held unconstitutional)]; MD. ANN. CODE art. 43, § 137 (1971); N.M. STAT. ANN. §§ 40A-5-1 (Supp. 1971); N.Y. PENAL LAW § 125.05 (Supp. 1971); N.C. GEN. STAT. § 14-45.1 (Supp. 1971); ORE. REV. STAT. § 435.415 (1971); S.C.

CODE ANN. § 16-87 (Supp. 1971); VA. CODE ANN. § 18.1-62.1 (Supp. 1971); WASH. REV. CODE § 9.02.010 (1961). *See* note 14 *infra* for a list of those states which follow the Model Penal Code.

6. For a comprehensive review of the abortion laws of the various states, see George, *The Evolving Law of Abortion*, pp. 3-62, in this volume.

7. Tietze & Lewit, *Abortion*, 220 SCIENTIFIC AM. 21, 23 (1969). The definitions of "therapeutic abortion" are various. Here, the term is taken to include those abortions which are performed for one or more of the medical or psychiatric indications allowed by a given state's law.

8. In People v. Belous, 71 Cal. 2d 954, 458 P.2d 194, 80 Cal. Rptr. 354 (1969), *cert. denied*, 397 U.S. 915 (1970), the court concluded that section 274 of the California Penal Code, which provides that a physician can administer an abortion only if he "deems it necessary" to save the patient's life, "is not susceptible of a construction that does not violate legislative intent and that is sufficiently certain to satisfy due process requirements without improperly infringing on fundamental [federal and California] constitutional rights." Cal. 2d at 960, 458 P.2d at 197, 80 Cal. Rptr. at 357.

9. *See* Halleck, *Excuse Makers to the Elite: Psychiatrists as Social Movers*, MED. OPINION Dec. 1971, at 48.

10. *See* Ayd, *Abortion: The Catholic Viewpoint*, in ABORTION: CHANGING VIEWS AND PRACTICE 48 (R. Sloane ed. 1970); Wilson, *The Abortion Problem in the General Hospital*, in THERAPEUTIC ABORTION 189 (H. Rosen ed. 1954).

11. It remains for the courts to decide whether this state of affairs is consistent with the equal protection clause of the 14th amendment. *Cf.* Lucas, *Federal Constitutional Limitations on the Enforcement and Administration of State Abortion Statutes*, 46 N.C. L. REV. 730, 769-75 (1968), for a discussion of the equal protection argument in terms of income and residential requirements.

12. The respective statutes of these states are: ARIZ. REV. STAT. ANN. § 13-211 (1956); CONN. GEN. STAT. ANN. § 53-29 (1958) [held unconstitutional in Abele v. Markel, ___ F. Supp. ___ (D. Conn. 1972)]; IDAHO CODE ANN. § 18-1506 (Supp. 1971); ILL. ANN. STAT. ch. 38, § 23-1 (1970) [held unconstitutional in Doe v. Scott, 321 F. Supp. 1385 (N.D. Ill. 1971); *appeals docketed sub. noms.* Hanrahan v. Doe and Heffernen v. Poe, 39 U.S.L.W. 3438 (U.S. Mar. 29, 1971)]; IND. ANN. STAT. § 10-105 (1956); IOWA CODE ANN. § 701.1 (1950); KY. REV. STAT. § 436.020 (1969); ME. REV. STAT. ANN. ch. 17, § 51 (1965); MICH. COMP. LAWS ANN. § 750.14 (1968); MINN. STAT. ANN. § 617.18 (1964); MO. ANN. STAT. § 559.100 (1953); MONT. REV. CODE ANN. § 94-401 (1969); NEB. REV. STAT. § 28-404 (1965); NEV. REV. STAT. § 201-120 (1967); N.D. CENT. CODE § 12-25-01 (1960); OHIO REV. CODE § 2901.15 (1953); OKLA. STAT. ANN. tit. 21, § 861 (Supp. 1971); R.I. GEN.

LAWS ANN. § 11-3-1 (1970); S.D. COMP. LAWS ANN. § 22-17-1
(1967); TENN. CODE ANN. § 39-301 (1955); TEX. PEN. CODE
ANN. art. 1191 (1961) [held unconstitutional in Roe v. Wade, 214
F. Supp. 1217 (N.D. Texas, 1970), *jurisdiction postponed*, 402 U.S.
941 (1971)]; UTAH CODE ANN. § 76-2-1 (1953); VT. STAT. ANN.
tit. 13, § 101 (1958) [held unconstitutional in Beecham v. Leahy, ___
Vt. ___, 287 A.2d 836 (1972)]; W. VA. CODE ANN. § 61-2-8
(1966); WIS. STAT. ANN. § 940.04 (1958) [held unconstitutional
in Babbitz v. McCann, 310 F. Supp. 293, 320 F. Supp. 219 (E.D.
Wis. 1970), *vacated and remanded*, 402 U.S. 903 (1971)]; WYO.
STAT. ANN. § 6-77 (1959).

13. MODEL PENAL CODE § 230.3 (Proposed Official Draft 1956). The
most pertinent part reads:
> A licensed physician is justified in terminating a pregnancy if
> he believes there is substantial risk that continuance of the
> pregnancy would gravely impair the physical or mental health
> of the mother or that the child would be born with grave
> physical or mental defect, or that the pregnancy resulted from
> rape, incest, or other felonious intercourse. All illicit inter-
> course with a girl below the age of 16 shall be deemed fe-
> lonious for purposes of this subsection. Justifiable abortions
> shall be performed only in a licensed hospital except in case of
> emergency when hospital facilities are unavailable. *Id.* §
> 203.3(2).

14. The respective statutes of these states are: ARK. STAT. ANN. § 41-304
(Supp. 1969); CAL. HEALTH & SAFETY CODE § 25951 (Supp. 1971);
COLO. REV. STAT. ANN. § 40-6-101 (1971); DEL. CODE ANN. tit. 24,
§ 1790 (Supp. 1970); FLA. SESS. LAWS ch. 72-196 (West 1972); GA.
CODE ANN. § 26-1202 (Rev. 1971) [portion of statute allowing abortion only when necessary to preserve life or health held unconstitutional
in Doe v. Bolton, 319 F. Supp. 1048 (N.D. Ga. 1970) (per curiam),
jurisdiction postponed, 402 U.S. 941 (1971)]; KAN. GEN. STAT.
ANN. § 21-3407 (Supp. 1971) [Poe v. Menghini, 40 U.S.L.W.
2666 (D. Kan. Mar. 10, 1972), held unconstitutional the requirement
that all abortions be approved by three physicians and performed in an
approved hospital]; MD. ANN. CODE art. 43, § 137 (1971); N.M.
STAT. ANN. § 40A-5-1 (Supp. 1971); N.C. GEN. STAT. § 14-45.1
(Supp. 1971); ORE. REV. STAT. § 435.415 (1971); S.C. CODE ANN.
§ 16-87 (Supp. 1971); VA. CODE ANN. § 18.1-62 (Supp. 1971).

15. N.Y. PENAL LAW § 125.5 (McKinney Supp. 1971).

16. Statement made by Dr. Iago Galdston at an abortion conference sponsored by the Planned Parenthood Federation of America, *reprinted in*
ABORTION IN THE UNITED STATES 119-20 (M. Calderone ed. 1959)
[hereinafter cited as ABORTION]. This belief has been shared by other
prominent psychiatrists such as Doctors Bolter and Wilson:

Despite protests to the contrary, we know that women's main role here on Earth is to conceive, deliver, and raise children. . . . When this function is interfered with, we see all sorts of emotional disorders and certainly the climax of these disorders is reached at the menopause when women recognize that they no longer can reproduce their kind and interpret the menopause as the end of life rather than the change of life. . . . The author has never seen a patient who has not had guilt feelings about a previous therapeutic abortion or illegal abortion. Bolter, *The Psychiatrist's Role in Therapeutic Abortion: The Unwitting Accomplice*, 119 AM. J. PSYCHIATRY 312, 314-15 (1962).

Many mothers who during the first weeks felt terrified at the thought of having a child, later bless the doctor who refused to allow them to proceed with their plans for abortion. It is also true that the woman who experiences an abortion, whether therapeutic or criminal, is traumatized by the act to such a degree that the memory becomes a potent factor in her future behavior pattern. Wilson, *supra* note 10, at 196. .

17. *See* notes 23-39 *infra* & accompanying table.

18. For example, Peck and Marcus found 19 percent of the patients to have such reactions. *See* note 25 *infra* & accompanying table.

19. *See* note 25 *infra* & accompanying table.

20. *See* notes 23, 24, 26, 28, 33, 34, 38, & 39 *infra* & accompanying table.

21. *Id.*

22. The Aren study found that 20 percent of the women regretted the abortion and would not go through the experience a second time if they again found themselves pregnant. *See* note 33 *supra* & accompanying table. Both studies suffer from the same methodological defect of failing to distinguish between symptoms resulting from abortion and those related to pre-existing psychiatric problems. In the Aren study, this distinction was not examined at all. In the Malmfors study, all the patients who showed psychiatric impairment after the abortion had a history of psychiatric symptoms prior to the abortion.

23. Ekblad, *Induced Abortion on Psychiatric Grounds*, ACTA PSYCHIATRICA ET NEUROLOGIC SCANDINAVICA 47 (Supp. No. 99, 1955).

24. Simon, Zenturia & Rothman, *supra* note 1, at 59-61.

25. Peck & Marcus, *supra* note 1.

26. Patt, Rapport & Barglow, *Follow-up of Therapeutic Abortion*, 20 ARCHIVES GEN. PSYCHIATRY 408 (1969).

27. Levene & Rigney, *supra* note 1.

28. Jansson, *Mental Disorders After Abortion*, 41 ACTA PSYCHIATRICA SCANDINAVICA 87, 90 (1965).

29. Clark, Forstner, Pond & Tredgold, *Sequels of Unwanted Pregnancy: A Follow-up of Patients Referred for Psychiatric Opinion*, 2 LANCET 501 (1968).

30. Mehlan, *Abstract*, in THE YEARBOOK OF OBSTETRICS & GYNECOLOGY 36 (1957-58).
31. Kolstad, *Therapeutic Abortion*, 36 ACTA OBSTERICIA ET GYNECOLOGICA SCANDINAVICA (Supp. No. 6, 1957).
32. Report of Dr. Brad Brekke, *summarized in* ABORTION, *supra* note 16, at 135-36.
33. Ford, Catelnuovo-Tedesco & Long, *Abortion: Is it a Therapeutic Procedure in Psychiatry?*, 218 J.A.M.A. 1173 (1971).
34. Barnes, Cohen, Stoeckle & McGuire, *Therapeutic Abortion: Medical and Social Sequels*, 75 ANNALS INTERNAL MED. 881 (1971).
35. Kretzschmar & Norris, *Psychiatric Implications of Therapeutic Abortion*, 98 AM. J. OBSTETRICS & GYNECOLOGY 368 (1967).
36. Gillis, *Follow-up After Abortion*, 1 BRIT. MED. J. 506 (1969).
37. Osofsky & Osofsky, *The Psychological Reaction of Patients to Legalized Abortion*, 42 AM. J. ORTHOPSYCHIATRY 48 (1972).
38. Malmfors, *The Problem of Woman Seeking Abortion*, *summarized in* ABORTION, *supra* note 16, at 133-35.
39. Aren, *On Legal Abortion in Sweden: Tentative Evaluation of Justification of Frequency During Last Decade*, 37 ACTA OBSTETRICIA ET GYNECOLOGICA SCANDINAVICA (Supp. No. 1, 1958).
40. It has been estimated that, in 1955, there were anywhere from 200,000 to 1,200,000 illegal abortions performed in the United States. Tietze & Lewit, *supra* note 5, at 29.
41. P. GEBBARD, W. POMEROY, C. MARTIN & C. CHRISTENSON, PREGNANCY, BIRTH AND ABORTION 119 (1958). This is based on a somewhat nonrandom sample of over 5,000 married women. Assuming that most women in the United States marry at some time in their lives and that the above sample of married women is reasonably representative of the country as a whole, it is not unreasonable to further estimate that one out of every five women has obtained an induced abortion by the time she has reached the age of 45.
42. Kummer, *supra* note 1, at 981.
43. David, *Abortion in Psychological Perspective*, 42 AM. J. ORTHOPSYCHIATRY 61, 62 (1972).
44. BUREAU OF THE CENSUS, U.S. DEP'T OF COMMERCE, STATISTICAL ABSTRACT OF THE UNITED STATES 49 (1971). In 1968 alone, a total of 339,000 illegitimate babies were born. The figure represents 9.7 percent of the total births. *Id.*
45. Cutright, *Illegitimacy: Myth, Causes and Cures*, 3 FAMILY PLANNING PERSPECTIVES 25 (1971).
46. The study was based on a sample of women aged 15 to 44 which represents most women's child bearing years. NATIONAL CENTER FOR HEALTH STATISTICS, U.S. DEP'T OF HEALTH, EDUCATION AND WELFARE, 18 MONTHLY VITAL STATISTICS REPORT 3 (Supp. No. 12, March 1970).
47. *Id.* at 1.

48. Christensen, *Child Spacing Analysis via Record Linkage: New Data Plus a Summing Up From Earlier Reports*, 25 MARRIAGE & FAMILY LIVING 272, 276 (1963).

49. Another possible outcome following the birth of an unwanted child to a mentally disturbed mother is that the mother will lose control of her aggressive impulses and beat or even murder the baby. It has been estimated that between 30,000 and 37,000 children are badly beaten by their parents each year. Zalba, *The Abused Child: A Survey of the Problem*, 11 SOCIAL WORK 3, 8 (1966). Furthermore, one study indicated that as many as 50 percent of these children may have been unwanted. *Id.* at 7.

A study by Resnick of 131 children murdered by a parent found that 14 percent of the murders were motivated by the child being unwanted. *See* Resnick, *Child Murder by Parents: A Psychiatric Review of Filicide*, 126 AM. J. PSYCHIATRY 325, 329 (1969). Another study by Resnick of 37 neonaticides (a child murdered by the parent within 24 hours of birth) found that 83 percent could be classified as resulting from the child's being unwanted. *See* Resnick, *Murder of the Newborn: A Psychiatric Review of Neonaticide*, 126 AM. J. PSYCHIATRY 1414 (1970).

50. Approximately 40 percent of all children born into poor families are unwanted. *See* Bumpass & Westoff, *The "Perfect Contraceptive" Population*, 169 SCI. 1177, 1179 (1970).

Surveys show that couples with incomes of less than $3000 desire the same number of children, three per family, as couples with incomes of greater than $10,000. Jaffe, *Family Planning and Poverty*, 26 J. MARRIAGE & FAMILY 467 (1964).

For more detailed discussion of the relationship between family planning and poverty, see H. SHEPPARD, EFFECTS OF FAMILY PLANNING ON POVERTY IN THE UNITED STATES (published by W. E. Upjohn Institute for Employment Research 1967); Campbell, *The Role of Family Planning in the Reduction of Poverty*, 30 J. MARRIAGE & FAMILY 236 (1968).

51. BUREAU OF THE CENSUS, *supra* note 44, at 140.

52. For further discussion of this point, see notes 75-89 *infra* & accompanying text.

53. Selected references representing literature showing the relationship between adverse experiences in childhood and subsequent mental disorders are: J. BOWLBY, CHILD CARE AND THE GROWTH OF LOVE (1965); I. CHEIN & D. WILNER, THE ROAD TO H (1964); S. GLUECK & E. GLUECK, UNRAVELLING JUVENILE DELINQUENCY (1950); Pavenstedt, *A Comparison of the Child Rearing Environment of the Upper-Lower, and Very-Low-Lower Class Families*, 35 AM. J. ORTHOPSYCHIATRY 89 (1965); Saul & Wenar, *Early Influences on Development and Disorders of Personality*, 34 PSYCHOANALYTIC Q. 327 (1965).

54. *See* Lieberman, *Preventive Psychiatry and Family Planning*, 26 J. MARRIAGE & FAMILY 471 (1964); Schwartz, *The Role of Family Planning in the Primary Prevention of Mental Illness*, 125 AM. J. PSYCHIATRY 1711 (1969).

55. Menninger, *Psychiatric Aspects of Contraception*, THERAPEUTIC ABORTION 250-51 (H. Rosen ed. 1954).

56. Responses to the question whether the couple wanted the child are not necessarily reliable. For further discussion of this problem see Pohlman, *"Wanted" and "Unwanted": Toward Less Ambiguous Definition*, 12 EUGENICS Q. 19 (1965).

57. Forssman & Thuwe, *One Hundred and Twenty Children Born After Application for Therapeutic Abortion Refused*, 42 ACTA PSYCHIATRICA SCANDINAVICA 71, 78-84 (1966).

58. *See* Barry & Barry, *Birth Order, Family Size and Schizophrenia*, 17 ARCHIVES GEN. PSYCHIATRY 435 (1967); Farina, Barry, Henry III, Garmez & Norman, *Birth Order of Recovered and Nonrecovered Schizophrenics*, 9 ARCHIVES GEN. PSYCHIATRY 224 (1963); Gregory, *An Analysis of Familial Data on Psychiatric Patients: Parental Age, Family Size, Birth Order, and Ordinal Position*, 12 BRIT. J. PREVENTIVE SOCIAL MED. 42 (1958); Gregory, *Family Data Concerning the Hypothesis of Hereditary Predisposition Toward Alcoholism*, 106 J. MENTAL SCI. 1068 (1960); Schooler, *Birth Order and Hospitalization for Schizophrenia*, 69 J. ABNORMAL & SOCIAL PSYCHOLOGY 574 (1964); Schooler, *Birth Order and Schizophrenia*, 4 ARCHIVES GEN. PSYCHIATRY 91 (1961).

59. *See* Schooler, *Birth Order and Hospitalization for Schizophrenia, supra* note 58.

60. P. WHELPTON, A. CAMPBELL & J. PATTERSON, FERTILITY AND FAMILY PLANNING IN THE UNITED STATES (1966).

61. *See, e.g.,* G. CAPLAN, PRINCIPALS OF PREVENTIVE PSYCHIATRY (1964).

62. 42 U.S.C. § 2809(a)(1) (1970) (originally enacted as Economic Opportunities Act of 1964, Pub. L. No. 88-452, tit. II, § 222(a)(1), 78 Stat. 508).

63. Economic Opportunity Amendments of 1971, S. 2007, 92d Cong., 1st Sess. (1971).

64. ECONOMIC OPPORTUNITY AMENDMENTS OF 1971 — VETO MESSAGE, H. DOC. NO. 92-48, 92d Cong., 1st Sess., S 21129 (1971).

65. *See* B. BETTELHEIM, THE CHILDREN OF THE DREAM (1969).

66. One indication of this is that suicide is one of the leading causes of death in the United States, claiming 22,000 lives in 1969. BUREAU OF THE CENSUS, *supra* note 44, at 58. Many authorities believe at least half of all suicides go unreported in order to protect survivors from embarrassment or to enable them to collect life insurance benefits.

67. In 1968, a total of 3,381,000 mental patients were treated in the nation's mental hospitals and outpatient clinics. The cost of mental ill-

ness, which would include the treatment for these three million patients, has been estimated at 20 billion dollars annually in the United States. BUREAU OF THE CENSUS, *supra* note 44, at 73. *See also* Conley, *An Approach to Measuring the Cost of Mental Illness*, 124 AM. J. PSYCHIATRY 755 (1967).

68. The number of alcoholics in the United States is estimated at nine million, making alcoholism far and away the nation's worst drug problem. U.S. DEP'T OF HEALTH, EDUCATION AND WELFARE, FIRST SPECIAL REPORT TO THE U.S. CONGRESS ON ALCOHOL AND HEALTH viii (1972). Alcohol also plays a major role in half the highway fatalities in the United States which each year claim thousands of lives. *Id.* Furthermore, public intoxication accounts for one-third of all arrests reported annually. *Id.* The percentage of arrests would rise to between 40 and 49 percent if such alcohol-related offenses such as driving while intoxicated, disorderly conduct, and vagrancy were considered.

Cirrhosis of the liver, most cases of which are the result of alcoholism, is one of the leading causes of death in the United States. BUREAU OF THE CENSUS, *supra* note 44, at 58.

69. The rate of addiction to hard narcotics has been growing in our large central cities and appears to be spreading to suburban areas. It has been estimated that there are 650,000 heroin addicts in the United States, and 400,000 in New York City alone. MED. WORLD NEWS, Feb. 16, 1971, at 20. Death from heroin overdose is a leading cause of death among teenagers in New York City. There were 447 of these deaths in 1970. MED. WORLD NEWS, April 16, 1971, at 6. Moreover, heroin addicts are responsible for a large proportion of "street crimes" in urban areas.

70. A high proportion of crimes of violence — aggravated assault, rape, robbery, and homicide — are committed by persons with a history of persistently antisocial behavior and other signs of severe maladjustment. *See* K. MENNINGER, THE CRIME OF PUNISHMENT 162-89 (1966), which contains an excellent discussion of the personality makeup of criminals. In the decade 1960 to 1970, the rate of violent crimes rose 157 percent. BUREAU OF THE CENSUS, *supra* note 44, at 140. In 1970, there were, according to FBI statistics, a total of 16,000 homicides, 37,000 forcible rapes, 330,000 aggravated assaults, and 348,000 robberies. *Id.*

71. An estimated two to three percent of our population is mentally retarded and in need of some support or supervision in order to live in the community. Seventy-five percent of these retarded persons have no demonstrable brain damage and are classed as "familial" (that is, their retardation is caused by a combination of genetic factors and inadequate child-rearing practices). Zigler, *Familial Mental Retardation: A Continuing Dilemma*, 155 SCI. 292 (1967).

72. *See Hearings on H.R. 3689 Before the Subcomm. on Public Health and Safety of the House Comm. on Interstate and Foreign Commerce*, 88th Cong., 1st Sess. 105 (1963). In 1968 alone, 3,381,000 mental patients were treated in the nation's mental hospitals and outpatient clinics. BUREAU OF THE CENSUS, *supra* note 44, at 73.

I would rank psychiatric illness second behind cardiovascular diseases, which cause 50 percent of all deaths, on the basis of the number of persons afflicted, the extent of their suffering, and the costs involved.

73. The women were asked whether, prior to the beginning of a given pregnancy, they and their husbands had decided that they did not want to have more children at any future time. If the answer was affirmative, the child was considered to have been unwanted. This assumes that, had the couple been using a perfect contraceptive, the child would not have been born.

The researchers believe that the true rate of unwanted births is higher than 19 percent because they assume that many women, not wishing to acknowledge that any of their children were in any sense unwanted, gave false responses to the interviewers.

In addition to the findings concerning unwanted births, Bumpass and Westoff also discovered that an additional 43 percent of births were timing failures (the couple did not want to have a child at that particular time, but had not necessarily decided to have no more children in the future). Only one-fourth of all the couples in the study were successful in preventing both unplanned and unwanted births. Bumpass & Westoff, *supra* note 50.

74. *See* notes 44-46 *supra* & accompanying text.

75. Segal & Tietze, *Contraceptive Technology: Current and Prospective Methods, reprinted in* REPORTS ON POPULATION/FAMILY PLANNING 4 (Oct. 1969).

76. *Id.*

77. Hardin, *The History and Future of Birth Control*, 10 PERSPECTIVES IN BIOLOGY & MED. 1, 11 (1966).

78. Segal & Tietze, *supra* note 75, at 9.

79. Djerassi, *Birth Control After 1984*, 169 SCI. 941 (1970).

80. Harkavy, et al., *Family Planning and Public Policy: Who Is Misleading Whom?*, 165 SCI. 367 (1969).

81. Black sociologist, Professor Charles V. Willie of Syracuse University has said:

> I must state categorically that many people in the black community are deeply suspicious of any family planning program initiated by whites. You probably have heard about but not taken seriously the call by some male-dominated black militant groups for females to eschew the use of contraceptives because they are pushed in the black community as "a method of ex-

terminating black people." While black females often take a
different view about contraceptives than their male companions, they too are concerned about the possibility of black genocide in America. The genocidal charge is neither "absurd"
nor "hollow" as some whites have contended. Neither is it
limited to residents of the ghetto, whether they be low-income
black militants or middle-aged black moderates. Position paper
by C. Willie, Professor and Chairman, Department of Sociol-
ogy at Syracuse, presented to the President's Commission on
Population Growth and the American Future, *reprinted in*
Population Reference Bureau, selection No. 37, Population
Reference Bureau, Inc. (1971).

82. Permitting unmarried teenagers to abort is not seen by the public as
encouraging promiscuity to quite the same extent as providing them
with contraceptives.

83. Pakter & Nelson, *Abortion in New York City: The First Nine Months,*
3 FAMILY PLANNING PERSPECTIVES 5 (1971).

84. *Id.* at 5.

85. *Id.* at 6.

86. The exact figures on marital status were not known at the time of this
study, but a sample survey showed that more than half of aborted resident women were unmarried. *Id.* at 8.

87. *Id.* at 6.

88. *Id.* at 12.

89. Tietze, The Potential Impact of Legal Abortion on Population Growth
in the United States, *prepared for* The Comm. on Population Growth
and the American Future (1971) (on file in the Case Western Reserve
Law Review office).

A PSYCHIATRIST'S VIEWS ON ABORTION

STEPHEN FLECK, M. D.

DISCUSSIONS OF THE PSYCHIATRIC ASPECTS of abortion have become rather frequent in the literature during recent years. Views have been offered by psychiatrists with little or only very occasional experience with this problem as well as by those who have had extensive, if not intensive, involvement with it.[1] To comment on a specific discussion, such as that of Dr. Richard Schwartz in this volume,[2] might be useful for a psychiatric audience but mean little to those more directly concerned with the clinical aspects of abortion or its sociopolitical parameters. In addition to some complementing remarks on items not covered by Dr. Schwartz, this article will concern the role of the psychiatrist in the field of abortion, tracing this role largely from a historical perspective. I shall indicate how far the profession has come and how much further I believe it should go in its contribution to the problem.

The past 100 years have seen the evolution of the psychiatrist from the status of an alienist — an isolated professional secluded in an institution, divorced professionally and geographically from the community — to various forms of participation in therapeutic and health-promoting programs. In this century the psychiatrist has come out of exile, so to speak, rejoining the profession in teaching hospitals and practicing increasingly in parallel with other medical personnel in the community. Yet this reintegration into medical pursuits has not been complete. Indeed, the psychiatric practitioner, especially under the influence of psychoanalytic guidelines, has typically sequestered himself in an office with relatively few patients. The relatively small and therapeutically oriented asylums of 100

179

years ago have given way to large state hospitals, where considerable attention is given to the bureaucratic issues and management of a large and complex subcommunity, quite often at the expense of therapeutic programs per se. In general hospitals and medical centers, however, the psychiatrist has enlarged his role as a teacher and consultant to other disciplines and as a therapist for emotionally disturbed patients. He has more and more become the guardian of person-focused medicine in these institutions.[3]

In the last two decades, if not since the end of World War II, psychiatrists have also been increasingly concerned with community-wide needs and preventive opportunities — not only for the prevention of mental illness but also for the prevention or correction of sociopathogenic conditions in various "communities," such as the military, industry, schools, or politically defined populations. Consequently, the psychiatrist's involvement with the abortion problem centers about two distinct parameters: the clinical level, through his involvement with obstetricians and patients in need or desirous of an abortion, and the community level, where abortion may be a preventive measure with regard to personally unwanted or socially undesirable reproduction. As to the latter, the psychiatrist's involvement may be such that he becomes an advocate of revision of the abortion statutes.[4]

Before discussing some of these roles in more detail, it should be asserted that from the standpoint of the clinician (whether obstetrician or psychiatrist), every woman — as an issue of health and of maximally appropriate self-determination of her life and fate — should have the opportunity to determine whether and when to become pregnant and whether and when to become a mother. I find it more difficult to speak of this as a right, since in every other respect matters of one's body, health, remedial health care, and the pursuit of one's life goals are (to the best of my knowledge) not spelled out anywhere as rights, but are a matter of social philosophy. They are legal issues only insofar as the Constitution and our laws reflect these basic tenets of being human.

I. THE PSYCHIATRIST AND THE
OBJECTIONS TO ABORTION

The traditional and historic interdiction of the performance of abortions derived from the known dangers of abortion to the health and the life of the abortee.[5] For at least a century this danger has been nonexistent, provided that the abortion is properly performed under sterile conditions and, when indicated, with the administration of antibiotic medication. Had there been any interest or foolhardy intent to perform organ transplants 500 or 5,000 years ago, we would probably have had to institute laws against such experimental surgery. But such laws would no longer be necessary because in principle the procedures are now more life-saving than life-endangering. Indeed, these very serious and potentially dangerous operations are performed throughout the world solely on the basis of clinical judgments and assessments; no laws govern them, despite new and very difficult ethical issues which have arisen in connection with organ transplants and even the definition of "death" itself.[6]

Abortion, if properly performed, is not in this dangerous category; it is almost 100 percent safe during the first trimester.[7] Religious or philosophical objections to abortion, therefore, must have no more influence on medical or clinical considerations than objections by certain religious sects have on transfusion or any surgery. In other words, such objections are certainly an individual's right, and should be protected, but no individual beliefs, whether shared by a minority or a majority, should entitle a group to dictate like standards of behavior for everybody.

Physicians, unfortunately, have failed to recognize how their cultural and ethical indoctrinations — which include discriminatory attitudes toward women — have influenced their clinical objectivity in this connection.[8] We do not punish people who have venereal disease or drink excessively; nor do we refuse to treat them because their behavior has deviated from the physician's standards of behavior and ethics. Indeed, doctors are morally enjoined to treat their enemies and those legally labeled criminal when in need. A physician or hospital which permits special beliefs to interfere with clinical objectivity is violating medico-ethical tenets when it refuses consideration and relief to a pregnant woman who does not wish to become a mother. Some doctors who would not dare refuse treatment to a patient with primary syphilis on the ground that he ought to bear the consequences and take a chance on developing paresis later on show no compunction about making the equivalent argument to a woman pregnant conceivably through her own carelessness, or even due to failure of a contraceptive prescribed by him.

No person can be harmed by a properly performed abortion — except possibly, but very improbably, the woman on whom it is performed. In England complications occur in less than 30 abortees per 100,000.[9]

There is much discussion about the destruction of the fetus, called murder by some. This is an important legal and ethical question, and abortion could be said to reflect an expression of unconcern for life and its value. But physicians and health professionals as a whole, being preoccupied with the preservation of life and health, are hardly guilty of any such lack of concern. Also, this particular form of murder, if it be that, seems a somewhat hypocritical concern in a society that does little to prevent some 30,000 annual criminal murders and that condones, as do most societies, murder in the service of the national goals determined by its leadership.

From the psychiatrist's vantage point, either a fetus or even a newborn baby can realize its potential to become a person only if its biological parents and society at large supply the essential psychosocial nutrients.[10] It is known that women who become mothers unwillingly, or who are unprepared for parenthood, more often fail to provide their children with the ingredients essential to becoming a person capable of an inner-directed life[11] and social adaptation than do mothers who have become so willingly.[12]

Unfortunately, the experience of some psychiatrists has been limited to the examination and study of psychological consequences of an abortion in patients who seek psychiatric treatment for reasons and symptoms quite unrelated to the abortion. Some of these "authorities" have argued that an abortion is a very traumatic experience. One even asserted, after disclaiming firsthand clinical experience with abortion, that only "sick women seek abortions because women are here to conceive and raise children."[13] I do not know who gave women this mandate or what evidence there is that child-bearing is the only healthful way for females to pursue happiness, but I do believe that such a restriction abridges the constitutionally guaranteed blessings of liberty and security of person. Psychiatrists who have had firsthand experience with the abortion problem know that, although it is a traumatic experience, it rarely has significant lasting consequences.[14]

This is true despite many legally imposed and sociocultural conditions which render the experience unnecessarily traumatic from the clinical standpoint. No operation can be performed without traumatizing both tissues and feelings; in fact, to be ill is an emotional trauma. The traumatic consequences of abortion are discernible through painstaking psychotherapeutic investigation but are of no gross clinical significance compared with 9 months of unwanted pregnancy and a lifetime of unwelcome motherhood, possibly unwelcome fatherhood, and a jeopardized life for the child-to-be.[15] Furthermore, what must be appreciated about such judgments is that they come mostly from male psychiatrists, whose clinical observations seem to be predetermined by inadequate knowledge of women and by disregard of the needs of children. Such "experts" also seem unduly influenced by religious philosophies promulgated for the most part by males who have eschewed sexual activity and by male legislators who waited 130 years after the birth of the Constitution before acknowledging that men and women are created equal for the purpose of suffrage.[16]

II. THE PSYCHIATRIST'S SPECIAL KNOWLEDGE

As a collaborator with and consultant to obstetrical colleagues, the psychiatrist should function as an expert with special knowledge and experience concerning all emotional and psychological aspects of fertility, infertility, and reproduction. In this connection, psychiatrists have contributed to the understanding of emotional changes and problems incident to menstruation and have studied in detail the psychological changes and personal maturation which occur during pregnancy. They have participated in research on infertility, which remains suspect to having some causal origins in emotional or psychoendocrine imbalances.[17] Furthermore, psychiatrists are concerned with the emotional impact of infertility on women and couples, no matter what its source or duration.

However, because of their special knowledge, psychiatrists are particularly aware that pregnancy, especially the first pregnancy, is a very central event in a woman's life. To be constructive for all concerned, this event demands not merely a willingness to go through pregnancy but the capacity to do so in a maturing manner and to assume the many emotional tasks necessary for endowing the infant with the essentials of life and growth. The same principles apply to a father-to-be, who must not only be motivated for fatherhood but capable of becoming a satisfied and satisfying member in the family triad.

Delivery or the post-partum period can precipitate or coincide with a major psychiatric disturbance, usually a psychosis. This occurs in 1 to 2 cases per 1000 deliveries.[18] In these circumstances, both psychiatric consultation and prolonged psychiatric hospital treatment are required. No such major psychiatric complications have been reported as a clear consequence of abortion. Moreover, 25 percent of all conceptions fail to reach term, mostly on an involuntary basis, without significant psychiatric sequellae.[19]

III. THE PSYCHIATRIST AND THE ABORTION DECISION

With regard to abortion, the psychiatrist's role has until recently been a minor one. He usually was consulted as to the advisability of abortion, if the law *and* the hospital rules permitted it, in patients with known psychiatric illness. Otherwise, his opinion and advice were rarely demanded or required, because the operation was usually performed for medical indications — that is, intercurrent or pre-existing illnesses which constituted a danger to the woman's life if complicated by pregnancy. With the advances in medical and surgical care, such indications have become very rare. But the increasing demand for abortion and the usual statutory requirements that the life of a woman must be threatened before an abortion can be performed have brought to the fore the contingency of self-destructive behavior induced by the pregnant state as an "indication" for abortion (*i.e.*, an indication required by law, rather than one arrived at on clinical grounds).[20]

The psychiatrist has therefore become increasingly involved in those hospitals where abortions are performed and where abortion committees made up of representatives of all major medical specialties review proposals for abortions presented by obstetricians or general practitioners. Psychiatric opinions as to the likelihood of a threat to life because of emotional distress have, unhappily, become the major justification for performing abortions. A statement to this effect is almost always sought from a psychiatrist. In this area he is, unfortunately, on slippery ground indeed: suicide during pregnancy is rather less common than in a comparable group of women of child-bearing age, whereas the suicide rate during the post-partum period, or certainly during the first year following delivery of a child, is higher than that of a comparable group without delivery.[21] Thus, the psychiatrist is called upon to make a predictive judgment about a risk of little statistical significance in an epidemiological sense, but a fifty-fifty proposition for each woman who presents herself as desiring an abortion and threatens that she will do anything to "get rid of that thing inside me." When relatively affluent pregnant women present themselves in this way, the physician's dilemma is not altogether absolute in terms of risk; they can travel to places where abortions can be performed safely if demanded and if the condition seems to warrant it in the judgment of the obstetrician consulted.

Therefore, the major burden of such decisions falls on women who cannot afford such freedom of movement and who would be likely to harm themselves by seeking an illegal abortion under frequently unfavorable and unsafe conditions. Some such women are well known to all large community hospitals, where they appear in emergency rooms bleeding, and often infected, from an incomplete abortion. Death rarely ensues, but it does occur in hundreds of women every year in the United States. In fact, they constitute the single largest category of pregnancy fatalities. Permanent health damage and even infertility may more often be the price the impecunious woman has to pay for terminating an unwanted pregnancy.

Any legal statutes that interfere with clinical judgment and its implementation in the matter of abortion, therefore, clearly work discriminatorily against women with limited resources. Such is the penalty of poverty. Deficient material and educational resources lead to impoverished lives, and sexual activity can become one of the few available satisfactions. When an unwanted pregnancy occurs and cannot be interrupted, the cycle repeats itself, as the child suffers the psychosocial and caloric malnutrition which was the fate of the mother, if not of both parents.

A further dilemma in the psychiatrist's role as a collaborator with the obstetrician derives from the fact that women whose emotional health is relatively strong may make appropriate decisions for themselves about a particular pregnancy without much help and with little emotional turmoil. Paradoxically, in most states such a woman has been required to feign emotional disturbance and threaten self-destructive behavior, even though she has no such intention in truth but is simply determined not to become a mother at that particular time.[22] It is legally easier but clinically more challenging for the psychiatrist to determine whether a woman who in fact was emotionally disturbed prior to becoming pregnant would be more endangered by an abortion than by the continuing pregnancy (and/or by the mother role in terms of her future health and adjustment). Thus, the psychiatrist and the obstetrician can help sick people reach clinically sound decisions, but they have been "legally" prevented from helping rather healthy women achieve clinically and personally sound solutions in the form of abortion.

Because the psychiatrist is often the sole key through which the obstetrician can implement his own clinical judgment, he often becomes the routine handmaiden for the obstetrician. This is a not altogether wholesome and clinically advantageous relationship. Furthermore, there is no doubt that after consulting with a psychiatrist over a period of time the obstetrician will be quite able to make sound clinical judgments about the emotional issues involved without any further psychiatric advice. But this educational role for the psychiatrist has been precluded by the nonclinical abortion rules and statutes.

While acknowledging that every woman who desires an abortion should have this request considered without legalistic hindrances, no physician acts responsibly unless he regards any treatment request as a complex issue. Motivation, ambivalences, and clinical realities in terms of consequences are the doctor's concern whether the request is for abortion, for other surgery, or for medication not necessarily indicated in the physician's judgment. Because pregnancy is an emotionally charged event not only for the woman but also for her partner and possibly other family members, a greater social field must be considered along with the individual personal features of the pregnant woman.

Again, I do not advocate consideration of a spouse's involvement, or that of other significant persons, as a "right," but often if not always as sound clinical practice. If the obstetrician himself does not want to consider these parameters, he should — aside from any psychiatric consultations — have a competent social worker or nurse-clinician collaborating with him.[23]

IV. THE PSYCHIATRIST AND BIRTH CONTROL

Another collaborative role between psychiatrists and obstetricians, also of recent origin, concerns the emotional aspects of reproductive control in general. Mixed attitudes toward sex and parenthood and inter-spouse conflicts in this respect are often involved in contraceptive failures. Birth control lapses often lead to the quest for abortion, which should serve only as a stopgap measure for contraceptive failures. It has become apparent since the introduction of widely available birth control measures that women — though culturally and ethically quite at ease about interfering with reproduction — still have complex psychological attitudes toward temporary or permanent infertility. Such ambivalences and conflicts often lead to contraceptive failure, either through various symptoms and discomforts attributed by the woman to the contraceptive or by direct interference with contraceptive activity by either partner.

Because many contraceptive failures derive from such rather subtle and covert conflicts around contraceptive practice, it must be pointed out here that the prescribing physician is under some obligation to help with the consequences of his "treatment failure," just as he would have to remedy any other untoward effects of his recommendations. Indeed, contraceptives that are almost completely effective in a technical sense are employed so erratically that their overall effectiveness is reduced to 25 percent in married couples.[24]

Obstetricians as well as psychiatrists must be aware of the common ambivalences in most women, especially in our society, toward sexual behavior, reproduction, and motherhood. Here, again, obstetricians must also learn how to deal with couples, instead of with only one partner, because the primary conflict may reside in the spouse. An imposition of even temporary infertility changes the equilibrium between marital partners. Psychiatric expertise and research are strongly required at this time to clarify these issues further and to help obstetricians and family physicians become readily aware of them so that they can advise and prescribe more sagaciously with regard to reproductive control, including abortion.

V. The Psychiatrist and the Hospital Setting

The psychiatrist generally has inherited certain elements of what is fondly referred to as "the old family doctor," still a valued physician role. Currently the psychiatrist is the only specialist whose primary concern is with the patient as a person. In our present medical care systems, most specialists, and even most general practitioners, often have little opportunity to know their patients as persons, or to learn much about their life in general. In addition, these modern doctors often do not treat other members of the family, as used to be routine. Consequently, they need guidance in the rapid assessment of character features and personality characteristics, procedures which are the psychiatrist's expertise. Especially in large community and teaching hospitals, which are manned primarily by specialists and student doctors, the psychiatrist has become the custodian and the teacher of person-focused care for all staff, including obstetricians. Through such education, young obstetricians can become familiar with the necessary considerations and approaches to women in general and to those seeking abortions in particular.[25]

But the psychiatrist must also appreciate that obstetricians and obstetrical nurses or midwives have usually chosen their specialty because they want to help create new human beings, not prevent them. Thus, conflicts about contraception and abortion among the staff may exist. These require expert attention in in-service training programs if such attitudes are not to burden patients.[26] Ideally, abortion should be managed by a special team or group of obstetricians, midwives or nurse-clinicians, and social workers, with psychiatric consultation available.

Of course, other specialist consultation should also be available, particularly the services of a geneticist. Parents or parents-to-be should be able to avoid reproduction if they do not wish to risk a genetically unwholesome offspring. The state should at least not interfere with parents who desire an abortion of a conceptus with a known risk of an hereditary handicap, or with a defect determined by amniocentesis, or which may have been inadvertently exposed to possible damage through radiation or drugs. To condemn people to assume parenthood of a child destined to an unhealthy life when it is preventable seems carrying "a concern for the right to live" to the absurd.[27]

Sharing these responsibilities through teamwork greatly reduces the burden of decision on any one individual in the group and can provide ideal care for the patient. A social worker or nurse-clinician can concern him- or herself (preferably the latter) with the applicant's history and life situation and discuss the pros and cons of the abortion requested. If a truly psychiatric issue exists, the patient can be referred by the intake worker to the consulting psychiatrist, just as she might be referred to any other medical specialist. The obstetrician then can make his decision about the abortion in a short time, based on the examination of the patient and the data provided. He may wish to confirm them or reestablish them in a brief interview for his own satisfaction.

The abortion could be performed then and there. Or if indicated — as it sometimes is for women whose decision is not firm — there may be an interim period followed by another interview before a final decision is made. Generally, however, such a waiting period should not be routinely imposed.

Unfortunately, the demand in many of these areas is great, so that no such comprehensive care and attention are given to many women seeking an abortion, and abortions may often be performed without sufficient clinical consideration of the woman's needs, wishes, possible conflicts, etc. On the other hand, because of anti-abortion laws, hospitals have typically erected elaborate safeguards against legal jeopardies by requiring several consultations and a final decision from an anonymous committee whose members do not have direct contact with the patient (to ensure "neutrality").

In such situations, the patient is subjected to a considerable amount of possible trauma, especially if (as discussed earlier) she is relatively healthy from an emotional standpoint. A more disturbed woman might justifiably be screened extensively. But on the whole, such an atmosphere suggests that the procedure is very critical, which naturally arouses fears and reinforces myths and guilt, especially if the woman's religion happens to interdict abortion. Even in states with "permissive" laws, however, the medical profession and hospital administration often continue with restrictive practices more stringent than the legal encumbrances.[28] Thus, education of our own professions remains an urgent task.

Another problem in many hospitals is that the abortee is mixed in with new mothers on the obstetrical floors or with women having major surgical illnesses on the gynecological floors. Such exposure is far from ideal, even if it lasts only a few hours. An abortion performed during the first trimester can be an outpatient procedure for most women, given a few hours' rest.[29] Again, it must be remembered that most obstetricians and obstetrical nurses do not seek their specialty in order to abort life, and they may unintentionally convey hostility to an abortee. It is important that 'abortions be performed in special areas of the hospital and by those who believe they are doing a service that is beneficial to the woman and to society at large, rather than by those who believe that such operations, albeit legal, are still sinful and disgraceful.

VI. The Psychiatrist's Ideal Roles

This brings us to some thoughts about the most effective functions for the psychiatrist in connection with abortion, both now and in the future.

A. Education

The psychiatrist can and should convey to colleagues, other health professionals, and the public in general (young people in particular) the issues raised by reproduction with consent. Only if it is clear that pregnancy and parenthood must become matters not of simple choice but of informed choice, in terms of what parenthood involves, can young people be expected to make decisions consistent with their self-interest and life goals as well as with societal prerogatives. There can be no room in a free society for enforced pregnancy, any more than there can be for any other enforced change of a person's body. Nor can enforced parenthood be reconciled with good mental and family health. People who are not ready, willing, or able to function as parents should be helped to avoid parenthood if possible, and abortion is one of the tools in this pursuit.[30]

B. Birth Control

There is at this time no more important issue before our society and before psychiatry than the prevention of unwanted offspring, which Dr. Schwartz has assessed in detail. Further population growth is probably not desirable; and most people would opt for small families if they had a choice, despite the myth that children are always a blessing. Children certainly can be a godsend, but many times are not.

Furthermore, this society's attitudes are far from consistent with the proposition that children invariably are a blessing. It is currently witnessing the unbelievably cruel spectacle of hundreds of thousands of children who are neglected, whom nobody wanted, and who are inadequately cared for in temporary foster homes because they are awaiting final disposition in the form of adoption. Nobody wants to adopt them, however, for any number of justifiable reasons. Yet had their mothers been permitted or helped to abort, this would have prevented that much social and emotional suffering.[31]

Even more significant evidence of our society's lack of concern for the child is that whenever the fiscal belt needs to be tightened, the first reduction of governmental outlay occurs in those services that most directly affect children: the educational systems, medical care, child welfare programs, aid to dependent children, etc. This would not be the case in a society that truly considers children a blessing. Our society may say that children are our first priority because they are "our future," but in actuality it behaves quite differently.

C. Informed Parenthood

Psychiatrists insist that parenthood should occur with the consent of both partners and that they should be informed of its consequences. Informed and planned parenthood, therefore, entails learning not only how to prepare formulas and a balanced diet, or bring home a paycheck, but how to enculturate young people of all ages and help them become independent, inner-directed adults who can cope with their environment productively. Because there is considerable biologically engendered striving for sexual activity, for pregnancy, and for early motherhood, young people must be helped to be aware of these feelings and to channel them appropriately, to reconcile them with their life goals, and to consider the evolutionary life cycle of babies. Parenthood is permanent, not just for the first year of the baby's life, and uncared-for children often become uncaring parents.[32]

Women in particular must be educated and helped to assert their needs in a society that still discriminates against them in many respects. They need to think clearly about their role in life. If they want to become mothers, they must understand that this entails some 20 to 30 years of maternal primacy, unless they can provide substitute care. This period must fit into their personal life goals and roles as workers or professionals. They must be helped to learn that there are no totally advantageous choices: postponing parenthood can carry as high a price as does parenthood that is premature in terms of the parents' development.

Our society as a whole must learn that life as a single person can be worthwhile, that childless marriages are not necessarily tragic or a failure, and that the single child need not be significantly disadvantaged compared to children who have siblings.[33]

VII. Conclusions and Predictions

The cultural, traditional, and possibly religious attitudes, myths, and shibboleths about child-bearing come within the province of a community-minded psychiatrist because they touch upon issues of the mental health of any population. More specifically, there are few psychiatric patients, even those whose condition is caused by an identifiable biological factor, who have not suffered to some degree, often a major degree, from feeling unwanted. While this is a loose and difficult concept, and although from the parents' standpoint such a person may have been wanted very much, the child's perception can deviate from that of his parents, often correctly. This is not to say that a child should never feel unwanted, but that many parents, because of anxiety or psychological disorders in themselves or because of disappointment over an unhealthy child (or even a child of the less desired sex), convey unwantedness in some significant way over a period of time.

The sense of unwantedness conveyed by some parents seems to relate to the national attitudes toward child care mentioned earlier and is also discernible in the widespread condemnation and apparent dislike of young people's behavior. Adults often express their anxiety about, if not dislike of, adolescents and young adults whose general views and values deviate from the parental generation. This has always been so and may be a necessary stage for young people in achieving full adulthood. Nevertheless, the older generation frequently reacts as if it has been indicted for failing as parents, and some respond to this challenge with wholesale condemnation of youth.

Today, young people are directing an especially strong challenge to the sexual standards of the past, and there has been a considerable upswing of sexual activity among them — or at least in the openness about sexual activity and a reduced concern with, and fear of, pregnancy and venereal disease. The increasing demand for abortion among young people is not likely to change soon unless contraception becomes highly effective *in practice*, which is not the case now. Effective sex education, family life preparation, and the prevention of unwelcome pregnancies are obviously the task and obligation of all those concerned with the education and health of the young and their future welfare. The benefits of unencumbered, clinically adjudged abortion practices have been demonstrated in New York City: during the first year of such practice, out-of-wedlock births were reduced by 7.5 percent.[34]

An ambivalence toward sexual activity will probably continue to beset even those young people whose attitudes toward sex have not been prejudiced by Victorian tenets. And because no birth control method is 100 percent effective, the need for abortion will remain with us. Furthermore, one must recognize a considerable tendency in some, if not many, women to at least find out whether they can become pregnant, without necessarily wishing to become mothers 9 months later. There are also some women who feel so much better when they are pregnant that they will become pregnant again and again, even though they may not actually wish to add to their families.[35] Repeated demands for abortion can be expected from these women unless their frustrations in other areas of life are relieved.[36] Obviously they need not only to obtain abortions, but to recognize and correct, if possible, their particular need to be pregnant.

In the sense of literally aborting unwanted pregnancies, abortion also remains an important stopgap for the psychiatrist's general proposition that unwanted parenthood is undesirable for the mental health of both parent and child. A significant decrease in the incidence of psychiatric illness might be accomplished if unwanted parenthood were prevented. We also know that unwilling parents are prone to exhibit violence toward their offspring and that people who commit violent acts often have been exposed to and have been the victims of such acts.

In brief, women's and children's "rights" to optimal opportunities in our society deserve our respect, if not our protection, and women need the opportunity for a regulated life pattern balanced between motherhood and other roles, just as children need an optimal environment in a parental home. These issues demand not only our verbal and intellectual consent, but also our actions. Abortion by a properly qualified professional or professional team·is one such act.

NOTES

1. *See generally* L. LADER, ABORTION (1966); H. ROSEN, ABORTION IN AMERICA (1967); THE TERRIBLE CHOICE: THE ABORTION DILEMMA (R. Cooke ed. 1968); Beck, Newman & Lewit, *Abortion — A National Public and Mental Health Problem,* 59 AM. J. PUB. HEALTH 2131, 2133-34 (1969); Fleck, *Some Psychiatric Aspects of Abortion,* 151 J. NERVOUS & MENTAL DISEASE 42 (1970); Ford et al., *Abortion: Is it a Therapeutic Procedure in Psychiatry?,* 218 J.A.M.A. 1173 (1971); Gabrielson et al., *Adolescent Attitudes Toward Abortion: Effects on Contraceptive Practice,* 61 AM. J. PUB. HEALTH 730 (1971); Heller & Whittington, *Colorado Story: Change in Law on Therapeutic Abortions — Denver General Hospital Experience,* 125 AM. J. PSYCHIATRY 809 (1968); Kimball, *Some Observations Regarding Unwanted Pregnancies and Therapeutic Abortions,* 35 OBSTETRICS & GYNECOLOGY 293 (1970); Niswander, Klein & Randall, *Changing Attitudes Toward Therapeutic Abortion,* 196 J.A.M.A. 1140 (1966); Senay, *Therapeutic Abortion — Clinical Aspects,* 23 ARCH. GEN. PSYCHIATRY 408 (1970); Sloane, *The Unwanted Pregnancy,* 280 NEW ENGLAND J. MED. 1206 (1969).
2. *See* Schwartz, *Abortion on Request: The Psychiatric Implications,* in this volume.
3. *See generally* G. BIBRING & R. KAHANA, LECTURES IN MEDICAL PSYCHOLOGY — AN INTRODUCTION TO THE CARE OF PATIENTS (1968); R. CAPLAN, PSYCHIATRY AND THE COMMUNITY IN NINETEENTH CENTURY AMERICA (1969); S. WERKMAN, THE ROLE OF PSYCHIATRY IN MEDICAL EDUCATION (1966); Lidz & Fleck, *Integration of Medical and Psychiatric Methods and Objectives on a Medical Service,* 12 PSYCHOSOMATIC MED. 103 (1950); Kahana, *Studies in Medical Psychology: A Brief Summary,* 3 PSYCHIATRIC MED. 1 (1972).
4. *See* GROUP FOR THE ADVANCEMENT OF PSYCHIATRY, THE DIMENSIONS OF COMMUNITY PSYCHIATRY, No. 69, Vol. VI (1968). *See also* Caplan, *supra* note 3.

5. H. ROSEN, THE TERRIBLE CHOICE: THE ABORTION DILEMMA, *supra* note 1.
6. *See generally* J. KATZ, EXPERIMENTATION WITH HUMAN BEINGS (1972).
7. INTERNATIONAL CONFERENCE ON ABORTION: HOT SPRINGS, VIRGINIA, 1968 (R. Hall ed. 1970); Connell, *Legal Abortions and the Hospital's Role*, 7 HOSPITAL PRACTICE 143 (1972); Ford et al., *supra* note 1; Niswander, Klein & Randall, *supra* note 1; Pakter & Nelson, *Abortion in New York City and the First Nine Months*, 3 FAMILY PLANNING PERSPECTIVES 5 (No. 3, 1971); Tietze & Lewit, *Legal Abortions: Early Medical Complications*, 3 FAMILY PLANNING PERSPECTIVES 4 (No. 10, 1971).
8. *See generally* Hardin, *Abortion or Compulsory Pregnancy?*, 30 J. MARRIAGE & FAMILY 246 (1968); Rossi, *Equality Between the Sexes: An Immodest Proposal*, 93 DAEDALUS 607 (1964).
9. Connell, *supra* note 7.
10. *See generally* J. BOWLBY, CHILD CARE AND THE GROWTH OF LOVE (1965); E. ERIKSON, INSIGHT AND RESPONSIBILITY (1964); E. ERIKSON, CHILDHOOD AND SOCIETY (1950); T. LIDZ, THE PERSON (1968).
11. By "inner-directed," I mean the capacity to plan one's own life and future in harmony with one's environment, as opposed to being directed primarily by external forces.
12. *See generally* T. LIDZ, *supra* note 9; Caplan, *The Disturbance of the Mother-Child Relationship by Unsuccessful Attempts at Abortion*, 38 MENTAL HYGIENE 67 (1954); Forssman & Thuwe, *One Hundred and Twenty Children Born After Application for Therapeutic Abortion Refused*, 42 ACTA PSYCHIATRICA SCANDINAVICA 71 (1966); Oppel & Roysten, *Teen Age Births: Some Social, Psychological and Physical Sequelae*, 61 AM. J. PUB. HEALTH 751 (1971); Pavenstedt, *A Comparison of the Child-Rearing Environment of the Upper-Lower and Very-Low-Lower Class Families*, 35 AM. J. ORTHOPSYCHIATRY 89 (1965).
13. Galdston, *Other Aspects (Psychiatric) of the Abortion Problem*, in ABORTION IN THE UNITED STATES (M. Calderone ed. 1959).
14. *See* sources cited in note 7 *supra*. *See also* Jansson, *Mental Disorders After Abortion*, 41 ACTA PSYCHIATRICA SCANDINAVICA 87 (1965); Kummer, *Post-Abortion Psychiatric Illness — A Myth?*, 119 AM. J. PSYCHIATRY 980 (1963); Osofsky & Osofsky, *The Psychological Reactions of Patients to Legalized Abortion*, 42 AM. J. PSYCHIATRY 48 (1972); Simon, Zenturio & Rothman, *Psychiatric Illness Following Therapeutic Abortion*, 124 AM. J. PSYCHIATRY 59 (1967).
15. *See* Lieberman, *Preventive Psychiatry and Family Planning*, 26 J. MARRIAGE & FAMILY 471 (1964).
16. *See, e.g.*, Lieberman, *supra* note 15; Rossi, *supra* note 8; Rossi, *Transition to Parenthood*, 30 J. MARRIAGE & FAMILY 26 (1968).

17. T. BENEDECK & B. RUBENSTEIN, THE SEXUAL CYCLE IN WOMEN (1942); Benedeck, *The Psychology of Pregnancy*, in PARENTHOOD 137 (E. Anthony & T. Benedeck eds. 1970). *See also* Fleck, *Pregnancy as a Symptom of Adolescent Maladjustment*, 2 INT. J. SOCIAL PSYCHIATRY 118 (1956).

18. J. HAMILTON, POSTPARTUM PSYCHIATRIC PROBLEMS (1962); Yalom et al., *"Post Partum" Blues Syndrome*, 18 ACTA. GEN. PSYCHIATRICA 16 (1969).

19. P. GEBHARD ET AL., PREGNANCY, BIRTH AND ABORTION (1958); F. TAUSSIG, ABORTION, SPONTANEOUS AND INDUCED: MEDICAL AND SOCIAL ASPECTS (1936).

20. *See, e.g.*, Lebensohn, *Abortion, Psychiatry and the Quality of Life*, 128 AM. J. PSYCHIATRY 946 (1972).

21. *See, e.g.*, Fleck, *supra* note 1.

22. *See, e.g.*, Lebensohn, *supra* note 20.

23. A woman is much preferred in this role because pregnancy and motherhood are female and feminine territory.

24. *See, e.g.*, Bumpass & Westoff, *The "Perfect Contraceptive" Population*, 169 SCIENCE 1177 (1970); Lehfeldt, *Willful Exposure to Unwanted Pregnancy*, 78 AM. J. OBSTETRICS & GYNECOLOGY 661 (1959); Lidz, *Emotional Factors in the Success of Contraception*, 20 STERILITY & FERTILITY 761 (1969); Sturgis, *Oral Contraceptives and Their Effect on Sex Behavior*, 2 MED. ASPECTS OF HUMAN SEXUALITY 8 (1968).

25. Since the psychiatrist knows how to work in teams with social workers and other health workers, he can also point the way to his colleagues in this respect.

26. *Cf.* Char & McDermott, *Abortions and Acute Identity Crisis in Nurses*, 128 AM. J. PSYCHIATRY 952 (1972).

27. *See* Fraser, *Genetic Counselling*, 6 HOSPITAL PRACTICE 49 (1971).

28. Fleck, *supra* note 1; Heller & Whittington, *supra* note 1.

29. *See, e.g.*, Gillis, *Follow-Up After Abortion*, 1 BRITISH MED. J. 506 (1969).

30. *Cf.* Brunswick, *Adolescent Health, Sex, and Fertility*, 61 AM. J. PUB. HEALTH 711 (1971); Lieberman, *Leveling with Young People About Sex*, 210 J.A.M.A. 711 (1969).

31. In addition, the problem is exacerbated by the tens of thousands of children who are beaten each year. *See generally* H. MAAS & R. ENGLER, CHILDREN IN NEED OF PARENTS (1959); Steele, *Parental Abuse of Infants and Small Children*, in PARENTHOOD, *supra* note 16, at 449-77.

32. *See generally* sources cited in notes 15, 16, 30 & 31 *supra*.

33. *Cf.* Rossi, *Transition to Parenthood*, 30 J. MARRIAGE & FAMILY 26 (1968).

34. Brunswick, *supra* note 30; Connell, *supra* note 7.

35. *See* Lehfeldt, *supra* note 24; Lidz, *supra* note 24.
36. For example, pregnancy may occur to ward off emotional pain or depression, and a significant coincidence has been noticed between an "unwanted pregnancy" and death of, or separation from, a close family member. (Unpublished data from ongoing research by M. Swigar.)

ABORTION PRACTICES IN THE UNITED STATES: A MEDICAL VIEWPOINT

KENNETH R. NISWANDER, M. D.

ACCORDING TO ALAN GUTTMACHER, "Illegal or criminal abortion is the only great pandemic disease which remains unrecognized and untreated by modern medicine."[1] Criminal abortion continues to be a major cause of maternal death. In fact, a 1965 study reported that criminal abortion over the previous 20 years in New York City accounted for an increasing percentage of puerperal deaths.[2] It also noted that the increased number of puerperal deaths seemed inversely proportional to the decreasing number of therapeutic abortions performed in New York at that time. One-third of the maternal deaths in California between 1957 and 1962 occurred following illegal abortions.[3] Happily, the number of legal abortions performed in New York and in California has increased significantly. Recent experience in New York, where abortion on demand is now available by statute,[4] suggests that the number of maternal deaths related to abortion has decreased precipitously.[5] A similar decrease in abortion-related maternal deaths has been noted in California, where abortion on demand is virtually available de facto.[6] Presumably, a similar decrease in the number of abortion-related maternal deaths could be expected if all states followed the lead of New York and California in making abortion more readily available.

The widespread prevalence of abortion has never been seriously questioned. A conservative estimate of the number of illegal abortions in the United States is 300,000 out of a total of 1,000,000 annually.[7] Kinsey found that 22 percent of the married women he interviewed had had one or more abortions *in marriage* by the age of 45.[8] Nearly 95 percent of the premarital pregnancies in

199

his sample were resolved by abortion.[9]   Obviously, modern society, like earlier ones, finds a frequent need for pregnancy interruption. Existing laws in many states prevent legal pregnancy interruption, and criminal abortion results. Since abortion that can be performed legally under the guise of existing medical and social sanctions is known to be safer than illegally procured interruption of pregnancy, it is important to study the historical background of abortions, the contemporary indications of therapeutic abortions, and the current legal abortion procedures in order to understand the contemporary medical abortion practices in the United States.

I. History

Abortion is an ancient practice.   The records of almost every civilization indicate knowledge of abortifacient agents and abortive techniques. Among primitive people, these were gruesome when practiced in the extreme, and they remain so among certain primitive tribes today. One tribe, for example, encouraged large ants to bite the woman's body, and on occasion the insects were taken internally.[10]   Gross traumatization of the pregnant abdomen was a popular method of attempting to induce abortion and is still used by some primitive groups. The early Hebrews knew abortive techniques, although they strongly disapproved of the practice.[11]   The Greeks, on the other hand, advocated abortion in order to control population size and ensure good social and economic conditions among the people. Hippocrates advised abortion in certain situations, but, as a general rule, condemned the practice because it so often resulted in the mother's injury or death.

Christian belief in the immortality of the viable fetus' soul has been largely responsible for the Church's condemnation of abortion. Doctrine has placed abortion in the same category as infanticide, and the unbaptized soul of the fetus, like that of the infant, was considered in danger of hellfire.   Many early canonists, however, did not feel that the soul entered the fetus at the time of conception; rather, the belief was prevalent that while the soul entered the body of a female fetus at 80 days gestation, the soul of the male fetus was present after the fortieth day of gestation. Because of this belief, interruption of the pregnancy before the fortieth day was punished only by a fine, whereas abortion when the soul was present was regarded as murder and was punished accordingly. In 1869 this distinction became unimportant, since abortion before the soul entered the fetus became "anticipated homicide."[12] In spite of the Church's opposition, abortion *was* practiced and not infrequently resulted in the mother's death.

The punishment for the poor Renaissance woman who induced abortion was death by crucifixion, whereas her rich sister might buy her way out of such punishment. Even today, the indigent patient may have a more difficult time in obtaining legal sanction for a medically indicated abortion, and as a result, criminal abortion still accounts for a disproportionately higher number of deaths among the underprivileged. A report on abortions in New York City covering a 20-year period indicated that 90 percent of the therapeutic abortions were performed on white women,[13] and a review of the abortions in two Buffalo, New York, hospitals attests to the paucity of therapeutic abortions among nonwhite patients.[14] Thus, although indications for abortion may have changed over the centuries, discrimination against the lower socio-economic classes and the very real dangers of criminal abortion remain.

Taussig, in his classic book on abortion, gives a good historical account of the medical indications for abortion and discusses some of the early authorities who refer to abortion.[15] Plato and Aristotle clearly encouraged abortion on social or economic grounds. Hippocrates practiced abortion but wanted only physicians to abort patients. In Rome, especially during the Empire, abortion was approved for social indications. The influence of Christianity, although it did not actually diminish the practice of abortion, did make it socially unacceptable. Early in the Christian era, Priscianus, a physician, recommended abortion to save the life of the mother, but writings about therapeutic abortion were scarce, and the ramifications of the abortion issue do not seem to have been reconsidered until 1772.[16] At that time William Cooper suggested therapeutic abortion for cases of contracted pelvis in order to prevent the horrors of attempted delivery through a malformed bony structure. Dewees, Velpeau, Hodge, and other prominent physicians continued to encourage abortion in cases of contracted pelvis. This suggestion was accepted by many obstetricians in Europe, and during the latter half of the nineteenth century "the indications, especially in Germany, were extended to include tuberculosis, heart disease, nephritis, and certain forms of psychosis".[17] These indications became more prevalent, and in recent years there has been a growing tendency to abort for fetal reasons. Psychogenic and socioeconomic factors have also undoubtedly exerted increasing influence in the decision to abort.[18]

II. CONTEMPORARY INDICATIONS FOR THERAPEUTIC ABORTION

Present day indications for therapeutic abortion can be conveniently divided into four categories, medical, fetal, psychiatric, and socioeconomic. Invariably, these categories overlap, for the gravida[19] with rubella[20] in the first trimester of pregnancy is likely to be psychiatrically, or at least emotionally, disturbed. Extreme poverty may be an important adjuvant reason to terminate pregnancy when organic disease decreases the mother's ability to care for a larger family.

A. *Medical Indications*

The medical indications for therapeutic abortion are so numerous that it is impossible to consider them all or to even mention those which were considered to indicate abortion in the past. A majority of them, however, can be included in one of the following types of disease: cardiovascular, gastrointestinal, renal, neurologic, pulmonary, diabetic, and malignant. Each will be briefly considered. The paucity of recent papers in the medical literature recommending abortion for medical disease or even describing the effect of medical diseases on pregnancy, however, undoubtedly reflects the infrequency with which medical disease now is thought to indicate abortion.

1. *Cardiovascular Disease* — Cardiovascular disease[21] has long been thought to increase the risk of maternal death during pregnancy, and, indeed, it has accounted for a significant percentage of maternal deaths.[22] Patients with rheumatic heart disease, congenital heart disorders, or chronic hypertensive disease must be watched closely by their physicians for signs of impending heart failure. In instances where the cardiac disease is severe, digitalis or other

cardiac supporting drugs are often used. Labor is frequently terminated earlier than in the normal pregnant patient. With improved prenatal care (including the significant advances recently provided by cardiac surgery), the number of women with cardiovascular disease whose life is actually in danger during pregnancy has decreased substantially. Some physicians feel that with adequate medical attention practically every pregnancy of a cardiac patient can be completed successfully with little risk of maternal death.[23] Others are less sanguine.[24] As with some of the other medical indications, a consultation suggesting interruption of pregnancy in a cardiac patient is not infrequently influenced by appreciation of the difficult situation that will eventually face the disabled cardiac patient who must try to take care of her new baby.

2. *Gastrointestinal Diseases* — Ulcerative colitis,[25] either active or quiescent, is perhaps the most common gastrointestinal disease which has been thought to indicate therapeutic abortion. There is general agreement that emotional factors affect the medical course of the patient with ulcerative colitis. Since pregnancy regularly and sometimes severely affects the emotional stability of women, it has been felt that pregnancy may adversely affect the outcome of this hazardous disease.[26] Fortunately, the disease is not a common one.

3. *Renal Disease* — Patients in this category[27] are likely to be the victims of chronic glomerulonephritis[28] or hypertension of renal origin;[29] less commonly, they may have only one functioning kidney or a history of nephrolithiasis.[30] Since the therapy of chronic nephritis[31] is still neither definitive nor effective, there are patients with nephritis whose lives will actually be shortened by the effects of pregnancy. Heroic measures, such as the use of the dialyzer, may see these women through severe life-threatening episodes; but all therapy will, in certain instances, eventually prove ineffective.[32] There are now a number of case reports in the medical literature of patients who have successfully completed a pregnancy following kidney transplantation because of kidney failure.[33] I know of no instance, however, in which the kidney transplantation has been performed *during* a pregnancy in which the pregnancy successfully went to term.

Some of the renal conditions which might seem to indicate therapeutic abortion, however, do not significantly affect the risk of maternal death. If one kidney has been removed there will often be little increased risk for the pregnant patient, as long as the remaining kidney functions well. The risk of nephrolithiasis cannot be minimized, but the instances when it might actually increase the risk of death in a pregnant patient seem remote.

4. *Neurologic Disease* — Diseases such as multiple sclerosis,[34] post poliomyelitis, paralysis, epilepsy, and various congenital neurologic disorders form the bulk of the neurologic indications for therapeutic abortion. It is unusual for a patient with multiple sclerosis to be made worse by pregnancy, but the effect of pregnancy on the disease is unpredictable.[35] Riva, Carpenter, and O'Grady have found no justifiable indication for pregnancy interruption in patients with multiple sclerosis.[36] There appears to be little evidence that the disease actually increases the risk of death during pregnancy. Much the same can be said about epilepsy in a pregnant patient. About one-third of the pregnant epileptics seem worse during pregnancy, but the effect of the pregnancy is unpredictable, and epilepsy does not seem to increase the risk of death for the pregnant woman.[37] As with cardiovascular disease, however, it is evident that a woman with a severe paralysis or a disabling sensory disorder will find it difficult, if not impossible, to care for·a newly born child once she leaves the hospital.

5. *Pulmonary Disease* — Tuberculosis accounts for nearly all of the pulmonary conditions thought to indicate therapeutic abortion. In former years, pregnancy was believed to affect the tubercular patient adversely and, in some instances, actually to increase the risk of death from tuberculosis. With the advent of drug therapy, tuberculosis has practically disappeared as an indication for therapeutic abortion. In addition to a possibly increased risk of maternal death, consultants often believed, as with some of the other diseases indicating abortion, that the tubercular patient could not properly care for her newborn child; and this consideration undoubtedly contributed to the decision to abort. With the current, relatively short period of hospitalization for tuberculosis and the relatively quick recovery, however, this consideration is no longer as important.

6. *Diabetes Mellitus* — Diabetes,[38] of varying degrees of severity, has often been an indication for therapeutic abortion. On

occasion poor medical control of the disease has indicated the abortion; at other times one of the complications of the disease, such as arteriosclerosis affecting the retina, heart, or brain, has been determined severe enough to interrupt the pregnancy. The maternal mortality rate, however, is currently considered to be essentially the same among diabetic patients as in the overall pregnant population. Fetal risk is distinctly increased in the diabetic patient, but this would seem to have little to do with the "health" or "life" of the mother. Loth and Hesseltine have stated that "it should be a rare instance in which the diabetic pregnant patient could not be carried to the time of fetal viability, if not to term, by adequate medical management."[39] As with other medical indications, the legal demand customary in most states that the "life" of the mother be endangered as a result of the disease necessitating an abortion is not always fulfilled.

7. *Malignancy* — Some physicians feel that pregnancy will adversely affect the patient's medical course when a prior malignancy has been treated.[40] The medical course of the patient with carcinoma[41] of the breast, for example, may be changed by the use of the female hormones, either estrogen or progesterone, which are present in high concentration in the bloodstream of a pregnant patient. The effect of hormones on the patient with carcinoma of the breast, however, is unpredictable, since these substances sometimes improve the clinical situation and at other times seem to contribute to the progression of the disease. There is little convincing evidence that they either prolong or shorten the patient's life. Majury says that "no convincing evidence has been produced which shows that subsequent pregnancy affects adversely the prognosis in extrauterine malignancy."[42] A history of carcinoma of the bowel (or, on occasion, carcinoma in other locations) has also been an accepted indication for therapeutic abortion; however, there is no convincing evidence that pregnancy in any way adversely affects the outcome of these neoplastic[43] diseases.

8. *Other Medical Diseases* — Rheumatoid arthritis,[44] hyperthyroidism,[45] lacerated cervix, multiple fibroids,[46] mumps in the first trimester, and other miscellaneous diseases too numerous to mention have also indicated therapeutic abortion. It is difficult to prove that

many of these diseases actually threaten the life of the pregnant patient, and social factors often seem to be a prominent consideration in the decision to abort.

B. *Fetal Indications*

Only those states with recently liberalized laws permit abortion because of an expected abnormality or death of the fetus. This is not surprising when one considers that most of the abortion laws were written many years before anything was known about the etiology of fetal defects. Some hospitals, however, will abort a pregnant woman, notwithstanding the patent illegality of the procedure, when there is a strong possibility that the baby will be abnormal.[47] The consultant who recommends an abortion may simply state that the danger of fetal malformation because of maternal rubella in the first trimester of pregnancy makes an abortion advisable. On other occasions, however, a psychiatric opinion will be sought, and this specialist may suggest that the patient's mental condition, influenced by the fear of fetal malformation from the rubella, may deteriorate with suicidal ideation if the pregnancy is not interruped. Whether to abort to prevent the birth of an abnormal baby or to protect the life of the mother, both approaches achieve the same result: interruption of the pregnancy.

Abortion for fetal indications may be recommended in five situations: (1) where there has been an ingestion of certain harmful drugs during pregnancy; (2) where certain viral infections have been contracted by the mother, especially rubella; (3) where the mother's abdomen has been exposed to radiation during pregnancy; (4) where there is a substantial risk of fetal malformation due to genetic factors; and (5) where there is a sensitization to the Rh factor.

1. *Drugs* — The tragedy that occurred following the ingestion of thalidomide by pregnant women both in Europe and in the United States is well known to everyone. Thalidomide, however, is not the first drug known to cause severe fetal abnormalities. The folic-acid antagonists, employed in the treatment of leukemia, had previously been found to produce severe anomalies because of their metabolic action. Certain other drugs are suspected of teratogenicity,[48] although none are as well established in this regard as thalidomide or the folic-acid antagonists. As the field of developmental

pharmacology progresses, however, there seems little doubt that other drugs will be implicated and will further aggravate the legal problem so vividly dramatized by thalidomide.

2. *Rubella* — An epidemic of rubella occurred in the eastern part of the United States in 1964, and this spread to the West Coast and to Hawaii in 1965. Although many pregnant women who contracted rubella were aborted during this epidemic, estimates indicate that about 30,000 defective children conceived during the epidemic were born.[49] When one considers the severity of the fetal abnormalities among these children, it would certainly seem more desirable, from an economic as well as a humanitarian viewpoint, to have terminated pregnancy when the odds were so relatively high that the child would be abnormal. Many parents desperately sought but failed to find a physician who would abort the pregnancy. The risk of rubella causation of an abnormal child is about 50 percent if the rubella occurs during the first month of pregnancy, 22 percent in the second month and 6 to 8 percent in the third month.[50] Even after the twelfth week, Hardy has shown that a substantial risk of fetal abnormality exists.[51] The administration of gamma globulin has not been a satisfactory preventative of the disease in the pregnant woman, partially because the commercial lots available vary so markedly in their effectiveness.[52]

The availability of an effective vaccine against rubella, however, has markedly decreased the risk that rubella infection will occur in a pregnant woman, but until the vaccine is universally used, instances of rubella in pregnancy will still sporadically appear. Certain other maternal infections may be associated with congenital fetal disease, but since diagnosis of the disease in the mother is virtually impossible, usually no consideration of abortion is possible.[53]

3. *Radiation* — It is generally agreed that when radiation is given in therapeutic doses to the mother in the first few months of pregnancy, malformation or death of the fetus may result.[54] According to Parlee, "it appears that ionizing radiation in therapeutic doses in the early months of pregnancy are grounds for the termination of the pregnancy."[55] Doses of radiation in therapeutic amounts are usually prescribed only for the treatment of a malignant neoplastic disease, such as carcinoma of the cervix. Fetal death and extrusion of the products of conception are the usual but not

inevitable result of such quantities of irradiation. A lesser dose of radiation, such as may be involved in an extensive diagnostic investigation, usually does not produce fetal death, but the risk of fetal malformation is uncertain.[56] When extensive diagnostic x-ray is used during the earliest weeks of an undiagnosed pregnancy, some physicians recommend therapeutic abortion. The possibility of having a malformed child under these circumstances does exist, but the actual risk has not been demonstrated. In such cases abortion seems justified on both psychiatric and humanitarian grounds, despite the fact that only uncertain evidence indicates how many of these children might be deformed.

4. *Genetic* — A large number of congenital malformations have a heredity basis.[57] Nadler and Gerbie feel that "firm diagnosis of all chromosome disorders can be established prenatally."[58] Since amniocentesis[59] is necessary to define the risk, however, and since amniocentesis is not totally innocuous, the decision of when to perform the procedure must rest on expert genetic counselling. Nadler and Gerbie caution that "the physician who detects a genetic disorder prenatally is committed to providing therapy," *i.e.* legal abortion if the prospective parents desire it.

5. *Erythroblastosis Fetalis*[60] — The hazard to the *fetus in utero* affected by Rh antibodies produced by the maternal organism is primarily anemia or lack of red blood cells. If this lack can be corrected by transfusing the *fetus in utero* at periodic intervals, there is a distinct possibility that the baby will be born alive and maintain good health through modern methods of exchange transfusion. Thus, abortion for fetal hemolytic disease is rarely indicated in contemporary medical practice. Of great medical importance is the discovery that the administration of the Rh antibody (Rhogam) to the nonsensitized gravida immediately following the delivery of an unaffected Rh positive infant usually prevents the formation of maternal antibodies thereby minimizing the risk of fetal sensitization during a subsequent pregnancy. Properly administered Rhogam should eliminate erythroblastosis fetalis almost totally.

C. *Psychiatric Indications*

Almost all reports on therapeutic abortion practice in the United States indicate an increasing frequency of abortion for psychogenic reasons. Since most state laws require that the "life" of the mother be endangered by pregnancy before abortion may be legally considered, the patient must have exhibited a genuine suicidal tendency to qualify for termination of her pregnancy. Despite the increase in this type of abortion, some psychiatrists believe that psychiatric indications are invalid. A paper in the British Medical Journal in 1963 by Dr. Myre Sim, and the correspondence in the same journal which this article engendered, illustrate the disagreement over psychogenic indications for abortion.[61] Dr. Sim stated in the original article that "there are no psychiatric grounds for termination of pregnancy."[62] Hoenig, commenting on Dr. Sim's paper, said that "termination of the pregnancy could well be indicated . . . in [specific] cases on psychiatric grounds within the meaning of the law."[63] Dr. Sim's reply to Dr. Hoenig stated that it was really the patient's socioeconomic condition which influenced the psychiatrist to recommend abortion. "If society wants abortion to be easier, it should have the courage to campaign for it honestly and not exploit the psychiatrist, who, I contend, has no factual basis for being associated with the problem."[64]

Psychiatrists have been in the forefront of the fight to expand the grounds for legal abortion. They were frequently willing (and of necessity are frequently *still* willing in the states with restrictive laws) to find that patients desiring abortion suffer from psychiatric disease severe enough to threaten the "life" of the mother. Rosenberg and Silver, in a paper on the attitudes and practices of psychiatrists in this regard, suggest that when a psychiatrist recommends therapeutic abortion, he is likely to be considering the socioeconomic factors at least as much as the psychiatric indications.[65]

D. *Socioeconomic Indications*

Throughout history, socioeconomic indications have been the predominate reason for interruption of pregnancy. Women have been aborted because they were afraid of childbirth, because they would not bear children before or after a certain age, in order to safeguard their beauty, and because of "improper" paternity. Nomadism, which made pregnancy inconvenient, and poverty have also played important roles in the motivation for abortion. With the advent of Christianity, all abortions were considered undesirable, if not criminal, and this was especially true of those performed for socioeconomic reasons. Therefore, legal abortion for social reasons virtually disappeared in civilized societies; there is little evidence, however, to suggest that illegal abortion for the same reasons decreased significantly.

Socioeconomic factors have undoubtedly influenced many doctors to recommend abortion for legitimate medical reasons. In days past, when tuberculosis responded slowly, or not at all, to treatment, Taussig believed that factors such as the willingness of the patient to cooperate with rigid therapy, the number of children she had, the amount of help she could get with her children, if any, and other related factors were important in the decision of whether or not to abort her.[66] Cardiac disease, while it may not actually increase the risk of death in the pregnant patient, may make it difficult or impossible for the mother to care adequately for her child. This problem has usually been an important consideration when the patient has cardiovascular disease, and the same problem arises with many other "medical" indications. Obviously, the fetal indications for abortion are primarily socioeconomic, since few, if any, actually threaten the life of the pregnant patient; however, the social as well as economic ramifications of a severely deformed infant are incalculable. It would seem too that socioeconomic factors play a predominant role in the decision to abort the psychiatric patient. Supporting this opinion is the fact that in 1969, before the liberal New York State law went into effect, 72 percent of the legal abortions done in New York City were done for psychiatric disease, while during the first 6 months of 1970, after the law allowed abortion on demand, 64 percent of the abortions were for sociologic indication and only 0.4 percent were for psychiatric disease.[67]

III.   CURRENT LEGAL ABORTION PRACTICES IN THE UNITED STATES

A.   *Changes in the Indications*

In the last 20 to 30 years, nearly all hospital surveys report a decrease in the percentage of therapeutic abortions performed for medical reasons.[68] Taussig, in his volume published in 1936, lists myriad medical indications for abortion.[69] Since the publication of

Taussig's book, there has been a gradual transition in medical thinking, and some of the diseases formerly used as indications for abortion no longer pertain. Taussig called tuberculosis "the most significant indication for therapeutic abortion in point of frequency,"[70] but this disease rarely gives reason to abort today. In a Buffalo abortion study, tuberculosis accounted for 33 to 50 percent of the abortions in the 1940's, about 10 percent in the 1950's, and none during the years 1958 to 1964.[71] In 1936 Taussig stated that "recently a tendency toward greater conservation has . . . been manifested with regard to the indications for therapeutic abortion in women with heart disease,"[72] although he felt that it was frequently a legitimate indication. In the same Buffalo study, cardiovascular indications were present in about 15 percent of the pregnancy interruptions in the 1940's, about 5 percent in the 1950's; they became practically nonexistent in the 1960's.[73]

In 1936 Taussig pointed out that psychiatric indications accounted for only a small percentage of therapeutic abortions, but that such abortions were occurring more often. He quoted Maier as saying that from 1929 to 1931 in Zurich, Switzerland, psychiatrically indicated therapeutic abortions were definitely on the increase.[74] Since Taussig's book was written, most of the reports on hospital experience document a gradually increasing percentage of abortions done for what are recorded as psychiatric indications. In one study, for example, the psychogenic indications increased in linear fashion from about 10 percent in 1943 to about 80 percent in 1963.[75] Of the legal abortions performed in the state of California during 1970, 98.2 percent were indicated for reasons of mental health.[76] As socioeconomic reasons for abortion become legal, we can expect to see the number of abortions for this reason increase and the number of abortions for psychiatric indication decrease.

An equally dramatic change occurred in those fetal indications that before the 1940's were practically unknown. For example, the first therapeutic abortion for rubella was performed in 1949, and although the incidence varied from year to year, depending apparently upon the prevalence of the disease, rubella accounted for an increasingly significant proportion of the abortions, particularly in an epidemic year, such as 1964. With the gradual disappearance of rubella, however, a reverse trend is undoubtedly underway.

Some psychiatrists feel that rarely, or indeed never, is psychiatric disease an absolute indication for therapeutic abortion.[77] Yet the number of such abortions gradually increases. A real suicidal risk must be present in the psychiatric patient to permit legal abortion in states with rigid laws, yet there is good evidence that the suicide rate among pregnant women is considerably lower than among the general population of nonpregnant women.[78] Further, although abortion for rubella is illegal in many states,[79] hospitals often choose to ignore the law for humanitarian reasons. Physicians performing these abortions believe that the patient has a right to make her own decision concerning a pregnancy which may result in the birth of an abnormal child. Social factors have thus become the prime consideration in the decision to terminate pregnancy for psychiatric or fetal indications.

Evidence also indicates that, except for New York state and perhaps a few other localities, the private patient has been much more likely to secure a legal interruption of pregnancy than has been the ward patient. Hall reported that at the Sloane Hospital for Women, the incidence of therapeutic abortion was four times greater on the private service than on the ward.[80] By sending a questionnaire to 65 randomly selected major hospitals, Dr. Hall discovered that this same discrepancy was widespread. In one study in the 1940's when the majority of abortions were done for medical reasons, the incidences on the ward and private services were about the same. In the 1950's when medical reasons accounted for fewer abortions, the incidence on the private service rose to twice that of the ward service. From 1960 to 1964, when the number of abortions for psychiatric or fetal reasons rose dramatically, the incidence on the private service soared to better than twenty times the number in the clinic service.[81] Recent experience in New York City has reversed this trend. During the first nine months of the experience under the liberal abortion law in New York City, 42 percent of the abortions on New York City residents were performed on nonwhite patients, although only 32 percent of the New York City births occurred in this group.[82] The precipitous decrease in the cost of an abortion, as well as the availability of Medicare coverage for abortion, undoubtedly accounts for this increase in the number of nonwhite women securing abortion.

Other interesting trends with regard to the maternal age, the parity, and the marital status of women securing legal abortion can be noted. In one series in the 1940's no girl under 20 years of age was aborted. In the 1950's about 7 percent of the patients were under 20 years of age, and from 1960 to 1964 almost 15 percent of the patients were in this younger age group.[83] Paralleling the decreasing age has been a change in parity. The proportion of nullipara[84] increased from about 20 percent during the 1940's to 36 percent in the early 1960's. The percentage of married patients dropped from 93.3 percent in the 1940's to 85.1 percent in the 1950's and to 58.9 percent in the 1960's. In the latter years, about 2 out of 5 of the patients aborted were either single, separated, or divorced.[85]

In a recent report of 42,598 legal abortions from 64 participating institutions in 12 states, Tietze and Lewit found that 25 percent of the patients were under 20 years of age, nearly 50 percent had had no prior pregnancies, and only about 25 percent of the patients were married at the time of the abortion.[86]

It is widely known that states, localities within the same state, and hospitals within the same locality vary greatly in their abortion policies. In the 1965 survey by Hall, hospital practices varied from no abortions in 24,417 deliveries to 1 in 36 deliveries.[87] It seems inconceivable that medical opinion at that time could have varied so widely. As recently as 1969, however, only 19 percent of the legal abortions in California were performed in the Los Angeles metropolitan area, whereas 44 percent of the state's live births occurred in the same area. San Francisco accounted for 59 percent of the abortions, but only 22 percent of the live births. An enormous change in 1970 increased Los Angeles' share of the legal abortions to 59 percent.[88] Certainly, the need for abortion did not change so markedly form 1969 to 1970. One can only presume that social factors encouraged the change.

B. *Medical Procedures Used to Produce Legal Abortion*

A variety of techniques are currently used to produce legal abortion. A number of variables influence the particular technique chosen. Length of gestation, combining sterilization with abortion, and the presence of pelvic pathology all influence the physician's choice. A list of the techniques used in the past two or three decades would include intracervical insertion of a foreign body, such as a hard, rubber catheter or a bougie; simple dilation and curettage (D & C); hysterectomy; hysterotomy (either vaginal or abdominal); the use of concentrated oxytocin solution;[89] the injection of hypertonic solutions into the uterus; and, more recently, suction curettage and the use in a variety of ways of a new group of substances called prostaglandins. Until recently the simple D & C accounted for the majority of abortions performed. Hysterectomy was used often in the 1940's, but then lost favor. In recent years it has been used somewhat more commonly when a sterilizing procedure was to be performed along with the abortion, or if the uterus itself was the site of some pathology. The use of bougies or intrauterine catheters has become obsolete since the 1940's. Concentrated oxytocin was first used in 1964, but never gained many followers. Intra-amniotic injection of hypertonic solutions, usually saline or glucose but more recently urea, have enjoyed increasing popularity since the mid-1960's. Prostaglandins must still be considered experimental pharmacologic agents, but they have been reported to successfully induce abortion if they are given by an intravenous or an intrauterine route.

C. Hazards of Therapeutic Abortion

Since the experience reported by various investigators concerning frequency of complications with abortion is so varied, it is difficult, if not impossible, to make any generalizations regarding the safety of legal abortion. Nevertheless, one can generalize that the safety of the particular procedure varies directly with its technical ease and the experience of the physician rendering the service.

Dilatation and curettage (D & C) seems to be a safe operation. A paper documenting experience with 320 D & C's performed from 1946 to 1964 included only two patients who became significantly ill.[90] One developed an abscess in the tissue adjacent to the uterus, an infection which responded rapidly to antibiotic therapy. The second patient developed pelvic peritonitis and a fistula between the bowel and the vagina; she required major abdominal surgery before she recovered. A more recent study was made of 812 patients aborted at Oxford University Hospital either by vacuum curettage (768 patients) or by D & C (44 patients).[91] Seventeen percent of the patients experienced hemorrhage of at least 500 cc of blood, 8.5 percent suffered a cervical laceration, 15 percent experienced a significant pyrexia,[92] and 1.7 percent suffered a perforated uterus. The recorded perforation rate was considered a minimum one, since in 3 of the 14 perforations reported the complication was not recognized until a planned laparotomy for tubal ligation. The investigators speculated that others might have been missed. Two patients required hysterectomy because of perforation.

In another study of 1000 vacuum curettages, only 6.1 percent of the patients suffered blood loss greater than 500 cc, and only 0.5 percent of the patients suffered a perforated uterus.[93] Tietze and Lewit reported on 42,598 abortions from 64 United States institutions, of which 75 percent were either suction curettage or the conventional D & C. They found a major complication rate of only 1.3 percent, except where a preexisting medical complication intervened.[94] Among 84,000 abortions performed in New York City during the first 9 months (July 1970-April 1971) following enactment of the liberal New York State abortion law, Pakter and Nelson recorded hemorrhage in only 0.15 percent of the patients and perforation in 0.17 percent of the patients. They also recorded a striking reduction in abortion-related deaths in 1971. There were 8 abortion-related maternal deaths during the first 4 months of 1969, 6 during the first 4 months of 1970, and 3 during the first 4 months of 1971. An interpolation of these figures indicates that there were approximately 4.6 maternal deaths per 100,000 abortions in New York City during the first half of 1971, a figure which compares favorably with the rate of abortion-related deaths in other countries.[95]

The intra-amniotic injection of formalin to produce abortion was first used many years ago, although the use of this drug is now known to be hazardous. After World War II hypertonic saline solution was substituted for formalin; the technique was used widely in Japan and later in other countries.[96] In 1958 hypertonic glucose was tried and the first successful termination of a midtrimester pregnancy using this solution was accomplished. No ill effects from either modality were reported in the English language literature the first few years, although several maternal deaths related to the use of intra-amniotic hypertonic saline solution in Japan were recorded.[97] A handful of deaths due to clostridium welchii infection were reported with dextrose.[98] In recent years an occasional death has occurred with the use of hypertonic saline, although the experience with this solution in general has been good. The deaths have been due primarily to brain damage related to inadvertent intravascular injection and hypernatremia. A number of cases of water intoxication due to the antidiuretic effect of oxytocin, usually coupled with the administration of large amounts of intravenous fluids, have also been recorded. The experience reported by MacKenzie, Roufa, and Tovell on 400 consecutive mid-trimester abortions induced by hypertonic saline is probably typical.[99] A small experience with the procedure from 1965 to June of 1970, was accompanied by several complications. The more extensive experience after the New York law liberalization in July, 1970, was associated with a marked decrease in the number of complications, and no deaths were reported in this series of patients. Karenyi[100] and Schulman[101] both reported experience with outpatients following intra-amniotic injection of hypertonic saline to procure abortion. In both series complications were rare and there were no deaths reported.

Experience with prostaglandins is too recent to appraise the hazards. Information to date has indicated a high percentage of complications (phlebitis[102] with PGE_2, and nausea and vomiting and fever with PGF_{2a}), but these have apparently not been serious.[103]

IV. CONCLUSION

Criminal abortion remains a major public health problem and cannot be ignored. It is doubtful that human nature or human society will ever permit the avoidance of all unsafe or unwanted pregnancies, and the need for abortion is likely to continue. Legalized abortion provides at least a partial answer.

An analysis of the reasons why physicians in the United States recommend legal abortion shows a changing philosophy over the past two decades. As medical disease has demanded less pregnancy interruption, psychiatric disease and risk of fetal malformation have required abortion more frequently. Social factors are apparently an important consideration with these indications. Groups of influential citizens — physicians, lawyers, psychologists, and social workers — are currently encouraging liberalization of abortion statutes in order to take into account factors other than the "life" of the pregnant patient.

Legal abortion in a well-equipped hospital is not hazardous, but criminal abortion in the United States annually accounts for hundreds of deaths and untold damage short of death. If liberalization of abortion statutes will decrease this toll of human potential, then society must offer this protection to women.

NOTES

1. Guttmacher, *Induced Abortion*, 63 N.Y. J. MEDICINE 2334 (1963) (editorial).
2. Gold, Erhardt, Jacobziner & Nelson, *Therapeutic Abortions in New York City: A 20 Year Review*, 55 AM. J. PUB. HEALTH 964, 965 (1965).
3. Montgomery & Hammersly, *Maternal Deaths in California, 1957-1962*, 100 CAL. MEDICINE 412, 415 (1964).
4. N.Y. PEN. LAW § 125.05(3) (McKinney Supp. 1971).
5. Pakter & Nelson, *Abortion in New York City: The First Nine Months*, 3 FAMILY PLANNING PERSPECTIVES 5, 10-11 (No. 3, 1971).
6. Personal communication from Walter Ballard, M.D., to the author, March, 1972.
7. Fisher, *Criminal Abortion*, in THERAPEUTIC ABORTION: MEDICAL, PSYCHIATRIC, LEGAL, ANTHROPOLOGICAL AND RELIGIOUS CONSIDERATIONS 3, 6 (H. Rosen ed. 1954) [hereinafter cited as THERAPEUTIC ABORTION].
8. ABORTION IN THE UNITED STATES 55 (M. Calderone ed. 1958).
9. *Id.*
10. *See generally* Devereux, *A Typological Study of Abortion in 350 Primitive, Ancient and Pre-Industrial Societies*, in THERAPEUTIC ABORTION 97, 121-34.
11. *See generally* F. TAUSSIG, ABORTION, SPONTANEOUS AND INDUCED: MEDICAL AND SOCIAL ASPECTS 31-45 (1936).
12. G. WILLIAMS, THE SANCTITY OF LIFE AND THE CRIMINAL LAW *passim* (1957).
13. Gold, *supra* note 2, at 966.
14. Niswander, Klein & Randall, *Changing Attitudes Toward Therapeutic Abortion*, 196 J.A.M.A. 1141, 1143 (1966).
15. *See generally* F. TAUSSIG, *supra* note 11, at 31-45.
16. *Id.* at 277.
17. *Id.* at 278.

18. *Id.*
19. A woman in her first pregnancy is referred to as *Gravida I*; in the second pregnancy *Gravida II*; etc. Medical definitions are from J. SCHMIDT, ATTORNEYS' DICTIONARY OF MEDICINE AND WORD FINDER 376 (1969) [hereinafter cited as J. SCHMIDT, DICTIONARY].
20. Commonly known as German measles. J. SCHMIDT, DICTIONARY at 712.
21. Disease involving the heart and the blood vessels, *i.e.*, the arteries and the veins. J. SCHMIDT, DICTIONARY at 155.
22. Gorenberg & Chesley, *Rheumatic Heart Disease in Pregnancy: The Remote Prognosis in Patients with "Functionally Severe" Disease*, 68 AM. J. OBSTETRICS & GYNECOLOGY 1151 (1954).
23. *Id.* at 1159.
24. Dack, Bader, Bader & Gelb, *Heart Disease*, in MEDICAL, SURGICAL, AND GYNECOLOGIC COMPLICATIONS OF PREGNANCY 37 (2d ed. J. Rovinsky & A. Guttmacher 1965). *See generally* Metcalfe, *Rheumatic Heart Disease in Pregnancy*, 11 CLINICAL OBSTETRICS & GYNECOLOGY (1968).
25. An inflammation of the colon (the large bowel) characterized by ulceration of its lining membrane. J. SCHMIDT, DICTIONARY at 900. 34.
26. Jacobs & Janowitz, *The Digestive Tract*, in MEDICAL, SURGICAL, AND GYNECOLOGIC COMPLICATIONS OF PREGNANCY 194 (2d ed. J. Rovinsky & A. Guttmacher 1965).
27. *I.e.*, with diseases pertaining to or involving the kidneys. J. SCHMIDT, DICTIONARY at 691.
28. A variety of kidney disease in mild form in which the tufts formed by the tiny blood vessels are inflamed. It leads to hypertension (high blood pressure) and eventually to uremia, a poisoning of the body due to failure of the kidneys to eliminate the toxic substances. J. SCHMIDT, DICTIONARY at 365.
29. *See* note 28 *supra.*
30. An abnormal condition marked by the presence of concretions or calculi (i.e., "stones") in the kidney or kidneys. Also, the various disorders resulting from the presence of the concretions. J. SCHMIDT, DICTIONARY at 545.
31. The prolonged and progressive form of nephritis (inflammation of the kidney or a deterioration of the tissue forming its delicate structure) which may follow an acute attack or may result from other diseases of the body, poisons, alcohol, germs, etc. The fine and delicate structure of the kidney becomes distorted; the fine blood vessels become thicker; the supporting tissue (the nonfunctional part) begins to overgrow the functional parts; and even the heart is affected. J. SCHMIDT, DICTIONARY at 544.
32. Herwig, Merrill, Jackson & Oken, *Chronic Renal Disease and Pregnancy*, 92 AM. J. OBSTETRICS & GYNECOLOGY 1117, 1120 (1965).

33. Caplan, Dossetor & Maughan, *Pregnancy Following Cadaver Kidney Homotransplantation*, 106 AM. J. OBSTETRICS & GYNECOLOGY 644 (1970).

34. A disease of the brain and spinal cord. In this condition, various parts of the brain and spinal cord are subjected to a type of deterioration called sclerosis. Sclerosis in this instance is a hardening of the nerve tissue and its displacement by overgrowing connective (supporting) tissue. Basically functional nerve tissue gives way to supporting, nonfunctional tissue. The disease progresses slowly but is incurable. J. SCHMIDT, DICTIONARY at 534.101.

35. Cohen & Kreuger, *Multiple Sclerosis and Pregnancy: Report of a Case*, 6 OBSTETRICS & GYNECOLOGY 144, 145 (1955).

36. Riva, Carpenter & O'Grady, *Pregnancy Associated with Multiple Sclerosis*, 66 AM. J. OBSTETRICS & GYNECOLOGY 403, 407 (1953).

37. Sabin & Oxorn, *Epilepsy and Pregnancy*, 7 OBSTETRICS & GYNECOLOGY 175, 179 (1956).

38. A disease in which the metabolism (body utilization) of sugars is greatly impaired due to the faulty secretion of insulin by the pancreas. J. SCHMIDT, DICTIONARY at 248.21.

39. Loth & Hesseltine, *Therapeutic Abortion at the Chicago Lying-in Hospital*, 72 AM. J. OBSTETRICS & GYNECOLOGY 304, 309 (1956).

40. *See, e.g., id.*

41. A malignant tumor or new growth (*i.e.*, a cancer) arising from cells that make up epithelium. Epithelium is the outer covering of the skin and the lining of the body cavities, such as the mouth, the rectum, the interior of the chest, etc. J. SCHMIDT, DICTIONARY at 149.

42. Majury, *Therapeutic Abortion in the Winnipeg General Hospital*, 82 AM. J. OBSTETRICS & GYNECOLOGY 10, 13 (1961). Other authors have agreed. *See, e.g.*, Holleb, *Breast Cancer and Pregnancy*, 15 CA. A. CANCER J. FOR CLINICIANS 182, 183 (1965).

43. Pertaining to a new growth or a tumor. J. SCHMIDT, DICTIONARY at 544.

44. A form of chronic arthritis usually affecting several joints. J. SCHMIDT, DICTIONARY at 702.

45. The condition resulting from an abnormal and/or excessive activity of the thyroid gland. J. SCHMIDT, DICTIONARY at 434.

46. Pertaining to, or composed of fibrous tissue. Fibroid is frequently used to refer to a tumor of the womb composed of muscle and fibrous tissue.

47. *Cf.* George, *The Evolving Law of Abortion*, in this volume. Guttmacher, *The Genesis of Liberalized Abortion in New York: A Personal Insight*, in this volume.

48. Tending to produce deformities of the body. J. SCHMIDT, DICTIONARY at 860.

49. Personal communication from John Sever to the author, October 1965.

50. Michaels & Mellin, *Prospective Experience with Maternal Rubella and the Associated Congenital Malformations*, 26 PEDIATRICS 200, 204 (1960). *See also* Lundstrom, *Rubella During Pregnancy: A Follow-Up Study of Children Born After an Epidemic of Rubella in Sweden, 1951 with Additional Investigations on Prophylaxis in Treatment of Maternal Rubella*, 81 ACTA PAEDIATRICA Supp. 133 at 1 (1962).

51. Hardy, McCracken, Gilkeson & Sever, *Adverse Fetal Outcome Following Maternal Rubella* AFTER *The First Trimester of Pregnancy*, 207 J.A.M.A. 2414, 2414-20 (1969).

52. Sever, Schiff & Huebner, *Frequency of Rubella Antibody Among Pregnant Women and Other Human and Animal Populations*, 23 OBSTETRICS & GYNECOLOGY 153, 158 (1964). *See also* Lundstrom, *supra* note 50, at 10.

53. D. Reid, K. Ryan & K. Benirschke, PRINCIPLES AND MANAGEMENT OF HUMAN REPRODUCTION 393 (1972).

54. Parlee, *Radiation Hazards in Obstetrics and Gynecology*, 75 AM. J. OBSTETRICS & GYNECOLOGY 327, 328 (1958).

55. *Id.* at 332.

56. THE EVALUATION OF RISKS FROM RADIATION 12 (1st ed. R. Russell Oxford 1966).

57. Reid, *supra* note 53, at 395.

58. Nadler, Nadler & Gerbie, *Present Status of Amniocentesis in Intrauterine Diagnosis of Genetic Defects*, 38 OBSTETRICS & GYNECOLOGY 796 (1971).

59. Perforating or tapping the *amnion* (*i.e.*, the inner of the two bags containing the fetus) with the use of a needle, the procedure is used to remove and study part of the amniotic fluid. J. SCHMIDT, DICTIONARY at 83.

60. A hemolytic anemia of the fetus or new born infant, caused by the transplacental transmission of maternally formed antibodies, usually secondary to an incompatability between the blood group of the mother and that of her offspring (usually an incompatability of the Rh factor). See J. SCHMIDT, DICTIONARY at 294.701.

61. Sim, *Abortion and the Psychiatrist*, 1963 Vol. II BRITISH MEDICAL J. 145.

62. *Id.* at 148.

63. Hoenig, *Correspondence*, 1963 Vol. II BRITISH MEDICAL J. 1125-26

64. Sim, *Correspondence*, 1963 Vol. II BRITISH MEDICAL J. 1062.

65. Rosenberg & Silver, *Suicide, Psychiatrists and Therapeutic Abortion*, 102 CAL. MEDICINE 407, 410 (1965).

66. F. TAUSSIG, *supra* note 11, at 293.

67. Pakter, Unpublished manuscript read at a meeting of the Population Association of America in Washington, D.C., April 23, 1971.

68. *E.g.*, Colpitts, *Trends in Therapeutic Abortion*, 68 AM. J. OBSTETRICS & GYNECOLOGY 988, 996 (1954); Routledge, Sparling & MacFarlane,

The Present Status of Therapeutic Abortion, 17 OBSTETRICS & GYNE-COLOGY 168, 171 (1961); Russell, *Changing Indications for Therapeutic Abortion*, 151 J.A.M.A. 108, 111 (1953).

69. F. TAUSSIG, *supra* note 11, at 282.
70. *Id.* at 292.
71. Niswander, *supra* note 14, at 1141.
72. F. TAUSSIG, *supra* note 11, at 297.
73. Niswander, *supra* note 14, at 1141.
74. F. TAUSSIG, *supra* note 11, at 313.
75. Niswander, *supra* note 14, at 1142.
76. BUREAU OF MATERNAL AND CHILD HEALTH, 4TH ANNUAL RE-PORT ON THE IMPLEMENTATION OF THE CALIFORNIA THERAPEUTIC ABORTION ACT, Table I (Berkeley, Cal. 1971) [hereinafter cited as CALIFORNIA ACT].
77. *See* Cheney, *Indications for Therapeutic Abortion From the Standpoint of the Neurologist and the Psychiatrist*, 103 J.A.M.A. 1914, 1918 (1934); Sim, *supra* note 61, at 148.
78. ABORTION IN THE UNITED STATES *supra* note 8, at 140; Rosenberg, *supra* note 65, at 409.
79. *Cf.* George, *supra* note 47 at 741 n.177.
80. Hall, *Therapeutic Abortion, Sterilization and Contraception*, 91 AM. J. OBSTETRICS & GYNECOLOGY 518 (1965).
81. Niswander, *supra* note 14, at 1142.
82. Pakter, *supra* note 5.
83. Niswander, *supra* note 14, at 1141.
84. A woman who has never given birth to a child. J. SCHMIDT, DIC-TIONARY at 567.
85. Niswander, *supra* note 14, at 1141.
86. Tietze & Lewit, *Legal Abortions: Early Medical Complications, an Interim Report of the Joint Program for the Study of Abortions*, 3 FAMILY PLANNING PERSPECTIVES 6, 7 (No. 4, 1971).
87. Hall, *supra* note 80, at 525.
88. *See* CALIFORNIA ACT, *supra* note 76, at Table II.
89. Oxytocin is a hormone which has the power to increase the contractions of the uterus in the late stages of pregnancy and during childbirth. J. SCHMIDT, DICTIONARY at 612.
90. Niswander, Klein & Randall, *Therapeutic Abortion: Indications and Techniques*, 28 OBSTETRICS & GYNECOLOGY 127 (1966).
91. Stallworthy, Moolgaoker & Walsh, *Legal Abortion: A Critical Assessment of its Risks*, II THE LANCET 1246 (1971).
92. An abnormal rise in the temperature of the body. J. SCHMIDT, DIC-TIONARY at 668.86.
93. Loung, Buckle & Anderson, *Results in 1,000 Cases of Therapeutic Abortion Managed by Vacuum Aspiration*, 4 BRITISH MEDICAL J. 478 (1971).

94. Tietze, *supra* note 86, at 12.

95. Pakter, *supra* note 5, at 9-11.

96. Wagatsuma, *Intra-Amniotic Injections of Saline for Therapeutic Abortion*, 93 AM. J. OBSTETRICS & GYNECOLOGY 743 (1965).

97. *Id.* at 743-44.

98. MacDonald, O'Driscoll & Geoghegan, *Intra-Amniotic Dextrose — A Maternal Death*, 20 OBSTETRICS & GYNECOLOGY SURVEY 776, 777 (1965).

99. MacKenzie, Roufa & Tovell, *Midtrimester Abortion: Clinical Experience with Amniocentesis and Hypertonic Instillation in 400 Patients*, 14 CLINICAL OBSTETRICS & GYNECOLOGY 107 (1971).

100. Kerenyi, *Outpatient Intra-Amniotic Injection of Hypertonic Saline*, 14 CLINICAL OBSTETRICS & GYNECOLOGY 124 (1971).

101. Schulman, Kaiser & Randolph, *Outpatient Saline Abortion*, 37 OBSTETRICS & GYNECOLOGY 521 (1971).

102. Inflammation of a vein. J. SCHMIDT, DICTIONARY at 668.3.

103. Hendricks, Brenner, Ekbladh, Brotanek & Fishburne, *Efficacy and Tolerance of Intravenous Prostaglandins, F_2a and E_2*, 111 AM. J. OBSTETRICS & GYNECOLOGY 564 (1971).

GENETIC RISK, PRENATAL DIAGNOSIS, AND SELECTIVE ABORTION

M. NEIL MACINTYRE

I. INTRODUCTION

IN THE BURGEONING DEBATE on the subject of therapeutic abortion and proposed changes in state abortion laws, numerous situations have been proposed as valid indications for interrupting a pregnancy. Of these, the one which ordinarily has received the least attention has been the risk that the child would be born with grave physical or mental defects.

In 1967, the California legislature passed a bill[1] modifying the abortion law of that state to accord generally with the Model Penal Code suggested by the American Law Institute (ALI) in 1962.[2] The California law is similar to the ALI proposal in that it accepts a threat to maternal health and a pregnancy resulting from rape or incest as grounds for interrupting a pregnancy. But it deviates from the ALI proposal by refusing to allow therapeutic abortions on the basis of a known risk that a child, if born, would have grievous defects.

The logic of this position is difficult to understand. Serious threat to a mother's life is widely accepted as an indication for therapeutic abortion; but in view of the capabilities of modern medicine, such a situation rarely arises. If "maternal health" is construed to include mental health, then it must be remembered that producing a mentally or physically defective child poses an extremely severe threat to the mental health not only of the mother but of the father and other family members as well. Rape is a socially unacceptable act, and pregnancy resulting from it may be emotionally threatening to the woman involved; but the unborn child can be expected to develop normally both physically and mentally. It is patently illogical to allow termination of such a pregnancy and to disallow termination of one involving a seriously defective child, which poses a greater emotional threat to the mother.[3]

It is difficult to understand why there has been such a lack of emphasis on the genetic risk of a defective child as an acceptable reason for interrupting a pregnancy. Perhaps legislators feel that such cases are so rare that they do not represent an important political issue. But if they considered the tremendous cost to society of caring for retarded and congenitally malformed children, they would find it easy to discern and recognize the political implications. Perhaps lawmakers have listened to the dire predictions of the extremists who insist that any legislation which discriminates against human beings on the basis of quality will inevitably lead to a state of degradation comparable to Nazi Germany. Whatever the reasons, I believe that the failure to accept the genetic risk of producing a defective child as one of the most valid reasons for considering the interruption of a pregnancy is based on a lack of understanding of the factors involved.

My purpose here is to share with the reader some of the knowledge and philosophy which I have gained through experience as a research scientist, clinical cytogeneticist, and genetic counselor. I hope that the reader will gain some insights that will enable him, whether he is legislator or an ordinary citizen, to make a more informed evaluation of therapeutic abortion in cases involving a known genetic risk that the child will be born with serious congenital defects, particularly in those cases where it can be shown that the fetus actually is genetically affected.

II. THE DEFECTIVE CHILD AS A THREAT TO THE MENTAL HEALTH OF THE FAMILY

A. *Effect on the Parents*

When a married couple decides to have a child, that decision and its outcome represent one of the most ego-involved situations known to our society. Such a couple is likely to look forward to the birth of the child with deep feelings of awe, satisfaction, delight, and pride. The partners feel that the infant will be among the most beautiful and perfect ever produced, for it is to be a combination of all that is best in each of them. It is their contribution to society and to posterity. Their hopes and aspirations for the child are high; they believe that, with the love and care which they are prepared to provide, the child will develop into a person of stature and that society will fully recognize and appreciate their reproductive and parental excellence.[4] In the context of such a psychological environment, the emotional shock that occurs when the child is born physically malformed and mentally defective is devastating.[5]

Although all parents in our society are expected to love and cherish their offspring, those who have produced a grossly defective child may experience strong feelings of fear, revulsion, and even hatred for the child. Among the questions that may, understandably, form in the mind of such a parent are: What are people going to think of me for having produced a child like this? Does it really represent a combination of all that is best in me and my mate? Can we accept this reproductive catastrophe as our contribution to society and to posterity? Is there something wrong with us? The most fundamental and emotionally destructive phenomenon is likely to be the terrible blow to the ego of each parent, and it is not unusual for them to wish that the child would die — and to suffer from the resulting feeling of guilt.

Instead of the socially acceptable and expected feelings of empathy and love for one's child, some very negative and socially abhorrent reactions dominate the thinking of the parents in such cases. The resultant feelings of guilt place the couple in an untenable situation, from which they must seek some means of relief. I am familiar with a case in which a couple produced a child with the D-1 trisomy syndrome, a particularly severe condition which results from a chromosomal abnormality and includes severe developmental anomalies of the face, such as complete cleft lip and cleft palate and abnormal development or absence of the eyes. Although the mother had shown no previous symptoms of emotional instability, she required extensive psychiatric treatment soon after the child had been born. The father demonstrated his inability to cope with the emotional stress of the situation by divorcing the mother and abandoning two normal siblings of the defective child.

In a more common reaction, the parents, attempting to resolve the disparity between their natural feelings and the unrealistic expectations of love imposed by society, overcompensate by loudly proclaiming the depth of their love for the child and the unifying effect that its presence has had upon the family. Of course, there are parents who can face the problem of a defective child fairly honestly and realistically, admitting that, despite their real and often deep feelings of love for the youngster, its presence has had a serious and lasting negative impact on their lives. They are earnestly concerned over the effect which the abnormal child will have on its siblings and will admit to feeling considerable bitterness at having had to bear such a burden. Moreover, they will strongly agree that under no circumstances do they wish a similar misfortune to occur to them again or to any of their children.

After the birth of a defective child, parents ordinarily feel a greater urge to compensate by initiating a subsequent pregnancy. If their only child is defective, the need to prove to themselves and the world that they are capable of producing something better can be almost overwhelming. When the basis for the child's abnormalities is known to be genetic — so that any future pregnancy carries with it a serious risk — the unfortunate couple almost invariably suffers from intense feelings of depression and a sense of being trapped. In such cases, there is a strong need for each individual to absolve himself of personal responsibility for the tragedy, which ordinarily leads to attempts to place the blame elsewhere.

Because of a general lack of understanding of the mechanisms of inheritance and an abundance of misinformation concerning heritable diseases, such conditions carry a definite stigma and are looked upon with a special sort of fear. Consequently, the carrier of a heritable disease may view him- or herself and be looked upon by others as somehow incomplete, less than human, or even unclean. It is little wonder that when the defects in an abnormal child are recognized as being genetic in origin, each of the parents is likely to say, "It must come from the other side of the family; it couldn't possibly come from mine." The same feelings are prevalent in the child's grandparents, who are also threatened and, because they belong to an even less-informed generation, tend to be even more unrealistic in their reactions. The unhealthy climate of accusations and recriminations surrounding the birth of a child with genetic problems places a very severe, sometimes intolerable, strain on the marital relationship of the parents.

Knowledge of the existence of a genetic risk is almost certain to engender some fear or concern regarding pregnancy. The resulting anxiety is potentially a serious threat to the stability of a couple's sexual relationship, and some degree of deterioration of this aspect of their marriage is almost inevitable. Indeed, the mere recognition of this phenomenon gives rise to additional anxiety, creating a self-generating cycle which may lead to the cessation of all sexual activity between the unfortunate partners.

B. *Effect upon Siblings*

A physically and mentally defective sibling can affect the sociopsychological development of a normal child in many ways. Some are subtle, some are brutally obvious, but most are undesirable. I could list these effects, but many of the important points can be made by presenting a case history from my files. It is representative of a common set of problems.

The young lady in question was an extremely attractive and intelligent 21-year-old nursing student with a 19-year-old sister and a 16-year-old brother. The latter was afflicted by Down's syndrome (mongolism). Through her studies, the oldest sibling had learned for the first time that, in a small percentage of cases, mongolism can be hereditary, the result of a chromosomal defect in the cells of one of the parents. This information had caused her concern, and she came to me for advice.

During the preliminary discussion she was calm and reserved. When I asked about her feelings with regard to her mongoloid brother, she indicated that she loved him, was sympathetic and solicitous toward him, and felt she had gained in maturity, understanding, and compassion by having been brought up with him. Superficial questioning with respect to her current environment established that she was enthusiastic about nurses' training, dedicated to preparing for her chosen profession, and doing well in her classes. She did not date a great deal and rarely went out with the same young man more than twice. When I commented that this seemed somewhat unusual for such an attractive girl, she responded that she was busy in school and that, furthermore, she had no interest in marriage.

I recommended a chromosome analysis of the mongoloid child, and he was brought to the laboratory by his mother. From her I learned that the young nursing student's attitude and behavior toward her retarded brother had always been exemplary. In praising the love that the girl had exhibited for her brother, her mother remarked on the things she had given up to spend time with him, the help that she had been to the mother in this respect, and her positive and mature acceptance of the entire situation.

Results of the chromosome analysis indicated that the basis for mongolism in the young boy was nonhereditary. Thus his sister carried no increased risk. To eliminate all possible doubt in her mind, she was also tested and proved to have a normal chromosome complement.

I had been somewhat concerned by some of the answers given by the young woman during the preliminary discussion and suggested additional talks. During several later counselling sessions, the girl became more and more relaxed and willing to talk. Ultimately, when she had come to trust me and recognized the depth of my understanding of her situation, she cast off her protective facade and spoke freely of the bitterness, anger, frustration, and hurt that she felt. She described her parents as somewhat conservative but warm and understanding people who had made it clear that she should accept her defective brother with love and should not demonstrate any aggression toward him. They had pointed out that a brother of this sort was a privilege of a sort and would serve as an enriching experience for her. They had praised her for her handling of the situation, and she had responded accordingly. But, in truth, she had hated it.

She described in detail her feelings as a younger girl in response to the candid comments and cruel humor of her peers, her embarrassment and shame at several incidents when her friends had been invited to play in her home, and her growing feeling of being stigmatized because of her brother's condition. She had resented the fact that an excessive amount of parental attention was focused on the brother, but she had never been allowed to express anger toward him or to her parents. In high school many young men had asked her for dates repeatedly, but she had accepted relatively few invitations and had never allowed her relationship with any boy to move beyond a superficial level. When asked to explain this diffidence, she said that she had felt that there somehow was something different about her that might be threatening to a marriage.

Furthermore, she had come to realize the frightening and depressing fact that when her parents died (and they were somewhat older than those of most of her classmates), she would inherit the responsibility for her mongoloid brother. She was certain that this would make her unacceptable as a wife for any young man.

In short, this young woman felt trapped and deeply concerned by the ambivalent feelings which she had developed for her parents and her brother. Once she found an outlet for her pent-up feelings, counseling progressed rapidly and positively. She is now a happily married practicing nurse and is looking forward to starting a family of her own.

The course taken by the girl's younger sister was completely different. She was described as quite wild, dating constantly and indiscriminately and experimenting with drugs. A poor student, she was a constant source of disappointment, anguish, and despair to her parents. She was also envied, in a way, by her older sister.

The contrast between the manner in which these two sisters reacted to their problem is interesting. Their reactions were almost completely opposite, yet neither was healthy. Although the older girl's behavior was considered exemplary by society and seemed to represent a particularly fine adjustment to the situation, in actual fact she was in serious trouble psychologically — perhaps more so than her sister, who has since received psychiatric help and is progressing toward emotional stability.[6]

III. DEVELOPMENT AND APPLICATION OF PRENATAL DIAGNOSTIC TECHNIQUES

A. *Background*

By the early 1960's, techniques for preparing human cells so that individual chromosomes could be studied had become available to medicine as an important diagnostic tool. Using these methods, various types of chromosomal abnormalities have been identified as the basis for genetic imbalance leading to grave congenital malformations and, in the majority of cases, serious mental retardation.

In most such instances, the chromosomal anomaly is not hereditary; *i.e.*, it is found in the cells of the congenitally malformed child although the chromosomes of the parents are normal. An example is the nonfamilial basis for Down's syndrome (mongolism), in which the cells of the mongoloid child each contain an extra chromosome which the parents' cells do not. The genetic accident leading to this chromosomal imbalance occurs either during the formation of the particular sperm or egg cell, which leads to the formation of the defective child, or shortly after fertilization.

In other cases, however, the chromosomal imbalance in the defective offspring does stem from heredity. When a parent is a carrier of a chromosomal rearrangement known as a translocation, there is no loss or gain of active genetic material. Consequently, the cells of a carrier are genetically balanced, and the individual is developmentally normal. But such a parent runs a risk as high as 50 percent of producing defective offspring.[7]

When the chromosome analysis of a malformed child indicates the presence of an hereditary chromosomal disorder, the child's parents are tested to ascertain which may be the carrier. The testing procedure is customarily extended to blood relatives of the carrier, because any or all of them could themselves be carriers and have no knowledge of their risk of producing defective offspring.[8]

When an individual learns that he or she is the carrier of a chromosomal rearrangement and is informed of the consequent risk of producing congenitally malformed children, there will almost certainly be a marked effect upon his or her thinking and behavior. In an unmarried person, fear of the high genetic risk may preclude typical dating activity, courtship, and marriage. Married couples carrying such a risk usually refuse to initiate a pregnancy willingly, particularly if they already have suffered the consequences of producing a defective child. Although pregnancies do occur in some such cases, the resulting anxiety and fear almost always impel the couple to elect therapeutic abortion. This decision usually is particularly distressing because of the knowledge that the developing child may be entirely normal.

B. *Prenatal Chromosome Analysis*

The frustration felt by a number of cytogeneticists because of their inability to offer assistance in such tragic cases as those just described stimulated research efforts to find a safe and reliable way of performing a chromosomal analysis on an unborn fetus as early in pregnancy as possible. In 1965, Dr. Harold Klinger and I, working independently, obtained the first successful fetal chromosome preparations from cultured fetal cells derived from amniotic fluid withdrawn from pregnant women.

Amniotic fluid for prenatal diagnosis is obtained by a procedure known as transabdominal amniocentesis. The obstetrician passes a needle through the abdominal and uterine walls of the mother and into the amniotic cavity containing the fluid and the fetus. Although to the layman the procedure might appear painful and hazardous, it is neither. Before the fetal cell culture technique was developed, amniocentesis was used to monitor the progress of Rh disease in affected fetuses during the third trimester of pregnancy.[9] In fact, the cells taken from such samples of amniotic fluid served as the research material in the development of the prenatal cell culture technique.

Amniotic fluid cell cultures and associated prenatal chromosome analyses are more and more widely used in the United States and abroad as an important diagnostic technique in the management of pregnancies with a suspected or known genetic risk. At this writing, almost 2000 such analyses have been performed, and no recorded case of maternal or fetal morbidity or mortality has been attributed to the procedure.[10]

Most cytogeneticists and genetic counsellors recommend chromosome analysis in three general categories of cases:

1. *Translocation Carrier Parent* — As indicated earlier, when one or the other parent is a carrier of a chromosomal translocation, the theoretical risk of producing a genetically unbalanced and congenitally malformed child is as high as 50 percent. Pregnancies in such cases are associated with such a high level of anxiety and fear that before prenatal diagnostic techniques were available, virtually all of the couples involved sought, and somehow obtained, therapeutic abortions on the basis of the risk.

2. *Previous Defective Child with Non-Hereditary Chromosome Abnormality* — The majority of cases in this group involve parents who have produced a mongoloid child of the nonhereditary type. In all such cases — unless an "older mother" is involved — the risk of recurrence of the tragedy is low. Nevertheless, the anxiety level of the parents is extremely high; in their minds the risk was 100 percent when they produced the defective child. The prenatal

chromosome analyses performed in such cases are intended primarily to remove the potentially dangerous fear and anxiety associated with the pregnancy, so that the remaining period of gestation can be relatively pleasant and healthy.

3. *Maternal Age Factor* — There is a positive correlation between an increase in maternal age and a heightened probability of producing a child with defects. This phenomenon is most clearly demonstrated by the nonhereditary type of mongolism: based on maternal age alone, the probability of producing such a child increases about 100-fold during the period of a woman's reproductive years. The risk is about 1 in 3000 at age 15 and rises to about 1 in 30 at age 45.

These facts are known to obstetricians, and the general phenomenon is widely recognized by laymen as well. Consequently, pregnancies in women over age 35 or 40 are likely to be associated with a great deal of anxiety in both parents. Chromosome analyses in such cases have led to the identification of several mongoloid fetuses.

Despite the obvious usefulness of prenatal chromosome analysis, there are certain limitations and pitfalls associated with the techniques. Occasionally the obstetrician has difficulty in obtaining the amniotic fluid sample, and amniocentesis must then be repeated. Also, it is fairly difficult to culture the relatively small number of living cells suspended in the amniotic fluid, and a culture failure or inadequate chromosome preparation may lead to an additional amniocentesis and delay of the final evaluation. A specific limitation arises in the case of multiple pregnancy. Although, almost without exception, a separate amniotic sac is associated with each developing fetus, the chromosome analysis obviously will be made on one fetus only.

A possible basis for an incorrect diagnosis is contamination of the tissue cultures by maternal cells dislodged during amniocentesis. This hazard can be virtually eliminated by setting up multiple cultures and by careful evaluation procedures. Finally, it must be recognized that even when the fetal chromosomes appear to be entirely normal, it is impossible to guarantee to the parents that the baby will be born without defects of any sort. Congenital malformations arise from a large number of causes, many of which have nothing to do with genetics.

From the ethical and legal standpoints, it is important that both parents be made aware not only of the techniques to be employed, but also of their limitations and potential hazards. An informative counselling session should be held prior to the amniocentesis if a prenatal chromosome analysis is to be performed.[11]

C. *Prenatal Analyses of Heritable Metabolic Disorders*

Following the development of the amniotic fluid cell culture techniques, it was recognized that such cultures — in addition to their application to prenatal chromosome analysis — could serve as the basis for the biochemical detection of certain heritable metabolic disorders.[12] These conditions arise from defects at the gene level and cannot be visualized as demonstrable chromosomal abnormalities.

Many of these genetic disorders are extremely serious, and some are predictably lethal in the first few years of a child's life. In Tay-Sachs disease, for example, the child is born apparently normal but within a few months starts to show the tragic effects of degeneration of the nervous system. These babies, who are as beautiful, lovable, alert, and reactive as any normal children, pass steadily and irrevocably through successive stages of mental and physical degeneration before the eyes of their horrified and distraught parents. During the degenerative period they develop a hypersensitivity to sound, so that even small noises will evoke violent reactions, and they frequently give the impression of suffering both physical pain and fear as they develop blindness and paralysis and lose mental contact with their environment. Usually death occurs before the age of 3, and the parents are left physically drained and emotionally devastated.

Tay-Sachs disease is inherited as an autosomal recessive and, when both parents are carriers, imposes a 1-in-4 risk of producing a child with the condition and a 1-in-2 risk of producing a carrier. By use of the appropriate biochemical testing procedures, it is possible to detect the carrier condition of this genetic trait in an individual and also to ascertain whether an unborn baby is affected by the disease.

Among the biochemical tests for the dozen or so heritable disorders that can be ascertained prenatally, some can be performed on the amniotic fluid itself, while others utilize uncultured amniotic fluid cells. However, most of them require cultured cells in much larger quantities than are needed for chromosome analysis.[13] Therefore, in addition to the problems of possible culture failure or maternal-cell contamination of the cultures (mentioned in connection with prenatal chromosome analysis), the final evaluation is delayed by the further problem of greater culture time, a major concern in biochemical analyses.

Because therapeutic abortion is a possible consequence when a prenatal genetic analysis is undertaken, there are both emotional and legal reasons for completing the evaluation as rapidly as possible. At the time of "quickening," when a pregnant woman first feels fetal movement (at between 16 and 20 weeks of gestation),[14] the event is very significant emotionally for her, and usually for her husband as well. Once the phenomenon of pregnancy becomes a proven reality, the parents focus emotionally on the fetus as a living, moving being. Ideally, prenatal diagnosis should be completed early enough to permit abortion, if necessary, before quickening occurs. In many cases, prenatal chromosome analyses can be completed early enough (though this is not the case when biochemical analyses require lengthier periods of fetal cell culture).

A point of legal importance in the chronology of pregnancy occurs at the twentieth week of gestation. As noted by Ryan:

> To the medical profession operating within its present framework, the conceptus, prior to 20 weeks of age, does not have the same legal status as one after that time. Should there be an untimely birth before 20 weeks, the act is considered an abortion, not a delivery, and is not listed on the mother's parity record. A birth or death certificate is not required and the body is handled as a pathological specimen without requiring legal interment.[15]

It appears likely that as the states liberalize their abortion laws, most of them will include some time limit in gestation beyond which abortion will not be permitted.[16] It also seems likely that in establishing such a cut-off date legislators will tend to favor that point at which the fetus is presumed to be viable. The term "viable" here refers to the capability of the fetus to survive outside the mother's womb, which is achieved at a point in time surrounded by considerable argument and confusion. It is frequently set at 20 weeks of gestation (giving rise to such laws as the one mentioned by Ryan) but a date several weeks later would probably be more realistic.

Confusion also arises from the use of the phrase "commencement of pregnancy." If pregnancy is considered to begin at the date of onset of the last menstrual period, the definition obviously is biologically incorrect. Although the time of fertilization would be biologically accurate, the specific date is extremely difficult to pinpoint in most cases. On the average, ovulation occurs approximately 2 weeks after the onset of the previous menstrual period, and fertilization, if it takes place, close to that point in time. This discrepancy of 2 weeks between the obstetrical and biological definitions of the beginning of pregnancy may prove to be a point of legal importance in some abortion cases (*e.g.*, where 2 weeks of leeway would spell the difference between whether or not a prenatal genetic evaluation could be completed).

Another potential problem in connection with the prenatal evaluation of heritable metabolic diseases arises from the fact that each disease requires a specific and different testing procedure. Consequently, if a subsequent prenatal evaluation is to be correct, it is of vital importance that the diagnosis of the disease in the original individual from whom it is learned that a genetic risk exists be absolutely accurate. For example, if a heritable neurologic disorder in a young child has been incorrectly diagnosed as Tay-Sachs disease, and the mother has her fetus evaluated for Tay-Sachs in a subsequent pregnancy, the testing will do no more than rule out Tay-Sachs disease, and the child may be born with the same disorder as its affected sibling.[17]

IV. The Life-Producing, Life-Enriching and Life-Saving Aspects of Prenatal Genetic Evaluation

When a couple learns that they carry a high genetic risk of producing a mentally and physically defective child, they do not initiate pregnancy willingly. This limitation on reproductive behavior is particularly tragic in those cases in which the couple has had nothing but genetic catastrophe. As noted earlier, under such circumstances there is a deep and pressing psychological need to compensate for the deficit by producing a normal child. The adoption of a child may prove of some value, but it does not solve the fundamental problem. Before prenatal diagnostic techniques were available, there was no way to help such unfortunate couples solve this dilemma. Now, prenatal evaluation and selective abortion can enable parents who otherwise would not undertake a pregnancy to do so, and to produce their own normal children. In this respect, prenatal genetic diagnoses may be looked upon as being life-producing.

I have placed considerable emphasis on the psychological damage which the presence of a defective child can cause to parents, siblings, and other members of the family, especially to those individuals known to be carriers of the genetic condition responsible for the child's defects. Prenatal evaluative techniques, coupled with effective genetic counselling, can markedly lessen the deleterious psychological effects on such families and, in time, should improve the attitude of our entire society. Thus, prenatal diagnosis can free individuals closely associated with a genetically based tragedy from the suspicion and condemnation they have confronted in the past and allow them to live far more pleasant and rewarding lives. Surely such procedures can be considered life-enriching.

Yet the most spectacular and important aspect of this new and exciting field of genetic diagnosis and management is that it preserves the lives of normal babies that would otherwise have been aborted because of a known genetic risk. Although couples with high genetic risk do not willingly undertake a pregnancy, pregnancies do occur in such cases. Furthermore, the genetic risk sometimes is not determined until after the fact of pregnancy. In virtually all such cases, the involved parents have sought and received therapeutic abortions, despite the fact that, even with the highest risk,[18] there remains a 50-50 chance that the child will be normal.

One may feel righteously enraged by the entire concept of therapeutic abortion and may be totally unsympathetic with the idea of interrupting a pregnancy under the circumstances just described. But the truth of the matter is that the attitude of the reader (or that of the author, for that matter) with respect to therapeutic abortion makes not one whit of difference when it comes to modifying the behavior of a distraught couple caught in the circumstance of a high-risk pregnancy. Experience has shown that, regardless of their previous attitude toward abortion, even when it was based on devout religious training and involvement, such couples seek and obtain abortions, legally or otherwise. Moreover, the more dogmatic and unyielding a couple's abhorrence of abortion is, the more destructive the post-abortion feelings of guilt are likely to be (particularly as they relate to the knowledge that the aborted child may well have been normal). The use of prenatal evaluative techniques in such cases not only eliminates much of the psychological damage to the parents but, more importantly, saves the lives of the unaffected children.

Theoretically, half of the fetuses in the highest-risk pregnancies are expected to be developmentally abnormal. But experience with the new techniques has demonstrated that notably fewer than 50 percent proved to be defective children. This interesting and important fact emerges because in a significant number of the cases involving a genetically unbalanced fetus, nature performs the abortion at an early stage. It is only when nature fails that the geneticist plays a role. A recent collection of data from various laboratories performing prenatal genetic evaluations indicates that the actual number of defective fetuses identified in high-risk cases has been about 20 percent. Since before prenatal diagnosis was used, virtually all of these would have ended in abortion, one is led to the irrefutable and heartwarming conclusion that prenatal diagnosis is literally saving the lives of 80 percent of the babies involved in even the highest-risk cases. Where the risk is lower, the percentage of babies saved is obviously higher.

Despite the fact that therapeutic abortion is performed in only a small percentage of the cases evaluated by prenatal diagnosis, such diagnoses should not and would not be performed if there were no legal way of obtaining an abortion when a fetus is found to be defective. Yet experience has shown that parents with a known genetic risk seek and obtain abortions, illegal if necessary, on the basis of the risk alone and despite the knowledge that the child might be normal. Taking these two facts together, and recognizing that prenatal diagnosis saves the lives of the normal babies in such cases, it could be argued that legislators who fail to recognize the risk of a defective child as an acceptable basis for legal abortion are dooming to destruction the lives of many wanted normal babies.

NOTES

1. CAL. HEALTH & SAFETY CODE §§ 25950-54 (Supp. 1971).
2. MODEL PENAL CODE § 230.3(2) (Proposed Official Draft, 1962).

3. A pregnancy resulting from incest carries with it a great increase in the genetic risk of physical and mental deformities. Yet social abhorrence of the initial act, rather than a recognition of genetic risk, is probably the basis for allowing therapeutic abortion in such cases.

4. Macintyre, *Counseling in Cases Involving Antenatal Diagnosis*, in ANTENATAL DIAGNOSIS (A. Dorfman ed. 1972).

5. It is probably impossible for anyone to recognize the full impact of such an event without actually experiencing it personally. Furthermore, it is natural for most uninvolved individuals to avoid the distress associated with a consideration of such unpleasant situations, and to protect themselves further by the reassuring thought that such a tragedy will never befall them. Consequently, society is prone to make pompous judgments with respect to the appropriate behavior for the principals in such a tragedy and to place unrealistic demands upon them.

6. One point that should be learned from this case is that the reactions of the normal siblings to the presence of a defective child are sometimes so controlled, in an effort to conform to societal expectations, that they may not be evident.

7. The mongoloid child was discussed here because it is the most familiar example. It should be noted, however, that among the types of cases of congenital malformations resulting from various kinds of chromosomal imbalance, the majority are more seriously abnormal than the mongoloid.

8. Macintyre, Staples, Steinberg & Hempel, *Familial Mongolism (Trisomy-21 Syndrome) Resulting from a "15/21" Chromosome Translocation in More Than Three Generations of a Large Kindred*, 14 AM. J. HUMAN GENETICS 335 (1962).

9. Stenchever & Cibils, *Management of the Rh-Sensitized Patient: A Three-Year Experience With Amniocentesis and Intrauterine Transfusion*, 100 AM. J. OBSTETRICS & GYNECOLOGY 554 (1968).

10. It cannot be assumed from present experience that amniocentesis is totally without risk, but the hazard is at least so small as to be immeasurable at this time.

11. In this connection, I use an "Informed Consent and Release" form which ensures that adequate information has been given and provides a significant degree of legal protection for the professionals involved. The form contains an explicit consent to the chromosome analysis and the penetration of the mother's abdominal and uterine walls. It also specifies that the following points must be explained to and understood by the parents: (1) that the procedure is considered extremely safe but it cannot be guaranteed that it will not cause damage to the mother or the fetus or initiate premature labor, possibly resulting in spontaneous abortion; (2) that any particular attempt to obtain amniotic fluid by transabdominal amniocentesis may be unsuccessful; (3) that an at-

tempt to obtain a viable tissue culture from the cells of any particular sample of amniotic fluid may be unsuccessful or that the chromosome preparations may be of poor quality and unusable; and (4) that although the likelihood of a misinterpretation of the chromosome karyotypes in this case is considered extremely small, a complete and correct diagnosis of the condition of the fetus based on the karyotypes obtained cannot be guaranteed. Finally, the form contains a release from liability for physical or mental injury resulting from the procedure.

See also Macintyre, *Chromosomal Problems of Intrauterine Diagnosis*, BIRTH DEFECTS: ORIGINAL ARTICLE SERIES, April 1971, at 10.

12. Nadler, *Patterns of Enzyme Development Utilizing Cultivated Human Fetal Cells Derived From Amniotic Fluid*, 2 BIOCHEM. GENET. 119 (1968).

13. Milunsky et al., *Prenatal Genetic Diagnosis*, 283 NEW ENGLAND J. MED. 1370, 1441, 1498 (1970).

14. In obstetrical practice, the chronology of pregnancy is considered to begin at the time of the onset of the last menstrual period.

15. Ryan, *Humane Abortion Laws and the Health Needs of Society*, in ABORTION AND THE LAW 61, 63 (D. Smith ed. 1967).

16. The New York law, for example, allows abortion on request "within 24 weeks from the commencement of pregnancy." N.Y. PENAL LAW § 125.05(3) (McKinney Supp. 1971).

17. All prenatal analyses present a unique problem in that the physician cannot ever examine the patient. In actual fact, therefore, prenatal evaluation is a prediction rather than a diagnosis, and this point should be made very clear to the parents in each case. Because the atmosphere surrounding such evaluations is very emotionally charged, the professionals involved in the procedures are particularly vulnerable to legal action by the involved parents in case of any presumed error in judg-.ment or management of the case.

The "Informed Consent and Release" form mentioned earlier (note 11 *supra*) was specifically designed for use in prenatal chromosome analyses. A similar form appropriate to prenatal biochemical analysis for specific heritable metabolic disorders is equally important.

18. In very rare cases of a particular kind of chromosomal translocation, the risk may be 100 percent.

ABORTION COUNSELLING: SHALL WOMEN BE PERMITTED TO KNOW?

GERALD A. MESSERMAN

I. INTRODUCTION

THE GROWING CONCERN of courts and legislatures with the wisdom and validity of anti-abortion laws has been accompanied by an increase in counselling services for women wishing to terminate unwanted pregnancies. Almost 200 affiliates of Planned Parenthood-World Population, operating throughout the country, have entered the abortion counselling field.[1] The Clergy Consultation Service, started in New York in 1967 by a group of ministers and rabbis, now has some 28 offices in 22 states and employs the services of over 1000 clergymen.[2] Numerous other groups throughout the country also provide abortion counselling.[3] Unfortunately, persons who participate in abortion counselling have found their activities to be somewhat hazardous. At least two criminal prosecutions have already been initiated against clergy counsellors,[4] and commercial counselling services have been charged with practicing medicine without a license, unlawful fee splitting, and unlawful advertising.[5]

Moreover, enormous pressure has been generated which, either intentionally or incidentally, has restricted the dissemination of information regarding the availability of legal abortions. Referral agencies have had little success in placing ads in daily metropolitan newspapers, and when intrepid student editors of college newspapers have published the names of abortion referral services, the threat of criminal prosecution has frequently been made. One such student editor was charged under a Florida law that prohibits the publishing of abortion information, despite the fact that referral services in Florida are legal.[6] When the Concordia College newspaper published an advertisement for an abortion clinic in New York, the president of the college immediately suspended publication of the newspaper.[7]

While the media have effectively blacked-out much information concerning abortion and abortion referral services, still other limitations on communication have been self-imposed. Planned Parenthood associations, for example, are reluctant to engage in public promotion of their services, believing that such activity does not conform to the image Planned Parenthood wishes to create.[8] By and large, however, it is the threat of criminal prosecution and media policies that have compelled a restrained approach by many of the counselling services, particularly the nonprofit ones.[9]

In practice, the relatively restricted access to abortion information has given rise to a number of important consequences. First, information regarding abortion services has been largely unavailable to all except the better-informed and more affluent members of the population. Second, referral agencies have often failed to provide the most effective counselling service appropriate to the needs of the counsellee.[10] And third, because of the unavailability of more conventional means of communication, referral services have been advertised in ways that offend the taste and sensibility of substantial segments of the population. For a period of time, for example, vacationers in Miami Beach could look up to the skies and see a low-flying airplane trailing a banner that read "Abortion Information" and listed the New York telephone number of a referral agency.[11]

Despite the pervasiveness of such problems and the variety of legal and practical issues they raise, legal scholars have focused little attention upon the questions presented. Existing law does provide significant guidelines for those engaged in abortion counselling. Yet most counsellors have had substantial difficulty determining precisely what the law permits or demands.[12] An exploration of relevant legal principles should assist in delineating and assessing the nature and magnitude of the risks involved in abortion counselling.[13]

II. THE CONSTITUTIONAL LIMITATIONS

One of the government's principal means for restricting abortion counselling is the criminal proscription of advertising and dissemination of abortion information.[14] The Supreme Court has not yet considered the validity of statutes which limit the public's access to abortion information,[15] but it is clear that such laws must be assessed in the context of first amendment principles. Appraisal of the constitutionality of limitations on advertising requires examination of two distinct but interrelated interests — the counsellor's right to speak, and the counsellee's right to hear and know.

A. *The Right of the Counsellor to Inform*

A preliminary inquiry concerning referral and counselling activities is whether the activity constitutes speech and is thus granted the protection of the first amendment, or whether the activity is conduct that is unprotected by the first amendment.[16] Counselling limited to the distribution of general information concerning abortions and specific information concerning the procurement of legal abortions is clearly speech.[17] When the counsellor actually arranges for performance of the abortion, however, his activity may well go beyond pure speech and become action which is beyond the protection of the first amendment.[18]

Where the counselling agency's activity falls within the realm of speech, any restrictions upon such activity can be constitutional only upon a showing of a compelling state interest. This conclusion follows from a long series of cases in which the Supreme Court

> has held that where fundamental personal liberties are involved, they may not be abridged by the states simply on a showing that a regulatory statute has some rational relationship to the effectuation of a proper state purpose. "Where there is significant encroachment upon personal liberty, the state may prevail only upon showing a subordinating interest which is compelling." *Bates v. Little Rock*, 361 U.S. 516, 524. The law must be shown "necessary, and not merely rationally related, to the accomplishment of a permissible state policy." *McLaughlin v. Florida*, 379 U.S. 184, 196.[19]

If a counselling service were merely to provide information regarding the circumstances in which an abortion could be lawfully procured in the state in which the service was operating, it is difficult to conceive of any legitimate basis for inhibiting the dissemination of such information. Thus, the communications would constitute protected first amendment expression. It would not fall within any of the areas of expression which may be regulated by the state: there would be no incitement of others to commit unlawful acts,[20] no utterance of inflammatory words,[21] no danger of shocking those who might be exposed to the words uttered,[22] and no obscenity.[23]

The same result should obtain where the counselling service provides similar information on the availability of abortions that are legal only in states other than the one in which the service is operating. Although a stronger state interest might arguably exist in this situation, it is doubtful that the state's interest would rise to the compelling nature required to warrant a restriction upon first amendment rights. Indeed, one federal court so concluded in the case of *Mitchell Family Planning, Inc. v. City of Royal Oak.*[24] *Mitchell* held unconstitutional a municipal ordinance which prohibited billboard advertising of any information concerning the procuring of an abortion. The court reasoned that "the City of Royal Oak has insufficient interest in an abortion to be performed in another state to warrant [such a] limitation of speech."[25]

Thus, where the agency's services do not include the actual arrangement of the abortion operation, it appears that a state could not meet the burden necessary to curtail the solely informational nature of the service. An even stronger case for this proposition can be made by examining the counselee's, or the public's, right to know.

B. *The Counsellee's Right to Be Informed*

That the first amendment protects more than the right to speak is a proposition most recently relied upon by the Supreme Court in invalidating a statute which prohibited the possession of pornographic literature: "It is now well established that the Constitution protects the right to receive information and ideas . . . , regardless of their social worth, [and that this right] is fundamental to our free society."[26] The public's right to receive information is a right of increasing prominence in contemporary America. It has been relied upon not only to protect an individual's right to possess pornographic materials, but also to justify publication of important classified government documents,[27] to bar prosecution of an agency advertising Mexican divorces,[28] and in a variety of other instances.

Within the context of the first amendment balancing test, the importance of the need for access to particular information is critical in determining whether there is a protected right to acquire such information. That factor should entitle dissemination of abortion information to a high degree of constitutional protection. The need to be informed of facts concerning abortion is at least as great to those seeking such information as is the need of others to possess pornographic material or to acquire information concerning Mexican divorces. Women concerned with terminating an unwanted pregnancy desperately desire information regarding how to do so, and whether a legal abortion is secured or not can be a question of extraordinary impact in a woman's life.[29] Indeed, the intensity with which a woman will search for an abortion, the urgency of the search, and the tragic frustration and indignities frequently encountered have been related by many.

The right to know is an integral aspect of the first amendment, and protection of that right requires that restrictions upon the dissemination of abortion information be struck down unless a state can demonstrate compelling reasons for such restrictions. Because such information does not fall within the categories of expression which heretofore have been validly regulated or prohibited, it is doubtful that a state could meet this burden. Furthermore, if the right to have an abortion is deemed a fundamental right, the right to know in the context of abortion counselling would assume an added dimension. Any restriction upon the dissemination of abortion information would infringe upon the right to abortion, and could therefore be justified only under the most limited circumstances, if any.[30]

C. *Advertising Abortion Information*

It may be of little solace to those involved in abortion counselling to know that the dissemination of abortion information is protected by the first amendment if the advertising of their services is not similarly protected. Nonetheless, this may be the case in certain instances. Relying on the commercial sector doctrine, courts have frequently held that advertisements and solicitations do not enjoy the protection of the first amendment. The commercial sector doctrine has its genesis in *Valentine v. Chrestensen*,[31] where the Supreme Court held that distribution of advertising handbills intended solely for a commercial purpose might legitimately be prohibited. In the words of the Court,

> the streets are proper places for the exercise of the freedom of communicating information and disseminating opinions and . . . though the states and municipalities may appropriately regulate the

> privilege in the public interest, they may not unduly burden or proscribe its employment in these public thoroughfares. [It is] equally clear that the Constitution imposes no such restraint on government as respects purely commercial advertising. Whether, and to what extent, one may promote or pursue a gainful occupation in the streets and to what extent such activities shall be judged a derogation of the public right of the user, are matters for legislative judgment.[32]

Many of the statutes which inhibit counselling activity[33] are written as restrictions on advertising. Should the commercial sector doctrine be invoked to uphold such statutes, the effectiveness of otherwise legal referral agencies would be seriously impaired. It is possible, however, that the statutory restrictions on advertising will not receive the judicial deference that would ensue from a rigid application of the commercial sector doctrine, particularly when the agencies in question operate on a nonprofit basis.

Courts have gone to great lengths to distinguish communication by professionals to their clients from aggressive, commercially motivated communication designed to promote the sale of particular goods or services. A case in point is *Planned Parenthood Committee v. Maricopa County*,[34] where the Supreme Court of Arizona rejected a constitutional challenge to a statute which prohibited the publication of "a notice or advertisement of any medicine or means for producing or facilitating a miscarriage or abortion, or for prevention of conception . . . ."[35] In upholding the Arizona statute, the court read the term "publishes a notice or advertisement" to apply only to an open appeal to the general public. General literature dealing with the population problem was held to be outside the proscription of the statute. Also excepted were such materials as "[a]rticles and press releases in newspapers and periodicals, including editorials, commentaries, and informational articles on matters of current public interest . . . ."[36] The statute would not apply, the court held, to "the dissemination of birth control information by a doctor to his patient, or by the Planned Parenthood Committee to those who seek such information from them . . . ."[37] This exception arises from the fact that "person-to-person consultation" would not be considered advertising. But if information describing the use and application of particular contraceptive devices were made available to the *general public*, "this would amount to advertising and fall within the prohibitive terms of the statute."[38]

The Arizona court distinguished aggressive solicitation of referrals "by the employment of touters or canvassers"[39] from referrals by physicians to Planned Parenthood that were made "to persons who . . . , of their own accord, sought birth control information from the referring party"[40] and referrals made in the course of the physician's treatment of the patient. Aggressive solicitation would constitute advertising, but professional referrals would not.

Given this construction of the statute, the constitutional challenge was dismissed by the court in summary fashion. The court concluded that the law did "not prohibit the public discussion or advocacy of the general ideas which plaintiff [sought] to promote,"[41] that it imposed no prior restraint upon the exercise of speech, and that it did not limit person-to-person conversation. The restriction in the statute was considered to be very limited: "The only limitation . . . is that plaintiff may not advertise, in the sense of publicly advocating, specific trade branded devices or preparations in the contraceptive field."[42] Suggesting that advertising "does not enjoy the same degree of protection under the first amendment as do other noncommercial forms of idea expression,"[43] the court found no defect in this limitation.

Furthermore, the court declared that the validity of any restraint upon the exercise of speech must be determined by balancing "the state's interest in the welfare and safety of its citizens against the individual's interest in free speech and the degree of impairment of this freedom caused by the governmental regulation."[44] To implement this balancing test, the court inquired whether there was any reasonable public interest which would justify the limitations upon expression imposed by the statute. Such a justification was found to exist in the state's objective of protecting the health and morals of the community by restricting sexual activity among unmarried persons. Considering the importance of this objective and the historical regulation of advertising that has been tolerated against first amendment challenges, the statutory proscription was deemed acceptable.

Although this approach to the advertising statutes potentially affords more protection to the abortion counsellor than would a rigid application of the commercial sector doctrine, it is still a serious impediment to those who desire counselling but do not know where it is available. A different and more realistic approach to the advertising issue was taken in *Mitchell Family Planning, Inc. v. City of Royal Oak*[45] where the court struck down a municipal ordinance prohibiting billboard advertising of abortion information. The nonprofit Mitchell Family Planning Agency had rented billboard space and put up an advertisement reading:

> Abortion Information
> Male and Female Sterilization Information
> Mitchell Family Planning Incorporated
> Niagara Falls, New York. Phone No.
> 716-285-9133.   Local Phone No. 358-4672.[46]

In response to the agency's request for an injunction restraining enforcement of the municipal ordinance, the court held that the ordinance was impermissibly broad because it seemed to prohibit advertising which could result in legal abortions as well as illegal ones. The court did not suggest that Mitchell's form of advertising was subject to any different tests than were other forms of expression. Then, because there was no indication that contacting the agency would imminently result in an illegal abortion, the court concluded that there was no clear and present danger that a substantive evil which the city had the power to prohibit would take place.[47]   Accordingly, no limitation of speech was justified.

While it remains to be seen what test is applied to advertising by nonprofit groups, a different test might well be applied to advertising by for-profit agencies as judicial hostility to money-making activities in the abortion field is manifested.   Although there is a certain dilution of first amendment protections when the balancing test is applied,[48] its utilization would still be preferable to reliance on the commercial sector doctrine, for under the balancing test it is possible that advertising even by commercial agencies will find an adequate measure of protection.

A recent case involving advertisements for Mexican divorces indicates how the public's right to acquire information may be balanced against the governmental power to regulate commercial solicitation.   In *Hiett v. United States*,[49] the defendant was convicted of using the mails to distribute written material "giving or offering to give information concerning where or how or through whom a divorce may be secured in a foreign country, and designed to solicit business in connection with the procurement thereof."[50] On appeal, the Government urged that this provision was a constitutionally permissible regulation of activity which went beyond the kind of expression protected by the first amendment. Solicitation, the Government argued, "is not a form of speech entitled to First Amendment protection, just as obscene, abusive language, and threats of fighting words are not protected."[51] The court rejected this contention and held that even purely commercial expression was entitled to some degree of first amendment protection.

The test to be applied, according to *Hiett*, is the same one used where courts are confronted with the validity of restraints upon expression which involve more than speech. Where speech is combined with conduct for the purpose of achieving communication, the court noted, such "nonpure" speech is afforded protection measured by balancing "the harm done by the overbreadth and vagueness of the statute against the legitimate interests the legislature was seeking to protect"[52] to determine whether the latter "are so overwhelming as to justify the encroachment."[53]

That the same test should be applied to commercial expression is the ultimate conclusion reached by the court: "[C]ases show that when speech is coupled with solicitation, as it is in the expression [the statute] prohibits, it is no longer pure speech and it is to be tested by the balancing approach."[54] Applying the balancing test to the commercial expression involved in solicitation of foreign divorce business, the court concluded that the statutory prohibition was intolerably broad, that the information it sought to remove from the public domain related to matters of great social importance, and that the Government's interest — the desire to preserve family integrity — could be achieved in a more reasonable way.[55]

The analogy is obvious between an interdiction against mailing information designed to solicit foreign divorce business and a prohibition against advertisements and dissemination of information regarding the availability of abortions in or outside of the state in which the information is distributed. If the information dispensed by the counselling service relates to lawful means of securing an abortion, it should not come within the state's legitimate power to bar expression which incites others to unlawful conduct. Furthermore, if the importance of the information to the public is realistically considered, it is likely that the purported governmental interest in prohibiting the advertising or dissemination of abortion information will prove inadequate to justify such a prohibition.

Simplistic application of the ill-defined and ambiguous commercial sector doctrine would clearly yield a far less desirable result. But the exclusion under that doctrine of commercial advertising from the protection of the first amendment cannot withstand analysis. The illogic of conditioning first amendment rights upon the motivating force impelling a particular expression is rather apparent. Any number of cases, for example, have recognized that newspapers, although profit-making businesses, are entitled to first amendment protection.[56] Similarly, picketing may be engaged in primarily for the purpose of achieving economic gain, but this fact does not place picketing outside the ambit of the first amendment.[57] And a book dealer, despite his profit motivation, retains first amendment protection: "It is . . . no matter that the dissemination [of books] takes place under commercial auspices."[58] Thus, the doctrine that commercial communication is outside the system of protected expression has been employed to justify controls over commercial advertising,[59] but the simplistic analysis which suggests that the first amendment becomes irrelevant upon a finding of commercialism does not withstand scrutiny.

Indeed, the commercial sector doctrine has little to commend it. It assumes that the motivation behind expression is different where the expression may be characterized as political, social, or literary, as opposed to expression which is crassly commercial. This assumption is simply not supported by fact.

> The profit motive should make no difference, for that is an element inherent in the very conception of a press under our system of free enterprise. Those who make their living through exercise of First Amendment rights are no less entitled to its protection than those whose advocacy or promotion is not hitched to a profit motive.[60]

Moreover, the commercial sector doctrine implicitly assumes that those who communicate information by way of advertising are offering facts less important to the public than is the information conveyed in noncommercial expression. This assumption also does not withstand scrutiny. It would be difficult to find, for example, information more intensely desired and more immediately relevant to a woman's life than the abortion information offered by counselling services. If there is to be a free flow of information regarding matters of great public importance and if that information cannot flow through noncommercial channels of communication, alternative commercial channels must be established and must be granted constitutional protection so that the information can find its way into the public domain.

Thus, to determine whether abortion advertising is protected first amendment activity, a number of different questions must be considered. First, is the counselling activity engaged in for commercial gain? Second, is the counselling activity advertised in a public manner? Third, what alternative means of gaining access to information are available to the public? And fourth, is the counselling service disseminating information dealing solely with legal abortion procedures? Where the counselling service is conducted for profit, the commercial sector doctrine may be applicable, for it still has vitality in the courts, ill-founded as that may be. At worst, application of the doctrine would exclude the counselling activity from first amendment protection. But more realistically, the validity of limitations upon the dissemination of information by a commercial counselling service would be evaluated by application of a balancing test only slightly different from that which is applied to restrictions upon other communication activities. And when nonprofit or noncommercial agencies are involved, traditional first amendment principles indicate that there would be little justification for restrictions.

III. Counselling as Aiding, Abetting, or Inducement of Abortion

A. *Culpability as an Accomplice of the Abortionist*

One of the problems that concerns abortion counselling and referral agencies is whether a counsellor who gives information leading to the performance of an illegal abortion may be convicted as an aider and abettor or as an accessory before the fact.[61] This issue was raised in *Commonwealth v. Hare*[62] in the prosecution of a clergyman who provided information to a woman seeking an abortion. In an indictment filed in 1969 in Middlesex County, Massachusetts, the clergyman was charged with abortion.[63] The indictment alleged that the minister, "with intent to procure the miscarriage of . . . [one woman], did aid or assist [another] in unlawfully using an instrument or other means upon the body of . . . [the woman]."[64] A bill of particulars was filed in which the commonwealth alleged that the minister, knowing that he was in violation of the laws of Massachusetts, "instructed" the woman and her companion to proceed to the alleged abortionist, "knowing he was an unlicensed physician," for the purpose of having him perform an unlawful abortion.[65]

A motion to dismiss the indictment was filed on the ground that the indictment and bill of particulars did not charge an offense under the laws of Massachusetts. The trial judge granted the motion to dismiss, stating:

> I do not regard the use of the word 'instructed', in the Bill of Particulars as implying that the defendant directed, advised, or induced . . . [the woman] to proceed to Brunelle, the alleged abortionist. An inspection of the evidence . . . before the Grand Jury confirms this view. In plain language, the defendant informed . . . [the woman] of the telephone number and address of Brunelle as one who would perform an abortion for $400. From the facts alleged in the Bill of Particulars and the reasonable inferences which may be drawn therefrom, no more can be concluded than that . . . [the woman] sought out the defendant, seeking information as to an abortion, and that the defendant furnished her with the name, address, and telephone number of the alleged abortionist, and the price. *There is no evidence of any connection or communication between the defendant and Brunelle.*[66]

The trial judge further pointed out that essential facts were missing from the commonwealth's case that would be necessary to find Hare guilty as an accessory. Namely, there had been no showing of "an association of the defendant with the venture or that he participated in it as in something that he wished to bring about and that he sought, by his action, to make it succeed."[67]

On appeal from the trial judge's order granting dismissal, the Supreme Judicial Court of Massachusetts reversed the lower court, but for reasons not really pertinent to the ultimate question of whether Hare's conduct was criminal. The court held that the dismissal order should have been denied because the indictment (considered without reference to the bill of particulars) adequately charged a crime.[68] But the supreme judicial court did provide dictum favorable to Hare's position:

> If the bill of particulars in the instant case in fact presents the total extent of the Commonwealth's proof, we think, without so deciding, that the allowance of a motion for a directed verdict might well be required at the conclusion of the Commonwealth's opening statement or at the close of the Commonwealth's case.[69]

Thus, although the trial judge erred procedurally in granting the defendant's motion, the supreme court apparently agreed in substance with the judge's conclusion that Hare's conduct did not make him culpable as an accessory.

Since remand, the *Hare* case has not yet followed its full course, but it does point out a critical problem which must be considered by all abortion counselling services in determining the manner in which they will operate. The Cleveland Consultation Service — of which Hare was a member — had been functioning before legal abortions were widely available in a number of states without concern for whether an abortion was necessary to preserve the life or health of the woman. Referrals were made to persons believed to be licensed physicians by the Consultation Service, although an effort was made to minimize the contact between the doctors and the Consultation Service on advice of counsel that this procedure would reduce exposure to criminal prosecution. The particular physician involved in the *Hare* case, as the facts developed, had lost his license as a consequence of an earlier abortion conviction. Consequently, the illegality of the abortion in Massachusetts was indisputable.[70] But there had been no actual contact by the minister-defendant and the unlicensed physician; no fee had been charged for the service by the minister; and no effort had been made by the minister to encourage the woman to have an abortion. Upon these facts, the question of whether or not the abortion counsellor could be convicted of being an accessory can be resolved on the basis of established legal principles.

A classic case concerning the requisites of culpability as an accessory is *United States v. Peoni*,[71] where Judge Learned Hand articulated the applicable standards in language that won approval in numerous subsequent decisions.[72] After reviewing statutory and common law history concerning the definitions and tests for determining whether one is guilty as an accessory, Judge Hand stated:

> It will be observed that all [the accepted] definitions have nothing whatever to do with the probability that the forbidden result would follow upon the accessory's conduct; and that they all demand that he in some sort associate himself with the venture, that he participate in it as in something that he wishes to bring about, that he seek by his action to make it succeed. All the words used — even the most colorless, "abet" — carry an implication of purposive attitude towards it.[73]

In *Peoni*, the court reversed a conviction on a charge of counterfeiting where guilt was predicated on the assertion that the defendant had acted as an accessory before the fact.[74] Judge Hand found that the defendant's conduct "was indeed a step in the causal chain which ended in [the principal's] possession [of counterfeit bills]," but it was nothing more.[75] The court thus rejected the "but-for" test as a means of determining whether evidence is sufficient to establish guilt: even if the Government could prove that the substantive offense would not have occurred without the participation of the alleged accessory, that in itself would not be sufficient to support conviction.[76]

Further guidance as to the risks involved in abortion counselling can be found in *Morei v. United States*,[77] where a government agent had sought to obtain narcotics from a physician. The physician did not give the agent the drugs, but he "did give the name of defendant Morei, and his address in Cleveland and told [the agent] to see Morei and tell him [the physician] had sent [the agent] and that 'he'll take care of you.' "[78] When Morei subsequently sold the narcotics to the agent, the physician was charged and convicted as an accessory to the sale, but his conviction was overturned on appeal. Because there had been no showing that the physician had any stake in the venture,[79] the appellate court would not permit an inference of the necessary interest in the outcome of the principal's criminal acts.[80] In evaluating the relationship shown by the evidence, the court observed: "This is not the purposive association with the venture that . . . brings [the physician] within the compass of the crime of purchasing or selling narcotics, either as principal, aider and abettor, or accessory before the fact."[81]

A similar decision was rendered by the Third Circuit Court of Appeals in *United States v. Moses*,[82] where the evidence demonstrated that the defendant introduced certain persons, at their request, to a seller of narcotics. The defendant had vouched for the buyers and a purchase was made. Nonetheless, the court found "[t]here was nothing to show that [the defendant] was associated in any way with the enterprise of the seller or that she had any personal or financial interest in bringing trade to him."[83] Thus, "[a]lthough appellant's conduct was prefatory to the sale, it was not collaborative with the seller. For this reason, the conviction [could not] be sustained."[84]

Transposing the principles developed in the cases described above to the typical abortion counselling situation, one can draw certain tentative conclusions. First, if the counsellor is not actually acting in concert with the abortionist, the probability of conviction as an aider and abettor or accessory before the fact is diminished. Second, if the counsellor is not profiting by the act of the abortionist, courts are apt to hold that he does not have a sufficient stake in the outcome of the venture to support a conviction. And third, where the counsellor either encouraged an abortion or had a personal interest in securing an abortion, the probability of a sustainable conviction is substantially increased.

Some of these tentative conclusions find direct support in the present case law. For example, in *Scott v. State*,[85] the Supreme Court of Delaware held that "the furnishing of the name of the person who later committed the abortion [is not] sufficient to convict one of aiding, abetting or procuring an abortion."[86] In *Scott*, the defendant secured the name and address of the abortionist and accompanied the patient to the apartment of the abortionist knowing that she intended to have an abortion performed. Despite these facts, the evidence was held insufficient to convict.[87]

On the other hand, if the evidence tends to support an inference of concerted action between the party making the referral and the person performing the abortion, the hazard of conviction is great. So, in *State v. Ellrich*,[88] conviction was sustained upon evidence demonstrating that the defendant-physician was contacted for the purpose of performing an abortion; that he gave the name and telephone number of the abortionist to the woman seeking the abortion;

and that he told her to call from a certain pay phone and to say that she was calling from a particular address, rather than use the defendant's name. These peculiar instructions, held the Supreme Court of New Jersey, showed a "prearranged code" between the defendant and the principal and "spell out quite clearly and convincingly a criminal concert of action."[89]

A personal interest sufficient to establish guilt as an aider and abettor may be found where the defendant seeks to bring about the abortion for personal reasons. Thus, in *Commonwealth v. Donoghue*,[90] the fact that the person who arranged the abortion was responsible for the pregnancy of the woman was held sufficient to establish his personal stake in the venture. Presumably, however, such a personal stake would not exist in the routine counselling situation.

B. *Culpability as an Accomplice of the Abortee*

In those cases in which the evidence has been held insufficient to support conviction of an individual as an aider and abettor to abortion where the principle offender was the abortionist, there was no issue before the court as to whether the individual who assisted in making arrangements could be convicted as an accomplice to the offense of unlawfully procuring an abortion. In several states the woman upon whom the abortion is performed may be charged with soliciting or submitting to an unlawful abortion.[91] In such an instance, it is possible that the counsellor may be charged as an accomplice to her offense. But here as well, the principles discussed above would pertain — *i.e.*, if the counsellor has a personal stake, financial or otherwise, in the outcome of the woman's effort to obtain an abortion, the chances of his conviction as an accomplice are increased.

In jurisdictions where the participation of the woman is considered innocent or noncriminal and the counsellor is concerned solely with assisting the woman, it is unlikely that any conviction of the counsellor would be possible. This conclusion derives from the established principle that "there can be no conviction for aiding and abetting someone to do an innocent act."[92] On the other hand, if there is a community of interest between the counsellor and the party performing an illegal abortion, the innocence of the woman will not save the counsellor from the risk of conviction as an accessory to the abortionist.

IV. Additional Hazards of Abortion Counselling

The manner in which an abortion counselling service operates bears not only upon the extent to which its participants are subjected to prosecution as accessories, but also upon the seriousness of other risks. For obvious reasons, those services which not only provide information, but also, and for a fee, make specific arrangements for the performance of the abortion invite the greatest possibility of legal interference.[93]

A. Commercial Services: Some Special Problems

Judicial hostility to abortion counselling services that operate for a profit has been strongly in evidence. For example, in State v. Abortion Information Agency, Inc., a temporary injunction was obtained in New York restraining a commercial abortion counselling service "from transacting business as a referral agency for performing abortions."[94] The agency operated by advertising, receiving telephone calls from women who wished to have abortions performed, advising the woman how an abortion might be obtained, informing the caller of the probable cost of the physician and hospital services, and charging the caller a fee for the referral and the operation.[95]

Women who used the service entered licensed hospitals and were examined and treated by licensed physicians. Nonetheless, the activities of the agency were found to be illegal on the following grounds: (1) the agency was acting as an intermediary or broker in the sale of professional services in violation of the public policy of the state;[96] (2) the agency was engaged in fee splitting contrary to the law and public policy of the state;[97] and (3) the agency was engaged in the unauthorized practice of medicine which, according to the court, involved some effort at determining the type of operation to be performed upon the women seeking abortions.[98] As a final justification for its decision, the court concluded that the agency was engaging in the unlicensed (and hence illegal) selling of insurance by providing abortion services at a "guaranteed flat charge that cover[ed] everything."[99]

The decision of the court bristles with hostility to the defendant's money-making activities. Indeed, the court concluded that the agency had "the appearance of one conceived in fraud," simply because its announced purpose, contained in the certificate of incorporation, was

> [t]o provide general information concerning legal abortions to the public and to women with problem pregnancies. The corporation, nor its agents, shall not [sic] undertake to diagnose pregnancy, or any other physical or mental condition of a client. The corporation shall not undertake to advise a client on the medical desirability of obtaining an abortion, nor shall it provide any information or perform any act which may constitute the practice of medicine.[100]

Fraud was inferred from the fact that, despite this assertion of purpose, a business was developed which engaged "extensively in the procurement of hospital services and . . . arrangements for abortions."[101] The court further concluded, although without pointing to any supporting evidence, that the defendant actually solicited and encouraged women to seek out abortions. Although the initial contact was always established as a result of a call from the woman, this fact was considered inconsequential:

> That the initial inquiry concerning the abortion is made by the patient does not negate the fact that the defendants' methodology once a patient contacted it was to further encourage the abortion, for the sole motive of financial gain to defendants, rather than to aid in giving objective and concerned advice to the patient.[102]

The conclusion that the agency was operating in violation of public policy derives from a plain and obvious antagonism to the profit-making nature of the agency's business.[103] This attitude was expressed by the trial court in unambiguous terms: "The law which sought to emancipate women from servitude as unwilling breeders, did not intend to deliver them as helpless victims of commercial operators for the exploitation of their misery."[104]

It is not unlikely that commercial referral agencies in other states may meet similar fates, if not similar rhetoric. Several courts have suggested that the practice of medicine should be protected from commercial exploitation.[105] It has been held to be against public policy, for example, to permit a "middleman" to intervene for profit in establishing the professional relationships between physicians and the public.[106] Such languuage parallels the charge leveled in *Abortion Information Agency, Inc.* that the agency was acting, in violation of public policy, as an intermediary or broker in the sale of professional services, and suggests that the commercial agencies may be in jeopardy.

Indeed, in the State of New York hostility toward commercial referral agencies was so intense that legislation was enacted to abolish these businesses.[107] Whether such broad, prohibitory legislation can be successfully challenged remains to be seen. The state clearly has the authority under its police power to prohibit business activities rationally deemed inimical to the public welfare. But no Supreme Court case has yet been decided under such a public welfare notion where the operators of the business could claim their activity was entitled to first amendment protection.[108]

If the general right to engage in business was all that was at stake, then the proscription of for-profit referral agencies would almost certainly be upheld as a rational legislative action, particularly when one considers the complaints typically directed at the agencies. Before the statutory ban on profit-making referral agencies was enacted in New York, the state had initiated a widespread investigation into the activities of commercial referral services. It was claimed by the New York Attorney General that the agencies engaged in deceptive advertising and failed to inform women of the true cost of the referral service. It was also claimed that the agencies illegally split their fees with the physicians and clinics performing the abortions.[109]

But if the referral agency can establish a first amendment claim — in addition to the general but unpersuasive claim of the right to do business — then more than a mere "rational-basis" justification for the legislative prohibition would be required. If the agency's activity constitutes speech, the validity of the proscriptive statute might turn on whether the state's interest in regulating the medical practice or eliminating the particular evils complained of is sufficient to justify the curtailment of first amendment rights. The fact that the state might eliminate abuses by regulation rather than by banning the agencies in toto would then be critical, for if regulation would suffice, there would seem to be insufficient justification for the infringement upon first amendment rights presented by a total prohibition, such as the one established by the New York legislation.[110]

B. *Subpoenas*

During the New York State Attorney General's investigation there was substantial litigation regarding issues of great importance to the counselling business, whether commercial or nonprofit. One issue that arose involved the right to subpoena hospital records containing the names and addresses of all patients referred by abortion counselling services, the type of operation performed, the name and address of the treating physician, and the duration of the stay of the patients. In *Montwill Corp. v. Lefkowitz,* the New York County Supreme Court held that the request for this information constituted "a proper demand and a valid exercise of the power vested in the Attorney-General."[111] The doctor-patient privilege asserted by the hospital was held to cover only information regarding the type of abortion performed. Furthermore, the court refused to impose formal conditions upon release of the information sought in order to keep the names of patients confidential. It felt "assured that the Attorney General [would] not release or make any public disclosure of the names of patients who have obtained abortions except as to such disclosure as may be necessary in the continued investigation . . . or the prosecution if any of any action arising out of the subject investigation."[112]

A similar result was reached in *Weitzner v. Lefkowitz,*[113] where the same New York court, speaking through a different judge, upheld a subpoena directed at a licensed physician who sought to withhold the names and addresses of his patients on the basis of the physician-patient privilege. Noting that the subpoena was issued in the course of an investigation into the activities of "private abortion referral agencies engaged in the business of commercial intermediaries or brokers between patient and doctor and patient and hospital in connection with abortion services,"[114] the court held that the issuance of the subpoena by the Attorney General constituted a legitimate exercise of his authority to investigate possible fraud and illegal business activity which might cause harm to the public.[115] The problems which might befall the patients whose names would be disclosed were dismissed with the simple comment that "the court has every confidence that the Attorney-General will prevent unnecessary disclosures."[116]

At least one New York case, however, has refused to order an abortion referral agency to disclose the names and addresses of the women with whom it had dealt. In *Lefkowitz v. Women's Pavillion, Inc.*,[117] the same New York County Supreme Court — now speaking through a third judge — observed that the Attorney General had presented no argument regarding the relevance and necessity of the names and addresses of clients who had obtained abortions through the referral agency. While casting no doubt upon the good faith of the Attorney General in conducting his investigation, the court held that good faith did not constitute justification "to embark on a roving course which would result in generally prying into the affairs of any person."[118] The court then added that

> the names of those who sought and received abortions are not protected by the umbrella of privilege within the meaning of the statute and judicial interpretation . . . . However, there is a delicate balance which must be maintained. Those persons who sought abortions approached the respondents in confidence with the intent of maintaining secrecy and avoiding embarrassment. This presents a proper case for the court to interfere and modify a subpoena to protect against an undue infringement upon the rights of private citizens . . . . Their right to privacy should be respected and protected. This is especially true in view of the fact that the fee arrangements under investigation by the Attorney-General will still be capable of full discovery.[119]

While the New York investigations have apparently ended, there is still the possibility that names and addresses of counsellees may be subpoenaed in other states in an official investigation or in civil or criminal litigation, that the privilege which exists between a physician and patient will not be deemed to encompass this information, and that exposure of the name of the counsellee may lead to substantial embarrassment. Unless a privilege protecting the confidentiality of such information can be successfully asserted on the basis of an independent legal or constitutional principle, referral agencies may be seriously jeopardizing those whom they serve.

C. Unauthorized Practice of Medicine

The question of whether abortion counselling falls within the prohibitions against the unauthorized practice of medicine is an issue which has arisen both in and out of New York. No doubt, the threat of criminal prosecution for practicing medicine without a license has been used as a practical means of inhibiting abortion counselling activities, but whether this approach will withstand judicial scrutiny remains to be seen. If the courts hold to the position that the practice of medicine includes only physical application of the healing arts and the prescribing of specific treatment, counselling services should be in no real jeopardy.[120] Indeed, this position has been accepted by some courts.[121] The majority of courts, however, have upheld statutes or regulations providing that any person who owns, maintains, operates, or manages a medical office is also engaged in the practice of medicine and must have a license therefor.[122] Presumably, such statutes are designed to protect the public against unqualified medical practitioners, and it has been the theory of most courts that such protection would be vitiated if the standards of ethics, the class of workmanship, and the price of services were subject to the control of lay managers.[123]

In those cases where management or operation of the "business side" does not include the exercise of any control or direction of the professional work, however, the lay manager has generally not been held to be practicing medicine.[124] Thus, in *Messner v. Board of Dental Examiners*, where the evidence showed only that the layman was the credit and advertising manager, that he superintended the laboratory to the extent of seeing that the work went out on time, and that he purchased dental and office supplies (but did not determine the grade or character of supplies to be ordered), the court found that he did not control the professional service and, consequently, was not practicing medicine.[125] On the other hand, in *Worlton v. Davis*,[126] the Supreme Court of Idaho held that a lay manager was engaged in the practice of medicine when he exercised control as a partner in determining who should be employed by the partnership and in determining remuneration of employees.

Thus, the test generally focuses on the degree of lay control over the professional services. If the layman exercises some power to hire, discharge, and fix the compensation of licensed practitioners, then he is likely to be considered to be practicing medicine without a license. If the control test is applied to counselling agencies, a similar result will obtain in those circumstances where the agency exercises such control and supervision over the physicians who actually perform the operations. In most cases, however, there is no such authority exercised by the counselling services.[127] Nor is there any actual dispensation of medical advice, medication, or treatment, as would ordinarily be involved in the practice of medicine. Even where the agency makes an initial determination of the probable kind of operation necessary and refers the woman to an appropriate clinic, if a final and independent determination of the kind of operation to be performed is made by a licensed physician, then little more is being offered by the referral agency than information about and easier access to the needed medical services. Since the medical practice statutes are presumably not intended to deprive the public of legitimate medical services or information regarding the availability of medical services, there would seem to be scant justification for holding that such agencies are engaged in the unauthorized practice of medicine.[128]

V. Conclusion

In many ways, the law has taken an approach to abortion counselling services which is intentionally designed to limit the public's access to information regarding the availability of abortions. By assuming this posture, the law has done nothing more than impose restrictions upon the uninformed. Those in the worst position to pay for a service which they consider necessary may be forced to pay the highest price for that service. The pressures which have been generated by the law have intimidated principally those who claim to be motivated by high purpose — those who see abortion counselling as a means of protecting the freedom of the individual and of dealing in a limited way with the enormous problems caused by the population explosion. Those who appear to be motivated by less lofty concerns have done a substantial service, if service is measured in terms of dissemination of desired information. Regardless of the motives of the counselling agencies, there is little or no justification for withholding information from the public regarding the availability of abortion services. There is equally little justification for the intimidation that derives from the ambiguities created by statutes and judicial decisions applicable to abortion counselling activities.

NOTES

1. N.Y. Times, July 1, 1971, at 42, col. 1.

2. Charlton, *Abortion Brokers Are Under Study*, N.Y. Times, Feb. 10, 1971, at 45, cols. 1, 3.

3. Counselling services fall into three broad categories. The first would include services, such as the Clergy Consultation Service, which are noncommercial and which merely provide a woman with specific information regarding how she can acquire an abortion. The second category would include those services which provide such information for a fee but have no close relationship with the physicians who actually perform abortions. Such services may or may not operate on a nonprofit basis. The third category would include services that not only provide information, but also make specific arrangements for the performance of the abortion. These arrangements may, and often do, include providing transportation, making direct contact with the physician, informing the woman of the cost of the abortion, and actually collecting the entire fee for the referral, the transportation and the medical service.

4. One of these cases is Commonwealth v. Hare, ___ Mass. ___, 280 N.E.2d 138 (1972).

5. *See, e.g.*, State v. Abortion Information Agency, Inc., 37 App. Div. 2d 142 (1971). *See also* N.Y. PUB. HEALTH LAW §§ 4400-03 (McKinney Supp. 1971).

6. N.Y. Times, Oct. 10, 1971, at 75, col. 2.

7. N.Y. Times, Dec. 8, 1970, at 10, col. 8.

8. The reluctance of Planned Parenthood associations to take an aggressive approach in the abortion counselling field probably derives from the fact that most affiliate associations are funded by broad-based organizations which include very conservative elements.

9. To a substantial extent, the only factor sufficient to overcome the enormous inhibition created by the threat of criminal prosecution is the desire for profit. The increase in the number of commercial services is largely a result of the unavailability of abortion information through noncommercial services. During an investigation of commercial agencies, the head of the consumer fraud division of the New York State Attorney General's Office observed that " '[t]he commercial agencies are able to operate because the out-of-state women are ignorant of the same facilities without a fee.' " Charlton, *supra* note 2, at 45, col. 3.

10. Thus, for a considerable period of time, the Clergy Consultation Service minimized its contacts with operating physicians for fear that such contacts might enhance the possibility of successful criminal prosecution. And detailed records were not kept because of a growing concern that such records may be unprotected by any privilege and subject to production upon subpoena. Little follow-up work was done because it was assumed that aggressive counselling would be more susceptible to a claim of active inducement.

11. *Id.* Billboards have also been used to advertise the availability of referral services.

12. The difficulties encountered and questions asked by new counselling services include the following:

(1) May the service offered be advertised? If it cannot be advertised, what can be done to make the public aware of the service? If advertising is not permissible for the purpose of achieving a commercial objective, is it permissible where the objective is solely humanitarian? Is a greater latitude permitted to those services which are plainly not conducted for profit?

(2) Do the unauthorized practice of medicine statutes prohibit abortion counselling? In determining whether such services are enjoined by the unauthorized practice of medicine statutes, is the availability of such services through established professional sources a relevant consideration?

(3) Is it improper to give information regarding the availability of legal abortions in a state other than that in which the counsellor is functioning?

(4) How far can the counsellor go in arranging for a legal abortion in a foreign state without subjecting himself to possible penalties for aiding, inducing, or causing an abortion in the state in which he operates?

(5) Is there some legal wisdom in limiting the counsellor's contact with the person who actually performs the abortion?

(6) If the abortion is unlawful where rendered, what risks are encountered by the counsellor?

(7) Are communications received by the counsellor privileged?

13. This article will not examine the constitutional challenges to current abortion laws. For a thorough discussion of those constitutional problems, see Lucas, *Federal Constitutional Limitations on the Enforcement and Administration of State Abortion Statutes*, 46 N.C.L. REV. 730 (1968). For an excellent discussion of the moral, social, religious, psychological, and economic issues relevant to the entire abortion question, see D. CALLAHAN, ABORTION: LAW, CHOICE AND MORALITY (1970).

14. Several state and federal statutes restrict the right to dispense information regarding abortions. An example, 18 U.S.C. § 1461 (1970), declares the following to be "nonmailable matter" which "shall not be conveyed in the mails or delivered from any post office by any letter carrier:"

Every article or thing designed, adapted, or intended for producing abortion, or for any indecent or immoral use; and

Every article, instrument, substance, drug, medicine, or thing which is advertised or described in a manner calculated to lead another to use or apply it for producing abortion, or for any indecent or immoral purpose; and

> Every written or printed card, letter, circular, book, pamphlet, advertisement or notice of any kind giving information, directly or indirectly, where, or how, or from whom, or by what means any of such mentioned matters, articles, or things may be obtained or made, or where or by whom any act or operation of any kind for the procuring or producing of abortion will be done or performed, or how or by what means abortion may be produced, whether sealed or unsealed. . . .

The penalty for violating this section is substantial — 5 thousand dollars and/or 5 years for the first offense and 10 thousand dollars and/or 10 years for each subsequent offense. The comprehensive prohibition and severe penalties contained in section 1461 are not unique to federal law. Virtually all states which have sought to prohibit dissemination of information regarding how to acquire an abortion have enacted equally comprehensive prohibitions. *See generally* George, *The Evolving Law of Abortion*, pp. 3-62, in this volume.

It should be noted that many, if not most, of these statutory limitations are on advertising. Counselling itself is not generally prohibited in such statutes.

15. Recent decisions however, have suggested some possible guidelines. In Eisenstadt v. Baird, 40 U.S.L.W. 4303 (U.S. March 22, 1972), the Court, on equal protection grounds, invalidated a Massachusetts statute which prohibited distribution of contraceptive devices to anyone but married persons. The Court concluded that there was no rational basis for affording different treatment to married persons than was afforded unmarried persons. Although the state might have a legitimate interest in protecting the health, safety, and morals of the community by discouraging sexual promiscuity among unmarried persons, the Court questioned whether that was the intended purpose of the statute: "Even on the assumption that the fear of pregnancy operates as a deterrent to fornication the Massachusetts statute is . . . so riddled with exceptions that deterrence of pre-marital sex cannot reasonably be regarded as its aim." *Id.* at 4307. The Court did not decide whether the Massachusetts statute might be upheld "simply as a prohibition on contraception," deferring resolution of that question with the observation that "whatever the rights of the individual to access to contraceptives may be, the rights must be the same for the unmarried and the married alike." *Id.* at 4308.

The relevance of *Baird* to the issues involved in abortion counselling is apparent. First, while the Court did not decide the constitutional arguments involved in the abortion controversy, it reaffirmed its commitment to the proposition that decisions regarding procreation should be left to the individual: "If the right of privacy means anything, it is the right of the individual, married or single, to be free from unwarranted governmental intrusion into matters so fundamentally affecting a person as the decision whether to bear or beget a child." *Id.* The term "unwarranted governmental intrusion" awaits interpretation, but the Court does insist that the same standard be applied with respect to single persons as is applied in determining the rights of married persons. A second important implication of *Baird* arises out of the Court's unwillingness (criticized by Chief Justice Burger) to accept at face value the state's assertion that legislation affecting exercise of the right to determine whether children will be born can be justified on the ground that such legislation is necessary to protect and promote public morality. Any such claim will be subjected to probing judicial scrutiny where the fundamental right of privacy is infringed upon.

16. The first amendment protects speech, but not action that goes beyond speech. *See, e.g.,* Street v. New York, 394 U.S. 576 (1969); Cantwell v. Connecticut, 310 U.S. 296, 303-04 (1940).

> [T]he theory [underlying the first amendment] rests upon a fundamental distinction between belief, opinion and communication of ideas on the one hand, and different forms of conduct on the other. For shorthand purposes we refer to this distinction hereafter as one between "expression" and "action." [I]n order to achieve its desired goals, a society or the state is entitled to exercise control over action — whether by prohibiting or compelling it — on an entirely different and vastly more extensive basis. But expression occupies a specially protected position. In this sector of human conduct, the social right of suppression or compulsion is at its lowest point, in most respects nonexistent. T. EMERSON, TOWARD A GENERAL THEORY OF THE FIRST AMENDMENT 6 (1966).

17. *See* Street v. New York, 394 U.S. 576 (1969), where the Court reversed a conviction under a flag desecration statute. *Compare* Tinker v. Des Moines Independent Community School District, 393 U.S. 503 (1969), *with* United States v. O'Brien, 391 U.S. 367 (1968) *and* Chaplinsky v. New Hampshire, 315 U.S. 568 (1942).

18. *But see* United States. v. O'Brien, 391 U.S. 367 (1968), where the Court indicated that speech, when mixed with "non-speech," may still be protected to some extent by the first amendment. *Id.* at 376. In any event, if the counsellor merely arranges or helps to arrange for a *legal* abortion, the due process clause of the 14th amendment would afford him some protection from criminal prosecution, for a state may not make criminal conduct which is no more than the facilitating of a legal act. *See, e.g.,* Shuttlesworth v. City of Birmingham, 373 U.S. 262, 265 (1963).

19. Griswold v. Connecticut, 381 U.S. 479, 497 (1965) (Douglas, J., concurring).

20. *See* DeJonge v. Oregon, 299 U.S. 353 (1937).

21. *See* Chaplinsky v. New Hampshire, 315 U.S. 568 (1942).
22. *See* Tinker v. Des Moines Independent Community School District, 393 U.S. 503 (1969); Benson v. Rich, 448 F.2d 1371 (10th Cir. 1971).
23. Roth v. United States, 354 U.S. 476 (1957).
24. 335 F. Supp. 738 (E.D. Mich. 1972).
25. *Id.* at 743.
26. Stanley v. Georgia, 394 U.S. 557, 564 (1969). A somewhat anomalous situation has been created by the decisions in *Stanley* and *Griswold*. *Stanley*, for example, establishes that the right to possess pornographic literature is protected by the concept of privacy implicit in the first amendment. On the other hand, acquisition of pornographic literature is rendered rather difficult by numerous decisions upholding the right of the government to regulate the sale of pornographic literature. *E.g.*, Roth v. United States, 354 U.S. 476 (1957). Likewise, the Court in *Griswold* rejected a prohibition against the use of contraceptive devices by married persons as an unwarranted invasion of marital privacy protected by the penumbra of the first amendment. The Court also held, in *Griswold*, that professional persons who prescribed the use of contraceptives for married persons had standing to assert the privacy interest of those persons and that they could not be convicted as aiders and abettors in light of the fact that the principal offense was unconstitutionally defined. Thus, the right of married persons to use contraceptives has been raised to constitutional dignity. And the right to prescribe such use has found incidental protection. But the Court has yet to determine whether a state may legitimately prohibit the sale of contraceptive devices to married and unmarried persons alike. As with pornography, the right to possess and use is protected, but not, as yet, the right to acquire. If sale is prohibited, of course, acquisition is rendered very difficult.

    The principle that the first amendment protects the right to know and receive information and ideas has long been recognized by the Court. *See, e.g.*, Pierce v. Society of Sisters, 268 U.S. 510 (1925); New York Times Co. v. Sullivan, 376 U.S. 254 (1964); Lamont v. Postmaster General, 381 U.S. 301 (1965).
27. New York Times Co. v. United States, 403 U.S. 713 (1971).
28. Hiett v. United States, 415 F.2d 664 (5th Cir. 1969).
29. *See generally* Schwartz, *Abortion on Request: The Psychiatric Implications*, pp. 139-178, in this volume.
30. *Cf.* Griswold v. Connecticut, 381 U.S. 479 (1965).
31. 316 U.S. 52 (1942).
32. *Id.* at 54.
33. *Cf.* note 14 *supra.*
34. 92 Ariz. 231, 375 P.2d 719 (1962).
35. Ariz. Rev. Stat. Ann. § 13-213 (1956).

Relying upon this provision, a county medical director instructed that distribution by the county health department of all information regarding birth control be terminated immediately, and the Planned Parenthood affiliate, a nonprofit corporation concerned with the dissemination of information which would permit parents to plan their families, cease distribution of literature dealing with contraception and birth control.

36. 92 Ariz. at 237, 375 P.2d at 723.
37. *Id.*
38. *Id.* at 238, 375 P.2d at 724.
39. *Id.*
40. *Id.*
41. *Id.* at 239, 375 P.2d at 725.
42. *Id.* at 239-40, 375 P.2d at 725.
43. *Id.* at 240, 375 P.2d at 725.
44. *Id.* at 241, 375 P.2d at 726.
45. 335 F. Supp. 738 (E.D. Mich. 1972).
46. *Id.* at 739.
47. *Id.* at 742.
48. *See* T. EMERSON, *supra* note 16, at 53-56.
49. 415 F.2d 664 (5th Cir. 1969).
50. *See* 18 U.S.C. § 1714 (1970).
51. 415 F.2d at 669.
52. *Id.* at 672.
53. *Id. See also* Street v. New York, 394 U.S. 576 (1969).
54. 415 F.2d at 672.
55. *Id.* at 671-73.
56. *See, e.g.,* Chicago Joint Board, Amalgamated Workers of America v. Chicago Tribune Co., 435 F.2d 470 (7th Cir. 1970); The Associates and Aldrich Co. v. Times-Mirror Co., 440 F.2d 133 (9th Cir. 1971).
57. Thornhill v. Alabama, 310 U.S. 88 (1940).
58. Smith v. California, 361 U.S. 147, 150 (1959).
59. *See, e.g.,* American Medicinal Products Inc. v. FTC, 136 F.2d 426 (9th Cir. 1943).
60. Cammarano v. United States, 358 U.S. 498, 514 (1959) (Douglas, J., concurring).
61. The common law divided guilty parties into principals and accessories; principals being those persons who actually perpetrated the offense, and accessories being those who contributed to the offense but did not actually perform the felonious act. *See* 1 M. HALE, PLEAS OF THE CROWN 612-21 (2d ed. 1800); R. PERKINS, PERKINS ON CRIMINAL LAW 643-48 (2d ed. 1969). Accessories were of three types: (1) before the fact; (2) at the fact (commonly called aiders and abettors); and (3) after the fact. While the distinctions of guilt between principals and accessories at or before the fact have been largely abolished

by statute, and all are charged and punishable as principals (*see, e.g.,* 18 U.S.C. § 2 (1970), the common law definitions are still pertinent in assessing whether one can be charged as an accessory. Thus, an accessory before the fact is one who, though absent at the commission of the felony, procures, counsels, commands, induces, or advises another to commit the felony. 1 F. WHARTON, CRIMINAL LAW § 263 (11th ed. 1912).

An aider and abettor is one who is present, either actually or constructively, and who (with mens rea) either assists the perpetrator in the commission of the crime, stands by with intent (known to the perpetrator) to render aid if needed, or commands, counsels, or otherwise encourages the perpetrator to commit the crime. R. PERKINS, *supra* at 645; F. WHARTON, *supra* at § 245.

An accessory after the fact is one who in no way is tainted with guilt of a crime when perpetrated, but who, with full knowledge of the facts, thereafter conceals the offender or gives him some assistance to save him from detection, arrest, trial, or punishment. R. PERKINS, *supra*, at 646; F. WHARTON, *supra*, at § 281.

62. Commonwealth v. Hare, ___ Mass. ___, 280 N.E.2d 138 (1972).
63. MASS. GEN. LAWS ANN. ch. 274, § 2 (1970) provides: "Whoever aids in commission of a felony, or is an accessory thereto before the fact by counselling, hiring or otherwise procuring such felony to be committed, shall be indicted, tried and punished as a principal."
64. ___ Mass. at ___, 280 N.E.2d at 140 n.4.
65. *Id.* at ___, 280 N.E.2d at 139.
66. *Id.* (emphasis added).
67. *Id.*
68. The error of the lower court was in considering facts alleged in the bill of particulars as limiting the commonwealth's indictment. The proper procedure, held the supreme court, was to look solely to the allegations in the indictment. The allegations in the *Hare* case (which were merely a general rephrasing of the criminal statute) were deemed adequate once the bill of particulars was ignored.
69. *Id.* at ___, 280 N.E.2d at 143.
70. If an abortion were legal (either because it was not proscribed by statute or because a proscriptive statute was unconstitutional), one presumably could not be charged with aiding and abetting. *See* Shuttlesworth v. City of Birmingham, 373 U.S. 262, 265 (1963).
71. 100 F.2d 401 (2d Cir. 1938).
72. *See, e.g.,* Nye & Nissen v. United States, 336 U.S. 613, 619 (1949); Morei v. United States, 127 F.2d 827, 831 (6th Cir. 1942).
73. 100 F.2d at 402. The same test was articulated by the Supreme Court in Nye & Nissen v. United States, 336 U.S. 613, 619 (1949), where the Court, quoting Judge Hand, stated: "In order to aid and abet another to commit a crime it is necessary that a defendant 'in some sort as-

sociate himself with the venture, that he participate in it as in something he wishes to bring about, that he seek by his action to make it succeed.' "

74. Peoni had sold counterfeit bills to one Regno; and Regno sold the same bills to one Dorsey. All three knew the bills were counterfeit and Dorsey was arrested while trying to pass the bills. The issue, then, was whether Peoni was guilty as an accessory to Dorsey's possession of the bills. 100 F.2d at 401.

75. *Id.* at 403.

76. *Id.* at 402-03.

77. 127 F.2d 827 (6th Cir. 1942).

78. *Id.* at 829-30.

79. The Court stated:

> There was no evidence that Dr. Platt planned with the other
> defendants or conspired directly or indirectly with them . . . .
> There was no community of scheme between [them] . . . nor
> was there any prearrangement or concert of action. Dr. Platt
> was payed nothing and it is not claimed that he . . . expected
> to receive anything from the claimed transaction. *Id.* at 831.

80. Like Judge Hand in the *Peoni* case, the *Morei* court also rejected the "but-for" test, stating that to accept such a standard "would open a vast field of offenses that have never been contemplated within the common law by aiding, abetting, inducing or procuring." *Id.* at 831.

81. *Id.* at 832. Nor could the physician be convicted of aiding and abetting the government agent, Beach. As the court remarked: "Giving Beach the name of Morei, under the circumstances of this case, and with no further connection with the offense, would not render Dr. Platt guilty of aiding and abetting Beach, or of being his accessory before the fact." *Id.*

82. 220 F.2d 166 (3d Cir. 1955).

83. *Id.* at 168.

84. *Id.*

85. 49 Del. 251, 113 A.2d 880 (1955).

86. *Id.* at 255, 113 A.2d at 882.

87. A similar conclusion was reached in People v. Northcott, 45 Cal. App. 706, 189 P. 704 (1920), where a physician who refused to perform an abortion gave his patient the name of a physician who did perform the abortion.

88. 10 N.J. 146, 89 A.2d 685 (1952).

89. *Id.* at 150, 89 A.2d at 687. *See also* McLure v. State, 214 Ark. 159, 215 S.W.2d 524 (1948) (concert of action established upon evidence that defendant-physician referred woman to another doctor for an abortion, that he stated "he had sent a million over there," that he instructed the woman to return to him for treatment, and that the woman returned to the defendant when the operation was completed).

90. 266 Mass. 391, 399-401 (1929).

91. *See, e.g.,* ARIZ. REV. STAT. ANN. § 13-212 (1956); MINN. STAT. ANN. § 617.19 (1963); WASH. REV. CODE ANN. § 9.02.020 (1961). *See also* George, *supra* note 14, at 723-24 & n.89 (1972); Annot., 34 A.I.R.3d 858 (1970).

92. Shuttlesworth v. City of Birmingham, 373 U.S. 262, 265 (1963).

93. As discussed earlier, actual arrangement of an abortion would constitute action rather than speech and would not be protected under the first amendment. *See* notes 16-18 *supra* & accompanying text.

94. 37 App. Div. 2d 142, 143 (1971).

95. The fee included a charge for all of the services, including the operation. The agency, not the patient, was billed by the hospital. *Id.*

96. *Id.* at 143-44. Later in the opinion, the court stated that "it is quite clear that plaintiff has made out a clear and convincing case concerning the inherent dangers to the public involved in this situation, considering the distinct probability of domination by the agency of the institutions." *Id.* at 144.

97. *Id.* Interestingly the court deemed irrelevant the fact that the fee splitting did not result in an increase in the cost to the patient. *Id.*

98. *Id.* at 145. In a dissenting opinion, Judge Steuer found that "there is absolutely no proof that the defendant is practicing or ever has practiced medicine. . . . The defendant makes no diagnosis, does not determine what operation is to be performed, does not perform it, and has nothing to do with the way it is performed or [how] the patient is treated thereafter." *Id.* at 147-48. In Judge Steuer's view, the practice of medicine did not encompass the activities engaged in by the agency; nor could he find any basis for the claim of fee splitting: "There is not even a suggestion that any doctor or hospital ever rebated any part of his fee or its charges to defendant or offered defendant an inducement of any kind to sent patients to it." *Id.* at 148.

As to the general public policy issue, Judge Steuer believed that it was an as yet undetermined factual question whether or not the agency was in a position, contrary to public policy, to dominate professional activity by substantially affecting the number and kind of patients admitted to a hospital. *Id.* at 150.

99. *Id.* at 145.

100. *Id.* at 145-46.

101. *Id.* at 146.

102. *Id.*

103. *See id.* at 147-50 (Judge Steuer, dissenting).

104. *Id.* at 149.

105. *See, e.g.,* Pac. Employers Ins. Co. v. Carpenter, 10 Cal. App. 2d 592, 52 P.2d 992 (1935); Parker v. Bd. of Dental Examiners, 216 Cal. 285, 298, 14 P.2d 67, 72 (1932).

106. Pac. Employers Ins. Co. v. Carpenter, 10 Cal. App. 2d 592, 52 P.2d 992 (1935).

107. N.Y. Pub. Health Law §§ 4400-03 (McKinney Supp. 1971). The statute discriminates between non-profit and for-profit agencies, the latter being absolutely banned. This discrimination survived constitutional challenge in S.P.S. Consultants v. Lefkowitz, 333 F. Supp. 1373 (1971).

108. Such a first amendment claim was raised and rejected by a lower federal court in S.P.C. Consultants v. Lefkowitz, 333 F. Supp. 1373 (S.D.N.Y. 1971).

109. See generally Charlton, supra note 2.

110. See, e.g., Griswold v. Connecticut, 381 U.S. 479, 485 (1965): "[A] 'governmental purpose to control or prevent activities constitutionally subject to state regulation may not be achieved by means which sweep unnecessarily broadly and hereby invade the area of protected freedoms.' NAACP v. Alabama, 377 U.S. 288, 307."

111. 66 Misc. 2d 724, 725, 321 N.Y.S.2d 975, 976 (N.Y. County Sup. Ct. 1971).

112. Id. at 726, 321 N.Y.S.2d at 977.

113. 66 Misc. 2d 721, 321 N.Y.S.2d 925 (N.Y. County Sup. Ct. 1971).

114. Id. at 722, 321 N.Y.S.2d at 926.

115. In light of the fact that the court found that the names and addresses of patients were "not confidential matters," id. at 723, 321 N.Y.S.2d at 927, it was somewhat surprising that the court went to such lengths to demonstrate the closeness of the relationship between the petitioner-physician and the referral agencies. The court acknowledged that the physician was a part owner and chief gynecologist of one of the clinics performing abortions for the agencies, that he was involved in setting up the referral corporations, that he was a major stockholder in two of the corporations which referred patients to his clinic, and that he derived "substantial income from referrals requiring his professional services." Id. at 722, 321 N.Y.S.2d at 926.

116. Id. at 723, 321 N.Y.S.2d at 927.

117. 66 Misc. 2d 743, 321 N.Y.S.2d 963 (N.Y. County Sup. Ct. 1971).

118. Id. at 744, 321 N.Y.S.2d at 965.

119. Id. at 745, 321 N.Y.S.2d at 965 (citations omitted).

120. Most counselling agencies do not actually prescribe or administer treatment. There are, however, those which have found themselves in extremely embarrassing positions because they dispensed tranquilizers to their clients.

121. See, e.g., State Electro-Medical Institute v. State, 74 Neb. 40, 103 N.W. 1078 (1905).

122. See State v. Boren, 36 Wash. 2d 522, 219 P.2d 566, appeal dismissed, 340 U.S. 881 (1950) (wherein the court held constitutional as a reasonable exercise of the police power a statute that a "person practices dentistry" within the meaning of certain license requirements if he "owns, maintains or operates an office for the practice of dentistry"); Taber v. State Bd. of Registration and Examination in Dentistry, 1 N.J.

343, 63 A.2d 535, *appeal dismissed*, 337 U.S. 922 (1949). *See also* Annot., 20 A.L.R.2d 808, 810 (1951).

In the absence of specific statutory provision to the contrary, it is well settled that neither a corporation nor any other unlicensed person may engage, directly or indirectly, in the practice of medicine. *See* Annot., 4 A.L.R.3d 383, 385 (1965). *See also* Pac. Employers Ins. Co. v. Carpenter, 10 Cal. App. 2d 592, 52 P.2d 992 (1935) *and* cases cited *id.* at 594-95, 52 P.2d at 993-94. As of 1965, professional corporations or associations had been authorized by statute in 31 states. Annot., 4 A.L.R.3d 383, 387-88 (1965). Of course, such statutes do not enable *unlicensed* practitioners to incorporate for the purpose of operating a medical practice.

123. *See, e.g.*, State v. Williams, 211 Ind. 186, 5 N.E.2d 961 (1937); Parker v. Bd. of Dental Examiners, 216 Cal. 285, 14 P.2d 67 (1932). Alternatively, the courts have felt that the practice of medicine should not be subject to commercial exploitation, at least not by persons other than licensed physicians. *See, e.g.*, Pac. Employers Ins. Co. v. Carpenter, 10 Cal. App. 2d 592, 595, 52 P.2d 992, 994 (1935).

124. *But see* Parker v. Bd. of Dental Examiners, 216 Cal. 285, 14 P.2d 67 (1932).

125. 87 Cal. App. 199, 262 P. 58 (1927). The court reached this result even though the manager in question shared in the profits of the office.

> Had it been shown, [however], that [the manager] had authority to participate in the employment or discharge of those engaged to do professional work and the fixing of their compensation a different question would arise. The power to hire and discharge and to fix the compensation of an employee necessarily implies the power to control his work. *Id.* at 204-05, 262 P. at 60.

126. 73 Idaho 217, 249 P.2d 810 (1952).

127. A distinction may be drawn, however, in the case of referral agencies which are able to obtain discounts in the price of the abortion operation. Conceivably, the ability to obtain a discount may be read to imply that the agency exercises control over the compensation of the licensed physician sufficient to bring it within the proscriptions of the unauthorized practice statutes.

128. Of course, when such agencies charge a fee for their services, which fee includes the price of the operation itself, the agency may be labeled a "broker" of medical services.

ABORTION AND
THE RIGHTS OF MINORS

HARRIET F. PILPEL AND
RUTH J. ZUCKERMAN

I. Introduction

DURING THE PAST SEVERAL YEARS, lawyers, legislators, and social agencies have shown a remarkable upsurge of interest in the legal rights of minors — both in a general context and particularly in connection with the receiving of medical services without parental consent. At common law minors were said to lack the capacity to consent to medical treatment.[1] Thus, unless one of the exceptions to the common law was applicable, physicians who undertook the examination or treatment of minors without first obtaining parental consent were subject to civil liability on the theory that any touching by the physician of the minor was done without "legal" consent and thus technically constituted a battery.[2] Although the rule was intended at least in part to protect minors, the practical result often was that the medical needs of minors were unmet. This was especially true in cases involving medical care or treatment connected with sexual activity, drug addiction, and alcoholism — medical problems which minors are often reluctant to reveal to a parent or guardian.

The question of permitting minors to obtain one particular type of medical treatment — abortion services — without parental consent has been brought into sharp focus by recent dramatic changes in the abortion laws of several states[3] and by a number of federal and state court decisions recognizing a constitutional basis for the right of women to terminate unwanted pregnancies.[4] With respect to abortion, the problems caused by a requirement of parental consent are exacerbated by: (1) the relatively short period of time

275

within which abortions can be safely performed; (2) the serious danger to the minor's health if she — unable to obtain a safe, legal abortion from a competent medical practitioner — resorts to the services of an unlicensed, incompetent abortionist or to the hazardous techniques of self-abortion; (3) the deleterious effect on the minor, the unwanted child, and society at large if she is forced to bear an unwanted child; and (4) the conflict between parent and child in values and beliefs which may be present where the medical treatment in question is abortion. Superimposed upon these related problems, and pervading every aspect of their resolution, are the philosophical-legal questions regarding the rights of the parent and the child vis-à-vis one another, and the state's role both as the arbiter of conflcts in those rights and as *parens patriae* or the guardian of the child's best interests.

The critical concern of this article is the right of a minor to obtain, without parental consent, an abortion in those states in which abortions are available to adult women as a result of liberalized legislation, therapeutic abortion provisions, or judicial mandate. Although the discussion is necessarily confined for the moment to those states, a Supreme Court decision as to a constitutional right to abortion is pending. At such time as that issue is decided in the affirmative by the United States Supreme Court, the question of the minor's rights will be of even greater significance.

First this article will explore general statutory and common law rules on parental consent to medical treatment in general and to abortion services in particular. It will then focus on the constitutional framework of the problem. Finally, it will propose a legislative reform which would permit a minor to obtain abortion services without parental consent in appropriate circumstances.

II. THE STATE LAW FRAMEWORK

A. *Parental Consent and Medical Treatment of Minors at Common Law*

As a general proposition, no state has by statute specifically prohibited the medical treatment of minors without parental consent. However, under the common law rule mentioned above, a physician who treated a minor without parental consent could be liable for damages, unless the facts brought the situation under an exception to the rule.[5] Liability did not rest on any actual harm to the minor; if such harm occurred, it could be redressed in an action for malpractice or negligence. Rather, liability was grounded on the legal fiction that, because a minor was incapable of consenting to the treatment, the touching which occurred in the course of treatment was nonconsensual and therefore constituted a technical battery.

There are, however, a number of exceptions to the common law rule requiring parental consent to a minor's medical treatment. The first of these exceptions, emancipation, focuses upon objective factors in the circumstances of the minor's life. The second, emergency, focuses upon the conditions requiring immediate treatment and the nature of that treatment. A third, more recently recognized exception, the mature minor doctrine, involves consideration of both the nature of the treatment and subjective factors, such as the minor's capacity for understanding the nature and consequences of the treatment.

A minor who is legally emancipated may give effective consent to medical treatment provided the minor understands the nature of the treatment in question and has requested it.[6] The question of what constitutes emancipation at common law is answered differently from state to state. For example, one circumstance which has commonly resulted in a finding of emancipation is a minor's marriage.[7] In addition, a minor will generally be deemed emancipated if he or she is living apart from his or her parents, is self-supporting, and is generally in control of his or her own life.[8] Other bases for a finding of emancipation are judicial decree and parental consent, express or implied.[9] Finally, emancipation by operation of law can occur where the parent's conduct is inconsistent with his parental obligations.[10]

The rule with respect to emergency treatment[11] constitutes another common law exception to the requirement of parental consent. Courts have defined an emergency, within the meaning of this rule, as existing when impending danger to life and limb would occur if treatment were not to begin immediately.[12]

In addition to the emergency and emancipation exceptions, there is developing in the case law of a number of jurisdictions a "mature minor" exception to the common law rule. The judge-made exception, in any particular case, will be based on the maturity and intelligence of the minor as well as his or her age and the nature of the treatment — *i.e.*, is it a simple procedure and is it for the minor's benefit? The cases so far indicate that when the minor has sufficient mental capacity and maturity to understand the nature and consequences of the medical procedure or treatment undertaken for his or her benefit, the minor's consent to treatment will be legally sufficient.[13]

B. *The Statutory Approach to Parental Consent*

1. *Parental Consent and State Abortion Laws* — At this writing, 13 states have enacted liberalized abortion laws[14] somewhat along the lines of the abortion statute found in the American Law Institute (ALI) Model Penal Code, under which abortions are permitted not only to preserve a mother's life, but to protect her mental and physical health and to avert the birth of defective offspring or those conceived through rape or incest.[15] The statutes in 9 of those states contain specific provisions with reference to parental consent for a minor's abortion.[16] More liberal than the ALI Model are the statutes in 4 other states which now eliminate, up to a certain point during pregnancy, all restrictions on the grounds for abortion.[17] In 2 of those, Washington[18] and Alaska,[19] the statutes deal with the question of parental consent.

In Maryland, Georgia, Kansas and California,[20] the remaining 4 of those states which have also passed some variation of the Model Penal Code provision, the laws say nothing on parental consent.[21] Similarly, in New York and Hawaii, where the restrictions upon availability of abortions have been all but completely eliminated, the abortion law is silent on the question of parental consent.[22] In these 6 states the question may arise whether the general common law rule which holds a minor incompetent to legally consent, absent an exception, is operative. Finally, none of the abortion laws of the 33 states which still retain the most restrictive abortion laws[23] contains any provision with respect to parental consent.

2. *Medical Treatment Statutes* — Where there is no statute specifically prohibiting or permitting abortions without parental consent, frequently there will be statutory or common law rules regarding medical treatment in general, which can be applied to fill

in the gaps in the abortion laws. Regarding the common law, many minors will fall under one of the exceptions mentioned above.[24] Although those exceptions to the common law rules on medical treatment without parental consent do in fact permit physicians to treat minors in a wide range of circumstances, as a practical matter the fear of civil litigation has been a deterrent to such treatment. This is so even though the reported cases fail to evidence a single instance in which a physician was successfully sued for battery after treating a minor 15 years of age or older without parental consent where the treatment was for the minor's benefit.[25]

The exceptions to the common law rule, although available as a defense in case of suit, have not provided reassurance to physicians sufficient for many of them to provide needed medical treatment to minors unwilling or unable to obtain parental consent. State legislators in the past several years have become increasingly alert to this problem, and in many states statutory provisions have been enacted which specifically permit all or various kinds of medical treatment of minors without parental consent.[26] Although it is beyond the scope of this article to analyze the statutory provisions of each of the states on medical treatment of minors, it will be useful here to review the general kinds of statutes which have been enacted, particularly as these statutes relate to the availability of abortion services to minors.

Only 2 states, New Hampshire and Wisconsin, presently lack any statutes specifically covering the medical treatment of minors. As to the other states, statutory coverage varies widely. At least 44 states and the District of Columbia have statutes which specifically authorize medical treatment of minors without parental consent for venereal disease.[27] These statutes vary somewhat from state to state. A few, for example, are applicable only to minors over a certain age.[28] In addition, a number of them permit or require notification of parents in some or all situations.[29] In some states, there are statutes which provide that minors who are over a certain age, or who are emancipated, or who meet certain qualifications, may consent to medical treatment of all kinds without parental consent.[30]

At least 13 states have passed statutes which specifically permit minors to consent to medical care and/or treatment related to pregnancy.[31] In only 2 of these states, Missouri and Hawaii, is abortion specifically excluded from the coverage of the special statute.[32] In the remaining 11 states, it seems clear that abortion for minors without parental consent is permitted (subject to the provisions of the abortion statutes which in some states deal specifically with parental consent). Thus far, however, only the courts of California have considered the question whether the "care related to pregnancy" statute[33] includes abortion services within its purview. In *Ballard v. Anderson*,[34] the Supreme Court of California specifically held that the California medical treatment statute emancipates unmarried pregnant minors for the purpose of obtaining therapeutic abortions without parental consent.[35] In the absence of contrary indications in the legislative histories of the treatment statues or in the abortion statutes themselves in the other 10 states, it is likely that if this question were to arise, it would be resolved as it was in *Ballard*.

A number of states have avoided some of the problems associated with the abortion of minors by lowering the age of majority from the usual 21 years. That approach effectively eliminates application of parental consent requirements to all medical treatment for those over the specified age.[36]

3. *Analogous Nonmedical Rules of Law* — Where state law is unclear, there may be state or local rules in related areas which furnish considerable support for the view that, irrespective of the laws on medical treatment, some or all minors should be deemed capable of consenting to abortion without parental consent, and that a requirement of parental consent is both inconsistent with such other laws and is contrary to public policy. For example, in most states a female minor above a specified age may marry without parental consent.[37] The laws on statutory rape also recognize, first, that unmarried minors above the age specified in the statutes do engage in sexual activity and, second, that they are able to consent to such sexual activity prior to the time when they are technically adults for all purposes.

In many states, by statute and administrative regulation, those under 21 may have access to contraceptive services without parental consent.[38] Thus, if a minor is legally able to obtain medical treatment to avoid an unwanted pregnancy, it makes little sense (and is legally inconsistent as well) to negate her implicit right of choice by denying her an abortion where contraception was unavailable or unsuccessful. Similarly, in many jurisdictions where a minor may consent to surrender her child for adoption,[39] it would not seem unreasonable to conclude that she should also have the right to terminate the pregnancy which could otherwise result in the birth of the child.

Clearly the laws in these related areas do not dispose of the question of whether a minor should be able to obtain an abortion without parental consent. They do, however, demonstrate that the law in many areas relating to sexual conduct deals with the realities of maturity and consent and that the legal fiction of infancy should be dispensed with where it is contrary to the best interests of the minor and where it is inconsistent with the general fabric of the law.

C. The Law on Parental Neglect

There are in a great many states statutory provisions which authorize the state to intervene on behalf of a minor child and to take custody of the minor as *parens patriae* when the parent has failed to provide adequate medical care.[40] Having taken custody of the child, the courts may then order medical treatment of both an emergency[41] and nonemergency[42] nature notwithstanding the absence of parental consent. These statutes manifest the state's judgment that the overriding consideration is the health and welfare of the child and that, where necessary, the parent's authority can and must be subordinated. Moreover, the fact that the parental objection is based on religious principles presents no impediment to the courts intervening when necessary.[43]

The clearest and most frequent cases of court intervention against parental opposition are those in which the treatment in question is of an emergency nature. This situation has occurred in a number of cases involving parental objection, based on religious beliefs, to blood transfusions where the threat to the child's life is direct and immediate. Where, however, the courts are faced with situations in which the "emergency" is not as clearly defined, or in which it is clear that the withholding of treatment would not be fatal, the decisions of the courts have involved both interpretation of the language of the statute giving them authority to act and an evaluation of the factual circumstances of each particular case as a prelude to *parens patriae*. For example, in *In re Seiferth*,[44] the New York Court of Appeals considered the propriety of an order declaring a 14-year-old boy to be a neglected child and temporarily transferring custody to the Commissioner of Social Welfare so that the Commissioner could consent to the performance of an operation to correct a cleft palate. In reversing the transfer of custody, the Court of Appeals noted that the child as well as his father was opposed to the surgery and that the child's cooperation was needed for post-surgery therapy. Since the court found that there was no emergency and that time was not of the essence, the state's interest in the health and welfare of the minor was subordinated to the private interest of the parent *and the minor*. It should be noted that in *Seiferth* the child and parent stood unified against the state, while in the abortion situation discussed here it is assumed that the minor's wishes are contrary to the position of the parent.

No unified stand by parent and child appears to have been present in another New York case involving the consent issue in a non-emergency context. In *In re Rotkowitz*,[45] a child's mother consented but the father refused consent to an operation to correct a serious deformity of the child's leg. The hospital refused to proceed without a court order. In ordering that the child be declared neglected and that the operation be performed, the court observed that:

> There are parents . . . who because of ignorance or prejudice or neglect or even sometimes viciousness, are either incapable or unwilling to do things necessary for the protection of their own offspring. There are parents who will by act do that which is harmful to the child and sometimes will fail to do that which is necessary to permit a child to live a normal life in the community.[46]

It should be noted that neglect has been even more broadly defined in some cases. One court has stated:

> [Neglect is] not only a failure to provide the necessaries of life — sustenance, clothing, shelter, food and warmth — but a failure to care, to look after, to guide, to supervise and . . . to direct the activities of a child . . . . [W]hen a parent is apprised of the conduct of the child just as if a parent were apprised of the physical ailments of the child and does nothing about correcting the conduct or correcting the condition which produced the physical ailment, that would constitute neglect . . . .[47]

Given such a broad view of neglect, one could rationally argue that parental inattentiveness to the sexual conduct which produced the pregnancy could constitute neglect, thus warranting a judicial order of temporary custody and treatment, where the minor is in favor of an abortion over the parents' opposition.[48]

In many cases, however, the best interests of the minor would make it undesirable for the parents to learn of the pregnancy at all. If the minor could obtain an abortion only by going through a court proceeding on the grounds of neglect, she might, rather than risk having her parents learn of her predicament, seek an unsafe illegal abortion, try to abort herself, or run away. In such circumstances, formal neglect proceedings which have as their very purpose the protection of the minor's best interests may actually be inimical to those interests. Thus, while in some instances neglect proceedings will provide an alternative to parental consent, in most cases — particularly those in which the minor is unwilling to have her parents learn of her pregnancy — these proceedings may not provide a realistic solution to the problem. But what is significant about neglect proceedings is that they demonstrate the state's awareness of the fact that at times it is necessary to override parental wishes and that they may provide a means in some cases for providing a minor with abortion services in the face of parental opposition.

III. THE CONSTITUTIONAL QUESTIONS

If the right to obtain an abortion is manifest in state statutes, or if it is determined to be a constitutional right, significant constitutional questions arise concerning the requirement of parental consent in the case of minors. If it is established by the United States Supreme Court, as it has been decided in several federal cases, that a woman has a constitutionally protected right to terminate an unwanted pregnancy, the constitutionality of parental consent requirements is likely to be questioned on the ground that allowing a state to enforce a parental veto over a minor's abortion amounts to a denial of the recognized constitutional right. Even disregarding any assumed constitutional right to abortion, parental consent requirements are still open to constitutional attack in those states having liberalized statutes which recognize a right to abortion. Moreover, if the statutes of a particular state were silent on the question of parental consent, or included a provision which allowed the performing of an abortion upon a female "with her consent,"[49] application of common law principles regarding a minor's consent could be constitutionally questioned. It is the purpose of this section to examine these constitutional questions, first on the basis of an assumed constitutional right to abortion, and then on the basis of the existing liberalized abortion laws.

A. A Minor's Constitutional Right to an Abortion

1. *Abortion as a Constitutional Right* — In addition to the statutory developments mentioned above, changes in the law surrounding abortions have come with judicial recognition of the woman's right to determine whether or not to bear a child.[50] Although the United States Supreme Court has not at the time of this writing ruled on the question of whether a woman has a fundamental constitutional right to terminate an unwanted pregnancy,[51] many state and federal courts have specifically held that laws which restrict or limit the availability and permissibility of abortions are unconstitutional as violations of the woman's fundamental rights under the ninth and fourteenth amendments.

The first case recognizing the fundamental nature of the right to have an abortion is *People v. Belous*.[52] That case declared unconstitutional a California statute previously in effect which limited legal abortions to those which were necessary in order to preserve the woman's life. The Supreme Court of California explicitly recognized a fundamental right to choose whether or not to bear a child, stating:

> The fundamental right of the woman to choose whether to bear children follows from the Supreme Court's and this court's repeated acknowledgment of a "right of privacy" or "liberty" in matters related to marriage, family, and sex. . . . That such a right is not enumerated in either the United States or California Constitutions is no impediment to the existence of the right.[53]

Decisions in a number of federal and state courts have followed the *Belous* decision in holding that abortion is a fundamental right. In six recent decisions,[54] three-judge federal courts held that the pertinent state law restrictions on abortion were unconstitutional because they interfered with a woman's right to choose whether or not to bear a child — a right the courts held to be secured by the ninth and fourteenth amendments. The question as to whether this right of privacy applies after as well as before conception, and thus includes abortion, has turned upon judicial analysis of the state's interest in the rights or welfare of the unborn. Once a court has concluded that the right to choose not to bear a child, including the right to terminate an unwanted pregnancy, is a fundamental right, the court has then usually asked whether the state has shown that the abortion statute's restrictions on this fundamental personal liberty are necessary in order to promote a compelling state interest.[55] The only asserted interest that has been seriously considered by courts in these cases has been the state's interest in protecting the fetus.[56] The six federal panels which struck down restrictive abortion laws explicitly held that this asserted interest was insufficient to overcome the woman's constitutional right.[57] Furthermore, the numerous state court cases which have declared restrictive abortion statutes unconstitutional have also rejected fetal interests as compelling.[58]

Those federal courts which have upheld restrictive abortion laws either have rejected the constitutional basis for a right to abortion[59] or have determined that the extent to which the fetus should be protected is a question for appropriate resolution by the legislature.[60] The result in these courts is, of course, the denial of any general constitutional right to an abortion. Although the Supreme Court has not yet spoken to the issue, the argument in favor of a constitutional right to an abortion is cogent and convincing. For purposes of the following discussion of whether a minor also has a constitutional right to an abortion, the reader should assume that the question will be finally resolved in the affirmative — *i.e.*, in favor of a woman's constitutional right to an abortion.

2. *The Constitutional Rights of Minors* — Assuming that the right to obtain an abortion is constitutionally protected, the logical next question is whether that right should also extend to minors. In a relatively recent line of cases, the United States Supreme Court has firmly established the principle that the protections of the Bill of Rights extend to minors. The decisions and their lower court interpretations make it clear that minors are indeed "persons" in the constitutional sense: thus the state must show a compelling reason to justify a limitation on the constitutional rights of a minor. For example, in the landmark case of *In re Gault*, the Supreme Court specifically rejected the notion that any alleged societal benefits resulting from informal juvenile court procedures constituted a

valid basis for depriving a minor of the right to procedural due process. In affirming those rights, the majority in *Gault* simply declared: "Neither the Fourteenth Amendment nor the Bill of Rights is for adults alone."[61] That a minor is a "person" to whom basic constitutional guarantees are extended is seen in a variety of other situations involving the exercise by minors of constitutionally protected rights. In the case of *In re Winship*,[62] the Court held that the due process clause of the fourteenth amendment applies in juvenile court proceedings so as to guarantee the safeguard of the "proof beyond a reasonable doubt" standard. In a number of cases, the Supreme Court has recognized that minors enjoy the first amendment guarantee of freedom of expression,[63] and the proscription against laws "respecting an establishment of religion."[64] The Court has similarly made it clear that the guarantees of the fourteenth amendment equal protection clause apply to minors.[65] The decisions thus make it clear that minors are "persons" entitled to at least some constitutional rights. What has not been decided as yet is the significant question whether a state, by vesting a parent with authority to deny certain rights of minors, and enforcing that parental veto through direct or indirect means, violates the constitutional rights of the minor. In those cases in which minors' constitutional rights have been considered, either there has been an express or implied unity of interest between the parent and child, or the fact of disparate interests was not at issue. There is evidence, however, that when the question is considered the Supreme Court is not likely to accept the notion that constitutional rights of minors are so easily subject to nullification by the acts of parents.[66]

3. *Parental Control v. Constitutional Rights* — Although the Supreme Court has made it clear that minors are "persons" entitled to the full enjoyment of constitutional rights, the Court has yet to consider the question whether states are free to enforce parental control over the exercise of some of those rights. Some insight into the issue can be gained by examining the extent to which courts have permitted parents to act in relation to the rights of their minor children in the absence of state legislation.

It has been established that parents have a constitutionally protected right to raise their children without unreasonable state interference,[67] and are empowered to discipline their children for disobeying reasonable commands.[68] Interpretations of the rights to raise and discipline children have included the right to allow the search of a child's room by police acting without a warrant and over the objections of the minor.[69]   Despite the fact that courts in many instances have been unwilling to interfere in the relationship between parent and child,[70] parental authority is neither absolute nor constitutionally insulated from some state regulation.   As the Supreme Court declared in *Prince v. Massachusetts*[71]: "Acting to guard the general interest in youths well being, the state, as *parens patriae* may restrict the parent's control by requiring school attendance, regulating or prohibiting the child's labor and in many other ways."[72]

There is no indication, however, that states may enforce unlimited parental authority to nullify the exercise of constitutional rights by minors especially where the public interest is not well defined, as in the case of a mature or emancipated minor.   A case somewhat to the point is *Rowan v. U.S. Post Office Dep't.*[73]   The case arose under a federal statute which permitted an addressee to direct the Postmaster General to issue an order prohibiting further mailings of certain types of matter to the addressee or any of the addressee's "minor children who have not attained their nineteenth birthday and who reside with the addressee."[74]   Although the portion of the statute dealing with minor children was not specifically challenged, Mr. Justice Brennan offered the following caveat:

> In light of the broad interpretation which the Court assigns to § 4009, . . . the possibility exists that parents could prevent their children, even if they are 18 years old, from receiving political, religious or other materials which the parents find offensive.   In my view, a statute so construed and applied is not without constitutional difficulties. . . . [I] understand the Court to leave open the question of the right of older children to receive materials through the mail without governmental interference and also the more specific question whether [the statute] may constitutionally be applied with respect to all materials and to all children under 19.[75]

Thus, Justice Brennan at least would have the courts be wary of permitting the state to enforce the parent's right to control, when that control would affect a constitutionally protected right otherwise enjoyed by the minor.

Also pertinent to the question of whether all minors may be subjected to parental authority in the exercise of constitutional rights is the question whether minors may effectively *waive* constitutional rights without parental involvement. Precedent makes it clear that a parent's right to speak for a minor is not exclusive. The Supreme Court of California, in *People v. Lara*,[76] rejected the contention that every minor is incompetent as a matter of law to waive constitutional rights to remain silent and to have an attorney unless the waiver is consented to by an attorney, a parent, or a guardian who has himself been advised of the rights. Instead, the court applied a totality of circumstances rule and declared that the validity of a waiver by a minor of the right to counsel and the right to remain silent "depends not on his age alone, but on a combination of that factor with such other circumstances as his intelligence, education, and ability to comprehend the meaning and the effect of his statement."[77] Thus, the question of the competence of a minor to waive his or her rights is one of fact, and while the age of the juvenile defendant is entitled to serious consideration, age per se is not conclusive.[78] When questions of waiver in the juvenile court setting have arisen, courts have considered age, education, and information available to the defendant juvenile as well as other pertinent facts.

When a court speaks of the competence to waive constitutional rights, it is clear that it is actually speaking of a *competence to decide* whether to waive *or assert* those rights, thus presuming an attendant competence to assert rights. If a mature minor is competent to waive his rights to counsel and his privilege against self-incrimination, such a minor should also be held to be competent to assert fundamental rights guaranteed by the Constitution, and should not be deprived of those rights by a state's delegating to the parent the decisional function.

While the courts have only infrequently considered the question of the parent's power to waive the child's rights, the few cases indicate that the interests of the child are paramount. In *Shioutaken v. District of Columbia*,[79] a case involving waiver of rights in a juvenile proceeding, the federal appellate court observed that "[t]he court would be well advised to consult the child's parents or guardian *where their interests are not adverse*."[80] That limitation was more fully developed in the later case of *McBride v. Jacobs*.[81] The court was willing to assume *arguendo* that the mother had been advised of the juvenile's right to counsel and that she had made an intelligent and competent waiver. In the absence of advice to and waiver by the minor in the circumstances of this case, however, the court held that the waiver by the mother was insufficient. The court observed:

> Obviously not all minors are capable of making a waiver. Where the court finds for any reason the minor is not capable of a waiver the parent may so waive *provided the court also finds there is no conflict of interest between them. . . .*[82]

This reasoning, coupled with the preceding analysis of the minor's competence to waive his constitutional rights, suggests that a parent should be permitted to waive the rights of a minor only when the minor is shown to be incapable of making an independent decision to waive or assert his rights, and in no case when the interest of the parent is adverse to that of the child. Extending that reasoning to the abortion question, a parent should not be able to block an independent choice by a minor to obtain an abortion where the minor is competent to make such a choice or where the interests of the parent and child are adverse.

Assuming that a constitutional right to an abortion does in fact exist, and also that a state-imposed parental consent requirement must be fulfilled if the minor is to exercise that right, the consent requirement must satisfy not merely a legitimate but a compelling state interest[83] and must be narrowly drawn.[84] Obviously, the state's consent requirement cannot be based upon state concern with the interest of the fetus in the case of minors when such an interest is not present in the case of adults. However, there arguably exist some other interests which might be asserted in support of the consent requirement. For example, a possible argument upon which the state might rely is that a rule requiring parental consent to abortion protects a minor from her own improvidence. There are two basic flaws in this rationale. First, the law in a variety of circumstances acknowledges that unmarried minors may consent to receive medical treatment and has legitimized such consent.[85] The extent to which state law does this varies, of course, from state to state. What is noteworthy here is that the "interest" of the state in protecting minors from improvidently consenting to medical treatment is not consistently asserted and appears not to be present in a variety of health situations (*e.g.*, venereal disease)[86] in most states. Second, in states other than those which have eliminated all restrictions on permissible grounds for abortion, informed medical authorities have concluded that a therapeutic abortion should be available where there is substantial risk of grave impairment to the physical and mental health or life of any female, especially a minor.[87] It is well known that the adverse consequences of childbirth to the minor's health and welfare increase as the minor's age decreases.[88] Moreover, even if in a given set of circumstances a minor's parents might agree, if asked, to consent to an abortion, the requirement of parental consent may adversely affect the mental or physical health and welfare of the minor, or perhaps drive her to an underground abortionist or self-abortion. Given these considerations, the requirement can hardly be rationalized as a means of protecting the minor from her own improvidence.

A second possible argument for a compelling interest of the state is that the denial of abortions and other forms of medical care to unmarried minors is necessary for the preservation of parental control. But the state has disregarded this parental interest in a variety of circumstances where the minor's health needs or the health interests of the community or both would be disserved by requiring parental consent. Under many state laws, broad groups of minors may give effective consent to receive *all* kinds of medical treatment if they meet certain requirements.[89] Moreover, in a great many states minors can also receive care related to pregnancy,[90] and it is difficult to see why, if that care may be provided without parental consent, abortion services cannot be. Where an unwanted teenage pregnancy occurs, a general interest of the state in assuring parents' control of their children does not appear compelling. Moreover, since the minor has become pregnant, it would appear that parental control has already been diminished,[91] and surely the state cannot intend the law to bolster parental control for punitive purposes.

B. *Alternative Constitutional Attacks on Parental Consent Requirements*

A ruling that the requirement of parental consent to a minor's abortion is unconstitutional — whether such requirement is imposed by statute or by state regulation or whether it is imposed by the practicalities of a physician's and/or hospital's fear of civil liability — need not necessarily rest upon the broad determination that there is a constitutional right to abortion as such. Alternative constitutional attacks on the parental consent requirement could be made under (1) the equal protection clause; (2) the constitutional right to life and health, and the physician's correlative right to practice medicine in accordance with the best medical standards; and (3) the prohibition against laws respecting an establishment of religion.

1. *The Equal Protection Clause* — Under the equal protection clause, states are free to legislate by classification among citizens so long as the classifications utilized rest upon some difference which bears a reasonable relation to the purpose of the statute which creates it.[92] If under the statute of a particular state, some or all minors are deprived of the right to obtain an abortion without getting parental consent, it could be argued that minors who are for that reason unable to obtain abortions are deprived of the equal protection of the law by virtue of an unreasonable classification. The precise manner in which such a claim could be raised would, of course, depend on the specific statutory and/or common law framework of a particular state; or, in the absence of a controlling state statute, upon whether the abortion services were denied by a private physician or a public or quasi-public facility which refused to perform an abortion for fear of civil liability.

In some states,[93] there are specific statutory prohibitions against the providing of abortion services to minors under a certain age without parental or spousal consent. In these states it is clear that the statutory framework divides women into at least three classes: (1) those who qualify for therapeutic abortions and for whom no consent other than their own is needed; (2) those who qualify for therapeutic abortions and who have been willing and able to obtain the required parental or spousal consent; and (3) those who qualify for therapeutic abortions but cannot obtain them because they are unwilling or unable to obtain the necessary parental or spousal consent. In other states the inability of some minors to obtain abortion services might rest upon a statutory provision which excludes abortion from the medical services for which a minor may consent.[94] In such states it could be argued that the statutory provision unreasonably discriminates against minors in need of a particular kind of medical care, namely an abortion. Finally, when abortions for minors are not singled out by any exclusionary statute, but are rather unavailable because of the general statutory medical care framework, two classes are created — adults and minors. The above examples of possible statutory frameworks, and the equal protection attacks thereunder indicate that the definition of offensive classifications will necessarily vary from state to state. It is clear, however, that where state laws regarding consent to medical treatment interfere in some manner with the rights of some women to obtain abortions otherwise permitted by state law, a classification is created which arguably offends the equal protection clause.

As indicated above, a statutory classification, to withstand attack under the equal protection clause, must at the very least be rationally related to a valid purpose of the statute creating it.[95] As the Supreme Court has recently declared, classifications "must be reasonable, not arbitrary, and must rest upon some ground of difference having a fair and substantial relation to the object of the legislation, so that all persons similarly circumstanced shall be treated alike."[96] However, where the particular statutory classification impinges upon the exercise of fundamental constitutional rights, a more stringent test of equal protection is applied as opposed to the simple rational relationship test. In these situations, the statutory classification must "be not merely rationally related to a valid public purpose but necessary to the achievement of a compelling state interest."[97] Assuming an affirmative answer to the question of whether there exists a constitutional right to abortion,[98] a classification limiting the exercise of that right by minors would necessarily be subject to the stricter compelling interest standard in order to survive scrutiny under the equal protection clause. As the discussion in an earlier portion of this article pointed out,[99] states would have considerable difficulty demonstrating that compelling interest. But the instant analysis is concerned with an alternative to the argument that there is a fundamental right to an abortion. Indeed, it is arguable that, in determining whether statutory parental consent requirements violate the equal protection clause, it is not necessary to reach the question of whether abortion is a constitutional right, since, in the writers' view, even the more lenient rational basis test cannot be met.

Reviewing the possible purposes for the state imposition of parental consent requirements upon the availability of abortions to minors,[100] it is reasonable to conclude that just as there is no compelling interest justifying the existence of such requirements, so too there is no rational relationship between the classification and the purpose of the statute creating it. For example, so far as any purpose to protect a minor from her own improvidence is concerned, arbitrarily restricting the right of a pregnant woman after the fact to obtain an abortion bears very little relation to the accomplishment of that goal. Similarly, any claimed purpose of assuring parental control bears little rational relationship to the statute: presumably the fact of sexual conduct leading to pregnancy would indicate that the parent had lost control of the child, and to enforce renewed control by means of a compelled continuation of pregnancy is both arbitrary and inhumane.[101]

One difficulty with this argument becomes apparent after consideration of judicial interpretation of the "rational relationship" concept. The Supreme Court has made it quite clear that rational relationship should be interpreted to mean that if any state of facts which would sustain the classification can be reasonably conceived, the classification should be allowed to stand.[102] Thus, only when there is a gross lack of correspondence between the classification and the purpose will the courts intervene under the equal protection clause. Yet, at the same time, the Court has declared that a gross lack of correspondence would be present when a classification drawn is *unreasonable* in light of its purpose.[103] It is the contention here that the restriction imposed upon the availability of abortions by consent requirements is indeed unreasonable in the equal protection sense.

2. *The Right of a Minor to Life and Health* — The minor's right to obtain needed medical services and more broadly, her right to life and health, arguably are also impinged upon by state laws which directly or indirectly condition the availability of abortion services upon parental consent.[104] The right to life is, of course, self-evident under the Constitution,[105] and the right to protect health appears to be equally fundamental.[106] Carrying the analysis one step further, freedom to obtain medical services for safeguarding health must be deemed an aspect of life and liberty if the fifth and fourteenth amendments are to have meaning. Given our constitutional framework, there can hardly be a more basic attribute of freedom than the right of the individual to be secure from physical or

emotional harm. With that in mind, the question of whether and how health should be protected is one uniquely suited to solution by the individual and his physician.

The extent to which state laws on abortion or on medical treatment for minors arguably interfere with the minor's constitutional right to life and health again vary with the particular state law framework. In the states which require parental or spousal consent to abortion where minors are below a certain age,[107] it is uncertain whether the common law emergency exception would apply or whether a neglect proceeding would be available for the minor's protection. The statutes of some of these states permit abortion only in certain situations. By foreclosing abortion (as they appear to do on their face) even in these limited circumstances in the absence of parental consent, they seem to ignore the health interest of minors. It is conceivable that a situation could arise in which a minor who is otherwise eligible for an abortion on the ground, for example, that pregnancy is a threat to her life or health would nonetheless be forced to risk injury to life and health — possibly of a permanent nature — in the event that she is unwilling or unable to obtain parental consent to the procedure.

In those states in which parental consent to abortion is not expressly required,[108] the common law and/or statutory framework might permit abortions without parental consent depending upon the particular circumstances. However, the uncertainty of the law, and the consequent reluctance of the medical profession to act in the face of such uncertainty, may effectively prevent the minor from obtaining abortion services — and thus foreclose her from enjoying her constitutional rights to life and health. Arguably, the state should at least be required to show a compelling state interest to justify this arbitrary interference with the minor's constitutional rights.[109]

Also involved here is the physician's right to evaluate the health needs of the pregnant minor who is his patient. Where parental consent to abortion is required, the health needs of the minor are relegated to secondary importance. Hence the physician who provides abortion services without parental consent may in some instances run the risk of civil liability or criminal penalties,[110] despite the fact that he has made a professional determination that the minor should have an abortion, the seeking of parental consent would be harmful to the minor, or parental consent cannot be obtained.

3. *The Prohibition against Laws Respecting an Establishment of Religion* — In some cases, parental refusal to consent to abortion may be based upon the parent's conviction that a fetus is a human being and that abortion is equivalent to murder.[111] Such a conviction is often based upon religious beliefs, particularly of the Roman Catholic Church.[112] In these circumstances, a third constitutional attack is available to the minor who seeks abortion services but is unable to obtain parental consent.

Where the minor wishes to have an abortion a fortiori, she does not subscribe to theological beliefs which would prohibit abortion. Where the grounds for parental objection are religious, the state, in enforcing it by means of criminal or civil sanctions, arguably interferes with the minor's rights in favor of the parents' religious beliefs. That such a course may violate the first and fourteenth amendment could follow from the Supreme Court's decisions in *Epperson v. Arkansas*,[113] and *Abington School District v. Schemmp*.[114] While those landmark decisions regarding the teaching of religious beliefs in public schools did not involve any question of parental consent, the basic mandate of the Court that states must refrain from the support of religious ideas could logically be extended to the context of minors' rights to obtain abortions. Thus, it could be argued that by enforcing the requirement of parental consent in cases where that consent is withheld by reason of the parents' religious beliefs, the state is not being "neutral in matters of religious theory, doctrine and practice."[115]

IV. LEGISLATIVE PROPOSALS FOR ABORTION AND PARENTAL CONSENT

The principle that the best interests of the minor are paramount should be kept foremost in mind when considering the question of what the law should be with respect to a minor's ability to consent for herself to the performance of an abortion. It was at least in part to protect these interests that the common law rules on parental consent to medical treatment were originally developed. Unfortunately, it is often the case that the interests of parent and child do not coincide but do, in fact, collide.

Where a minor seeks abortion services and indicates to a physician that she is unwilling or unable to seek parental consent, the physician should discuss the matter fully with her. If the physician is satisfied that she wants an abortion, and that she is unwilling or unable to obtain parental consent, and if he believes that it will be in her best interest to terminate the unwanted pregnancy, he should be free to perform the abortion without the threat of civil or criminal penalty. The physician should, of course, carefully explain the nature and consequences of the abortion procedure to the patient and should take special pains with young minors to make his explanations clear. Social service and contraceptive counselling should also be provided to the minor, as well as other medical and psychiatric or psychological treatment where needed.

While in an ideal family parent and child would have the kind of relationship which would encourage the pregnant minor to take her parents into her confidence and seek their help, the real life situation of many minors may not permit such confidences. For example, the minor may have become pregnant through an act of incest and be unwilling to have this known to her mother. Or the minor may have reasonable grounds for believing that knowledge of her pregnancy would result in severe punitive sanctions by her family. The minor may know that her parents, on religious grounds, will refuse to consent to abortion. A minor may be living away from her parents or may have been abandoned by her parents and thus be unable to obtain parental consent. There are many other situations in which the seeking of parental consent would be at best futile and at worst harmful. Faced with an absolute requirement of parental consent, many minors, rather than risk parental knowledge of and adverse reaction to the pregnancy, will either run away from home, try to abort themselves, or find a quack abortionist who is willing to perform a nonmedical, unsafe abortion without parental consent. No state law should encourage that result.

The choice between permitting safe, legal abortions by physicians without parental consent and forcing a minor to either bear an unwanted child or undertake to have an unsafe illegal abortion seems to be one that can only be satisfactorily resolved by permitting abortions without parental consent. Since the rights of the minor — her privacy, her health and safety, and indeed her very life — may depend upon her ability to consent for herself to the performance of abortion, the law should permit her to do so. Unless it does, both the minor and the physician, who would, but for the negative effect of the law (whether such negative effect stems from ambiguity or outright prohibition) be able to provide the needed services, are placed in an impossible dilemma under the present laws in many states. The elimination of laws negating the rights of the minor as to abortion seems dictated by constitutional considerations as well as considerations of humanitarianism and public well-being.

It may be that some variation of the Illinois statute on birth control services would be appropriate for providing abortion services.[116] Such a statute would provide that abortion services may be provided to any minor (1) who is married, is a parent, or has had a prior pregnancy; (2) who has the consent of her parent or legal guardian; (3) who has graduated from high school; (4) who is living away from home under such circumstances that she makes most of her own decisions; (5) as to whom the failure to provide such services would create a serious health hazard; or (6) who is referred for such services by a physician, clergyman, social worker, or family planning agency. Adoption of this type of statute in the abortion area might help to assuage the fear sometimes expressed that a very young minor may act precipitously in relation to abortion if she is neither relatively independent nor has had the benefit of adult advice in relation to the decision-making process.

Although a great many minors can now obtain abortions in a variety of states under a number of different laws and legal theories, we contend that the best interests of the minor would be served by a statutory provision which makes crystal clear the availability of abortion services without parental knowledge or consent, and which includes protection for the servicing physician and/or health facility from criminal or civil liability where such liability would be based solely on the absence of parental consent.

NOTES

1. *See, e.g.*, Bonner v. Moran, 126 F.2d 121 (D.C. Cir. 1941).

2. *Id.*; Zoski v. Gaines, 271 Mich. 1, 260 N.W. 99 (1935); Perry v. Hodgson, 168 Ga. 678, 148 S.E. 659 (1929).

3. *See* notes 14-22 *infra* & accompanying text.

4. *See* notes 50-58 *infra* & accompanying text.

5. For a statement of the general rule on liability of physicians who treat minors without parental consent see Bonner v. Moran, 126 F.2d 121 (D.C. Cir. 1941) and Younts v. St. Francis Hospital & School of Nursing, Inc., 205 Kan. 292, 469 P.2d 330 (1970).

6. *See, e.g.*, Smith v. Selby, 72 Wash. 2d 16, 21, 431 P.2d 719, 723 (1967).

7. *E.g.*, Bach v. Long Island Jewish Hosp., 49 Misc. 2d 207, 267 N.Y.S.2d 289 (Sup. Ct. 1966). *See also In re* Palumbo, 172 Misc. 55, 14 N.Y.S.2d 329 (Dom. Rel. Ct. 1939).

8. *See, e.g.*, Cohen v. Delaware Lackawanna & W. R.R., 150 Misc., 450, 269 N.Y.S. 667 (Sup. Ct. 1934). It is unclear whether financial dependence on parents would by itself totally undercut a claim of emancipation. *See* Tremper v. Tremper, 35 Misc. 2d 846, 848, 231 N.Y.S.2d 430, 433 (Sup. Ct. 1962). Case law also indicates that a minor, while in military service, is considered emancipated. Swenson v. Swenson, 241 Mo. App. 21, 25, 227 S.W.2d 103, 105 (1950). There is also case authority which indicates that a minor who is still living in the parental home may be considered emancipated if he or she pays living expenses to the parents and has full discretion with respect to the rest of his or her earnings. *See, e.g.*, Crosby v. Crosby, 230 App. Div. 651, 652, 246 N.Y.S. 384, 386 (1930); Giovagnioli v. Fort Orange Construction Co., 148 App. Div. 489, 493, 133 N.Y.S. 92, 94 (1911).

9. *See* Tremper v. Tremper, 35 Misc. 2d 846, 848, 231 N.Y.S.2d 430, 433 (Sup. Ct. 1962).

10. *E.g.*, Murphy v. Murphy, 206 Misc. 228, 229, 133 N.Y.S.2d 796, 797 (Sup. Ct. 1954).

11. *E.g.*, Luka v. Lowrie, 171 Mich. 122, 136 N.W. 1106 (1912); Sullivan v. Montgomery, 155 Misc. 488, 279 N.Y.S. 575 (N.Y. City Ct. 1935). In *Sullivan v. Montgomery*, a 20 year old boy had injured his ankle during a football game and after being taken to a physician for an examination, consented to being anaesthetized and to having his ankle set. Despite the fact that the physician had not obtained parental consent, the court denied recovery by the minor in an action for assault and stated:

> [I]f a physician or surgeon is confronted with an emergency which endangers the life or health of the patient, it is his duty to do that which the occasion demands within the usual and

customary practice among physicians and surgeons in the same locality. Many persons are injured daily in our city and emergency cases constantly arise. To hold that a physician or surgeon must wait until perhaps he may be able to secure the consent of the parents, who may not be available, before administering an anaesthetic or giving to the person injured the benefit of his skill and learning to the end that pain and suffering may be alleviated may result in the loss of many lives and pain and suffering which might otherwise be prevented. I do not believe that those who have devoted their lives to humanity will wantonly administer an anaesthetic where such consent may reasonably be obtained in view of the exigency; it would be altogether too harsh a rule to say that under the circumstances disclosed by the testimony in the instant case, the defendant should be held liable because he did not obtain the consent of the father to the administration of an anaesthetic; as the defendant was confronted with an emergency and as he obtained the consent of his patient, I hold that the consent of the father was not necessary. 155 Misc. at 449-50, 279 N.Y.S. at 577-78 (citation omitted).

12. *See, e.g.,* Luka v. Lowrie, 171 Mich. 122, 136 N.W. 1106 (1912).

13. *See, e.g.,* Younts v. St. Francis Hospital & School of Nursing, Inc., 205 Kan. 292, 301, 469 P.2d 330, 337 (1970); Bakker v. Welsh, 144 Mich. 632, 635-36, 108 N.W. 94, 96 (1906), *limited in* Zoski v. Gaines, 271 Mich. 1, 10, 260 N.W. 99, 103 (1935); Gulf & S.I.R. Co. v. Sullivan, 155 Miss. 1, 10, 119 So. 501, 502 (1928); Bishop v. Shurly, 237 Mich. 76, 78-79, 211 N.W. 75, 85-86 (1926); Bach v. Long Island Jewish Hosp., 49 Misc. 2d 207, 267 N.Y.S.2d 289 (Sup. Ct. 1966); Lacey v. Laird, 166 Ohio St. 12, 21, 139 N.E.2d 25, 31 (1956) (Taft, J., concurring). *See also* RESTATEMENT OF TORTS § 59(a) (1934): "If a child . . . is capable of appreciating the nature, extent and consequences of the invasion . . . his assent prevents the invasion from creating liability, though the assent of the parent, guardian or other person is not obtained or is expressly refused."

14. ARK. STAT. ANN. § 41-305 (Supp. 1969); CAL. HEALTH & SAFETY CODE § 25951 (West Supp. 1970); COLO. REV. STAT. ANN. § 40-6-101(3)(a) (1971); DEL. CODE ANN. tit. 24, § 1790(b)(3) (Supp. 1970); FLA. SESS. LAWS ch. 72-196 (1972); GA. CODE ANN. § 26-9923 (1971); KAN. GEN. STAT. ANN. § 21-3407 (Supp. 1971); MD. ANN. CODE art. 43, § 137(a) (1971); N.M. STAT. ANN. §§ 40A-5-1 to 3 (Supp. 1971); N.C. GEN. STAT. § 14-45.1 (Supp. 1971); ORE. REV. STAT. ANN. § 435.415 (1971); S.C. CODE ANN. § 16-87 (Supp. 1971); VA. CODE ANN. § 18.1-62.1(c)(1)(i) (Supp. 1971).

15. *See* MODEL PENAL CODE § 230.3(2) (Proposed Official Draft, 1962). That section provides in pertinent part:

(2) *Justifiable Abortion.* A licensed physician is justified in terminating a pregnancy if he believes there is substantial risk that continuance of the pregnancy would gravely impair the physical or mental health of the mother or that the child would be born with grave physical or mental defect, or that the pregnancy resulted from rape, incest, or other felonious intercourse.

16. Specific consent provisions are included in the statutes of Arkansas, Colorado, Delaware, Florida, New Mexico, North Carolina, Oregon, South Carolina, and Virginia. The statutes vary in their mechanics, and the statute of Virginia may be said to be the most complete in meeting all possibilities. It provides that if the woman "shall be an infant or incompetent as adjudicated by any court of competent jurisdiction . . . permission [must be] . . . given in writing by a parent, or if married, by her husband, guardian or person standing in loco parentis to such infant or incompetent." VA. CODE ANN. § 18.1-62.1(e) (Supp. 1971). The statute then goes on to state that: "For purposes of this section any married woman over the age of eighteen years shall be deemed competent to give her consent in the same manner as though she were twenty-one years of age or older notwithstanding the provisions of § 32-137 of the code of Virginia." *Id.*

In Delaware, parental consent is required if the woman is under 19 or mentally incompetent. DEL. CODE ANN. tit. 24, § 1790(b)(3) (Supp. 1970). Oregon requires parental consent if the woman is under 21 and unmarried. ORE. REV. STAT. § 435.415(1) (Supp. 1971-72). Colorado and New Mexico require the parent or guardian to concur in the request for an abortion if the woman is under 18. COLO. REV. STAT. ANN. § 40-2-50 (Supp. 1971); N.M. STAT. ANN. § 40A-5-1(c) (Supp. 1971). Arkansas, North Carolina, and South Carolina require the consent of the parent, guardian, or husband if the woman is under 21 or incompetent as adjudicated by a court. ARK. STAT. ANN. § 41-305 (Supp. 1969); N.C. GEN. STAT. § 14-45.1 (1969); S.C. CODE ANN. § 16-87 (Supp. 1971). Florida requires both parental consent and the woman's written consent if she is under the age of 18 and is unmarried. The provision does not apply, however, if the physician, with a corroborating medical opinion, determines that the continuation of the pregnancy would threaten the life of the woman. FLA. SESS. LAWS ch. 72-196 (1972).

The MODEL PENAL CODE § 230.31(2) (Proposed Official Draft, 1962) itself does not require parental consent for abortion; nor does the Uniform Abortion Act approved by the Commissioners on Uniform State laws, which statute was in turn adopted by the American Bar Association in 1972. The Uniform Abortion Act basically permits, up to a certain period of gestation, abortion without limitation as to the permissible grounds; after the specified gestational period, the grounds for abortion are more limited.

17. *See* ALASKA STAT. § 11.15.060 (1970); HAWAII REV. LAWS § 453.16 (Supp. 1971); N.Y. PENAL LAW § 125.05 (McKinney Supp. 1971); WASH. REV. CODE ANN. § 9.02.060 (Supp. 1971).

18. Washington provides that in addition to the woman's consent, the prior consent of a legal guardian is required if the woman is unmarried and under the age of 18. WASH. REV. CODE ANN. § 9.02.060 (Supp. 1971).

19. Alaska requires parental consent "from the parent or guardian of an unmarried woman less than 18 years of age." ALASKA STAT. § 11.15.060 (1970).

20. MD. ANN. CODE art. 43, § 137 (1971); GA. CODE ANN. § 26-9925 (Supp. 1971); KAN. STAT. ANN. § 21-3407 (Supp. 1971); CAL. HEALTH & SAFETY CODE § 25951 (West Supp. 1970).

21. Mississippi also "liberalized" its abortion law in 1966; however, the revised law, which now permits abortion in cases of rape as well as in those cases when it is deemed necessary to save the life of the woman, is not properly considered an ALI type bill. In any case, the Mississippi abortion statute is silent on the question of parental consent. MISS. CODE ANN. § 2223 (Supp. 1971).

22. In such states it is therefore necessary to look to the general statutory, common law and administrative law framework as well as local rules. In New York City, for example, the Health and Hospitals corporation (which has responsibility for the operation of the municipal hospitals) has adopted a policy with respect to minors and abortions which provides that only the patient's consent is required for abortion procedures on all females who are married, emancipated or at least 17 years of age. (An emancipated minor is defined as one "who is self supporting, or living away from home under such circumstances that she makes most of her own decisions.") In all other cases parental consent is required *except* when "in the opinion of the attending physician the seeking of parental consent would endanger the physical or mental health of the patient." City of New York, Interdepartmental Memorandum To Hospital Administrators from Robert A. Derzon Acting Commissioner, June 29, 1970.

23. *See generally* George, *The Evolving Law of Abortion*, pp. 3-62, *supra*.

24. *See* text accompanying notes 6-13 *supra*.

25. Nor is there any reported case in which a physician was held liable for providing a minor with medical examination and treatment for family planning services. For a review of state statutory provisions on medical treatment of minors which emphasizes the availability of contraceptive services see Pilpel & Wechsler, *Birth Control, Teenagers and the Law: A New Look, 1971*, 3 FAMILY PLANNING PERSPECTIVES 37 (No. 3, 1971). *See also* Pilpel & Wechsler, *Birth Control, Teenagers and the Law*, 1 FAMILY PLANNING PERSPECTIVES 29 (No. 1, 1969).

26. *See generally* Pilpel & Wechsler, *supra* note 25 (two articles). As an example of current provisions, the California Civil Code, in

addition to specifically dealing with venereal disease and pregnancy, provides:

> [A] minor 15 years of age or older who is living separate and apart from his parents or legal guardian, whether with or without the consent of a parent or guardian and regardless of the duration of such separate residence, and who is managing his own financial affairs, regardless of the source of his income, may give consent to hospital care . . . or medical or surgical diagnosis or treatment to be rendered by a physician and surgeon licensed under the provision of the State Medical Practice Act. . . . Such consent shall not be subject to disaffirmance because of minority. CAL. CIVIL CODE § 34.6 (West Supp. 1971).

A similar statutory framework exists in Minnesota, except that Minnesota's statute does not contain as low an age limit as California's does. *See* MINN. STAT. ANN. § 144.341 (Minn. Session Law Service 1971). In addition, in Minnesota a minor who has borne a child may give effective consent to medical treatment for the child and for herself. *Id.* § 144.342.

27. The states which at the time of this writing appear to have no special statute covering venereal disease treatment for minors are: West Virginia, Wyoming, Vermont, Tennessee, New Hampshire, and Wisconsin.

28. *See* CAL. CIV. CODE ANN. § 34.7 (West Supp. 1971) (12 years or older); DEL. CODE ANN. tit. 13, § 708(a) & (b) (Supp. 1970) (12 years or older); HAWAII REV. LAWS §§ 577A-1, 577A-2 (Supp. 1971); ILL. ANN. STAT. ch. 91, § 18-1 (Supp. 1972) (12 years or older); IOWA CODE ANN. § 140.9 (Supp. 1972) (16 years or older); N.D. CENT. CODE § 14-10-17 (1971) (14 years or older); ORE. REV. STAT. § 109.105 (1971-72) (14 years or older); WASH. REV. CODE ANN. § 70.24.110 (Supp. 1971) (14 years or older).

29. For statutes in which parental notification is permitted see GA. CODE ANN. § 17.104.3 (Supp. 1971); ILL. ANN. STAT. ch. 91, § 18-1 (Supp. 1971); LA. REV. STAT. ANN. § 1065.1 (Supp. 1971); MD. ANN. CODE art. 43, § 135 (Supp. 1971); MO. ANN. STAT. § 431.062 (Supp. 1971). Parental notification is required in: HAWAII REV. LAWS §§ 577A-1, 577A-3 (Supp. 1971) (if minor is under 18); IOWA CODE ANN. § 140.9 (Supp. 1972) (if it appears that minor may communicate disease to members of his family); NEB. REV. STAT. § 71-1120 (1969) (if minor is under 16 or if minor is unemancipated and over 16).

30. *See, e.g.,* CAL. CIV. CODE ANN. § 34.6 (West Supp. 1971) (Minors 15 and over who meet certain minimal qualifications); ILL. ANN. STAT. ch. 91, § 18.1 (Supp. 1972) (married, or pregnant minors or persons 18 or older); MD. ANN. CODE, art. 43, § 135 (Supp. 1971) (18 or over or married or the parent of a child); MISS. CODE ANN. §§ 7129-

81, 7129-82 (Supp. 1971) (married — common law as well as unmarried or emancipated or of sufficient intelligence to understand and appreciate the consequences of the proposed surgical or medical treatment); MONT. REV. CODE ANN. § 69-6101 (1970) (is or professes to be married or pregnant); NEV. REV. STAT. § 129.030 (1969) (emancipated or married); N.M. STAT. ANN. § 12-12-1 (1968) (married or emancipated); N.C. GEN. STAT. § 90-21.5 (Supp. 1971) (18 years or older or emancipated); PA. STAT. ANN. tit. 35, § 10103 (Supp. 1971) (18 years or older or graduated from high school or who has been pregnant or who has married); WASH. REV. CODE ANN. § 26.28.010 (Supp. 1971) (18 years or older).

31. ALA. ACT 2281 (1972); CAL. CIV. CODE ANN. § 25.6 (West Supp. 1971), § 34.5 (West 1954); DEL. CODE ANN. tit. 13, § 708 (Supp. 1970) (12 years or older); GA. CODE ANN. § 88-2904(f) (1971); HAWAII REV. STAT. §§ 577A, 577A-2 (Supp. 1971) (but physician must inform spouse, parent, custodian or guardian of any minor actually found to be pregnant); KAN. STAT. ANN. § 38-123 (Supp. 1971) (where no parent or guardian is available); MD. CODE ANN. art. 43, § 135 (Supp. 1971) (notification of parent permitted by physician); MINN. STAT. ANN. § 144.343 (Minn. Sess. Laws Service 1971); MISS. CODE ANN. § 7129-81(i) (Supp. 1971); MO. ANN. STAT. § 431.062 (Supp. 1971); N.J. REV. STAT. § 9:17A-1 (Supp. 1971-72); PA. STAT. ANN. tit. 35, § 10103 (Supp. 1971); VA. CODE ANN. § 32-137 (Supp. 1971).

32. HAWAII REV. STAT. §§ 577A, 577A-2 (Supp. 1971); MO. ANN. STAT. § 431.062 (Supp. 1971).

33. CAL. CIV. CODE ANN. § 25.6 (West Supp. 1971), § 34.5 (West 1954).

34. 4 Cal. 3d 873, 484 P.2d 1345, 95 Cal. Rptr. 1 (1971).

35. 4 Cal. 3d at 884, 484 P.2d at 1353, 95 Cal. Rptr. at 9.

36. See, e.g., HAWAII REV. LAWS § 577-1 (1968) (age 20); NEV. REV. STAT. § 129.010 (1969) (age 18 females, age 21 males); MICH. COMP. LAWS § 722.52 (Supp. 1972) (age 18).

37. See, e.g., N.Y. DOM. REL. §§ 2, 7 (McKinney 1964).

38. See generally Pilpel & Wechsler, supra note 25 (two articles). See also George, supra note 23, at 723 n.89.

39. See, e.g., N.Y. DOM. REL. § 111 (McKinney Supp. 1971-72).

40. See, e.g., ILL. ANN. STAT. ch. 37 §§ 701-1, -2, 702-4(1)(a), 703-1, -7 (Smith-Hurd Supp. 1972); N.J. REV. STAT. §§ 9:2-9 to -11 (1960); N.Y. FAMILY CT. ACT § 232 (McKinney 1963).

41. See, e.g., State v. Perricone, 37 N.J. 463, 181 A.2d 751, cert. denied, 371 U.S. 890 (1962).

42. See, e.g., In re Carstairs, 115 N.Y.S.2d 314 (Dom. Rel. Ct. 1952) (psychiatric observation for possible emotional instability); In re Sampson, 65 Misc. 2d 658, 317 N.Y.S.2d 641 (Dom. Rel. Ct. 1970) (blood transfusion during corrective surgery on child's deformed face).

43. *See, e.g.,* Jacobson v. Massachusetts, 197 U.S. 11 (1904); State v. Perricone, 37 N.J. 463, 181 A.2d 751, *cert. denied,* 371 U.S. 890 (1962).
44. 309 N.Y. 80, 127 N.E.2d 820 (1955).
45. 175 Misc. 948, 25 N.Y.S.2d 624 (Dom. Rel. Ct. 1941).
46. *Id.* at 949, 25 N.Y.S.2d at 626. *See also In re* Vasko, 238 App. Div. 128, 263 N.Y.S. 552 (1933).
47. *In re* Carstairs, 115 N.Y.S.2d 314, 316 (Dom. Rel. Ct. 1952).
48. The consequences of such unwanted pregnancies and births have been well documented. *See, e.g.,* GIL, VIOLENCE AGAINST CHILDREN — PHYSICAL CHILD ABUSE IN THE UNITED STATES (1970); Campbell, *The Role of Family Planning in the Reduction of Poverty,* 30 J. MARRIAGE & FAMILY 236, 245 (1968); BERNSTEIN & HERZOG, HEALTH SERVICES FOR THE UNMARRIED MOTHER, UNITED STATES DEPARTMENT OF HEALTH, EDUCATION AND WELFARE, WELFARE ADMINISTRATION (Children's Bureau) (1964); Anderson, Jenss, Mosher & Richter, *The Medical, Social and Educational Implications of the Increase in Out of Wedlock Births,* 56 AM. J. PUB. HEALTH, 1868, 1869 (1966); Newcombe & Tavendale, *Maternal Age & Birth Order Correlations,* I MUTATION RESEARCH 446, 452 (1964); Perkin, *Assessment of Reproductive Risk in Non-Pregnant Women,* 101 AM. J. OBSTETRICS & GYNECOLOGY 709, 710 (1968). It is also clear that a very significant number of out-of-wedlock births occur to minors. The distribution by age of the illegitimate births in 1968 was as follows:

Under 15 years	7,700
15 - 17 years	77,900
18 - 19 years	80,100
20 - 24 years	107,900
25 - 29 years	35,200
30 - 34 years	17,200
35 - 39 years	9,700
40 years and over	3,300

U.S. DEP'T OF HEALTH, EDUCATION AND WELFARE, DIVISION OF VITAL STATISTICS, PUBLIC HEALTH SERVICE, MONTHLY VITAL STATISTICS REPORT — 10: "Estimated Number of Illegitimate Live Births and Ratios by Age of Mother and Color — United States [Based on a 50 percent sample of births]" (1968). *See also* Yurdin, *Recent Trends in Illegitimacy — Implications for Practice,* 49 CHILD WELFARE 373, 373-75 (1970).
49. N.Y. PENAL LAW § 125.05 (McKinney Supp. 1971).
50. *See, e.g.,* People v. Belous, 71 Cal. 2d 954, 458 P.2d 194, 80 Cal. Rptr. 354 (1969), *cert. denied,* 397 U.S. 915 (1970).
51. The Supreme Court has heard oral argument in two cases in which restrictive state statutes were held to be unconstitutional. *See* Roe v.

Wade, 314 F. Supp. 1217 1221-23 (N.D. Tex. 1970) (per curiam), *jurisdiction postponed*, 402 U.S. 941 (1971) (No. 808, 1970 Term; renumbered No. 70-18, 1971 Term); Doe v. Bolton, 319 F. Supp. 1048, 1054-55 (N.D. Ga. 1970) (per curiam), *jurisdiction postponed*, 402 U.S. 941 (No. 971, 1970 Term; renumbered 70-40, 1971 Term), *restored to calendar for reargument*, 40 U.S.L.W. 3617 (U.S. June 27, 1972).

52. 71 Cal. 2d 954, 458 P.2d 194, 80 Cal. Rptr. 354 (1969), *cert. denied*, 397 U.S. 915 (1970). The court grounded its holding on the fundamental right of privacy as laid down in Griswold v. Connecticut, 381 U.S. 479 (1969).

It should be noted that the decision actually effected no change in the California law on abortion, since the statute on which the defendant's conviction was based and which was declared unconstitutional in *Belous*, had previously been repealed by the legislature. The statute in effect since 1967 allows abortion when necessary to prevent grave impairment of the woman's physical or mental health, or when the pregnancy is the result of rape or incest, or when the woman is under the age of 15. CAL. HEALTH & SAFETY CODE §§ 25951, 25952(C) (Supp. 1972).

53. 71 Cal. 2d at 963, 458 P.2d at 199, 80 Cal. Rptr. at 359.

54. Abele v. Markle, ___ F. Supp. ___ (D. Conn. April 18, 1972); Young Women's Christian Ass'n v. Kugler, 10 Crim. L. Rptr. 2469 (D.N.J. Feb. 29, 1972); Doe v. Scott, 321 F. Supp. 1385 (N.D. Ill. 1971), *appeals docketed sub. noms.* Hanrahan v. Doe *and* Heffernan v. Doe, 39 U.S.L.W. 3438 (U.S. Mar. 29, 1971) (Nos. 1522, 1523, 1970 Term; renumbered Nos. 70-105, 70-106, 1971 Term); Doe v. Bolton, 319 F. Supp. 1048 (N.D. Ga. 1970) (per curiam), *appeal granted*, 402 U.S. 941 (1971) (No. 971, 1970 Term; renumbered No. 70-40, 1971 Term); Roe v. Wade, 314 F. Supp. 1217 (N.D. Tex. 1970) (per curiam) *appeal granted*, 402 U.S. 941 (1971) (No. 808, 1970 Term, renumbered 70-18, 1971 Term); Babbitz v. McCann, 310 F. Supp. 293 (E.D. Wis.) (per curiam), *appeal dismissed*, 400 U.S. 1 (1970) (per curiam).

55. *See generally* cases cited note 54 *supra*. On the question of the state's compelling interest burden, see Bates v. Little Rock, 361 U.S. 516, 527 (1960).

56. There are three other hypothetical state interests that could conceivably be put forward to support statutory limitations on the permissible grounds for the performance of abortions. They are the state's interest in: (1) enforcing morals; (2) increasing population; and (3) protecting the health of the pregnant woman. As to enforcing morals through anti-abortion statutes, it should be noted that the statutes in restricting abortions draw no distinctions between married and unmarried women, and are thus overbroad if their purpose is the deterrence of sexual

misconduct. In any case, "to prescribe . . . [an unwanted pregnancy] as punishment for illicit intercourse would be a monstrous thing." State v. Baird, 50 N.J. 376, 383, 235 A.2d 673, 677 (1967) (concurring opinion Weintraub C.J.). *See also* Eisenstadt v. Baird, 429 F.2d 1398, 1402 (1st Cir. 1970), *aff'd*, 40 U.S.L.W. 4303 (1972). As to increasing population, given the present concern with problems of overpopulation, the assertion of this interest is extremely improbable and would in fact be ludicrous. Finally, as to protecting health interests of pregnant women, laws restricting the grounds for abortion serve no such purpose; instead they disregard health by defining the availability of abortion narrowly so that many women whose health is threatened by pregnancy and childbirth are unable to terminate pregnancy. Alternatively, women who for health or other reasons are unwilling to bear an unwanted child may seek the services of an unskilled, quack abortionist or resort to dangerous techniques of self-abortion and may thus cause serious, permanent injury to their health or even death.

57. *See* cases cited note 54 *supra.*

58. *See, e.g.*, State v. Walsingham, 250 So.2d 857 (Fla. 1971); People v. Barksdale, 18 Cal. App. 3rd 948, 96 Cal. Rptr. 265, *appeal docketed*, No. 1 Crim. 9526 (Cal. Dist. Ct., July 22, 1971); Shively v. Board of Medical Examiners, Calif. Super. Ct., Dkt. No. 59033 (San Francisco Co., Sept. 24, 1968); Commonwealth v. Page, 6 Center Co. Legal J. 285 (Pa. C.P. July 23, 1970); State v. Munson, Dkt. No. 24949 (S. Dak. 7th Cir. Ct., Pennington Co., April 6, 1970); State v. Ketchum (Mich. Dist. Ct., March 30, 1970).

59. *See* Steinberg v. Brown, 321 F. Supp. 741 (N.D. Ohio 1970).

60. *See* Doe v. Rampton, Civil No. 324-70 (D. Utah, filed Sept. 29, 1971); Corkey v. Edwards, 322 F. Supp. 1248, 1251 (W.D.N.C. 1971), *appeal docketed*, 40 U.S.L.W. 3048 (U.S. July 17, 1971) (No. 71-92); Steinberg v. Brown, 321 F. Supp. 741, 746 (N.D. Ohio 1970); Rosen v. Louisiana State Bd. of Medical Examiners, 318 F. Supp. 1217, 1225 (E.D. La. 1970), *appeal docketed*, 39 U.S.L.W. 3247 (U.S. No. 27, 1970) (No. 1010, 1970 Term; renumbered No. 70-42, 1971 Term).

61. 387 U.S. 1, 13 (1967).

62. 397 U.S. 358 (1970).

63. *See, e.g.*, Tinker v. Des Moines School District, 393 U.S. 503 (1969) (right to freedom of expression extended to wearing black arm bands as protest against Vietnam war); Board of Education v. Barnette, 319 U.S. 624 (1943) (state regulation compelling students to salute the flag held unconstitutional).

64. *See, e.g.*, School District of Abbington Township v. Schempp, 374 U.S. 203 (1963); Engel v. Vitale, 370 U.S. 421 (1962).

65. *See* Brown v. Bd. of Education, 347 U.S. 483 (1954) (school children

protected from racial discrimination and unequal education); Levy v. Louisiana, 391 U.S. 68 (1968) (statute discriminating against illegitimate children held unconstitutional).

66. Wisconsin v. Yoder, 40 U.S.L.W. 4476 (U.S. May 16, 1972).
67. *See* Pierce v. Society of Sisters, 268 U.S. 510 (1925); Meyer v. Nebraska, 262 U.S. 390 (1923).
68. *See, e.g.*, Commonwealth v. Brasker, ___ Mass. ___, 270 N.E.2d 389 (Mass. 1971) (statute punishing "stubborn children" held not unconstitutionally vague).
69. Vandenberg v. Superior Court, 8 Cal. App. 3d 1048, 87 Cal. Rptr. 876 (1970). *See also In re* Donaldson, 269 Cal. App. 2d 509, 75 Cal. Rptr. 220 (Ct. App. 1969) (holding that a school acting in loco parentis has the right to search a student's locker without a warrant).
70. *See, e.g.*, Roe v. Doe, 29 N.Y.2d 188, 324 N.Y.S. 2d 71, 272 N.E.2d 567 (1971) where the New York Court of Appeals declared:
> It is the natural right, as well as the legal duty, of a parent to care for, control and protect his child from potential harm, whatever the source, and absent a clear showing of misfeasance, abuse or neglect, courts should not interfere with that delicate responsibility. *Id.* at 193, 272 N.E.2d at 570, 324 N.Y.S. 2d at 75.
71. 321 U.S. 158 (1944).
72. *Id.* at 166.
73. 397 U.S. 728 (1970).
74. 39 U.S.C. § 4009(g) (1970).
75. 397 U.S. at 741.
76. 67 Cal. 2d 365, 432 P.2d 202, 62 Cal. Rptr. 586 (1967).
77. *Id.* at 383, 432 P.2d at 215, 62 Cal. Rptr. at 599.
78. *See* Williams v. Huff, 142 F.2d 91 (D.C. Cir. 1944); *In re* Dennis M., 70 Cal. 2d 444, 450 P.2d 296, 75 Cal. Rptr. 1 (1969).
79. 236 F.2d 666 (D.C. Cir. 1956).
80. *Id.* at 670 n.26 (emphasis added).
81. 247 F.2d 595 (D.C. Cir. 1957).
82. *Id.* at 596 (emphasis added).
83. *Cf.* Bates v. Little Rock, 361 U.S. 516 (1960).
84. *See, e.g.*, Griswold v. Connecticut, 381 U.S. 479, 485 (1969), *citing* NAACP v. Alabama, 377 U.S. 288, 307 (1963).
85. *See* notes 27-31 *supra* & accompanying text.
86. *Cf.* note 27 *supra* & accompanying text.
87. *See generally* authorities cited note 48 *supra*.
88. *Cf.* Pilpel & Wechsler (1971), *supra* note 25, at 37 n.3.
89. *See generally* statutes cited note 30 *supra*.
90. *See* statutes cited note 31 *supra*.
91. *Cf.* text accompanying notes 47-48 *supra*.

92. *See* McLaughlin v. Florida, 379 U.S. 184 (1964); McGowan v. Maryland, 366 U.S. 420 (1961); *Developments in the Law, Equal Protection*, 82 HARV. L. REV. 1065 (1969).

93. *See* notes 16, 18, 19 *supra* & accompanying text.

94. *See, e.g.*, HAWAII REV. STAT. §§ 577A, 577A-2 (Supp. 1971); MO. REV. STAT. § 431.062 (Supp. 1971).

95. The rational relationship test will be applicable if the right in question is deemed not to be a "fundamental" right. *See* Dandridge v. Williams, 397 U.S. 471 (1970).

96. Reed v. Reed, 404 U.S. 71 (1971), *quoting* Royster Guano Co. v. Virginia, 253 U.S. 412, 415 (1920).

97. Eisenstadt v. Baird, 40 U.S.L.W. 4303, 4306 n.7, *citing* Shapiro v. Thompson, 394 U.S. 618 (1969) and Loving v. Virginia, 388 U.S. 1 (1967).

98. *See* text accompanying notes 49-60 *supra.*

99. *See* text accompanying notes 55-58 *supra.*

100. *See* text accompanying notes 85-91 *supra.*

101. *Cf.* State v. Baird, 50 N.J. 376, 383, 235 A.2d 673, 677 (1967), where Chief Judge Weintraub, concurring, states that "to prescribe . . . [an unwanted pregnancy] . . . as a punishment for illicit intercourse would be a monstrous thing."

102. *See* McLaughlin v. Florida, 379 U.S. 184 (1964).

103. 379 U.S. at 191.

104. To a degree the right to life and health overlaps with the right to abortion. However, if the Supreme Court were ultimately to reject the separate constitutional basis of the right to abortion, the right of life and health would still provide the basis not only for attack on the old restrictive abortion statutes but also on the laws preventing minors from obtaining abortions without parental consent. In the case of adults this ground might not be as all-inclusive as the privacy ground discussed above. However, so far as minors are concerned — particularly those who are very young — the dangers to life and health of pregnancy are more readily apparent. *See* note 48 *supra.*

105. Thus, in People v. Belous, 71 Cal. 2d 954, 458 P.2d 194, 80 Cal. Rptr. 354 (1969) *cert. denied*, 397 U.S. 915 (1970), the Supreme Court of California, in considering the constitutionality of that state's restrictive anti-abortion statute, specifically found that if the law (which in that case permitted abortions only where necessary to preserve the life of the woman) was read to require "certainty of death," the statute "would work an invalid abridgment of the woman's constitutional rights. The rights involved . . . are the woman's right to life and to choose whether to bear children. The woman's right to life is involved, because childbirth involves risk of death." *Id.* at 963, 458 P.2d at 199, 80 Cal. Rptr. at 359 (footnotes omitted).

106. *Cf.* Jacobson v. Massachusetts, 197 U.S. 11 (1905). *See also* United

States v. Vuitch, 402 U.S. 62 (1971) in which the Supreme Court acknowledged that health includes all aspects of physical and mental well-being. While the Supreme Court in *Vuitch* was construing the District of Columbia statute against a claim that it was unconstitutionally vague, a fair implication from that construction is that the Court recognized that people must be free to safeguard health as broadly defined in that case.

107. *See* notes 16, 18, 19 *supra* & accompanying text.

108. *See* notes 20-22 *supra*.

109. *See* note 97 *supra* & accompanying text.

110. *See* statutes cited note 16 *supra*.

111. See Tinnelly, *Abortion and Penal Law*, 5 CATHOLIC LAW, 187, 190 (1959).

112. The official Catholic position opposes any direct interruption of the reproductive process at any time before or after conception. This position (Humane Vitae) was stated by Pope Paul VI as follows:

> [W]e must once again declare that the direct interruption of the generative process already begun, and, above all, directly willed and procured abortion, even if for therapeutic reasons, are to be absolutely excluded as a licit means of regulating birth. The 7th Encyclical of Pope Paul VI (as made public by the Vatican, July 29, 1968, in translation from the Latin).

Even if these beliefs are not grounded upon an established religion but are rather based on conscientious scruples held by a parent, the same basic objection could be made, namely that the parents' freedom of conscience is being implemented at the expense of the minor's equally cogent claim to freedom of conscience.

113. 393 U.S. 97 (1968).

114. 374 U.S. 203 (1965).

115. 393 U.S. at 103-04.

116. The Illinois birth control statute provides as follows:

> Birth control services and information may be rendered by doctors licensed in Illinois to practice medicine in all of its branches to any minor:
> 1. who is married; or
> 2. who is a parent; or
> 3. who is pregnant; or
> 4. who has the consent of his parent or legal guardian; or
> 5. as to whom the failure to provide such services would create a serious health hazard; or
> 6. who is referred for such services by a physician, clergyman or a planned parenthood agency. ILL. ANN. STAT. 91, § 18.7 (1969).

SUPPLEMENT

DECISIONS OF THE UNITED STATES SUPREME COURT
IN JANUARY 1973 WITH RESPECT TO THE TEXAS
AND GEORGIA ABORTION STATUTES

On January 22, 1973, the United States Supreme Court handed down its long-awaited rulings with respect to the constitutionality of the criminal abortion laws in Texas and Georgia. As a result of these two landmark decisions, not only the Texas and Georgia abortion statutes but those of several dozen additional states were overturned, and some form of revision of the abortion laws was mandated in almost every other state. The Court's decision in each case was 7-2, with Justice Blackman (joined by Justices Burger, Douglas, Brennan, Stewart, Marshall, and Powell) delivering the opinion of the Court and Justices White and Rehnquist dissenting. The following is a transcript of the Supreme Court's rulings in the Texas and Georgia cases.

No. 70–18

Jane Roe et al., Appellants,	On Appeal from the United
v.	States District Court for the
Henry Wade.	Northern District of Texas.

[January 22, 1973]

SYLLABUS

A PREGNANT SINGLE WOMAN (Roe) brought a class action challenging the constitutionality of the Texas criminal abortion laws, which proscribe procuring or attempting an abortion except on medical advice for the purpose of saving the mother's life. A licensed physician (Hallford), who had two state abortion prosecutions pending against him, was permitted to intervene. A childless married couple (the Does), the wife not being pregnant, separately attacked the laws, basing alleged injury on the future possibilities of contraceptive failure, pregnancy, unpreparedness for parenthood, and impairment of the wife's health. A three-judge District Court, which consolidated the actions, held that Roe and Hallford, and members of their classes, had standing to sue and presented justiciable controversies. Ruling that declaratory, though not injunctive, relief was warranted, the court declared the abortion statutes void as vague and overbroadly infringing those plaintiffs' Ninth and Fourteenth Amendment rights. The court ruled the Does' complaint not justiciable. Appellants directly appealed to this Court on the injunctive rulings, and appellee cross-appealed from the District Court's grant of declaratory relief to Roe and Hallford. *Held:*

1. While 28 U.S.C. § 1253 authorizes no direct appeal to this Court from the grant or denial of declaratory relief alone, review is not foreclosed when the case is properly before the Court on appeal from specific denial of injunctive relief and the arguments as to both injunctive and declaratory relief are necessarily identical.

2. Roe has standing to sue; the Does and Hallford do not.

(a) Contrary to appellee's contention, the natural termination of Roe's pregnancy did not moot her suit. Litigation involving pregnancy, which is "capable of repetition, yet evading review," is an exception to the usual federal rule that an actual controversy must exist at review stages and not simply when the action is initiated.

(b) The District Court correctly refused injunctive, but erred in granting declaratory, relief to Hallford, who alleged no federally protected right not assertable as a defense against the good-faith state prosecutions pending against him. *Samuels v. Mackell,* 401 U.S. 66.

(c) The Does' complaint, based as it is on contingencies, any one or more of which may not occur, is too speculative to present an actual case or controversy.

3. State criminal abortion laws, like those involved here, that except from criminality only a life-saving procedure on the mother's behalf without regard to the stage of her pregnancy and other in-

terests involved violate the Due Process Clause of the Fourteenth Amendment, which protects against state action the right to privacy, including a woman's qualified right to terminate her pregnancy. Though the State cannot override that right, it has legitimate interests in protecting both the pregnant woman's health and the potentiality of human life, each of which interests grows and reaches a "compelling" point at various stages of the woman's approach to term.

(a) For the stage prior to approximately the end of the first trimester, the abortion decision and its effectuation must be left to the medical judgment of the pregnant woman's attending physician.

(b) For the stage subsequent to approximately the end of the first trimester, the State, in promoting its interest in the health of the mother, may, if it chooses, regulate the abortion procedure in ways that are reasonably related to maternal health.

(c) For the stage subsequent to viability the State, in promoting its interest in the potentiality of human life, may, if it chooses, regulate, and even proscribe, abortion except where necessary, in appropriate medical judgment, for the preservation of the life or health of the mother.

4. The State may define the term "physician" to mean only a physician currently licensed by the State, and may proscribe any abortion by a person who is not a physician as so defined.

5. It is unnecessary to decide the injunctive relief issue since the Texas authorities will doubtless fully recognize the Court's ruling that the Texas criminal abortion statutes are unconstitutional.

314 F. Supp. 1217, affirmed in part and reversed in part.

BLACKMUN, J., delivered the opinion of the Court, in which BURGER, C. J., and DOUGLAS, BRENNAN, STEWART, MARSHALL, and POWELL, JJ., joined. BURGER, C. J., and DOUGLAS and STEWART, JJ., filed concurring opinions. WHITE, J., filed a dissenting opinion, in which REHNQUIST, J., joined. REHNQUIST, J., filed a dissenting opinion.

MR. JUSTICE BLACKMUN delivered the opinion of the Court.

This Texas federal appeal and its Georgia companion, *Doe v. Bolton, post* ——, present constitutional challenges to state criminal abortion legislation. The Texas statutes under attack here are typical of those that have been in effect in many States for approximately a century. The Georgia statutes, in contrast, have a modern cast and are a legislative product that, to an extent at least, obviously reflects the influences of recent attitudinal change, of advancing medical knowledge and techniques, and of new thinking about an old issue.

We forthwith acknowledge our awareness of the sensitive and emotional nature of the abortion controversy, of the vigorous opposing views, even among physicians, and of the deep and seemingly absolute convictions that the subject inspires. One's philosophy, one's experiences, one's exposure to the raw edges of human existence, one's religious training, one's attitudes toward life and family and their values, and the moral standards one establishes and seeks to observe, are all likely to influence and to color one's thinking and conclusions about abortion.

In addition, population growth, pollution, poverty, and racial overtones tend to complicate and not to simplify the problem.

Our task, of course, is to resolve the issue by constitutional measurement free of emotion and of predilection. We seek earnestly to do this, and, because we do, we have inquired into, and in this opinion place some emphasis upon, medical and medical-legal history and what that history reveals about man's attitudes toward the abortive procedure over the centuries. We bear in mind, too, Mr. Justice Holmes' admonition in his now vindicated dissent in *Lochner v. New York*, 198 U.S. 45, 76 (1905):

> It [the Constitution] is made for people of fundamentally differing views, and the accident of our finding certain opinions natural and familiar or novel and even shocking ought not to conclude our judgment upon the question whether statutes embodying them conflict with the Constitution of the United States.

I

The Texas statutes that concern us here are Arts. 1191-1194 and 1196 of the State's Penal Code.[1] These make it a crime to

---

[1] "Article 1191. Abortion

"If any person shall designedly administer to a pregnant woman or knowingly procure to be administered with her consent any drug or medicine, or shall use towards her any violence or means whatever externally or internally applied, and thereby procure an abortion, he shall be confined in the penitentiary not less than two nor more than five years; if it be done without her consent, the punishment shall be doubled. By

"procure an abortion," as therein defined, or to attempt one, except with respect to "an abortion procured or attempted by medical advice for the purpose of saving the life of the mother." Similar statutes are in existence in a majority of the States.[2]

Texas first enacted a criminal abortion statute in 1854. Texas Laws 1854, c. 49, § 1, set forth in 3 Gammel, Laws of Texas, 1502 (1898). This was soon modified into language that has remained

---

'abortion' is meant that the life of the fetus or embryo shall be destroyed in the woman's womb or that a premature birth thereof be caused.
"Art. 1192. Furnishing the means
"Whoever furnishes the means for procuring an abortion knowing the purpose intended is guilty as an accomplice.
"Art. 1193. Attempt at abortion.
"if the means used shall fail to produce an abortion, the offender is nevertheless guilty of an attempt to produce abortion, provided it be shown that such means were calculated to produce that result, and shall be fined not less than one hundred nor more than one thousand dollars.
"Art. 1194. Murder in producting abortion
"If the death of the mother is occasioned by an abortion so produced or by an attempt to effect the same it is murder.
"Art. 1196. By medical advice
"Nothing in this chapter applies to an abortion procured or attempted by medical advice for the purpose of saving the life of the mother."
The foregoing Articles, together with Art. 1195, comprise Chapter 9 of Title 15 of the Penal Code. Article 1195, not attacked here, reads:
"Art. 1195. Destroying unborn child
"Whoever shall during parturition of the mother destroy the vitality or life in a child in a state of being born and before actual birth, which child would otherwise have been born alive, shall be confined in the penitentiary for life or for not less than five years."

[2] Ariz. Rev. Stat. Ann. § 13-211 (1971); Conn. Pub. Act. No. 1 (May 1972 special session) (in 4 Conn. Leg. Serv. 677 (1972)), and Conn. Gen. Stat. Rev. §§ 53-29, 53-30 (1968) (or unborn child); Idaho Code § 18-1505 (App. to Supp. 1971); Ill. Rev. Stats. c. 38, § 23-1 (1971); Ind. Code § 35-1-58-1 (1971); Iowa Code § 701.1 (1971); Ky. Rev. Stat. § 436.020 (1963); La. Rev. Stat. § 37:1285 (6) (1964) (loss of medical license) (but see § 14-87 (1972 Supp.) containing no exception for the life of the mother under the criminal statute); Me. Rev. Stat. Ann. Tit. 17, § 51 (1964); Mass. Gen. Laws Ann. c. 272, § 19 (1970) (using the term "unlawfully," construed to exclude an abortion to save the mother's life, *Kudish* v. *Bd. of Registration*, 356 Mass. 98, 248 N. E. 2d 264 (1969)); Mich. Comp. Laws § 750.14 (1948); Minn. Stat. § 617.18 (1971); Mo. Rev. Stat. § 559.100 (1969); Mont. Rev. Codes Ann. § 94-401 (1961); Neb. Rev. Stat. § 28-405 (1964); Nev. Rev. Stat. § 200:220 (1967); N. H. Rev. Stat. Ann. § 585.13 (1955); N. J. Stat. Ann. § 2A:87-1 (1969) ("without lawful justification"); N. D. Cent. Code §§ 12-25-01, 12-25-02 (1960); Ohio Rev. Code § 2901.16 (1953); Okla. Stat. Ann., Tit. 21, § 861 (1972-1973 Supp.); Pa. Stat. Ann., Tit. 18, §§ 4718, 4719 (1963) ("unlawful"); R. I. Gen. Laws Ann. § 11-3-1 (1969); S. D. Compiled Laws § 22-17-1 (1967); Tenn. Code Ann. §§ 39-301, 39-302 (1956); Utah Code Ann. §§ 76-2-1, 76-2-2 (1953); Vt. Stat. Ann., Tit. 13, § 101 (1958); W. Va. Code Ann. § 61-2-8 (1966); Wis Stat. § 940.04 (1969); Wyo. Stat. Ann. §§ 6-77, 6-78 (1957).

substantially unchanged to the present time. See Texas Penal Code
of 1857, Arts. 531-536; Paschal's Laws of Texas, Arts. 2192-2197
(1866); Texas Rev. Stat., Arts. 536-541 (1879); Texas Rev. Crim.
Stat., Arts. 1071-1076 (1911). The final article in each of these
compilations provided the same exception, as does the present Article 1196, for an abortion by "medical advice for the purpose of saving the life of the mother."[3]

II

Jane Roe,[4] a single woman who was residing in Dallas County,
Texas, instituted this federal action in March 1970 against the District Attorney of the county. She sought a declaratory judgment
that the Texas criminal abortion statutes were unconstitutional on
their face, and an injunction restraining the defendant from enforcing the statutes.

Roe alleged that she was unmarried and pregnant; that she
wished to terminate her pregnancy by an abortion "performed by a
competent, licensed physician, under safe, clinical conditions"; that
she was unable to get a "legal" abortion in Texas because her life did
not appear to be threatened by the continuation of her pregnancy;
and that she could not afford to travel to another jurisdiction in

---

[3] Long ago a suggestion was made that the Texas statutes were unconstitutionally
vague because of definitional deficiencies. The Texas Court of Criminal Appeals disposed of that suggestion peremptorily, saying only,
"It is also insisted in the motion in arrest of judgment that the statute is unconstitutional and void in that it does not sufficiently define or describe the offense of abortion.
We do not concur in respect to this question." *Jackson* v. *State*, 55 Tex. Crim. R. 79,
89, 115 S. W. 262, 268 (1908).
The same court recently has held again that the State's abortion statutes are not unconstitutionally vague or overbroad. *Thompson* v. *State*, —— Tex. Crim. App. ——,
—— S. W. 2d —— (1971), appeal pending. The court held that "the State of Texas
has a compelling interest to protect fetal life"; that Art. 1191 "is designed to protect
fetal life"; that the Texas homicide statutes, particularly Art. 1205 of the Penal Code,
are intended to protect a person "in existence by actual birth" and thereby implicitly
recognize other human life that is not "in existence by actual birth"; that the definition
of human life is for the legislature and not the courts; that Art. 1196 "is more definite
that the District of Columbia statute upheld in [*United States* v.] *Vuitch*" (402 U. S.
62); and that the Texas statute is not vague and indefinite or overbroad." A physician's
abortion conviction was affirmed.
In n. 2, —— Tex. Crim. App., at ——, —— S. W. 2d at ——, the court observed
that any issue as to the burden of proof under the exemption of Art. 1196 "is not before us." But see *Veevers* v. *State*, 172 Tex. Crim. App. 162, 168-169, 354 S. W. 2d
161 (1962). Cf. *United States* v. *Vuitch*, 402 U. S. 62, 69-71 (1971).
[4] The name is a pseudonym.

order to secure a legal abortion under safe conditions. She claimed that the Texas statutes were unconstitutionally vague and that they abridged her right of personal privacy, protected by the First, Fourth, Fifth, Ninth, and Fourteenth Amendments. By an amendment to her complaint Roe purported to sue "on behalf of herself and all other women" similarly situated.

James Hubert Hallford, a licensed physician, sought and was granted leave to intervene in Roe's action. In his complaint he alleged that he had been arrested previously for violations of the Texas abortion statutes and that two such prosecutions were pending against him. He described conditions of patients who came to him seeking abortions, and he claimed that for many cases he, as a physician, was unable to determine whether they fell within or outside the exception recognized by Article 1196. He alleged that, as a consequence, the statutes were vague and uncertain, in violation of the Fourteenth Amendment, and that they violated his own and his patients' rights to privacy in the doctor-patient relationship and his own right to practice medicine, rights he claimed were guaranteed by the First, Fourth, Fifth, Ninth, and Fourteenth Amendments.

John and Mary Doe,[5] a married couple, filed a companion complaint to that of Roe. They also named the District Attorney as defendant, claimed like constitutional deprivations, and sought declaratory and injunctive relief. The Does alleged that they were a childless couple; that Mrs. Doe was suffering from a "neuralchemical" disorder; that her physician had "advised her to avoid pregnancy until such time as her condition has materially improved" (although a pregnancy at the present time would not present "a serious risk" to her life); that, pursuant to medical advice, she had discontinued use of birth control pills; and that if she should become pregnant, she would want to terminate the pregnancy by an abortion performed by a competent, licensed physician under safe, clinical conditions. By an amendment to their complaint, the Does purported to sue "on behalf of themselves and all couples similarly situated."

The two actions were consolidated and heard together by a duly convened three-judge district court. The suits thus presented the situations of the pregnant single woman, the childless couple, with the wife not pregnant, and the licensed practicing physician, all

---

[5] These names are pseudonyms.

joining in the attack on the Texas criminal abortion statutes. Upon the filing of affidavits, motions were made to dismiss and for summary judgment. The court held that Roe and Dr. Hallford, and members of their respective classes, had standing to sue, and presented justiciable controversies, but that the Does had failed to allege facts sufficient to state a present controversy and did not have standing. It concluded that, with respect to the requests for a declaratory judgment, abstention was not warranted. On the merits, the District Court held that the "fundamental right of single women and married persons to choose whether to have children is protected by the Ninth Amendment, through the Fourteenth Amendment," and that the Texas criminal abortion statutes were void on their face because they were both unconstitutionally vague and constituted an overbroad infringement of the plaintiffs' Ninth Amendment rights. The court then held that abstention was warranted with respect to the requests for an injunction. It therefore dismissed the Doe complaint, declared the abortion statutes void, and dismissed the application for injunctive relief. 314 F. Supp. 1217 (ND Tex. 1970).

The plaintiffs Roe and Doe and the intervenor Hallford, pursuant to 28 U.S.C. § 1253, have appealed to this Court from that part of the District Court's judgment denying the injunction. The defendant District Attorney has purported to cross appeal, pursuant to the same statute, from the court's grant of declaratory relief to Roe and Hallford. Both sides also have taken protective appeals to the United States Court of Appeals for the Fifth Circuit. That court ordered the appeals held in abeyance pending decision here. We postponed decision on jurisdiction to the hearing on the merits. 402 U.S. 941 (1971).

III

It might have been preferable if the defendant, pursuant to our Rule 20, had presented to us a petition for certiorari before judgment in the Court of Appeals with respect to the granting of the plaintiffs' prayer for declaratory relief. Our decisions in *Mitchell v. Donovan*, 398 U.S. 427 (1970), and *Gunn v. University Committee*, 399 U.S. 383 (1970), are to the effect that § 1253 does not authorize an appeal to this Court from the grant or denial of declaratory relief alone. We conclude, nevertheless, that those decisions do not foreclose our review of both the injunctive and the declaratory aspects of a case of this kind when it is properly here, as this one is, on appeal under § 1253 from specific denial of injunctive relief, and the arguments as to both aspects are necessarily identical. See *Carter v. Jury Commission*, 396 U.S. 320 (1970); *Florida Lime and Avocado Growers, Inc. v. Jacobsen*, 362 U.S. 73, 80-81 (1960). It would be destructive of time and energy for all concerned were we to rule otherwise. Cf. *Doe v. Bolton, post,* ——.

IV

We are next confronted with issues of justiciability, standing, and abstention. Have Roe and the Does established that "personal stake in the outcome of the controversy," *Baker v. Carr*, 369 U.S. 186, 204 (1962), that insures that "the dispute sought to be adjudicated will be presented in an adversary context and in a form historically viewed as capable of judicial resolution," *Flast v. Cohen*, 392 U.S. 83, 101 (1968), and *Sierra Club v. Morton*, 405 U.S 727, 732 (1972)? And what effect did the pendency of criminal abortion charges against Dr. Hallford in state court have upon the propriety of the federal court's granting relief to him as a plaintiff-intervenor?

A. *Jane Roe.* Despite the use of the pseudonym, no suggestion is made that Roe is a fictitious person. For purposes of her case, we accept as true, and as established, her existence; her pregnant state, as of the inception of her suit in March 1970 and as late as May 21 of that year when she filed an alias affidavit with the District Court; and her inability to obtain a legal abortion in Texas.

Viewing Roe's case as of the time of its filing and thereafter until as late as May, there can be little dispute that it then presented a case or controversy and that, wholly apart from the class aspects, she, as a pregnant single woman thwarted by the Texas criminal abortion laws, had standing to challenge those statutes. *Abele v. Markle*, 452 F. 2d 1121, 1125 (CA2 1971); *Crossen v. Breckenridge*, 446 F. 2d 833, 838-839 (CA6 1971); *Poe v. Menghini*, 339 F. Supp. 986, 990-991 (Kans. 1972). See *Truax v. Raich*, 239 U.S. 33 (1915). Indeed, we do not read the appellee's brief as really asserting anything to the contrary. The "logical nexus between the status asserted and the claim sought to be adjudicated," *Flast v.*

Cohen, 392 U.S., at 102, and the necessary degree of contentiousness, *Golden v. Zwickler,* 394 U.S. 103 (1969), are both present.

The appellee notes, however, that the record does not disclose that Roe was pregnant at the time of the District Court hearing on May 22, 1970,[6] or on the following June 17 when the court's opinion and judgment were filed. And he suggests that Roe's case must now be moot because she and all other members of her class are no longer subject to any 1970 pregnancy.

The usual rule in federal cases is that an actual controversy must exist at stages of appellate or certiorari review, and not simply at the date the action is initiated. *United States v. Munsingwear, Inc.,* 340 U.S. 36 (1950); *Golden v. Zwickler, supra; SEC v. Medical Committee for Human Rights,* 404 U.S. 403 (1972).

But when, as here, pregnancy is a significant fact in the litigation, the normal 266-day human gestation period is so short that the pregnancy will come to term before the usual appellate process is complete. If that termination makes a case moot, pregnancy litigation seldom will survive much beyond the trial stage, and appellate review will be effectively denied. Our law should not be that rigid. Pregnancy often comes more than once to the same woman, and in the general population, if man is to survive, it will always be with us. Pregnancy provides a classic justification for a conclusion of non-mootness. It truly could be "capable of repetition, yet evading review." *Southern Pacific Terminal Co. v. ICC,* 219 U.S. 498, 515 (1911). See *Moore v. Ogilvie,* 394 U.S. 814, 816 (1969); *Carroll v. President and Commissioners,* 393 U.S. 175, 178-179 (1968); *United States v. W. T. Grant Co.,* 345 U.S. 629, 632-633 (1953).

We therefore agree with the District Court that Jane Roe had standing to undertake this litigation, that she presented a justiciable controversy, and that the termination of her 1970 pregnancy has not rendered her case moot.

B. *Dr. Hallford.* The doctor's position is different. He entered Roe's litigation as a plaintiff-intervenor alleging in his complaint that he:

---

[6] The appellee twice states in his brief that the hearing before the District Court was held on July 22, 1970. Appellee's Brief 13. The docket entries, Appendix, at 2, and the transcript, Appendix, at 76, reveal this to be an error. The July date appears to be the time of the reporter's transcription. See Appendix, at 77.

In the past has been arrested for violating the Texas Abortion Laws and at the present time stands charged by indictment with violating said laws in the Criminal District Court of Dallas County, Texas to-wit: (1) The State of Texas vs. James H. Hallford, No. C-69-5307-IH, and (2) The State of Texas vs. James H. Hallford, No. C-69-2524-H. In both cases the defendant is charged with abortion. . . .

In his application for leave to intervene the doctor made like representations as to the abortion charges pending in the state court. These representations were also repeated in the affidavit he executed and filed in support of his motion for summary judgment.

Dr. Hallford is therefore in the position of seeking, in a federal court, declaratory and injunctive relief with respect to the same statutes under which he stands charged in criminal prosecutions simultaneously pending in state court. Although he stated that he has been arrested in the past for violating the State's abortion laws, he makes no allegation of any substantial and immediate threat to any federally protected right that cannot be asserted in his defense against the state prosecutions. Neither is there any allegation of harassment or bad faith prosecution. In order to escape the rule, articulated in the cases cited in the next paragraph of this opinion, that, absent harassment and bad faith, a defendant in a pending state criminal case cannot affirmatively challenge in federal court the statutes under which the State is prosecuting him, Dr. Hallford seeks to distinguish his status as a present state defendant from his status as a "potential future defendant" and to assert only the latter for standing purposes here.

We see no merit in that distinction. Our decision in *Samuels v. Mackell*, 401 U.S. 66 (1971), compels the conclusion that the District Court erred when it granted declaratory relief to Dr. Hallford instead of refraining from so doing. The court, of course, was correct in refusing to grant injunctive relief to the doctor. The reasons supportive of that action, however, are those expressed in *Samuels v. Mackell, supra*, and in *Younger v. Harris*, 401 U.S. 37 (1971); *Boyle v. Landry*, 401 U.S. 77 (1971); *Perez v. Ledesma*, 401 U.S. 82 (1971); and *Byrne v. Karalexis*, 401 U.S. 216 (1971). See also *Dombrowski v. Pfister*, 380 U.S. 479 (1965). We note, in passing, that *Younger* and its companion cases were decided after the three-judge District Court decision in this case.

Dr. Hallford's complaint in intervention, therefore, is to be dismissed.[7] He is remitted to his defenses in the state criminal proceedings against him. We reverse the judgment of the District Court insofar as it granted Dr. Hallford relief and failed to dismiss his complaint in intervention.

C. *The Does.* In view of our ruling as to Roe's standing in her case, the issue of the Does' standing in their case has little significance. The claims they assert are essentially the same as those of Roe, and they attack the same statutes. Nevertheless, we briefly note the Does' posture.

Their pleadings present them as a childless married couple, the woman not being pregnant, who have no desire to have children at this time because of their having received medical advice that Mrs. Doe should avoid pregnancy, and for "other highly personal reasons." But they "fear . . . they may face the prospect of becoming parents." And if pregnancy ensues, they "would want to terminate" it by an abortion. They assert an inability to obtain an abortion legally in Texas and, consequently, the prospect of obtaining an illegal abortion there or of going outside Texas to some place where the procedure could be obtained legally and competently.

We thus have as plaintiffs a married couple who have, as their asserted immediate and present injury, only an alleged "detrimental effect upon [their] marital happiness" because they are forced to "the choice of refraining from normal sexual relations or of endangering Mary Doe's health through a possible pregnancy." Their claim is that sometime, in the future, Mrs. Doe might become pregnant because of possible failure of contraceptive measures, and at that time in the future, she might want an abortion that might then be illegal under the Texas statutes.

This very phrasing of the Does' position reveals its speculative character. Their alleged injury rests on possible future contracep-

---

[7] We need not consider what different result, if any, would follow if Dr. Hallford's intervention were on behalf of a class. His complaint in intervention does not purport to assert a class suit and makes no reference to any class apart from an allegation that he "and others similarly situated" must necessarily guess at the meaning of Art. 1196. His application for leave to intervene goes somewhat further for it asserts that plaintiff Roe does not adequately protect the interest of the doctor "and the class of people who are physicians . . . and the class of people who are . . . patients . . . ." The leave application, however, is not the complaint. Despite the District Court's statement to the contrary, 314 F. Supp., at 1225, we fail to perceive the essentials of a class suit in the Hallford complaint.

tive failure, possible future pregnancy, possible future unprepared-ness for parenthood, and possible future impairment of health. Any one or more of these several possibilities may not take place and all may not combine. In the Does' estimation, these possibilities might have some real or imagined impact upon their marital happiness. But we are not prepared to say that the bare allegation of so indi-rect an injury is sufficient to present an actual case or controversy. *Younger v. Harris*, 401 U.S., at 41-42; *Golden v. Zwickler,* 394 U.S., at 109-110 (1969); *Abele v. Markle*, 452 F. 2d, at 1124-1125; *Crossen v. Breckenridge*, 446 F.2d, at 839. The Does' claim falls far short of those resolved otherwise in the cases that the Does urge upon us, namely, *Investment Co. Institute v. Camp*. 401 U.S. 617 (1971); *Data Processing Service v. Camp*, 397 U.S. 150 (1970); and *Epperson v. Arkansas*, 393 U.S. 97 (1968). See also *Truax v. Raich, supra.*

The Does therefore are not appropriate plaintiffs in this litiga-tion. Their complaint was properly dismissed by the District Court, and we affirm that dismissal.

V

The principal thrust of appellant's attack on the Texas statutes is that they improperly invade a right, said to be possessed by the pregnant woman, to choose to terminate her pregnancy. Appellant would discover this right in the concept of personal "liberty" em-bodied in the Fourteenth Amendment's Due Process Clause; or in personal, marital, familial, and sexual privacy said to be protected by the Bill of Rights or its penumbras, see *Griswold v. Connecticut*, 381 U.S. 479 (1965); *Eisenstadt v. Baird*, 405 U.S. 438 (1972); *id.*, at 460 (WHITE, J., concurring); or among those rights reserved to the people by the Ninth Amendment, *Griswold v. Connecticut*, 381 U.S. at 486 (Goldberg, J., concurring). Before addressing this claim, we feel it desirable briefly to survey, in several aspects, the history of abortion, for such insight as that history may afford us, and then to examine the state purposes and interests behind the crim-inal abortion laws.

VI

It perhaps is not generally appreciated that the restrictive crim-inal abortion laws in effect in a majority of States today are of relatively recent vintage. Those laws, generally proscribing abortion or its attempt at any time during pregnancy except when necessary to preserve the pregnant woman's life, are not of ancient or even of common law origin. Instead, they derive from statutory changes effected, for the most part, in the latter half of the 19th century.

1. *Ancient attitudes.* These are not capable of precise determination. We are told that at the time of the Persian Empire abortifacients were known and that criminal abortions were severely punished.[8] We are also told, however, that abortion was practiced in Greek times as well as in the Roman Era,[9] and that "it was resorted to without scruple."[10] The Ephesian, Soranos, often described as the greatest of the ancient gynecologists, appears to have been generally opposed to Rome's prevailing free-abortion practices. He found it necessary to think first of the life of the mother, and he resorted to abortion when, upon this standard, he felt the procedure advisable.[11] Greek and Roman law afforded little protection to the unborn. If abortion was prosecuted in some places, it seems to have been based on a concept of a violation of the father's right to his offspring. Ancient religion did not bar abortion.[12]

2. *The Hippocratic Oath.* What then of the famous Oath that has stood so long as the ethical guide of the medical profession and that bears the name of the great Greek (460(?)-377(?) B.C.), who has been described as the Father of Medicine, the "wisest and the greatest practitioner of his art," and the "most important and most complete medical personality of antiquity" who dominated the medical schools of his time, and who typified the sum of the medi-

---

[8] A. Castiglioni, A History of Medicine 84 (2d ed. 1947), E. Krumbhaar, translator and editor (hereinafter "Castiglioni").

[9] J. Ricci, The Genealogy of Gynaecology 52, 84, 113, 149 (2d ed. 1950) (hereinafter "Ricci"); L. Lader, Abortion 75-77 (1966) (hereinafter "Lader"); K. Niswander, Medical Abortion Practices in the United States, in Abortion and the Law 27, 38-40 (D. Smith, editor, 1967); G. Williams, The Sanctity of Life 148 (1957) (hereinafter "Williams"); J. Noonan, An Almost Absolute Value in History, in The Morality of Abortion 1, 3-7 (J. Noonan ed. 1970) (hereinafter "Noonan"); E. Quay, Justifiable Abortion — Medical and Legal Foundations, II, 49 Geo. L. J. 395, 406-422 (1961) (hereinafter "Quay").

[10] L. Edelstein, The Hippocratic Oath 10 (1943) (hereinafter "Edelstein"). But see Castiglioni 227.

[11] Edelstein 12; Ricci 113-114, 118-119; Noonan 5.

[12] Edelstein 13-14.

cal knowledge of the past?[13]   The Oath varies somewhat according to the particular translation, but in any translation the content is clear: "I will give no deadly medicine to anyone if asked, nor suggest any such counsel; and in like manner I will not give to a woman a pessary to produce abortion,"[14] or "I will neither give a deadly drug to anybody if asked for it, nor will I make a suggestion to this effect.   Similarly, I will not give to a woman an abortive remedy."[15]

Although the Oath is not mentioned in any of the principal briefs in this case or in *Doe v. Bolton, post,* it represents the apex of the development of strict ethical concepts in medicine, and its influence endures to this day.   Why did not the authority of Hippocrates dissuade abortion practice in his time and that of Rome?   The late Dr. Edelstein provides us with a theory:[16] The Oath was not uncontested even in Hippocrates' day; only the Pythagorean school of philosophers frowned upon the related act of suicide.   Most Greek thinkers, on the other hand, commended abortion, at least prior to viability. See Plato, *Republic*, V, 461; Aristotle, *Politics*, VII, 1335 b 25.   For the Pythagoreans, however, it was a matter of dogma.   For them the embryo was animate from the moment of conception, and abortion meant destruction of a living being.   The abortion clause of the Oath, therefore, "echoes Pythagorean doctrines," and "[i]n no other stratum of Greek opinion were such views held or proposed in the same spirit of uncompromising austerity."[17]

Edelstein then concludes that the Oath originated in a group representing only a small segment of Greek opinion and that it certainly was not accepted by all ancient physicians.   He points out that medical writings down to Galen (130-200 A.D.) "give evidence of the violation of almost every one of its injunctions."[18]   But with the end of antiquity a decided change took place.   Resistance against suicide and against abortion became common.   The Oath came to be popular.   The emerging teachings of Christianity were in agreement

---

[13] Castiglioni 148.

[14] *Id.,* at 154.

[15] Edelstein 3.

[16] *Id.,* at 12, 15-18.

[17] *Id.,* at 18; Lader 76.

[18] Edelstein 63.

with the Pythagorean ethic. The Oath "became the nucleus of all medical ethics" and "was applauded as the embodiment of truth." Thus, suggests Dr. Edelstein, it is "a Pythagorean manifesto and not the expression of an absolute standard of medical conduct."[19]

This, it seems to us, is a satisfactory and acceptable explanation of the Hippocratic Oath's apparent rigidity. It enables us to understand, in historical context, a long accepted and revered statement of medical ethics.

3. *The Common Law.* It is undisputed that at the common law, abortion performed *before* "quickening" — the first recognizable movement of the fetus *in utero*, appearing usually from the 16th to the 18th week of pregnancy[20] — was not an indictable offense.[21] The absence of a common law crime for pre-quickening abortion appears to have developed from a confluence of earlier philosophical, theological, and civil and canon law concepts of when life begins. These disciplines variously approached the question in terms of the point at which the embryo or fetus became "formed" or recognizably human, or in terms of when a "person" came into being, that is, infused with a "soul" or "animated." A loose consensus evolved in early English law that these events occurred at some point between conception and live birth.[22] This was "mediate animation." Al-

[19] *Id.*, at 64.

[20] Dorland's Illustrated Medical Dictionary 1261 (24th ed. 1965).

[21] E. Coke, Institutes III *50 (1948); 1 W. Hawkins, Pleas of the Crown c. 31, § 16 (1762); 1 Blackstone, Commentaries *129-130 (1765); M. Hale, Pleas of the Crown 433 (1778). For discussions of the role of the quickening concept in English common law, see Lader 78; Noonan 223-226; C. Means, The Law of New York Concerning Abortion and the Status of the Foetus, 1664-1968: A Case of Cessation of Constitutionality, 14 N. Y. L. Forum 411, 418-428 (1968) (hereinafter "Means I"); L. Stern, Abortion: Reform and the Law, 59 J. Crim. L. C. & P. S. 84 (1968) (hereinafter "Stern"); Quay 430-432; Williams 152.

[22] Early philosophers believed that the embryo or fetus did not become formed and begin to live until at least 40 days after conception for a male, and 80 to 90 days for a female. See, for example, Aristotle, Hist. Anim. 7.3.583b; Gen. Anim. 2.3.736, 2.5.741; Hippocrates, Lib. de Nat. Puer., No. 10. Aristotle's thinking derived from his three-stage theory of life: vegetable, animal, rational. The vegetable stage was reached at conception, the animal at "animation," and the rational soon after live birth. This theory, together with the 40/80 day view, came to be accepted by early Christian thinkers.

The theological debate was reflected in the writings of St. Augustine, who made a distinction between *embryo inanimatus*, not yet endowed with a soul, and *embryo animatus*. He may have drawn upon Exodus xxi, 22. At one point, however, he expresses the view that human powers cannot determine the point during fetal development at which the critical change occurs. See Augustine, De Origine Animae 4.4 (Pub. Law

though Christian theology and the canon law came to fix the point of animation at 40 days for a male and 80 days for a female, a view that persisted until the 19th century, there was otherwise little agreement about the precise time of formation or animation.   There was agreement, however, that prior to this point the fetus was to be regarded as part of the mother and its destruction, therefore, was not homicide.   Due to continued uncertainty about the precise time when animation occurred, to the lack of any empirical basis for the 40-80 day view, and perhaps to Acquinas' definition of movement as one of the two first principles of life, Bracton focused upon quickening as the critical point.   The significance of quickening was echoed by later common law scholars and found its way into the received common law in this country.

Whether abortion of a *quick* fetus was a felony at common law, or even a lesser crime, is still disputed.   Bracton, writing early in the 13th century, thought it homicide.[23]   But the later and predominant view, following the great common law scholars, has been that it was at most a lesser offense.   In a frequently cited passage, Coke took the position that abortion of a woman "quick with childe" is "a great misprision and no murder."[24]   Blackstone followed, saying that while abortion after quickening had once been considered manslaughter (though not murder), "modern law" took a less severe view.[25]   A recent review of the common law precedents argues, how-

---

44.527).   See also Reany, The Creation of the Human Soul, c. 2 and 83-86 (1932); Huser, The Crime of Abortion in Common Law 15 (Catholic Univ. of America, Canon Law Studies No. 162, Washington, D. C. 1942).

Galen, in three treatises related to embryology, accepted the thinking of Aristotle and his followers.   Quay 426-427.   Later, Augustine on abortion was incorporated by Gratian into the Decretum, published about 1140.   Decretum Magistri Gratiani 2.32.2.7 to 2.32.2.10, in 1 Corpus Juris Canonici 1122, 1123 (2d ed. Friedberg ed. 1879). Gratian, together with the decretals that followed, were recognized as the definitive body of canon law until the new Code of 1917.

For discussions of the canon law treatment, see Means I, at 411-412; Noonan, 20-26; Quay 426-430; see also Noonan, Contraception: A History of Its Treatment by the Catholic Theologians and Canonists 18-29 (1965).

[23] Bracton took the position that abortion by blow or poison was homicide "if the foetus be already formed and animated, and particularly if it be animated." 2 H. Bracton, De Legibus et Consuetudinibus Angliae 279 (Twiss ed. 1879), or, as a later translation puts it, "if the foetus is already formed or quickened, especially if it is quickened," II Bracton, On the Laws and Customs of England 341 (Thorne ed. 1968).   See Quay 431; see also 2 Fleta 60-61 (Book I, c. 23) (Selden Society ed. 1955).

[24] E. Coke, Institutes III *50 (1648).

[25] 1 Blackstone, Commentaries *129-130 (1765).

ever, that those precedents contradict Coke and that even post-quickening abortion was never established as a common law crime.[26] This is of some importance because while most American courts ruled, in holding or dictum, that abortion of an unquickened fetus was not criminal under their received common law,[27] others followed Coke in stating that abortion of a quick fetus was a "misprision," a term they translated to mean "misdemeanor."[28] That their reliance on Coke on this aspect of the law was uncritical and, apparently in all the reported cases, dictum (due probably to the paucity of common law prosecutions for post-quickening abortion), makes it now appear doubtful that abortion was ever firmly established as a common law crime even with respect to the destruction of a quick fetus.

4. *The English statutory law.* England's first criminal abortion statute, Lord Ellenborough's Act, 43 Geo. 3, c. 58, came in 1803. It made abortion of a quick fetus, § 1, a capital crime, but in § 2 it provided lesser penalties for the felony of abortion before quickening, and thus preserved the quickening distinction. This contrast was continued in the general revision of 1828, 9 Geo. 4, c. 31, § 13, at 104. It disappeared, however, together with the death penalty,

---

[26] C. Means, The Phoenix of Abortional Freedom: Is a Penumbral or Ninth-Amendment Right About to Arise from the Nineteenth-Century Legislative Ashes of a Fourteenth-Century Common-Law Liberty?, 17 N. Y. L. Forum 335 (1971) (hereinafter "Means II"). The author examines the two principal precedents cited marginally by Coke, both contrary to his dictum, and traces the treatment of these and other cases by earlier commentators. He concludes that Coke, who himself participated as an advocate in an abortion case in 1601, may have intentionally misstated the law. The author even suggests a reason: Coke's strong feelings about abortion, coupled with his reluctance to acknowledge common law (secular) jurisdiction to assess penalties for an offence that traditionally had been an exclusively ecclesiastical or canon law crime. See also Lader 78-79, who notes that some scholars doubt the common law ever was applied to abortion; that the English ecclesiastical courts seem to have lost interest in the problem after 1527; and that the preamble to the English legislation of 1803, 43 Geo. 3, c. 58, § 1, at 203, referred to in the text, *infra*, states that "no adequate means have been hitherto provided for the prevention and punishment of such offenses."

[27] *Commonwealth v. Bangs*, 9 Mass. 387, 388 (1812); *Commonwealth v. Parker*, 50 Mass. (9 Met.) 263, 265-266 (1845); *State v. Cooper*, 22 N. J. L. 52, 58 (1849); *Abrams v. Foshee*, 3 Iowa 274, 278-280 (1856); *Smith v. Gaffard*, 31 Ala. 45, 51 (1857); *Mitchell v. Commonwealth*, 78 Ky. 204, 210 (1879); *Eggart v. State*, 40 Fla. 527, 532, 25 So. 144, 145 (1898); *State v. Alcorn*, 7 Idaho 599, 606, 64 P. 1014, 1016 (1901); *Edwards v. State*, 79 Neb. 251, 252, 112 N. W. 611, 612 (1907); *Gray v. State*, 77 Tex. Crim. R. 221, 224, 178 S. W. 337, 338 (1915); *Miller v. Bennett*, 190 Va. 162, 169, 56 S. E. 2d 217, 221 (1949). Contra, *Mills v. Commonwealth*, 13 Pa. 631, 633 (1850); *State v. Slagle*, 83 N. C. 630, 632 (1880).

[28] See *Smith v. State*, 33 Me. 48, 55 (1851); *Evans v. People*, 49 N. Y. 86, 88 (1872); *Lamb v. State*, 67 Md. 524, 533, 10 A. 208 (1887).

in 1837, 7 Will. 4 & 1 Vic., c. 85, § 6, at 360, and did not reappear in the Offenses Against the Person Act of 1861, 24 & 25 Vic., c. 100, § 59, at 438, that formed the core of English anti-abortion law until the liberalizing reforms of 1967. In 1929 the Infant Life (Preservation) Act, 19 & 20 Geo. 5, c. 34, came into being. Its emphasis was upon the destruction of "the life of a child capable of being born alive." It made a willful act performed with the necessary intent a felony. It contained a proviso that one was not to be found guilty of the offense "unless it is proved that the act which caused the death of the child was not done in good faith for the purpose only of preserving the life of the mother."

A seemingly notable development in the English law was the case of *Rex v. Bourne*, [1939] 1 K. B. 687. This case apparently answered in the affirmative the question whether an abortion necessary to preserve the life of the pregnant woman was excepted from the criminal penalties of the 1861 Act. In his instructions to the jury Judge Macnaghten referred to the 1929 Act, and observed, p. 691, that that Act related to "the case where a child is killed by a willful act at the time when it is being delivered in the ordinary course of nature." *Id.*, at 91. He concluded that the 1861 Act's use of the word "unlawfully" imported the same meaning expressed by the specific proviso in the 1929 Act even though there was no mention of preserving the mother's life in the 1861 Act. He then construed the phrase "preserving the life of the mother" broadly, that is, "in a reasonable sense," to include a serious and permanent threat to the mother's *health*, and instructed the jury to acquit Dr. Bourne if it found he had acted in a good faith belief that the abortion was necessary for this purpose. *Id.*, at 693-694. The jury did acquit.

Recently Parliament enacted a new abortion law. This is the Abortion Act of 1967, 15 & 16 Eliz., 2, c. 87. The Act permits a licensed physician to perform an abortion where two other licensed physicians agree (a) "that the continuance of the pregnancy would involve risk to the life of the pregnant woman, or of injury to the physical or mental health of the pregnant woman or any existing children of her family, greater than if the pregnancy were terminated," or (b) "that there is a substantial risk that if the child were born it would suffer from such physical or mental abnormalities as to be seriously handicapped." The Act also provides that, in making this determination, "account may be taken of the pregnant woman's actual or reasonably foreseeable environment." It also permits a physician, without the concurrence of others, to terminate a pregnancy where he is of the good faith opinion that the abortion "is immediately necessary to save the life or to prevent grave permanent injury to the physical or mental health of the pregnant woman."

5. *The American law.* In this country the law in effect in all but a few States until mid-19th century was the pre-existing English common law. Connecticut, the first State to enact abortion legislation, adopted in 1821 that part of Lord Ellenborough's Act that related to a woman "quick with child."[29] The death penalty was not imposed. Abortion before quickening was made a crime in that State only in 1860.[30] In 1828 New York enacted legislation[31] that, in two respects, was to serve as a model for early anti-abortion statutes. First, while barring destruction of an unquickened fetus as well as a quick fetus, it made the former only a misdemeanor, but the latter second-degree manslaughter. Second, it incorporated a concept of therapeutic abortion by providing that an abortion was excused if it "shall have been necessary to preserve the life of such mother, or shall have been advised by two physicians to be necessary for such purpose." By 1840, when Texas had received the common law,[32] only eight American States had statutes dealing with abortion.[33] It was not until after the War Between the States that legislation began generally to replace the common law. Most of these initial statutes dealt severely with abortion after quickening but were lenient with it before quickening. Most punished attempts equally with completed abortions. While many statutes included the exception for an abortion thought by one or more physicians to be necessary to save the mother's life, that provision soon disappeared and the typical law required that the procedure actually be necessary for that purpose.

---

[29] Conn. Stat., Tit. 20, § 14 (1821).

[30] Conn. Pub. Acts, c. 71, § 1 (1860).

[31] N. Y. Rev. Stat., pt. IV, c. I, Tit. II, Art. 1, § 9, at 661, and Tit. VI, § 21, at 694 (1829).

[32] Act of January 20, 1840, § 1, set forth in 2 Gammel, Laws of Texas 177-178 (1898); see *Grigsby v. Reib*, 105 Tex. 597, 600, 153 S. W. 1124, 1125 (1913).

[33] The early statutes are discussed in Quay 435-438. See also Lader 85-88; Stern 85-86; and Means II 375-376.

Gradually, in the middle and late 19th century the quickening distinction disappeared from the statutory law of most States and the degree of the offense and the penalties were increased. By the end of the 1950's, a large majority of the States banned abortion, however and whenever performed, unless done to save or preserve the life of the mother.[34] The exceptions, Alabama and the District of Columbia, permitted abortion to preserve the mother's health.[35] Three other States permitted abortions that were not "unlawfully" performed or that were not "without lawful justification," leaving interpretation of those standards to the courts.[36] In the past several years, however, a trend toward liberalization of abortion statutes has resulted in adoption, by about one-third of the States, of less stringent laws, most of them patterned after the ALI Model Penal Code, § 230.3,[37] set forth as Appendix B to the opinion in *Doe v. Bolton, post* ——.

It is thus apparent that at common law, at the time of the adoption of our Constitution, and throughout the major portion of the 19th century, abortion was viewed with less disfavor than under

---

[34] Criminal abortion statutes in effect in the States as of 1961, together with historical statutory development and important judicial interpretations of the state statutes, are cited and quoted in Quay 447-520. See Note, A Survey of the Present Statutory and Case Law on Abortion: The Contradictions and the Problems, 1972 Ill. L. Forum 177, 179, classifying the abortion statutes and listing 25 States as permitting abortion only if necessary to save or preserve the mother's life.

[35] Ala. Code, Tit. 14, § 9 (1958); D. C. Code Ann. § 22-201 (1967).

[36] Mass. Gen. Laws Ann., c. 272, § 19 (1970); N. J. Rev. Stat. Ann. 2A:87-1 (1969); Pa. Stat. Ann., Tit. 18, §§ 4718, 4719 (1963).

[37] Fourteen States have adopted some form of the ALI statute. See Ark. Stat. Ann. §§ 41-303 to 41-310 (Supp. 1971); Calif. Health and Safety Code §§ 25950-25955.5 (West Supp. 1972); Colo. Rev. Stats. Ann. §§ 40-2-50 to 40-2-53 (Perm. Cum. Supp. 1967); Del. Code Ann., Tit. 24, §§ 1790-1793 (Supp. 1972); Florida Law of Apr. 13, 1972, c. 72-196, 1972 Fla. Sess. Law Serv., at 380-382; Ga. Code §§ 26-1201 to 26-1203 (1972); Kan. Stat. Ann. § 21-3407 (Supp. 1971); Md. Ann. Code, Art. 43, §§ 137-139 (Repl. 1971); Miss. Code Ann. § 2223 (Supp. 1972); N. M. Stat. Ann. §§ 40A-5-1 to 40A-5-3 (Repl. 1972); N. C. Gen. Stat. § 14-45.1 (Supp. 1971); Ore. Rev. Stat. §§ 435.405 at 435.495 (1971); S. C. Code Ann. §§ 16-82 to 16-89 (Supp. 1971); Va. Code Ann. §§ 18.1-62 to 18.1-62.3 (Supp. 1972). Mr. Justice Clark described some of these States as having "led the way." Religion, Morality and Abortion: A Constitutional Appraisal, 2 Loyola U. (L. A.) L. Rev. 1, 11 (1969).

By the end of 1970, four other States had repealed criminal penalties for abortions performed in early pregnancy by a licensed physician, subject to stated procedural and health requirements. Alaska Stat. § 11.15.060 (1970); Haw. Rev. Stat. § 453-16 (Supp. 1971); N. Y. Penal Code § 125.05 (McKinney Supp. 1972-1973); Wash. Rev. Code §§ 9.02.060 to 9.02.080 (Supp. 1972). The precise status of criminal abortion laws in some States is made unclear by recent decisions in state and federal courts striking down existing state laws, in whole or in part.

most American statutes currently in effect. Phrasing it another way, a woman enjoyed a substantially broader right to terminate a pregnancy than she does in most States today. At least with respect to the early stage of pregnancy, and very possibly without such a limitation, the opportunity to make this choice was present in this country well into the 19th century. Even later, the law continued for some time to treat less punitively an abortion procured in early pregnancy.

6. *The position of the American Medical Association.* The anti-abortion mood prevalent in this country in the late 19th century was shared by the medical profession. Indeed, the attitude of the profession may have played a significant role in the enactment of stringent criminal abortion legislation during that period.

An AMA Committee on Criminal Abortion was appointed in May 1857. It presented its report, 12 Trans. of the Am. Med. Assn. 73-77 (1859), to the Twelfth Annual Meeting. That report observed that the Committee had been appointed to investigate criminal abortion "with a view to its general suppression." It deplored abortion and its frequency and it listed three causes "of this general demoralization":

> The first of these causes is a wide-spread popular ignorance of the true character of the crime — a belief, even among mothers themselves, that the foetus is not alive till after the period of quickening.
> The second of the agents alluded to is the fact that the profession themselves are frequently supposed careless of foetal life . . . .
> The third reason of the frightful extent of this crime is found in the grave defects of our laws, both common and statute, as regards the independent and actual existence of the child before birth, as a living being. These errors, which are sufficient in most instances to prevent conviction, are based, and only based, upon mistaken and exploded medical dogmas. With strange inconsistency, the law fully acknowledges the foetus in utero and its inherent rights, for civil purposes; while personally and as criminally affected, it fails to recognize it, and to its life as yet denies all protection. *Id.*, at 75-76.

The Committee then offered, and the Association adopted, resolutions protesting "against such unwarrantable destruction of human life," calling upon state legislatures to revise their abortion laws, and requesting the cooperation of state medical societies "in pressing the subject." *Id.*, at 28, 78.

In 1871 a long and vivid report was submitted by the Committee on Criminal Abortion. It ended with the observation, "We had to deal with human life. In a matter of less importance we could entertain no compromise. An honest judge on the bench would call things by their proper names. We could do no less." 22 Trans. of the Am. Med. Assn. 258 (1871). It proffered resolutions, adopted by the Association, *id.*, at 38-39, recommending, among other things, that it "be unlawful and unprofessional for any physician to induce abortion or premature labor, without the concurrent opinion of at least one respectable consulting physician, and then always with a view to the safety of the child — if that be possible," and calling "the attention of the clergy of all denominations to the perverted views of morality entertained by a large class of females — aye, and men also, on this important question."

Except for periodic condemnation of the criminal abortionist, no further formal AMA action took place until 1967. In that year the Committee on Human Reproduction urged the adoption of a stated policy of opposition to induced abortion except when there is "documented medical evidence" of a threat to the health or life of the mother, or that the child "may be born with incapacitating physical deformity or mental deficiency," or that a pregnancy "resulting from legally established statutory or forcible rape or incest may constitute a threat to the mental or physical health of the patient," and two other physicians "chosen because of their recognized professional competence have examined the patient and have concurred in writing," and the procedure "is performed in a hospital accredited by the Joint Commission on Accreditation of Hospitals." The providing of medical information by physicians to state legislatures in their consideration of legislation regarding therapeutic abortion was "to be considered consistent with the principles of ethics of the American Medical Association." This recommendation was adopted by the House of Delegates. Proceedings of the AMA House of Delegates, 40-51 (June 1967).

In 1970, after the introduction of a variety of proposed resolutions, and of a report from its Board of Trustees, a reference committee noted "polarization of the medical profession on this controversial issue"; division among those who had testified; a difference of opinion among AMA councils and committees; "the remarkable shift in testimony" in six months, felt to be influenced "by the rapid changes in state laws and by the judicial decisions which tend to make abortion more freely available;" and a feeling "that this trend will continue." On June 25, 1970, the House of Delegates adopted preambles and most of the resolutions proposed by the reference committee. The preambles emphasized "the best interests of the patient," "sound clinical judgment," and "informed patient consent," in contrast to "mere acquiescence to the patient's demand." The resolutions asserted that abortion is a medical procedure that should be performed by a licensed physician in an accredited hospital only after consultation with two other physicians and in conformity with state law, and that no party to the procedure should be required to violate personally held moral principles.[38] Proceedings of the AMA House of Delegates 221 (June 1970). The AMA Judicial Council rendered a complementary opinion.[39]

7. *The position of the American Public Health Association.* In October 1970, the Executive Board of the APHA adopted Standards for Abortion Services. These were five in number:

---

[38] "Whereas, Abortion, like any other medical procedure, should not be performed when contrary to the best interests of the patient since good medical practice requires due consideration for the patient's welfare and not mere acquiescence to the patient's demand; and

"Whereas, The standards of sound clinical judgment, which, together with informed patient consent should be determinative according to the merits of each individual case; therefore be it

"*RESOLVED*, That abortion is a medical procedure and should be performed only by a duly licensed physician and surgeon in an accredited hospital acting only after consultation with two other physicians chosen because of their professional competency and in conformance with standards of good medical practice and the Medical Practice Act of his State; and be it further

"*RESOLVED*, That no physician or other professional personnel shall be compelled to perform any act which violates his good medical judgment. Neither physician, hospital, nor hospital personnel shall be required to perform any act violative of personally-held moral principles. In these circumstances good medical practice requires only that the physician or other professional personnel withdraw from the case so long as the withdrawal is consistent with good medical practice." Proceedings of the AMA House of Delegates 221 (June 1970).

[39] "The Principles of Medical Ethics of the AMA do not prohibit a physician from performing an abortion that is performed in accordance with good medical practice and under circumstances that do not violate the laws of the community in which he practices.

"In the matter of abortions, as of any other medical procedure, the Judicial Council becomes involved whenever there is alleged violation of the Principles of Medical Ethics as established by the House of Delegates."

a. Rapid and simple abortion referral must be readily available through state and local public health departments, medical societies, or other non-profit organizations.

b. An important function of counseling should be to simplify and expedite the provision of abortion services; it should not delay the obtaining of these services.

c. Psychiatric consultation should not be mandatory. As in the case of other specialized medical services, psychiatric consultation should be sought for definite indications and not on a routine basis.

d. A wide range of individuals from appropriately trained, sympathetic volunteers to highly skilled physicians may qualify as abortion counselors.

e. Contraception and/or sterilization should be discussed with each abortion patient. Recommended Standards for Abortion Services, 61 Am. J. Pub. Health 396 (1971).

Among factors pertinent to life and health risks associated with abortion were three that "are recognized as important":

a. the skill of the physician,

b. the environment in which the abortion is performed, and above all

c. the duration of pregnancy, as determined by uterine size and confirmed by menstrual history. *Id.*, at 397.

It was said that "a well-equipped hospital" offers more protection "to cope with unforeseen difficulties than an office or clinic without such resources. . . . The factor of gestational age is of overriding importance." Thus it was recommended that abortions in the second trimester and early abortions in the presence of existing medical complications be performed in hospitals as inpatient procedures. For pregnancies in the first trimester, abortion in the hospital with or without overnight stay "is probably the safest practice." An abortion in an extramural facility, however, is an acceptable alternative "provided arrangements exist in advance to admit patients promptly if unforeseen complications develop." Standards for an abortion facility were listed. It was said that at present abortions should be performed by physicians or osteopaths who are licensed to practice and who have "adequate training." *Id.*, at 398.

8. *The position of the American Bar Association.* At its meeting in February 1972 the ABA House of Delegates approved, with 17 opposing votes, the Uniform Abortion Act that had been drafted and approved the preceding August by the Conference of Commissioners on Uniform State Laws. 58 A. B. A. J. 380 (1972). We

set forth the Act in full in the margin.[40]   The conference has appended an enlightening Prefatory Note.[41]

VII

Three reasons have been advanced to explain historically the enactment of criminal abortion laws in the 19th century and to justify their continued existence.

---

[40]   "UNIFORM ABORTION ACT
"SECTION 1.   [*Abortion Defined; When Authorized.*]
"(a) 'Abortion' means the termination of human pregnancy with an intention other than to produce a live birth or to remove a dead fetus.
"(b) An abortion may be performed in this state only if it is performed:
"(1) by a physician licensed to practice medicine [or osteopathy] in this state or by a physician practicing medicine [or osteopathy] in the employ of the government of the United States or of this state, [and the abortion is performed [in the physician's office or in a medical clinic, or] in a hospital approved by the [Department of Health] or operated by the United States, this state, or any department, agency, or political subdivision of either;] or by a female upon herself upon the advice of the physician; and
"(2) within [20] weeks after the commencement of the pregnancy [or after [20] weeks only if the physician has reasonable cause to believe (i) there is a substantial risk that continuance of the pregnancy would endanger the life of the mother or would gravely impair the physical or mental health of the mother, (ii) that the child would be born with grave physical or mental defect, or (iii) that the pregnancy resulted from rape or incest, or illicit intercourse with a girl under the age of 16 years of age].
"SECTION 2.   [*Penalty.*]   Any person who performs or procures an abortion other than authorized by this Act is guilty of a [felony] and, upon conviction thereof, may be sentenced to pay a fine not exceeding [$1,000] or to imprisonment [in the state penitentiary] not exceeding [5 years], or both.
"SECTION 3.   [*Uniformity of Interpretation.*]   This Act shall be construed to effectuate its general purpose to make uniform the law with respect to the subject of this Act among those states which enact it.
"SECTION 4.   [*Short Title.*]   This Act may be cited as the Uniform Abortion Act.
"SECTION 5.   [*Severability.*]   If any provision of this Act or the application thereof to any person or circumstance is held invalid, the invalidity does not affect other provisions or applications of this Act which can be given effect without the invalid provision or application, and to this end the provisions of this Act are severable.
"SECTION 6.   [*Repeal.*]   The following acts and parts of acts are repealed:
"(1)
"(2)
"(3)
"SECTION 7.   [*Time of Taking Effect.*]   This Act shall take effect ———————."
[41] "This Act is based largely upon the New York abortion act following a review of the more recent laws on abortion in several states and upon recognition of a more liberal trend in laws on this subject.   Recognition was given also to the several decisions in state and federal courts which show a further trend toward liberalization of abortion laws, especially during the first trimester of pregnancy.
"Recognizing that a number of problems appeared in New York, a shorter time period for 'unlimited' abortions was advisable.   The time period was bracketed to per-

It has been argued occasionally that these laws were the product of a Victorian social concern to discourage illicit sexual conduct. Texas, however, does not advance this justification in the present case, and it appears that no court or commentator has taken the argument seriously.[42] The appellants and *amici* contend, moreover, that this is not a proper state purpose at all and suggest that, if it were, the Texas statutes are overbroad in protecting it since the law fails to distinguish between married and unwed mothers.

A second reason is concerned with abortion as a medical procedure. When most criminal abortion laws were first enacted, the procedure was a hazardous one for the woman.[43] This was particularly true prior to the development of antisepsis. Antiseptic techniques, of course, were based on discoveries by Lister, Pasteur, and others first announced in 1867, but were not generally accepted and employed until about the turn of the century. Abortion mortality was high. Even after 1900, and perhaps until as late as the development of antibiotics in the 1940's, standard modern techniques such as dilation and curettage were not nearly so safe as they are today. Thus it has been argued that a State's real concern in enacting a criminal abortion law was to protect the pregnant woman, that is, to restrain her from submitting to a procedure that placed her life in serious jeopardy.

Modern medical techniques have altered this situation. Appellants and various *amici* refer to medical data indicating that abor-

---

mit the various states to insert a figure more in keeping with the different conditions that might exist among the states. Likewise, the language limiting the place or places in which abortions may be performed was also bracketed to account for different conditions among the states. In addition, limitations on abortions after the initial 'unlimited' period were placed in brackets so that individual states may adopt all or any of these reasons, or place further restrictions upon abortions after the initial period.

"This Act does not contain any provision relating to medical review committees or prohibitions against sanctions imposed upon medical personnel refusing to participate in abortions because of religious or other similar reasons, or the like. Such provisions, while related, do not directly pertain to when, where, or by whom abortions may be performed; however, the Act is not drafted to exclude such a provision by a state wishing to enact the same."

[42] See, for example, *YWCA v. Kugler*, 342 F. Supp. 1048, 1074 (N. J. 1972); *Abele v. Markle*, 342 F. Supp. 800, 805-806 (Conn. 1972) (Newman, J., concurring), appeal pending; *Walsingham v. Florida*, 250 So. 2d 857, 863 (Ervin, J., concurring) (Fla. Supp. 1972); *State v. Gedicke*, 43 N. J. L. 86, 80 (Sup. St. 1881); Means II, at 381-382.

[43] See C. Haagensen & W. Lloyd, A Hundred Years of Medicine 19 (1943).

tion in early pregnancy, that is, prior to the end of first trimester, although not without its risk, is now relatively safe. Mortality rates for women undergoing early abortions, where the procedure is legal, appear to be as low as or lower than the rates for normal childbirth.[44] Consequently, any interest of the State in protecting the woman from an inherently hazardous procedure, except when it would be equally dangerous for her to forgo it, has largely disappeared. Of course, important state interests in the area of health and medical standards do remain. The State has a legitimate interest in seeing to it that abortion, like any other medical procedure, is performed under circumstances that insure maximum safety for the patient. This interest obviously extends at least to the performing physician and his staff, to the facilities involved, to the availability of after-care, and to adequate provision for any complication or emergency that might arise. The prevalence of high mortality rates at illegal "abortion mills" strengthens, rather than weakens, the State's interest in regulating the conditions under which abortions are performed. Moreover, the risk to the woman increases as her pregnancy continues. Thus the State retains a definite interest in protecting the woman's own health and safety when an abortion is proposed at a late stage of pregnancy.

The third reason is the State's interest — some phrase it in terms of duty — in protecting prenatal life. Some of the argument for this justification rests on the theory that a new human life is present from the moment of conception.[45] The State's interest and general obligation to protect life then extends, it is argued, to prenatal life. Only when the life of the pregnant mother herself is at stake, balanced against the life she carries within her, should the interest of the embryo or fetus not prevail. Logically, of course, a

---

[44] Potts, Postconception Control of Fertility, 8 Int'l J. of G. & O. 957, 967 (1970) (England and Wales); Abortion Mortality, 20 Morbidity and Morality, 208, 209 (July 12, 1971) (U. S. Dept. of HEW, Public Health Service) (New York City); Tietze, United States: Therapeutic Abortions, 1963-1968, 59 Studies in Family Planning 5, 7 (1970); Tietze, Mortality with Contraception and Induced Abortion, 45 Studies in Family Planning 6 (1969) (Japan, Czechoslovakia, Hungary); Tietze & Lehfeldt, Legal Abortion in Eastern Europe, 175 J. A. M. A. 1149, 1152 (April 1961). Other sources are discussed in Lader 17-23.

[45] See Brief of Amicus National Right to Life Foundation; R. Drinan, The Inviolability of the Right to Be Born, in Abortion and the Law 107 (D. Smith, editor, 1967); Louisell, Abortion, The Practice of Medicine, and the Due Process of Law, 16 UCLA L. Rev. 233 (1969); Noonan 1.

legitimate state interest in this area need not stand or fall on acceptance of the belief that life begins at conception or at some other point prior to live birth. In assessing the State's interest, recognition may be given to the less rigid claim that as long as at least *potential* life is involved, the State may assert interests beyond the protection of the pregnant woman alone.

Parties challenging state abortion laws have sharply disputed in some courts the contention that a purpose of these laws, when enacted was to protect prenatal life.[46] Pointing to the absence of legislative history to support the contention, they claim that most state laws were designed solely to protect the woman. Because medical advances have lessened this concern, at least with respect to abortion in early pregnancy, they argue that with respect to such abortions the laws can no longer be justified by any state interest. There is some scholarly support for this view of original purpose.[47] The few state courts called upon to interpret their laws in the late 19th and early 20th centuries did focus on the State's interest in protecting the woman's health rather than in preserving the embryo and fetus.[48] Proponents of this view point out that in many States, including Texas,[49] by statute or judicial interpretation, the pregnant woman herself could not be prosecuted for self-abortion or for cooperating in an abortion performed upon her by another.[50] They claim that adoption of the "quickening" distinction through received common law and state statutes tacitly recognizes the greater health hazards inherent in late abortion and impliedly repudiates the theory that life begins at conception.

---

[46] See, *e. g.*, *Abele v. Markle*, 342 F. Supp. 800 (Conn. 1972), appeal pending.

[47] See discussions in Means I and Means II.

[48] See, *e. g.*, *State v. Murphy*, 27 N. J. L. 112, 114 (1858).

[49] *Watson v. State*, 9 Tex. App. 237, 244-245 (1880); *Moore v. State*, 37 Tex. Crim. R. 552, 561, 40 S. W. 287, 290 (1897); *Shaw v. State*, 73 Tex. Crim. R. 337, 339, 165 S. W. 930, 931 (1914); *Fondren v. State*, 74 Tex. Crim. R. 552, 557, 169 S. W. 411, 414 (1914); *Gray v. State*, 77 Tex. Crim. R. 221, 229, 178 S.W. 337, 341 (1915). There is no immunity in Texas for the father who is not married to the mother. *Hammett v. State*, 84 Tex. Crim. R. 635, 209 S. W. 661 (1919); *Thompson v. State*, —— Tex. Crim. R. —— (1971), appeal pending.

[50] See *Smith v. State*, 33 Me. 48, 55 (1851); *In re Vince*, 2 N. J. 443, 450, 67 A.2d 141, 144 (1949). A short discussion of the modern law on this issue is contained in the Comment to the ALI's Model Penal Code § 207.11, at 158 and nn. 35-37 (Tent. Draft No. 9, 1959).

It is with these interests, and the weight to be attached to them, that this case is concerned.

VIII

The Constitution does not explicitly mention any right of privacy. In a line of decisions, however, going back perhaps as far as *Union Pacific R. Co. v. Botsford*, 141 U.S. 250, 251 (1891), the Court has recognized that a right of personal privacy, or a guarantee of certain areas or zones of privacy, does exist under the Constitution. In varying contexts the Court or individual Justices have indeed found at least the roots of that right in the First Amendment, *Stanley v. Georgia*, 394 U.S. 557, 564 (1969); in the Fourth and Fifth Amendments, *Terry v. Ohio*, 392 U.S. 1, 8-9 (1968), *Katz v. United States*, 389 U.S. 347, 350 (1967), *Boyd v. United States*, 116 U.S. 616 (1886), see *Olmstead v. United States*, 277 U.S. 438, 478 (1928) (Brandeis, J. dissenting); in the penumbras of the Bill of Rights, *Griswold v. Connecticut*, 381 U.S. 479, 484-485 (1965); in the Ninth Amendment, *id.*, at 486 (Goldberg, J., concurring); or in the concept of liberty guaranteed by the first section of the Fourteenth Amendment, see *Meyer v. Nebraska*, 262 U.S. 390, 399 (1923). These decisions make it clear that only personal rights that can be deemed "fundamental" or "implicit in the concept of ordered liberty," *Palko v. Connecticut*, 302 U.S. 319, 325 (1937), are included in this guarantee of personal privacy. They also make it clear that the right has some extension to activities relating to marriage, *Loving v. Virginia*, 388 U.S. 1, 12 (1967), procreation, *Skinner v. Oklahoma*, 316 U.S. 535, 541-542 (1942), contraception, *Eisenstadt v. Baird*, 405 U.S. 438, 453-454 (1972); *id.*, at 460, 463-465 (WHITE, J., concurring), family relationships, *Prince v. Massachusetts*, 321 U.S. 158, 166 (1944), and child rearing and education, *Pierce v. Society of Sisters*, 268 U.S. 510, 535 (1925), *Meyer v. Nebraska, supra.*

This right of privacy, whether it be founded in the Fourteenth Amendment's concept of personal liberty and restrictions upon state action, as we feel it is, or, as the District Court determined, in the Ninth Amendment's reservation of rights to the people, is broad enough to encompass a woman's decision whether or not to terminate her pregnancy. The detriment that the State would impose upon the pregnant woman by denying this choice altogether is apparent. Specific and direct harm medically diagnosable even in early pregnancy may be involved. Maternity, or additional offspring, may force upon the woman a distressful life and future. Psychological harm may be imminent. Mental and physical health may be taxed by child care. There is also the distress, for all concerned, associated with the unwanted child, and there is the problem of bringing a child into a family already unable, psychologically and otherwise, to care for it. In other cases, as in this one, the additional difficulties and continuing stigma of unwed motherhood may be involved. All these are factors the woman and her responsible physician necessarily will consider in consultation.

On the basis of elements such as these, appellants and some *amici* argue that the woman's right is absolute and that she is entitled to terminate her pregnancy at whatever time, in whatever way, and for whatever reason she alone chooses. With this we do not agree. Appellants' arguments that Texas either has no valid interest at all in regulating the abortion decision, or no interest strong enough to support any limitation upon the woman's sole determination, is unpersuasive. The Court's decisions recognizing a right of privacy also acknowledge that some state regulation in areas protected by that right is appropriate. As noted above, a state may properly assert important interests in safeguarding health, in maintaining medical standards, and in protecting potential life. At some point in pregnancy, these respective interests become sufficiently compelling to sustain regulation of the factors that govern the abortion decision. The privacy right involved, therefore, cannot be said to be absolute. In fact, it is not clear to us that the claim asserted by some *amici* that one has an unlimited right to do with one's body as one pleases bears a close relationship to the right of privacy previously articulated in the Court's decisions. The Court has refused to recognize an unlimited right of this kind in the past. *Jacobson v. Massachusetts*, 197 U.S. 11 (1905) (vaccination); *Buck v. Bell*, 274 U.S. 200 (1927) (sterilization).

We therefore conclude that the right of personal privacy includes the abortion decision, but that this right is not unqualified and must be considered against important state interests in regulation.

We note that those federal and state courts that have recently considered abortion law challenges have reached the same conclusion. A majority, in addition to the District Court in the present case, have held state laws unconstitutional, at least in part, because of vagueness or because of overbreadth and abridgement of rights. *Abele v. Markle*, 342 F. Supp. 800 (Conn. 1972), appeal pending; *Abele v. Markle*, —— F. Supp. —— (Conn. Sept. 20, 1972) appeal pending; *Doe v. Bolton*, 319 F. Supp. 1048 (ND Ga. 1970), appeal decided today, *post* ——; *Doe v. Scott*, 321 F. Supp. 1385 (ND Ill. 1971), appeal pending; *Poe v. Menghini*, 339 F. Supp. 986 (Kan. 1972); *YWCA v. Kugler*, 342 F. Supp. 1048 (NJ 1972); *Babbitz v. McCann*, 310 F. Supp. 293 (ED Wis. 1970), appeal dismissed, 400 U.S. 1 (1970); *People v. Belous*, 71 Cal. 2d 954, 458 P.2d 194 (1969), cert. denied, 397 U.S. 915 (1970); *State v. Barquet*, 262 S. 2d 431 (Fla. 1972).

Others have sustained state statutes. *Crossen v. Attorney General*, 344 F. Supp. 587 (ED Ky. 1972), appeal pending; *Rosen v. Louisiana State Board of Medical Examiners*, 318 F. Supp. 1217 (ED La. 1970), appeal pending; *Corkey v. Edwards*, 322 F. Supp. 1248 (WDNC 1971), appeal pending; *Steinberg v. Brown*, 321 F. Supp. 741 (ND Ohio 1970); *Doe v. Rampton*, —— F. Supp. —— (Utah 1971), appeal pending; *Cheaney v. Indiana*, —— Ind. ——, 285 N. E. 2d 265 (1972); *Spears v. State*, 257 So. 2d 876 (Miss. 1972); *State v. Munson*, —— S. D. ——, 201 N. W. 2d 123 (1972), appeal pending.

Although the results are divided, most of these courts have agreed that the right of privacy, however based, is broad enough to cover the abortion decision; that the right, nonetheless, is not absolute and is subject to some limitations; and that at some point the state interests as to protection of health, medical standards, and pre-natal life, become dominant. We agree with this approach.

Where certain "fundamental rights" are involved, the Court has held that regulation limiting these rights may be justified only by a "compelling state interest," *Kramer v. Union Free School District*, 395 U.S. 621, 627 (1969); *Shapiro v. Thompson*, 394 U.S. 618, 634 (1969), *Sherbert v. Verner*, 374 U.S. 398, 406 (1963), and that legislative enactments must be narrowly drawn to express only the legitimate state interests at stake. *Griswold v. Connecticut*,

381 U.S. 479, 485 (1965); *Aptheker v. Secretary of State,* 378 U.S. 500, 508 (1964); *Cantwell v. Connecticut,* 310 U.S. 296, 307-308 (1940); see *Eisenstadt v. Baird,* 405 U.S. 438, 460, 463-464 (1972) (WHITE, J., concurring).

In the recent abortion cases, cited above, courts have recognized these principles. Those striking down state laws have generally scrutinized the State's interest in protecting health and potential life and have concluded that neither interest justified broad limitations on the reasons for which a physician and his pregnant patient might decide that she should have an abortion in the early stages of pregnancy. Courts sustaining state laws have held that the State's determinations to protect health or prenatal life are dominant and constitutionally justifiable.

IX

The District Court held that the appellee failed to meet his burden of demonstrating that the Texas statute's infringement upon Roe's rights was necessary to support a compelling state interest, and that, although the defendant presented "several compelling justifications for state presence in the area of abortions," the statutes outstripped these justifications and swept "far beyond any areas of compelling state interest." 314 F. Supp., at 1222-1223. Appellant and appellee both contest that holding. Appellant, as has been indicated, claims an absolute right that bars any state imposition of criminal penalties in the area. Appellee argues that the State's determination to recognize and protect prenatal life from and after conception constitutes a compelling state interest. As noted above, we do not agree fully with either formulation.

A. The appellee and certain *amici* argue that the fetus is a "person" within the language and meaning of the Fourteenth Amendment. In support of this they outline at length and in detail the well-known facts of fetal development. If this suggestion of personhood is established, the appellant's case, of course, collapses, for the fetus' right to life is then guaranteed specifically by the Amendment. The appellant conceded as much on reargument.[51] On the other hand, the appellee conceded on reargument[52] that no case

---

[51] Tr. of Rearg. 20-21.
[52] Tr. of Rearg. 24.

could be cited that holds that a fetus is a person within the meaning of the Fourteenth Amendment.

The Constitution does not define "person" in so many words. Section 1 of the Fourteenth Amendment contains three references to "person." The first, in defining "citizens," speaks of "persons born or naturalized in the United States." The word also appears both in the Due Process Clause and in the Equal Protection Clause. "Person" is used in other places in the Constitution: in the listing of qualifications for representatives and senators, Art. I, § 2, cl. 2, and § 3, cl. 3; in the Apportionment Clause, Art. I, § 2, cl. 3;[53] in the Migration and Importation provision, Art. I, § 9, cl. 1; in the Emolument Clause, Art. I, § 9, cl. 8; in the Electors provisions, Art. II, § 1, cl. 2, and the superseded cl. 3; in the provision outlining qualifications for the office of President, Art. II, § 1, cl. 5; in the Extradition provisions, Art. IV, § 2, cl. 2, and the superseded Fugitive Slave cl. 3; and in the Fifth, Twelfth, and Twenty-second Amendments as well as in §§ 2 and 3 of the Fourteenth Amendment. But in nearly all these instances, the use of the word is such that it has application only postnatally. None indicates, with any assurance, that it has any possible pre-natal application.[54]

All this, together with our observation, *supra*, that throughout the major portion of the 19th century prevailing legal abortion practices were far freer than they are today, persuades us that the word "person," as used in the Fourteenth Amendment, does not include

---

[53] We are not aware that in the taking of any census under this clause, a fetus has ever been counted.

[54] When Texas urges that a fetus is entitled to Fourteenth Amendment protection as a person, it faces a dilemma. Neither in Texas nor in any other State are all abortions prohibited. Despite broad proscription, an exception always exists. The exception contained in Art. 1196, for an abortion procured or attempted by medical advice for the purpose of saving the life of the mother, is typical. But if the fetus is a person who is not to be deprived of life without due process of law, and if the mother's condition is the sole determinant, does not the Texas exception appear to be out of line with the Amendment's command?

There are other inconsistencies between Fourteenth Amendment status and the typical abortion statute. It has already been pointed out, n. 49, *supra*, that in Texas the woman is not a principal or an accomplice with respect to an abortion upon her. If the fetus is a person, why is the woman not a principal or an accomplice? Further, the penalty for criminal abortion specified by Art. 1195 is significantly less than the maximum penalty for murder prescribed by Art. 1257 of the Texas Penal Code. If the fetus is a person, may the penalties be different?

the unborn.[55] This is in accord with the results reached in those few cases where the issue has been squarely presented. *McGarvey v. Magee-Womens Hospital,* 340 F. Supp. 751 (WD Pa. 1972); *Byrn v. New York City Health & Hospitals Corp.,* 31 N.Y. 2d 194, 286 N.E. 2d 887 (1972), appeal pending; *Abele v. Markle,* —— F. Supp. —— (Conn. Sept. 20, 1972), appeal pending. Compare *Cheaney v. Indiana,* —— Ind. ——, 285 N.E. 265, 270 (1972); *Montana v. Rogers,* 278 F. 2d 68, 72 (CA7 1960), aff'd *sub nom. Montana v. Kennedy,* 366 U.S. 308 (1961); *Keeler v. Superior Court,* —— Cal. ——, 470 P. 2d 617 (1970); *State v. Dickinson,* 23 Ohio App. 2d 259, 275 N.E. 2d 599 (1970). Indeed, our decision in *United States v. Vuitch,* 402 U.S. 62 (1971), inferentially is to the same effect, for we there would not have indulged in statutory interpretation favorable to abortion in specified circumstances if the necessary consequence was the termination of life entitled to Fourteenth Amendment protection.

This conclusion, however, does not of itself fully answer the contentions raised by Texas, and we pass on to other considerations.

B. The pregnant woman cannot be isolated in her privacy. She carries an embryo and, later, a fetus, if one accepts the medical definitions of the developing young in the human uterus. See Dorland's Illustrated Medical Dictionary, 478-479, 547 (24th ed. 1965). The situation therefore is inherently different from marital intimacy, or bedroom possession of obscene material, or marriage, or procreation, or education, with which *Eisenstadt, Griswold, Stanley, Loving, Skinner, Pierce,* and *Meyer* were respectively concerned. As we have intimated above, it is reasonable and appropriate for a State to decide that at some point in time another interest, that of health of the mother or that of potential human life, becomes significantly involved. The woman's privacy is no longer sole and any right of privacy she possesses must be measured accordingly.

Texas urges that, apart from the Fourteenth Amendment, life begins at conception and is present throughout pregnancy, and that, therefore, the State has a compelling interest in protecting that

---

[55] Cf. the Wisconsin abortion statute, defining "unborn child" to mean "a human being from the time of conception until it is born alive," Wis. Stat. § 940.04(6) (1969), and the new Connecticut statute, Public Act No. 1, May 1972 Special Session, declaring it to be the public policy of the State and the legislative intent "to protect and preserve human life from the moment of conception."

life from and after conception. We need not resolve the difficult question of when life begins. When those trained in the respective disciplines of medicine, philosophy, and theology are unable to arrive at any consensus, the judiciary, at this point in the development of man's knowledge, is not in a position to speculate as to the answer.

It should be sufficient to note briefly the wide divergence of thinking on this most sensitive and difficult question. There has always been strong support for the view that life does not begin until live birth. This was the belief of the Stoics.[56] It appears to be the predominant, though not the unanimous, attitude of the Jewish faith.[57] It may be taken to represent also the position of a large segment of the Protestant community, insofar as that can be ascertained; organized groups that have taken a formal position on the abortion issue have generally regarded abortion as a matter for the conscience of the individual and her family.[58] As we have noted the common law found greater significance in quickening. Physicians and their scientific colleagues have regarded that event with less interest and have tended to focus either upon conception or upon live birth or upon the interim point at which the fetus becomes "viable," that is, potentially able to live outside the mother's womb, albeit with artificial aid.[59] Viability is usually placed at about seven months (28 weeks) but may occur earlier, even at 24 weeks.[60] The Aristotelian theory of "mediate animation" that held sway throughout the Middle Ages and the Renaissance in Europe, continued to be official Roman Catholic dogma until the 19th century, despite opposition to this "ensoulment" theory from those in the Church who would recognize the existence of life from the moment of conception.[61] The latter is now, of course, the official belief of

[56] Edelstein 16.

[57] Lader 97-99; D. Feldman, Birth Control in Jewish Law 251-294 (1968). For a stricter view, see I. Jakobovits, Jewish Views on Abortion, in Abortion and the Law 124 (D. Smith ed. 1967).

[58] Amicus Brief for the American Ethical Union et al. For the position of the National Council of Churches and of other denominations, see Lader 99-101.

[59] L. Hellman & J. Pritchard, Williams Obstetrics 493 (14th ed. 1971); Dorland's Illustrated Medical Dictionary 1689 (24th ed. 1965).

[60] Hellman & Pritchard, *supra*, n. 58, at 493.

[61] For discussions of the development of the Roman Catholic position, see D. Callahan, Abortion: Law, Choice and Morality 409-447 (1970); Noonan 1.

the Catholic Church. As one of the briefs *amicus* discloses, this is a view strongly held by many non-Catholics as well, and by many physicians. Substantial problems for precise definition of this view are posed, however, by new embryological data that purport to indicate that conception is a "process" over time, rather than an event, and by new medical techniques such as menstrual extraction, the "morning-after" pill, implantation of embryos, artificial insemination, and even artificial wombs.[62]

In areas other than criminal abortion the law has been reluctant to endorse any theory that life, as we recognize it, begins before live birth or to accord legal rights to the unborn except in narrowly defined situations and except when the rights are contingent upon live birth. For example, the traditional rule of tort law had denied recovery for prenatal injuries even though the child was born alive.[63] That rule has been changed in almost every jurisdiction. In most States recovery is said to be permitted only if the fetus was viable, or at least quick, when the injuries were sustained, though few courts have squarely so held.[64] In a recent development, generally opposed by the commentators, some States permit the parents of a stillborn child to maintain an action for wrongful death because of prenatal injuries.[65] Such an action, however, would appear to be one to vindicate the parents' interest and is thus consistent with the view that the fetus, at most, represents only the potentiality of life. Similarly, unborn children have been recognized as acquiring rights or interests by way of inheritance or other devolution of property, and have been represented by guardians *ad litem*.[66] Perfection of the inter-

---

[62] See D. Brodie, The New Biology and the Prenatal Child, 9 J. Fam. L. 391, 397 (1970); R. Gorney, The New Biology and the Future of Man, 15 UCLA L. Rev. 273 (1968); Note, Criminal Law — Abortion — the "Morning-After" Pill and Other Pre-Implantation Birth-Control Methods and the Law, 46 Ore. L. Rev. 211 (1967); G. Taylor, The Biological Time Bomb 32 (1968); A. Rosenfeld, The Second Genesis 138-139 (1969); G. Smith, Through a Test Tube Darkly: Artificial Insemination and the Law, 67 Mich. L. Rev. 127 (1968); Note, Artificial Insemination and the Law, U. Ill. L. F. 203 (1968).

[63] Prosser, Handbook of the Law of Torts 335-338 (1971); 2 Harper & James, The Law of Torts 1028-1031 (1956); Note, 63 Harv. L. Rev. 173 (1949).

[64] See cases cited in Prosser, *supra,* n. 62, at 336-338; Annotation, Action for Death of Unborn Child, 15 A. L. R. 3d 992 (1967).

[65] Prosser, *supra,* n. 62, at 338; Note, The Law and the Unborn Child, 46 Notre Dame Law. 349, 354-360 (1971).

[66] D. Louisell, Abortion, The Practice of Medicine, and the Due Process of Law, 16

ests involved, again, has generally been contingent upon live birth. In short, the unborn have never been recognized in the law as persons in the whole sense.

X

In view of all this, we do not agree that, by adopting one theory of life, Texas may override the rights of the pregnant woman that are at stake. We repeat, however, that the State does have an important and legitimate interest in preserving and protecting the health of the pregnant woman, whether she be a resident of the State or a nonresident who seeks medical consultation and treatment there, and that it has still *another* important and legitimate interest in protecting the potentiality of human life. These interests are separate and distinct. Each grows in substantiality as the woman approaches term and, at a point during pregnancy, each becomes "compelling."

With respect to the State's important and legitimate interest in the health of the mother, the "compelling" point, in the light of present medical knowledge, is at approximately the end of the first trimester. This is so because of the now established medical fact, referred to above at p. 34, that until the end of the first trimester mortality in abortion is less than mortality in normal childbirth. It follows that, from and after this point, a State may regulate the abortion procedure to the extent that the regulation reasonably relates to the preservation and protection of maternal health. Examples of permissible state regulation in this area are requirements as to the qualifications of the person who is to perform the abortion; as to the licensure of that person; as to the facility in which the procedure is to be performed, that is, whether it must be a hospital or may be a clinic or some other place of less-than-hospital status; as to the licensing of the facility; and the like.

This means, on the other hand, that, for the period of pregnancy prior to this "compelling" point, the attending physician, in consultation with his patient, is free to determine, without regulation by

UCLA L. Rev. 233, 235-238 (1969); Note, 56 Iowa L. Rev. 994, 999-1000 (1971); Note, The Law and the Unborn Child, 46 Notre Dame Law, 349, 351-354 (1971).

the State, that in his medical judgment the patient's pregnancy should be terminated. If that decision is reached, the judgment may be effectuated by an abortion free of interference by the State.

With respect to the State's important and legitimate interest in potential life, the "compelling" point is at viability. This is so because the fetus then presumably has the capability of meaningful life outside the mother's womb. State regulation protective of fetal life after viability thus has both logical and biological justifications. If the State is interested in protecting fetal life after viability, it may go so far as to proscribe abortion during that period except when it is necessary to preserve the life or health of the mother.

Measured against these standards, Art. 1196 of the Texas Penal Code, in restricting legal abortions to those "procured or attempted by medical advice for the purpose of saving the life of the mother," sweeps too broadly. The statute makes no distinction between abortions performed early in pregnancy and those performed later and it limits to a single reason, "saving" the mother's life, the legal justification for the procedure. The statute, therefore, cannot survive the constitutional attack made upon it here.

This conclusion makes it unnecessary for us to consider the additional challenge to the Texas statute asserted on grounds of vagueness. See *United States v. Vuitch*, 402 U.S. 62, 67-72 (1971).

XI

To summarize and to repeat:

1. A state criminal abortion statute of the current Texas type, that excepts from criminality only a *life saving* procedure on behalf of the mother, without regard to pregnancy stage and without recognition of the other interests involved, is violative of the Due Process Clause of the Fourteenth Amendment.

(a) For the stage prior to approximately the end of the first trimester, the abortion decision and its effectuation must be left to the medical judgment of the pregnant woman's attending physician.

(b) For the stage subsequent to approximately the end of the first trimester, the State, in promoting its interest in the health of the mother, may, if it chooses, regulate the abortion procedure in ways that are reasonably related to maternal health.

(c) For the stage subsequent to viability the State, in promoting its interest in the potentiality of human life, may, if it chooses, regulate, and even proscribe, abortion except where it is necessary, in appropriate medical judgment, for the preservation of the life or health of the mother.

2. The State may define the term "physician," as it has been employed in the preceding numbered paragraphs of this Part XI of this opinion, to mean only a physician currently licensed by the State, and may proscribe any abortion by a person who is not a physician as so defined.

In *Doe v. Bolton, post,* procedural requirements contained in one of the modern abortion statutes are considered. That opinion and this one, of course, are to be read together.[67]

This holding, we feel, is consistent with the relative weights of the respective interests involved, with the lessons and example of medical and legal history, with the lenity of the common law, and with the demands of the profound problems of the present day. The decision leaves the State free to place increasing restrictions on abortion as the period of pregnancy lengthens, so long as those restrictions are tailored to the recognized state interests. The decision vindicates the right of the physician to administer medical treatment according to his professional judgment up to the points where important state interests provide compelling justifications for intervention. Up to those points the abortion decision in all its aspects is inherently, and primarily, a medical decision, and basic responsibility for it must rest with the physician. If an individual practitioner abuses the privilege of exercising proper medical judgment, the usual remedies, judicial and intra-professional, are available.

---

[67] Neither in this opinion nor in *Doe v. Bolton, post,* do we discuss the father's rights, if any exist in the constitutional context, in the abortion decision. No paternal right has been asserted in either of the cases, and the Texas and the Georgia statutes on their face take no cognizance of the father. We are aware that some statutes recognize the father under certain circumstances. North Carolina, for example, 1B N. C. Gen. Stat. § 14-45.1 (Supp. 1971), requires written permission for the abortion from the husband when the woman is a married minor, that is, when she is less than 18 years of age, 41 N. C. A. G. 489 (1971); if the woman is an unmarried minor, written permission from the parents is required. We need not now decide whether provisions of this kind are constitutional.

XII

Our conclusion that Art. 1196 is unconstitutional means, of course, that the Texas abortion statutes, as a unit, must fall. The exception of Art. 1196 cannot be stricken separately, for then the State is left with a statute proscribing all abortion procedures no matter how medically urgent the case.

Although the District Court granted plaintiff Roe declaratory relief, it stopped short of issuing an injunction against enforcement of the Texas statutes. The Court has recognized that different considerations enter into a federal court's decision as to declaratory relief, on the one hand, and injunctive relief, on the other. *Zwickler v. Koota*, 389 U.S. 241, 252-255 (1967); *Dombrowski v. Pfister*, 380 U.S. 479 (1965). We are not dealing with a statute that, on its face, appears to abridge free expression, an area of particular concern under *Dombrowski* and refined in *Younger v. Harris*, 401 U.S., at 50.

We find it unnecessary to decide whether the District Court erred in withholding injunctive relief, for we assume the Texas prosecutorial authorities will give full credence to this decision that the present criminal abortion statutes of that State are unconstitutional.

The judgment of the District Court as to intervenor Hallford is reversed, and Dr. Hallford's complaint in intervention is dismissed. In all other respects the judgment of the District Court is affirmed. Costs are allowed to the appellee.

It is so ordered.

MR. JUSTICE STEWART, concurring

In 1963, this Court, in *Ferguson v. Skrupa*, 372 U.S. 726, purported to sound the death knell for the doctrine of substantive due process, a doctrine under which many state laws had in the past been held to violate the Fourteenth Amendment. As Mr. Justice Black's opinion for the Court in *Skrupa* put it: "We have returned to the original constitutional proposition that courts do not substitute their social and economic beliefs for the judgment of legislative bodies, who are elected to pass laws." *Id.*, at 730.[1]

---

[1] Only Mr. Justice Harlan failed to join the Court's opinion, 372 U. S. at 733.

Barely two years later, in *Griswold v. Connecticut*, 381 U.S. 479, the Court held a Connecticut birth control law unconstitutional. In view of what had been so recently said in *Skrupa*, the Court's opinion in *Griswold* understandably did its best to avoid reliance on the Due Process Clause of the Fourteenth Amendment as the ground for decision. Yet, the Connecticut law did not violate any provision of the Bill of Rights, nor any other specific provision of the Constitution.[2] So it was clear to me then, and it is equally clear to me now, that the *Griswold* decision can be rationally understood only as a holding that the Connecticut statute substantively invaded the "liberty" that is protected by the Due Process Clause of the Fourteenth Amendment.[3] As so understood, *Griswold* stands as one in a long line of pre-*Skrupa* cases decided under the doctrine of substantive due process, and I now accept it as such.

"In a Constitution for a free people, there can be no doubt that the meaning of 'liberty' must be broad indeed." *Board of Regents v. Roth*, 408 U.S. 564, 572. The Constitution nowhere mentions a specific right of personal choice in matters of marriage and family life, but the "liberty" protected by the Due Process Clause of the Fourteenth Amendment covers more than those freedoms explicitly named in the Bill of Rights. See *Schware v. Board of Bar Examiners*, 353 U.S. 232, 238-239; *Pierce v. Society of Sisters*, 268 U.S. 510, 534-535; *Meyer v. Nebraska*, 262 U.S. 390, 399-400. Cf. *Shapiro v. Thompson*, 394 U.S. 618, 629-630; *United States v. Guest*, 383 U.S. 745, 757-758; *Carrington v. Rash*, 380 U.S. 89, 96; *Aptheker v. Secretary of State*, 378 U.S. 500, 505; *Kent v. Dulles*, 357 U.S. 116, 127; *Bolling v. Sharpe*, 347 U.S. 497, 499-500; *Truax v. Raich*, 239 U.S. 33, 41.

---

[2] There is no constitutional right of privacy, as such. "[The Fourth] Amendment protects individual privacy against certain kinds of governmental intrusion, but its protections go further, and often have nothing to do with privacy at all. Other provisions of the Constitution protect personal privacy from other forms of governmental invasion. But the protection of a person's *general* right to privacy — his right to be let alone by other people — is, like the protection of his property and of his very life, left largely to the law of the individual States." *Katz v. United States*, 389 U. S. 347, 350-351 (footnotes omitted).

[3] This was also clear to Mr. Justice Black, 381 U. S., at 507 (dissenting opinion); to Mr. Justice Harlan, 381 U. S., at 499 (opinion concurring in the judgment); and to MR. JUSTICE WHITE, 381 U. S., at 502 (opinion concurring in the judgment). See also Mr. Justice Harlan's thorough and thoughtful opinion dissenting from dismissal of the appeal in *Poe v. Ullman*, 367 U. S. 497, 522.

As Mr. Justice Harlan once wrote: "[T]he full scope of the liberty guaranteed by the Due Process Clause cannot be found in or limited by the precise terms of the specific guarantees elsewhere provided in the Constitution. This 'liberty' is not a series of isolated points pricked out in terms of the taking of property; the freedom of speech, press, and religion; the right to keep and bear arms; the freedom from unreasonable searches and seizures; and so on. It is a rational continuum which, broadly speaking, includes a freedom from all substantial arbitrary impositions and purposeless restraints, . . . and which also recognizes, what a reasonable and sensitive judgment must, that certain interests require particularly careful scrutiny of the state needs asserted to justify their abridgment." *Poe v. Ullman*, 367 U.S. 497, 543 (opinion dissenting from dismissal of appeal) (citations omitted). In the words of Mr. Justice Frankfurter, "Great concepts like . . . 'liberty' . . . were purposely left to gather meaning from experience. For they relate to the whole domain of social and economic fact, and the statesmen who founded this Nation knew too well that only a stagnant society remains unchanged." *National Mutual Ins. Co. v. Tidewater Transfer Co., Inc.*, 337 U.S. 582, 646 (dissenting opinion).

Several decisions of this Court make clear that freedom of personal choice in matters of marriage and family life is one of the liberties protected by the Due Process Clause of the Fourteenth Amendment. *Loving v. Virginia*, 388 U.S. 1, 12; *Griswold v. Connecticut, supra*; *Pierce v. Society of Sisters, supra*; *Meyer v. Nebraska, supra*. See also *Prince v. Massachusetts*, 321 U.S. 158, 166; *Skinner v. Oklahoma*, 316 U.S. 535, 541. As recently as last Term, in *Eisenstadt v. Baird*, 405 U.S. 438, 453, we recognized "the right of the *individual*, married or single, to be free from unwarranted governmental intrusion into matters so fundamentally affecting a person as the decision whether to bear or beget a child." That right necessarily includes the right of a woman to decide whether or not to terminate her pregnancy. "Certainly the interests of a woman in giving of her physical and emotional self during pregnancy and the interests that will be affected throughout her life by the birth and raising of a child are of a far greater degree of significance and personal intimacy than the right to send a child to private school protected in *Pierce v. Society of Sisters*, 268 U.S. 510 (1925), or the right to teach a foreign language protected in *Meyer v. Nebraska,* 262 U.S. 390 (1923)." *Abele v. Markle,* —— F. Supp. ——, —— (Conn. 1972).

Clearly, therefore, the Court today is correct in holding that the right asserted by Jane Roe is embraced within the personal liberty protected by the Due Process Clause of the Fourteenth Amendment.

It is evident that the Texas abortion statute infringes that right directly. Indeed, it is difficult to imagine a more complete abridgment of a constitutional freedom than that worked by the inflexible criminal statute now in force in Texas. The question then becomes whether the state interests advanced to justify this abridgment can survive the "particularly careful scrutiny" that the Fourteenth Amendment here requires.

The asserted state interests are protection of the health and safety of the pregnant woman, and protection of the potential future human life within her. These are legitimate objectives, amply sufficient to permit a State to regulate abortions as it does other surgical procedures, and perhaps sufficient to permit a State to regulate abortions more stringently or even to prohibit them in the late stages of pregnancy. But such legislation is not before us, and I think the Court today has thoroughly demonstrated that these state interests cannot constitutionally support the broad abridgment of personal liberty worked by the existing Texas law. Accordingly, I join the Court's opinion holding that that law is invalid under the Due Process Clause of the Fourteenth Amendment.

MR. JUSTICE REHNQUIST, dissenting

The Court's opinion brings to the decision of this troubling question both extensive historical fact and a wealth of legal scholarship. While its opinion thus commands my respect, I find myself nonetheless in fundamental disagreement with those parts of it which invalidate the Texas statute in question, and therefore dissent.

I

The Court's opinion decides that a State may impose virtually no restriction on the performance of abortions during the first trimester of pregnancy. Our previous decisions indicate that a necessary predicate for such an opinion is a plaintiff who was in her first trimester of pregnancy at some time during the pendency of her law suit. While a party may vindicate his own constitutional rights, he may not seek vindication for the rights of others. *Moose Lodge v. Irvis*, 407 U.S. 163 (1972); *Sierra Club v. Morton*, 405 U.S. 727 (1972). The Court's statement of facts in this case makes clear, however, that the record in no way indicates the presence of such a plaintiff. We know only that plaintiff Roe at the time of filing her complaint was a pregnant woman; for aught that appears in this record, she may have been in her *last* trimester of pregnancy as of the date the complaint was filed.

Nothing in the Court's opinion indicates that Texas might not constitutionally apply its proscription of abortion as written to a woman in that stage of pregnancy. Nonetheless, the Court uses her complaint against the Texas statute as a fulcrum for deciding that States may impose virtually no restrictions on medical abortions performed during the *first* trimester of pregnancy. In deciding such a hypothetical lawsuit the Court departs from the longstanding admonition that it should never "formulate a rule of constitutional law broader than is required by the precise facts to which it is to be applied." *Liverpool, New York and Philadelphia Steamship Co. v. Commissioners of Emigration*, 113 U.S. 33, 39 (1885). See also *Ashwander v. TVA*, 297 U.S. 288, 345 (1936) (Brandeis, concurring).

II

Even if there were a plaintiff in this case capable of litigating the issue which the Court decides, I would reach a conclusion opposite to that reached by the Court. I have difficulty in concluding, as the Court does, that the right of "privacy" is involved in this case. Texas by the statute here challenged bars the performance of a medical abortion by a licensed physician on a plaintiff such as Roe. A transaction resulting in an operation such as this is not "private" in the ordinary usage of that word. Nor is the "privacy" which the Court finds here even a distant relative of the freedom from searches and seizures protected by the Fourth Amendment to the Constitution which the Court has referred to as embodying a right to privacy. *Katz v. United States*, 389 U.S. 347 (1967).

If the Court means by the term "privacy" no more than that the claim of a person to be free from unwanted state regulation of consensual transactions may be a form of "liberty" protected by the Fourteenth Amendment, there is no doubt that similar claims have been upheld in our earlier decisions on the basis of that liberty. I agree with the statement of MR. JUSTICE STEWART in his concurring opinion that the "liberty," against deprivation of which without due process the Fourteenth Amendment protects, embraces more than the rights found in the Bill of Rights. But that liberty is not guaranteed absolutely against deprivation, but only against deprivation without due process of law. The test traditionally applied in the area of social and economic legislation is whether or not a law such as that challenged has a rational relation to a valid state objective. *Williamson v. Lee Optical Co.*, 348 U.S. 483, 491 (1955). The Due Process Clause of the Fourteenth Amendment undoubtedly does place a limit on legislative power to enact laws such as this, albeit a broad one. If the Texas statute were to prohibit an abortion even where the mother's life is in jeopardy, I have little doubt that such a statute would lack a rational relation to a valid state objective under the test stated in *Williamson, supra*. But the Court's sweeping invalidation of any restrictions on abortion during the first trimester is impossible to justify under that standard, and the conscious weighing of competing factors which the Court's opinion apparently substitutes for the established test is far more appropriate to a legislative judgment than to a judicial one.

The Court eschews the history of the Fourteenth Amendment in its reliance on the "compelling state interest" test. See *Weber v. Aetna Casualty & Surety Co.*, 406 U.S. 164, 179 (1972) (dissenting opinion). But the Court adds a new wrinkle to this test by transposing it from the legal considerations associated with the Equal Protection Clause of the Fourteenth Amendment to this case arising under the Due Process Clause of the Fourteenth Amendment. Unless I misapprehend the consequences of this transplanting of the "compelling state interest test," the Court's opinion will accomplish the seemingly impossible feat of leaving this area of the law more confused than it found it.

While the Court's opinion quotes from the dissent of Mr. Justice Holmes in *Lochner v. New York*, 198 U.S. 45 (1905), the result it reaches is more closely attuned to the majority opinion of Mr. Justice Peckham in that case. As in *Lochner* and similar cases applying substantive due process standards to economic and social welfare legislation, the adoption of the compelling state interest standard will inevitably require this Court to examine the legislative policies and pass on the wisdom of these policies in the very process of deciding whether a particular state interest put forward may or may not be "compelling." The decision here to break the term of pregnancy into three distinct terms and to outline the permissible retrictions the State may impose in each one, for example, partakes more of judicial legislation than it does of a determination of the intent of the drafters of the Fourteenth Amendment.

The fact that a majority of the States, reflecting after all the majority sentiment in those States, have had restrictions on abortions for at least a century seems to me as strong an indication there is that the asserted right to an abortion is not "so rooted in the traditions and conscience of our people as to be ranked as fundamental," *Snyder v. Massachusetts*, 291 U.S. 97, 105 (1934). Even today, when society's views on abortion are changing, the very existence of the debate is evidence that the "right" to an abortion is not so universally accepted as the appellants would have us believe.

To reach its result the Court necessarily has had to find within the scope of the Fourteenth Amendment a right that was apparently completely unknown to the drafters of the Amendment. As early as 1821, the first state law dealing directly with abortion was enacted by the Connecticut legislature. Conn. Stat. Tit. 22, §§ 14, 16 (1821). By the time of the adoption of the Fourteenth Amendment in 1868 there were at least 36 laws enacted by state or territorial legislatures limiting abortion.[1] While many States have amended or updated

---

[1] States having enacted abortion laws prior to the adoption of the Fourteenth Amendment in 1868:

    1. Alabama—Ala. Acts. c. 6, § 2 (1840-1841).

    2. Arizona—Howell Code, c. 10, § 45 (1865).

    3. Arkansas—Ark. Rev. Stat., c. 44, div. III, Art. II, § 6 (1838).

    4. California—Cal. Sess. Stats., c. 99, § 45, at 233 (1849-1850).

    5. Colorado (Terr.)—Colo. Gen. Laws of Terr. of Colo., 1st Sess., § 42, at 296-297 (1861).

    6. Connecticut—Conn. Stat. Tit. 22, §§ 14, 16, at 152, 153 (1821). By 1868 this statute had been replaced by another abortion law. Conn. Pub. Acts, c. LXXI, §§ 1, 2, at 65 (1860).

their laws, 21 of the laws on the books in 1868 remain in effect to-day.[2] Indeed, the Texas statute struck down today was, as the ma-

---

7. Florida—Fla. Acts 1st Sess., c. 1637, III, § 10, § 11, VIII, § 9, § 10, § 11, as amended now in Fla. Stat. Ann. §§ 782.09, 782.10, 797.01, 797.02, 782.16 (1944).

8. Georgia—Ga. Pen. Code §§ 56, 57, 58, 67, 68, 69 (1833).

9. Kingdom of Hawaii—Hawaii Pen. Code §§ 1, 2, 3 (1850).

10. Idaho (Terr.)—Idaho (Terr.) Laws §§ 33, 34, 42, at 435 (1863).

11. Illinois—Ill. Rev. Code §§ 40, 41, 46, at 130, 131 (1827). By 1868 this statute had been replaced by a subsequent enactment. Ill. Pub. Laws §§ 1, 2, 3, at 89 (1867).

12. Indiana—Ind. Rev. Stat. §§ 1, 3, at 224 (1838). By 1868 this statute had been superseded by a subsequent enactment. Ind. Laws c. LXXXI, § 2 (1859).

13. Iowa (Terr.)—Iowa (Terr.) Stat. 1st Legis., 1st Sess., § 18, at 145 (1838). By 1868 this statute had been superseded by a subsequent enactment. Iowa (Terr.) Rev. Stat. §§ 10, 13 (1843).

14. Kansas (Terr.)—Kan. (Terr.) Stat. c. 48, §§ 9, 10, 39 (1855). By 1868 this statute had been superseded by a subsequent enactment. Kan. Gen. Laws c. 28, §§ 9, 10 (1859).

15. Louisiana—La. Rev. Stat. § 24, at 138 (1856).

16. Maine—Me. Rev. Stat. c. 160, §§ 11, 12, 13, 14 (1840).

17. Maryland—Md. Laws c. 179, § 2, at 318 (1868).

18. Massachusetts—Mass. Acts & Resolves c. 27 (1845).

19. Michigan—Mich. Rev. Stat. c. 153, §§ 32, 33, 34, at 662 (1846).

20. Minn. (Terr.)—Minn. (Terr.) Rev. Stat. c. 100, §§ 10, 11, at 493 (1851).

21. Mississippi—Miss. Code §§ 8, 9, at 958 (1848).

22. Missouri—Mo. Rev. Stat. Art. II, §§ 9, 10, 36, at 168 (1835).

23. Montana (Terr.)—Mont. (Terr.) Laws § 41, at 184 (1864).

24. Nevada (Terr.)—Nev. (Terr.) Laws c. 28, § 42, at 63 (1861).

25. New Hampshire—N. H. Laws c. 743, § 1, at 708 (1848).

26. New Jersey—N. J. Laws, at 266 (1849).

27. New York—N. Y. Rev. Stat. pt. IV, c. I, Tit. II, §§ 8, 9, at 550 (1828). By 1868 this statute had been superseded by subsequent enactments. N. Y. Laws c. 260, §§ 1, 2, 3, 4, 5, 6, at 285 (1845); N. Y. Laws c. 22, § 1, at 19 (1846).

28. Ohio—Ohio Gen. Stat. §§ 111 (1), 112 (2), at 252 (1841).

29. Oregon—Ore. Gen. Laws. Crim. Code, c. 43, § 509, at 528 (1845-1864).

30. Pennsylvania—Pa. Laws No. 374, §§ 87, 88, 89 (1860).

31. Texas—Tex. Gen. Stat. Dig. c. VII, Arts. 531-536, at 524 (Oldham & White 1859).

32. Vermont—Vt. Acts No. 33, § 1 (1846). By 1868 this statute had been amended by a subsequent enactment. Vt. Acts No. 57, §§ 1, 3 (1867).

33. Virginia—Va. Acts Tit. II, c. 3, § 9, at 96 (1848).

34. Washington (Terr.)—Wash. (Terr.) Stats. c. II, §§ 37, 38, at 81 (1854).

35. West Virginia—Va. Acts. Tit. II, c. 3, § 9, at 96 (1848).

36. Wisconsin—Wis. Rev. Stat. c. 133, §§ 10, 11 (1849). By 1868 this statute had been superseded by a subsequent enactment. Wis. Rev. Stat. c. 164, §§ 10, 11; c. 169, §§ 58, 59 (1858).

[2] Abortion laws in effect in 1868 and still applicable as of August 1970:

1. Arizona (1865).

2. Connecticut (1860).

3. Florida (1868).

4. Idaho (1863).

jority notes, first enacted in 1857 and "has remained substantially unchanged to the present time." *Ante*, at ——.

There apparently was no question concerning the validity of this provision or of any of the other state statutes when the Fourteenth Amendment was adopted. The only conclusion possible from this history is that the drafters did not intend to have the Fourteenth Amendment withdraw from the States the power to legislate with respect to this matter.

III

Even if one were to agree that the case which the Court decides were here, and that the enunciation of the substantive constitutional law in the Court's opinion were proper, the actual disposition of the case by the Court is still difficult to justify. The Texas statute is struck down *in toto*, even though the Court apparently concedes that at later periods of pregnancy Texas might impose these self-same statutory limitations on abortion. My understanding of past practice is that a statute found to be invalid as applied to a particular plaintiff, but not unconstitutional as a whole, is not simply "struck down" but is instead declared unconstitutional as applied to the fact situation before the Court. *Yick Wo v. Hopkins*, 118 U.S. 356 (1886); *Street v. New York*, 394 U.S. 576 (1969).

For all of the foregoing reasons, I respectfully dissent.

5. Indiana (1838).
6. Iowa (1843).
7. Maine (1840).
8. Massachusetts (1845).
9. Michigan (1846).
10. Minnesota (1851).
11. Missouri (1835).
12. Montana (1864).
13. Nevada (1861).
14. New Hampshire (1848).
15. New Jersey (1849).
16. Ohio (1841).
17. Pennsylvania (1860).
18. Texas (1859).
19. Vermont (1867).
20. West Virginia (1848).
21. Wisconsin (1858).

No. 70–40

Mary Doe et al., Appellants, *v.* Arthur K. Bolton, as Attorney General of the State of Georgia, et al.	On Appeal from the United States District Court for the Northern District of Georgia.

[January 22, 1973]

Syllabus

Georgia law proscribes an abortion except as performed by a duly licensed Georgia physician when necessary in "his best clinical judgment" because continued pregnancy would endanger a pregnant woman's life or injure her health; the fetus would likely be born with serious defects; or the pregnancy resulted from rape. § 26-1202(a) of Ga. Criminal Code. In addition to a requirement that the patient be a Georgia resident and certain other requirements, the statutory scheme poses three procedural conditions in § 26-1202(b): (1) that the abortion be performed in a hospital accredited by the Joint Committee on Accreditation of Hospitals (JCAH); (2) that the procedure be approved by the hospital staff abortion committee; and (3) that the performing physician's judgment be confirmed by independent examinations of the patient by two other licensed physicians. Appellant Doe, an indigent married Georgia citizen, who was denied an abortion after eight weeks of pregnancy for failure to meet any of the § 26-1202(a) conditions, sought declaratory and injunctive relief, contending that the Georgia laws were unconstitutional. Others joining in the complaint included Georgia-licensed physicians (who claimed that the Georgia statutes "chilled and deferred" their practices), registered nurses, clergymen, and social workers. Though holding that all the plaintiffs had standing, the District Court ruled that only Doe presented a justiciable controversy. In Doe's case the court gave declaratory, but not injunctive, relief, invalidating as an infringement of privacy and personal liberty the limitation to the three situations specified in § 26-1202(a) and certain other provisions but holding that the State's interest in health protection and the existence of a "*potential* of independent human existence" justified regulation through § 26-1202(b) of the "manner of performance as well as the quality of the final decision to abort." The appellants, claiming entitlement to broader relief, directly appealed to this Court. *Held*:

1. Doe's case presents a live, justiciable controversy and she has standing to sue, *Roe v. Wade, ante*, p. ——, as do the physician-appellants (who, unlike the physician in *Wade*, were not charged with abortion violations), and it is therefore unnecessary to resolve the issue of the other appellants' standing.

2. A woman's constitutional right to an abortion is not absolute. *Roe v. Wade, supra*.

3. The requirement that a physician's decision to perform an abortion must rest upon "his best clinical judgment" of its necessity is not unconstitutionally vague, since that judgment may be made in the light of *all* the attendant circumstances. *United States v. Vuitch*, 402 U.S. 62, 71-72.

4. The three procedural conditions in § 26-1202(b) violate the Fourteenth Amendment.

(a) The JCAH accreditation requirement is invalid, since the State has not shown that only hospitals (let alone those with JCAH accreditation) meet its interest in fully protecting the patient; and a hospital requirement failing to exclude the first trimester of pregnancy would be invalid on that ground alone, see *Roe v. Wade, supra*.

(b) The interposition of a hospital committee on abortion, a procedure not applicable as a matter of state criminal law to other surgical situations, is unduly restrictive of the patient's rights, which are already safeguarded by her personal physician.

(c) Required acquiescence by two co-practitioners also has no rational connection with a patient's needs and unduly infringes on her physician's right to practice.

5. The Georgia residence requirement violates the Privileges and Immunities Clause by denying protection to persons who enter Georgia for medical services there.

6. Appellants' equal protection argument centering on the three procedural conditions in § 26-1202(b), invalidated on other grounds, is without merit.

7. No ruling is made on the question of injunctive relief. Cf. *Roe v. Wade, supra.*

319 F. Supp. 1048, modified and affirmed.

BLACKMUN, J., delivered the opinion of the Court, in which BURGER, C. J., and DOUGLAS, BRENNAN, STEWART, MARSHALL, and POWELL, J. J., joined. BURGER, C. J., and DOUGLAS and STEWART, J. J., filed concurring opinions. WHITE, J., filed a dissenting opinion, in which REHNQUIST, J., joined. REHNQUIST, J., filed a dissenting opinion.

MR. JUSTICE BLACKMUN delivered the opinion of the Court.

In this appeal the criminal abortion statutes recently enacted in Georgia are challenged on constitutional grounds. The statutes are §§ 26-1201 through 26-1203 of the State's Criminal Code, formulated by Georgia Laws, 1968 Session, 1249, 1277-1280. In *Roe v. Wade, ante* ——, we today have struck down, as constitutionally defective, the Texas criminal abortion statutes that are representative of provisions long in effect in a majority of our States. The Georgia legislation, however, is different and merits separate consideration.

I

The statutes in question are reproduced as Appendix A, *post* ——.[1] As the appellants acknowledge,[2] the 1968 statutes are patterned upon the American Law Institute's Model Penal Code, § 230.3 (Proposed Official Draft, 1962), reproduced as Appendix B, *post* ——. The ALI proposal has served as the model for recent legislation in approximately one-fourth of our States.[3] The new Georgia provisions replaced statutory law that had been in effect for more than 90 years. Georgia Laws 1876, No. 130, § 2, at 113.[4] The pre-

---

[1] The portions italicized in Appendix A are those held unconstitutional by the District Court.

[2] Appellants' Brief 25 n. 5; Tr. of Oral Arg. 9.

[3] See *Roe v. Wade, ante* —— n. 37.

[4] The active provisions of the 1876 statute were:

"Section I. *Be it enacted, etc.,* That from and after the passage of this Act, the wilful killing of an unborn child, so far developed as to be ordinarily called 'quick,' by any injury to the mother of such child, which would be murder if it resulted in the

decessor statute paralleled the Texas legislation considered in *Roe v. Wade, ante,* and made all abortions criminal except those necessary "to preserve the life" of the pregnant woman. The new statutes have not been tested on constitutional grounds in the Georgia state courts.

Section 26-1201, with a referenced exception, makes abortion a crime, and § 26-1203 provides that a person convicted of that crime shall be punished by imprisonment for not less than one nor more than 10 years. Section 26-1202(a) states the exception and removes from § 1201's definition of criminal abortion, and thus makes non-criminal, an abortion "performed by a physician duly licensed" in Georgia when, "based upon his best clinical judgment . . . an abortion is necessary because

"(1) A continuation of the pregnancy would endanger the life of the pregnant woman or would seriously and permanently injure her health, or
"(2) The fetus would very likely be born with a grave, permanent, and irremediable mental or physical defect, or
"(3) The pregnancy resulted from forcible or statutory rape."[5]

Section 26-1202 also requires, by numbered subdivisions of its subsection (b), that, for an abortion to be authorized or performed as

---

death of such mother, shall be guilty of a felony, and punishable by death or imprisonment for life, as the jury trying the case may recommend.

"Sec. II. *Be it further enacted,* That every person who shall administer to any woman pregnant with a child, any medicine, drug, or substance whatever, or shall use or employ any instrument or other means, with intent thereby to destroy such child, unless the same shall have been necessary to preserve the life of such mother, or shall have been advised by two physicians to be necessary for such purpose, shall, in case the death of such child or mother be thereby produced, be declared guilty of an assault with intent to murder.

"Sec. III. *Be it further enacted,* That any person who shall wilfully administer to any pregnant woman any medicine, drug or substance, or anything whatever, or shall employ any instrument or means whatever, with intent thereby to procure the miscarriage or abortion of any such woman, unless the same shall have been necessary to preserve the life of such woman, or shall have been advised by two physicians to be necessary for that purpose, shall, upon conviction, be punished as prescribed in section 4310 of the Revised Code of Georgia."

It should be noted that the second section, in contrast to the first, makes no specific reference to quickening. The section was construed, however, to possess this line of demarcation. *Taylor v. State,* 105 Ga. 846, 33 S. E. 190 (1899).

[5] In contrast with the ALI model, the Georgia statute makes no specific reference to pregnancy resulting from incest. We were assured by the State at reargument that this was because the statute's reference to "rape" was intended to include incest. Tr. of Rearg. 32.

a noncriminal procedure, additional conditions must be fulfilled. These are (1) and (2) residence of the woman in Georgia; (3) reduction to writing of the performing physician's medical judgment that an abortion is justified for one or more of the reasons specified by § 26-1202(a), with written concurrence in that judgment by at least two other Georgia-licensed physicians, based upon their separate personal medical examinations of the woman; (4) performance of the abortion in a hospital licensed by the State Board of Health and also accredited by the Joint Commission on Accreditation of Hospitals; (5) advance approval by an abortion committee of not less than three members of the hospital's staff; (6) certifications in a rape situation; and (7), (8), and (9) maintenance and confidentiality of records. There is a provision (subsection (c)) for judicial determination of the legality of a proposed abortion on petition of the judicial circuit law officer or of a close relative, as therein defined, of the unborn child, and for expeditious hearing of that petition. There is also a provision (subsection (e)) giving a hospital the right not to admit an abortion patient and giving any physician and any hospital employee or staff member the right, on moral or religious grounds, not to participate in the procedure.

II

On April 16, 1970, Mary Doe,[6] 23 other individuals (nine described as Georgia-licensed physicians, seven as nurses registered in the State, five as clergymen, and two as social workers), and two nonprofit Georgia corporations that advocate abortion reform, instituted this federal action in the Northern District of Georgia against the State's attorney general, the district attorney of Fulton County, and the chief of police of the city of Atlanta. The plaintiffs sought a declaratory judgment that the Georgia abortion statutes were unconstitutional in their entirety. They also sought injunctive relief restraining the defendants and their successors from enforcing the statutes.

Mary Doe alleged:

(1) She was a 22-year-old Georgia citizen, married, and nine weeks pregnant. She had three living children. The two older

---

[6] Appellants by their complaint, Appendix 7, allege that the name is a pseudonym.

ones had been placed in a foster home because of Doe's poverty and inability to care for them. The youngest, born July 19, 1969, had been placed for adoption. Her husband had recently abandoned her and she was forced to live with her indigent parents and their eight children. She and her husband, however, had become reconciled. He was a construction worker employed only sporadically. She had been a mental patient at the State Hospital. She had been advised that an abortion could be performed on her with less danger to her health than if she gave birth to the child she was carrying. She would be unable to care for or support the new child.

(2) On March 25, 1970, she applied to the Abortion Committee of Grady Memorial Hospital, Atlanta, for a therapeutic abortion under § 26-1202. Her application was denied 16 days later, on April 10, when she was eight weeks pregnant, on the ground that her situation was not one described in § 26-1202(a).[7]

(3) Because her application was denied, she was forced either to relinquish 'her right to decide when and how many children she will bear' or to seek an abortion that was illegal under the Georgia statutes. This invaded her rights of privacy and liberty in matters related to family, marriage, and sex, and deprived her of the right to choose whether to bear children. This was a violation of rights guaranteed her by the First, Fourth, Fifth, Ninth, and Fourteenth Amendments. The statutes also denied her equal protection and procedural due process and, because they were unconstitutionally vague, deterred hospitals and doctors from performing abortions. She sued 'on her own behalf and on behalf of all others similarly situated.'

The other plaintiffs alleged that the Georgia statutes "chilled and deterred" them from practicing their respective professions and deprived them of rights guaranteed by the First, Fourth, and Fourteenth Amendments. These plaintiffs also purported to sue on their own behalf and on behalf of others similarly situated.

A three-judge district court was convened. An offer of proof as to Doe's identity was made, but the court deemed it unnecessary to receive that proof. The case was then tried on the pleadings and interrogatories.

The District Court, *per curiam*, 319 F. Supp. 1048 (ND Ga. 1970), held that all the plaintiffs had standing but that only Doe presented a justiciable controversy. On the merits, the court concluded that the limitation in the Georgia statute of the "number of

---

[7] In answers to interrogatories Doe stated that her application for an abortion was approved at Georgia Baptist Hospital on May 5, 1970, but that she was not approved as a charity patient there and had no money to pay for an abortion. Appendix 64.

reasons for which an abortion may be sought," *id.*, at 1056, improperly restricted Doe's rights of privacy articulated in *Griswold v. Connecticut*, 381 U.S. 479 (1965), and of "personal liberty," both of which it thought "broad enough to include the decision to abort a pregnancy," *id.*, at 1055. As a consequence, the court held invalid those portions of §§ 26-1202(a) and (b)(3) limiting legal abortions to the three situations specified; § 26-1202(b)(6) relating to certifications in a rape situation; and § 26-1202(c) authorizing a court test. Declaratory relief was granted accordingly. The court, however, held that Georgia's interest in protection of health, and the existence of a *"potential* of independent human existence" (emphasis in original), *id.*, at 1055, justified state regulation of "the manner of performance as well as the quality of the final decision to abort," *id.*, at 1056, and it refused to strike down the other provisions of the statutes. It denied the request for an injunction, *id.*, at 1057.

Claiming that they were entitled to an injunction and to broader relief, the plaintiffs took a direct appeal pursuant to 28 U.S.C. § 1253. We postponed decision on jurisdiction to the hearing on the merits. 402 U.S. 941 (1971). The defendants also purported to appeal, pursuant to § 1253, but their appeal was dismissed for want of jurisdiction. 402 U.S. 936 (1971). We are advised by the defendant-appellees, Brief 42, that an alternative appeal on their part is pending in the United States Court of Appeals for the Fifth Circuit. The extent, therefore, to which the District Court decision was adverse to the defendants, that is, the extent to which portions of the Georgia statutes were held to be unconstitutional, technically is not now before us.[8] *Swarb v. Lennox*, 405 U.S. 191, 201 (1972).

III

Our decision in *Roe v. Wade, ante* ——, establishes (1) that, despite her pseudonym, we may accept as true, for this case, Mary Doe's existence and her pregnant state on April 16, 1970; (2) that the constitutional issue is substantial; (3) that the interim termination of Doe's and all other Georgia pregnancies in existence in 1970 has not rendered the case moot; and (4) that Doe presents a justiciable controversy and has standing to maintain the action.

---

[8] What we decide today obviously has implications for the issues raised in the defendants' appeal pending in the Fifth Circuit.

Inasmuch as Doe and her class are recognized, the question whether the other appellants — physicians, nurses, clergymen, social workers, and corporations — present a justiciable controversy and have standing is perhaps a matter of no great consequence. We conclude, however, that the physician-appellants, who are Georgia-licensed doctors consulted by pregnant women, also present a justiciable controversy and do have standing despite the fact that the record does not disclose that any one of them has been prosecuted, or threatened with prosecution, for violation of the State's abortion statutes. The physician is the one against whom these criminal statutes directly operate in the event he procures an abortion that does not meet the statutory exceptions and conditions. The physician-appellants, therefore, assert a sufficiently direct threat of personal detriment. They should not be required to await and undergo the criminal prosecution as the sole means of seeking relief. *Crossen v. Breckenridge*, 446 F. 2d 833, 839-840 (CA6 1971); *Poe v. Menghini*, 339 F. Supp. 986, 990-991 (Kans. 1972).

In holding that the physicians, while theoretically possessed of standing, did not present a justiciable controversy, the District Court seems to have relied primarily on *Poe v. Ullman*, 367 U.S. 497 (1961). There a sharply divided Court dismissed an appeal from a state court on the ground that it presented no real controversy justifying the adjudication of a constitutional issue. But the challenged Connecticut statute, deemed to prohibit the giving of medical advice on the use of contraceptives, had been enacted in 1879, and, apparently with a single exception, no one had ever been prosecuted under it. Georgia's statute, in contrast, is recent and not moribund. Furthermore, it is the successor to another Georgia abortion statute under which, we are told,[9] physicians were prosecuted. The present case, therefore, is closer to *Epperson v. Arkansas*, 393 U.S. 97 (1968), where the Court recognized the right of a school teacher, though not yet charged criminally, to challenge her State's anti-evolution statute. See also *Griswold v. Connecticut*, 381 U.S., at 481.

The parallel claims of the nurse, clergy, social worker, and corporation-appellants are another step removed and as to them, the Georgia statutes operate less directly. Not being licensed physicians, the nurses and the others are in no position to render medical advice.

---

[9] Tr. of Oral Arg. 21-22.

They would be reached by the abortion statutes only in their capacity as accessories or as counselor-conspirators. We conclude that we need not pass upon the status of these additional appellants in this suit, for the issues are sufficiently and adequately presented by Doe and the physician-appellants, and nothing is gained or lost by the presence or absence of the nurses, the clergymen, the social workers, and the corporations. See *Roe v. Wade, ante,* at ———.

IV

The appellants attack on several grounds those portions of the Georgia abortion statutes that remain after the District Court decision: undue restriction of a right to personal and marital privacy; vagueness; deprivation of substantive and procedural due process; improper restriction to Georgia residents; and denial of equal protection.

A. *Roe v. Wade, ante,* sets forth our conclusion that a pregnant woman does not have an absolute constitutional right to an abortion on her demand. What is said there is applicable here and need not be repeated.

B. The appellants go on to argue, however, that the present Georgia statutes must be viewed historically, that is, from the fact that prior to the 1968 Act an abortion in Georgia was not criminal if performed to "preserve the life" of the mother. It is suggested that the present statute, as well, has this emphasis on the mother's rights, not on those of the fetus. Appellants contend that it is thus clear that Georgia has given little, and certainly not first, consideration to the unborn child. Yet it is the unborn child's rights that Georgia asserts in justification of the statute. Appellants assert that this justification cannot be advanced at this late date.

Appellants then argue that the statutes do not adequately protect the woman's right. This is so because it would be physically and emotionally damaging to Doe to bring a child into her poor "fatherless"[10] family, and because advances in medicine and medical techniques have made it safer for a woman to have a medically induced abortion than for her to bear a child. Thus, "a statute which requires a woman to carry an unwanted pregnancy to term infringes

---

[10] Appellants' Brief 25.

not only on a fundamental right of privacy but on the right to life itself." Brief 27.

The appellants recognize that a century ago medical knowledge was not so advanced as it is today, that the techniques of antisepsis were not known, and that any abortion procedure was dangerous for the woman. To restrict the legality of the abortion to the situation where it was deemed necessary, in medical judgment, for the preservation of the woman's life was only a natural conclusion in the exercise of the legislative judgment of that time. A State is not to be reproached, however, for a past judgmental determination made in the light of then-existing medical knowledge. It is perhaps unfair to argue, as the appellants do, that because the early focus was on the preservation of the woman's life, the State's present professed interest in the protection of embryonic and fetal life is to be downgraded. That argument denies the State the right to readjust its views and emphases in the light of the advanced knowledge and techniques of the day.

C. Appellants argue that § 26-1202(a) of the Georgia statute, as it has been left by the District Court's decision, is unconstitutionally vague. This argument centers in the proposition that, with the District Court's having stricken the statutorily specified reasons, it still remains a crime for a physician to perform an abortion except when, as § 26-1202(a) reads, it is "based upon his best clinical judgment that an abortion is necessary." The appellants contend that the word "necessary" does not warn the physician of what conduct is proscribed; that the statute is wholly without objective standards and is subject to diverse interpretation; and that doctors will choose to err on the side of caution and will be arbitrary.

The net result of the District Court's decision is that the abortion determination, so far as the physician is concerned, is made in the exercise of his professional, that is, his "best clinical" judgment in the light of *all* the attendant circumstances. He is not now restricted to the three situations originally specified. Instead, he may range farther afield wherever his medical judgment, properly and professionally exercised, so dictates and directs him.

The vagueness argument is set at rest by the decision in *United States v. Vuitch*, 402 U.S. 62, 71-72 (1971), where the issue was raised with respect to a District of Columbia statute making abortions criminal "unless the same were done as necessary for the preservation of the mother's life or health and under the direction of a competent licensed practitioner of medicine." That statute has been construed to bear upon psychological as well as physical well-being. This being so, the Court concluded that the term "health" presented no problem of vagueness. "Indeed, whether a particular operation is necessary for a patient's physical or mental health is a judgment that physicians are obviously called upon to make routinely whenever surgery is considered." 402 U.S., at 72. This conclusion is equally applicable here. Whether, in the words of the Georgia statute, "an abortion is necessary," is a professional judgment that the Georgia physician will be called upon to make routinely.

We agree with the District Court, 319 F. Supp., at 1058, that the medical judgment may be exercised in the light of all factors — physical, emotional, psychological, familial, and the woman's age — relevant to the well-being of the patient. All these factors may relate to health. This allows the attending physician the room he needs to make his best medical judgment. And it is room that operates for the benefit, not the disadvantage, of the pregnant woman.

D. The appellants next argue that the District Court should have declared unconstitutional three procedural demands of the Georgia statute: (1) that the abortion be performed in a hospital accredited by the Joint Commission on Accreditation of Hospitals:[11] (2) that the procedure be approved by the hospital staff abortion committee; and (3) that the performing physician's judgment be confirmed by the independent examinations of the patient by two other licensed physicians. The appellants attack these provisions not only on the ground that they unduly restrict the woman's right of privacy, but also on procedural due process and equal protection grounds. The physician-appellants also argue that, by subjecting a doctor's individual medical judgment to committee approval and to confirming consultations, the statute impermissibly restricts the physician's right to practice his profession and deprives him of due process.

1. *JCAH Accreditation.* The Joint Commission on Accreditation of Hospitals is an organization without governmental sponsorship or overtones. No question whatever is raised concerning the

[11] We were advised at reargument, Tr. of Rearg. 10, that only 54 of Georgia's 159 counties have a JCAH accredited hospital.

integrity of the organization or the high purpose of the accreditation process.[12] That process, however, has to do with hospital standards generally and has no present particularized concern with abortion as a medical or surgical procedure.[13] In Georgia there is no restriction of the performance of non-abortion surgery in a hospital not yet accredited by the JCAH so long as other requirements imposed by the State, such as licensing of the hospital and of the operating surgeon, are met. See Georgia Code §§ 88-1901(a) and 88-1905 (1971) and 84-907 (Supp. 1971). Furthermore, accreditation by the Commission is not granted until a hospital has been in operation at least one year. The Model Penal Code, § 230.3, Appendix B hereto, contains no requirement for JCAH accreditation. And the Uniform Abortion Act (Final Draft, August 1971),[14] approved by the American Bar Association in February 1972, contains no JCAH accredited hospital specification.[15] Some courts have held

---

[12] Since its founding, JCAH has pursued the "elusive goal" of defining the "optimal setting" for "quality of service in hospitals." JCAH, Accreditation Manual for Hospitals, Foreword (Dec. 1970). The Manual's Introduction states the organization's purpose to establish standards and conduct accreditation programs that will afford quality medical care "to give patients the optimal benefits that medical science has to offer." This ambitious and admirable goal is illustrated by JCAH's decision in 1966 "to raise and strengthen the standards from their present level of minimum essential to the level of optimum achievable . . . ." Some of these "optimum achievable" standards required are: disclosure of hospital ownership and control; a dietetic service and written dietetic policies; a written disaster plan for mass emergencies; a nuclear medical services program; facilities for hematology, chemistry, microbiology, clinical microscopy, and sero-immunology; a professional library and document delivery service; a radiology program; a social services plan administered by a qualified social worker; and a special care unit.

[13] "The Joint Commission neither advocates nor opposes any particular position with respect to elective abortions." Letter dated July 9, 1971, from John L. Brewer, M. D. Commissioner, JCAH, to the Rockefeller Foundation. Brief for *amici*, American College of Obstetricians and Gynecologists, et al., p. A-3.

[14] See *Roe v. Wade, ante* ——, n. 49.

[15] Some state statutes do not have the JCAH accreditation requirement. Alaska Stat. § 11.15.060 (1970); Hawaii Rev. Stat. § 453.16 (Supp. 1971); N. Y. Penal Code § 125.05.3 (McKinney Supp. 1972-1973). Washington has the requirement but couples it with the alternative of "a medical facility approved . . . by the state board of health." Wash. Rev. Code § 9.02.070 (Supp. 1972). Florida's new statute has a similar provision. Law of Apr. 13, 1972, c. 72-196, § 1 (2). Others contain the specification. Ark. Stat. Ann. §§ 41-303 to 41-310 (Supp. 1971); Cal. Health and Safety Code §§ 25950-25955.5 (West Supp. 1972); Colo. Rev. Stats. Ann. §§ 40-2-50 to 40-2-53 (Perm. Cum. Supp. 1967); Kan. Stat. Ann § 21-3047 (Supp. 1971); Md. Ann. Code Art. 43, §§ 137-139 (Repl. 1971). Cf. Del. Code Ann. § 1790-1793 (Supp. 1970) specifying "a nationally recognized medical or hospital accreditation authority," § 1790 (a).

that a JCAH accreditation requirement is an overbroad infringement of fundamental rights because it does not relate to the particular medical problems and dangers of the abortion operation. *Poe v.*
Menghini, 339 F. Supp. 986, 993-994 (Kan. 1972); *People v. Barks-*
dale, 96 Cal. Rptr. 265, 273-274 (Cal. App. 1971).

We hold that the JCAH accreditation requirement does not withstand constitutional scrutiny in the present context. It is a requirement that simply is not "based on differences that are reasonably
related to the purposes of the Act in which it is found." *Morey v.*
Doud, 354 U.S. 457, 465 (1957).

This is not to say that Georgia may not or should not, from and
after the end of the first trimester, adopt standards for licensing all
facilities where abortions may be performed so long as those standards are legitimately related to the objective the State seeks to accomplish. The appellants contend that such a relationship would be
lacking even in a lesser requirement that an abortion be performed
in a licensed hospital, as opposed to a facility, such as a clinic, that
may be required by the State to possess all the staffing and services
necessary to perform an abortion safely (including those adequate to
handle serious complications or other emergency, or arrangements
with a nearby hospital to provide such services). Appellants and
various *amici* have presented us with a mass of data purporting to
demonstrate that some facilities other than hospitals are entirely adequate to perform abortions if they possess these qualifications. The
State, on the other hand, has not presented persuasive data to show
that only hospitals meet its acknowledged interest in insuring the
quality of the operation and the full protection of the patient. We
feel compelled to agree with appellants that the State must show
more than it has in order to prove that only the full resources of a
licensed hospital, rather than those of some other appropriately licensed institution, satisfy these health interests. We hold that the
hospital requirement of the Georgia law, because it fails to exclude
the first trimester of pregnancy, see *Roe v. Wade, ante,* p. ——, is
also invalid. In so holding we naturally express no opinion on the
medical judgment involved in any particular case, that is, whether
the patient's situation is such that an abortion should be performed
in a hospital rather than in some other facility.

2. *Committee Approval.* The second aspect of the appellants'
procedural attack relates to the hospital abortion committee and to

the pregnant woman's asserted lack of access to that committee. Relying primarily on *Goldberg v. Kelly*, 397 U.S. 254 (1970), concerning the termination of welfare benefits, and *Wisconsin v. Constantineau*, 400 U.S. 433 (1971), concerning the posting of an alcoholic's name, Doe first argues that she was denied due process because she could not make a presentation to the committee. It is not clear from the record, however, whether Doe's own consulting physician was or was not a member of the committee or did or did not present her case, or, indeed, whether she herself was or was not there. We see nothing in the Georgia statute that explicitly denies access to the committee by or on behalf of the woman. If the access point alone were involved, we would not be persuaded to strike down the committee provision on the unsupported assumption that access is not provided.

Appellants attack the discretion the statute leaves to the committee. The most concrete argument they advance is their suggestion that it is still a badge of infamy "in many minds" to bear an illegitimate child, and that the Georgia system enables the committee members' personal views as to extramarital sex relations, and punishment therefor, to govern their decisions. This approach obviously is one founded on suspicion and one that discloses a lack of confidence in the integrity of physicians. To say that physicians will be guided in their hospital committee decisions by their predilections on extramarital sex unduly narrows the issue to pregnancy outside marriage. (Doe's own situation did not involve extramarital sex and its product.) The appellants' suggestion is necessarily somewhat degrading to the conscientious physician, particularly the obstetrician, whose professional activity is concerned with the physical and mental welfare, the woes, the emotions, and the concern of his female patients. He, perhaps more than anyone else, is knowledgeable in this area of patient care, and he is aware of human frailty, so-called "error," and needs. The good physician — despite the presence of rascals in the medical profession, as in all others, we trust that most physicians are "good" — will have a sympathy and an understanding for the pregnant patient that probably is not exceeded by those who participate in other areas of professional counseling.

It is perhaps worth noting that the abortion committee has a function of its own. It is a committee of the hospital and it is composed of members of the institution's medical staff. The membership usually is a changing one. In this way its work burden is shared and is more readily accepted. The committee's function is protective. It enables the hospital appropriately to be advised that its posture and activities are in accord with legal requirements. It is to be remembered that the hospital is an entity and that it, too, has legal rights and legal obligations.

Saying all this, however, does not settle the issue of the constitutional propriety of the committee requirement. Viewing the Georgia statute as a whole, we see no constitutionally justifiable pertinence in the structure for the advance approval by the abortion committee. With regard to the protection of potential life, the medical judgment is already completed prior to the committee stage, and review by a committee once removed from diagnosis is basically redundant. We are not cited to any other surgical procedure made subject to committee approval as a matter of state criminal law. The woman's right to receive medical care in accordance with her licensed physician's best judgment and the physician's right to administer it are substantially limited by this statutorily imposed overview. And the hospital itself is otherwise fully protected. Under § 26-1202(e) the hospital is free not to admit a patient for an abortion. It is even free not to have an abortion committee. Further, a physician or any other employee has the right to refrain, for moral or religious reasons, from participating in the abortion procedure. These provisions obviously are in the statute in order to afford appropriate protection to the individual and to the denominational hospital. Section 26-1202(e) affords adequate protection to the hospital and little more is provided by the committee prescribed by § 26-1202(b)(5).

We conclude that the interposition of the hospital abortion committee is unduly restrictive of the patient's rights and needs that, at this point, have already been medically delineated and substantiated by her personal physician. To ask more serves neither the hospital nor the State.

3. *Two-Doctor Concurrence.* The third aspects of the appellants' attack centers on the "time and availability of adequate medical facilities and personnel." It is said that the system imposes substantial and irrational roadblocks and "is patently unsuited" to prompt determination of the abortion decision. Time, of course, is

critical in abortion. Risks during the first trimester of pregnancy are admittedly lower than during later months.

The appellants purport to show by a local study[16] of Grady Memorial Hospital (serving indigent residents in Fulton and DeKalb Counties) that the "mechanics of the system itself forced . . . discontinuation of the abortion process" because the median time for the workup was 15 days. The same study shows, however, that 27% of the candidates for abortion were already 13 or more weeks pregnant at the time of application, that is, they were at the end of or beyond the first trimester when they made their applications. It is too much to say, as appellants do, that these particular persons "were victims of [a] system over which they [had] no control." If higher risk was incurred because of abortions in the second rather than the first trimester, much of that risk was due to delay in application, and not to the alleged cumbersomeness of the system. We note, in passing, that appellant Doe had no delay problem herself; the decision in her case was made well within the first trimester.

It should be manifest that our rejection of the accredited hospital requirement and, more important, of the abortion committee's advance approval eliminates the major grounds of the attack based on the system's delay and the lack of facilities. There remains, however, the required confirmation by two Georgia-licensed physicians in addition to the recommendation of the pregnant woman's own consultant (making under the statute, a total of six physicians involved, including the three on the hospital's abortion committee). We conclude that this provision, too, must fall.

The statute's emphasis, as has been repetitively noted, is on the attending physician's "best clinical judgment that an abortion is necessary." That should be sufficient. The reasons for the presence of the confirmation step in the statute are perhaps apparent, but they are insufficient to withstand constitutional challenge. Again, no other voluntary medical or surgical procedure for which Georgia requires confirmation by two other physicians has been cited to us. If a physician is licensed by the State, he is recognized by the State as capable of exercising acceptable clinical judgment. If he fails in this, professional censure or deprivation of his license are avail-

---

16 L. Baker & M. Freeman, Abortion Surveillance at Grady Memorial Hospital Center for Disease Control (June and July 1971) (U. S. Dept. of HEW, PHS).

able remedies. Required acquiescence by co-practitioners has no rational connection with a patient's needs and unduly infringes on the physician's right to practice. The attending physician will know when a consultation is advisable — the doubtful situation, the need for assurance when the medical decision is a delicate one, and the like. Physicians have followed this routine historically and know its usefulness and benefit for all concerned. It is still true today that "[r]eliance must be placed upon the assurance given by his license, issued by an authority competent to judge in that respect, that he [the physician] possesses the requisite qualifications." *Dent v. West Virginia*, 129 U.S. 114, 122-123 (1889). See *United States v. Vuitch*, 402 U.S., at 71.

E. The appellants attack the residency requirement of the Georgia law, §§ 26-1202(b)(1) and (b)(2), as violative of the right to travel stressed in *Shapiro v. Thompson*, 394 U.S. 618, 629-631 (1969), and other cases. A requirement of this kind, of course, could be deemed to have some relationship to the availability of post-procedure medical care for the aborted patient.

Nevertheless, we do not uphold the constitutionality of the residence requirement. It is not based on any policy of preserving state-supported facilities for Georgia residents, for the bar also applies to private hospitals and to privately retained physicians. There is no intimation, either, that Georgia facilities are utilized to capacity in caring for Georgia residents. Just as the Privileges and Immunities Clause, Const. Art. IV, § 2, protects persons who enter other States to ply their trade, *Ward v. Maryland*, 79 U.S. (12 Wall.) 418, 430 (1870); *Blake v. McClung*, 172 U.S. 239, 248-256 (1898), so must it protect persons who enter Georgia seeking the medical services that are available there. See *Toomer v. Witsell*, 334 U.S. 385, 396-397 (1948). A contrary holding would mean that a State could limit to its own residents the general medical care available within its borders. This we could not approve.

F. The last argument on this phase of the case is one that often is made, namely, that the Georgia system is violative of equal protection because it discriminates against the poor. The appellants do not urge that abortions should be performed by persons other than licensed physicians, so we have no argument that because the wealthy can better afford physicians, the poor should have non-physicians made available to them. The appellants acknowledged that the procedures are "nondiscriminatory in . . . express terms" but they suggest that they have produced invidious discriminations. The District Court rejected this approach out of hand. 319 F. Supp., at 1056. It rests primarily on the accreditation and approval and confirmation requirements, discussed above, and on the assertion that most of Georgia's counties have no accredited hospital. We have set aside the accreditation, approval, and confirmation requirements, however, and with that, the discrimination argument collapses in all significant aspects.

V

The appellants complain, finally, of the District Court's denial of injunctive relief. A like claim was made in *Roe v. Wade, ante.* We declined decision there insofar as injunctive relief was concerned, and we decline it here. We assume that Georgia's prosecutorial authorities will give full recognition to the judgment of this Court.

In summary, we hold that the JCAH accredited hospital provision and the requirements as to approval by the hospital abortion committee, as to confirmation by two independent physicians, and as to residence in Georgia are all violative of the Fourteenth Amendment. Specifically, the following portions of § 26-1202(b), remaining after the District Court's judgment, are invalid:

(1) Subsections (1) and (2).

(2) That portion of Subsection (3) following the words "such physician's judgment is reduced to writing."

(3) Subsections (4) and (5).

The judgment of the District Court is modified accordingly and, as so modified, is affirmed. Costs are allowed to the appellants.

Criminal Code of Georgia

(The italicized portions are those held unconstitutional by the District Court)

CHAPTER 26–12. ABORTION.

26-1201. Criminal Abortion. Except as otherwise provided in section 26-1202, a person commits criminal abortion when he administers any medicine, drug or other substance whatever to any woman or when he uses any instrument or other means whatever upon any woman with intent to produce a miscarriage or abortion.

26-1202. Exception. (a) Section 26-1201 shall not apply to an abortion performed by a physician duly licensed to practice medicine and surgery pursuant to Chapter 84-9 or 84-12 of the Code of Georgia of 1933, as amended, based upon his best clinical judgment that an abortion is necessary *because:*

(1) *A continuation of the pregnancy would endanger the life of the pregnant woman or would seriously and permanently injure her health; or*

(2) *The fetus would very likely be born with a grave, permanent, and irremediable mental or physical defect; or*

(3) *The pregnancy resulted from forcible or statutory rape.*

(b) No abortion is authorized or shall be performed under this section unless each of the following conditions is met;

(1) The pregnant woman requesting the abortion certifies in writing under oath and subject to the penalties of false swearing to the physician who proposes to perform the abortion that she is a bona fide legal resident of the State of Georgia.

(2) The physician certifies that he believes the woman is a bona fide resident of this State and that he has no information which should lead him to believe otherwise.

(3) Such physician's judgment is reduced to writing and concurred in by at least two other physicians duly licensed to practice medicine and surgery pursuant to Chapter 84-9 of the Code of Georgia of 1933, as amended, who certify in writing that based upon their separate personal medical examinations of the pregnant woman, the abortion is, in their judgment, necessary *because of one or more of the reasons enumerated above.*

(4) Such abortion is performed in a hospital licensed by the State Board of Health and accredited by the Joint Commission on Accreditation of Hospitals.

(5) The performance of the abortion has been approved in advance by a committee of the medical staff of the hospital in which the operation is to be performed. This committee must be one established and maintained in accordance with the standards promulgated by the Joint Commission on the Accreditation of Hospitals, and its approval must be by a majority vote of a membership of not less than three members of the hospital's staff; the physician proposing to perform the operation may not be counted as a member of the committee for this purpose.

(6) *If the proposed abortion is considered necessary because the woman has been raped, the woman makes a written statement under oath, and subject to the penalties of false swearing, of the date, time and place of the rape and the name of the rapist, if known. There must be attached to this statement a certified copy of any report of the rape made by any law enforcement officer or agency and a statement by the solicitor general of the judicial circuit where the rape occurred or allegedly occurred that, according to his best information, there is probable cause to believe that the rape did occur.*

(7) Such written opinions, statements, certificates, and concurrences are maintained in the permanent files of such hospital and are available at all reasonable times to the solicitor general of the judicial circuit in which the hospital is located.

(8) A copy of such written opinions, statements, certificates, and concurrences is filed with the Director of the State Department of Public Health within ten (10) days after such operation is performed.

(9) All written opinions, statements, certificates, and concurrences filed and maintained pursuant to paragraphs (7) and (8) of

this subsection shall be confidential records and shall not be made available for public inspection at any time.

(*c*) *Any solicitor general of the judicial circuit in which an abortion is to be performed under this section, or any person who would be a relative of the child within the second degree of consanguinity, may petition the superior court of the county in which the abortion is to be performed for a declaratory judgment whether the performance of such abortion would violate any constitutional or other legal rights of the fetus. Such solicitor general may also petition such court for the purpose of taking issue with compliance with the requirements of this section. The physician who proposes to perform the abortion and the pregnant woman shall be respondents. The petition shall be heard expeditiously and if the court adjudges that such abortion would violate the constitutional or other legal rights of the fetus, the court shall so declare and shall restrain the physician from performing the abortion.*

(d) If an abortion is performed in compliance with this section, the death of the fetus shall not give rise to any claim for wrongful death.

(e) Nothing in this section shall require a hospital to admit any patient under the provisions hereof for the purpose of performing an abortion, nor shall any hospital be required to appoint a committee such as contemplated under subsection (b)(5). A physician, or any other person who is a member of or associated with the staff of a hospital, or any employee of a hospital in which an abortion has been authorized, who shall state in writing an objection to such abortion on moral or religious grounds shall not be required to participate in the medical procedures which will result in the abortion, and the refusal of any such person to participate therein shall not form the basis of any claim for damages on account of such refusal or for any disciplinary or recriminatory action against such person.

26-1203. Punishment. A person convicted of criminal abortion shall be punished by imprisonment for not less than one nor more than 10 years.

APPENDIX B

American Law Institute

MODEL PENAL CODE

Section 230.3. Abortion.

(1) *Unjustified Abortion.* A person who purposely and unjustifiably terminates the pregnancy of another otherwise than by a live birth commits a felony of the third degree or, where the pregnancy has continued beyond the twenty-sixth week, a felony of the second degree.

(2) *Justifiable Abortion.* A licensed physician is justified in terminating a pregnancy if he believes there is substantial risk that continuance of the pregnancy would gravely impair the physical or mental health of the mother or that the child would be born with grave physical or mental defect, or that the pregnancy resulted from rape, incest, or other felonious intercourse. All illicit intercourse with a girl below the age of 16 shall be deemed felonious for purposes of this subsection. Justifiable abortions shall be performed only in a licensed hospital except in case of emergency when hospital facilities are unavailable. [Additional exceptions from the requirement of hospitalization may be incorporated here to take account of situations in sparsely settled areas where hospitals are not generally accessible.]

(3) *Physicians' Certificates; Presumption from Non-Compliance.* No abortion shall be performed unless two physicians, one of whom may be the person performing the abortion, shall have certified in writing the circumstances which they believe to justify the abortion. Such certificate shall be submitted before the abortion to the hospital where it is to be performed and, in the case of

abortion following felonious intercourse, to the prosecuting attorney or the police. Failure to comply with any of the requirements of this Subsection gives rise to a presumption that the abortion was un-justified.

(4) *Self-Abortion.* A woman whose pregnancy has contin-ued beyond the twenty-sixth week commits a felony of the third de-gree if she purposely terminates her own pregnancy otherwise than by a live birth, or if she uses instruments, drugs or violence upon her-self for that purpose. Except as justified under Subsection (2), a person who induces or knowingly aids a woman to use instruments, drugs or violence upon herself for the purpose of terminating her pregnancy otherwise than by a live birth commits a felony of the third degree whether or not the pregnancy has continued beyond the twenty-sixth week.

(5) *Pretended Abortion.* A person commits a felony of the third degree if, representing that it is his purpose to perform an abor-tion, he does an act adapted to cause abortion in a pregnant woman although the woman is in fact not pregnant, or the actor does not believe she is. A person charged with unjustified abortion under Subsection (1) or an attempt to commit that offense may be convicted thereof upon proof of conduct prohibited by this Subsection.

(6) *Distribution of Abortifacients.* A person who sells, of-fers to sell, possesses with intent to sell, advertises, or displays for sale anything specially designed to terminate a pregnancy, or held out by the actor as useful for that purpose, commits a misdemeanor, unless:

(a) the sale, offer or display is to a physician or druggist or to an intermediary in a chain of distribution to physicians or drug-gists; or

(b) the sale is made upon prescription or order of a physi-cian; or

(c) the possession is with intent to sell as authorized in paragraphs (a) and (b); or

(d) the advertising is addressed to persons named in para-graph (a) and confined to trade or professional channels not likely to reach the general public.

(7) *Section Inapplicable to Prevention of Pregnancy.* Noth-ing in this Section shall be deemed applicable to the prescription, ad-

ministration or distribution of drugs or other substances for avoiding pregnancy, whether by preventing implantation of a fertilized ovum or by any other method that operates before, at or immediately after fertilization.

Nos. 70–18 AND 70–40

MR. CHIEF JUSTICE BURGER, concurring.

I agree that, under the Fourteenth Amendment to the Constitution, the abortion statutes of Georgia and Texas impermissibly limit the performance of abortions necessary to protect the health of pregnant women, using the term health in its broadest medical context. See *Vuitch v. United States*, 402 U.S. 62, 71–72 (1971). I am somewhat troubled that the Court has taken notice of various scientific and medical data in reaching its conclusion; however, I do not believe that the Court has exceeded the scope of judicial notice accepted in other contexts.

In oral argument, counsel for the State of Texas informed the Court that early abortive procedures were routinely permitted in certain exceptional cases, such as nonconsensual pregnancies resulting from rape and incest. In the face of a rigid and narrow statute, such as that of Texas, no one in these circumstances should be placed in a posture of dependence on a prosecutorial policy or prosecutorial discretion. Of course, States must have broad power, within the limits indicated in the opinions, to regulate the subject of abortions, but where the consequences of state intervention are so severe, uncertainty must be avoided as much as possible. For my part, I would be inclined to allow a State to require the certification of two physicians to support an abortion, but the Court holds otherwise. I do not believe that such a procedure is unduly burdensome, as are the complex steps of the Georgia statute, which require as many as six doctors and the use of a hospital certified by the JCAH.

I do not read the Court's holding today as having the sweeping consequences attributed to it by the dissenting Justices; the dissenting views discount the reality that the vast majority of physicians observe the standards of their profession, and act only on the basis of carefully deliberated medical judgments relating to life and health. Plainly, the Court today rejects any claim that the Constitution requires abortion on demand.

MR. JUSTICE DOUGLAS, concurring.

While I join the opinion of the Court,[1] I add a few words.

The questions presented in the present cases go far beyond the issues of vagueness, which we considered in *United States v. Vuitch*, 402 U.S. 62. They involve the right of privacy, one aspect of which we considered in *Griswold v. Connecticut*, 381 U.S. 479, 484, when we held that various guarantees in the Bill of Rights create zones of privacy.[2]

The *Griswold* case involved a law forbidding the use of contraceptives. We held that law as applied to married people unconstitutional:

> We deal with a right of privacy older than the Bill of Rights — older than our political parties, older than our school system. Marriage is a coming together for better or for worse, hopefully enduring, and intimate to the degree of being sacred. *Id.*, 486.

The District Court in *Doe* held that *Griswold* and related cases "establish a constitutional right to privacy broad enough to encom-

---

[1] I disagree with the dismissal of Dr. Hallford's complaint in intervention in *Roe v. Wade*, because my disagreement with *Younger v. Harris*, 401 U. S. 37, revealed in my dissent in that case, still persists and extends to the progeny of that case.

[2] There is no mention of privacy in our Bill of Rights but our decisions have recognized it as one of the fundamental values those amendments were designed to protect. The fountainhead case is *Boyd v. United States*, 116 U. S. 616, holding that a federal statute which authorized a court in tax cases to require a taxpayer to produce his records or to concede the Government's allegations offended the Fourth and Fifth Amendments. Justice Bradley, for the Court, found that the measure unduly intruded into the "sanctity of a man's home and the privacies of life." *Id.*, 630. Prior to *Boyd*, in *Kilbourn v. Thompson*, 103 U. S. 168, 195, Mr. Justice Miller held for the Court that neither House of Congress "possesses the general power of making inquiry into the private affairs of the citizen." Of *Kilbourn* Mr. Justice Field later said, "This case will stand for all time as a bulwark against the invasion of the right of the citizen to protection in his private affairs against the unlimited scrutiny of investigation by a congressional committee." *In re Pacific Ry. Comm'n*, 32 F. 231, 253 (cited with approval in *Sinclair v. United States*, 279 U. S. 263, 293). Mr. Justice Harlan, also speaking for the Court, in *Interstate Commerce Comm'n v. Brimson*, 154 U. S. 447, 478, thought the same was true of administrative inquiries, saying the Constitution did not permit a "general power of making inquiry into the private affairs of the citizen." In a similar vein were *Harriman v. Interstate Commerce Comm'n*, 211 U. S. 407; *United States v. Louisville & Nashville R. R.*, 236 U. S. 318, 335; and *Federal Trade Comm'n v. American Tobacco Co.*, 264 U. S. 298.

pass the right of a woman to terminate an unwanted pregnancy in its early stages, by obtaining an abortion." 319 F. Supp., at 1054.

The Supreme Court of California expressed the same view in *People v. Belous*,[3] 71 Cal. 2d 954, 963.

The Ninth Amendment obviously does not create federally enforceable rights. It merely says, "The enumeration in the Constitution of certain rights shall not be construed to deny or disparage others retained by the people." But a catalogue of these rights includes customary, traditional, and time-honored rights, amenities, privileges, and immunities that come within the sweep of "the Blessings of Liberty" mentioned in the preamble to the Constitution. Many of them in my view come within the meaning of the term "liberty" as used in the Fourteenth Amendment.

First is the autonomous control over the development and expression on one's intellect, interests, tastes, and personality.

These are rights protected by the First Amendment and in my view they are absolute, permitting of no exceptions. See *Terminiello v. Chicago*, 337 U.S. 77; *Roth v. United States*, 354 U.S. 476, 508 (dissent); *Kingsley Pictures Corp. v. Regents*, 360 U.S. 684, 697 (concurring); *New York Times Co. v. Sullivan*, 376 U.S. 254, 293 (Black, J., concurring in which I joined). The Free Exercise Clause of the First Amendment is one facet of this constitutional right. The right to remain silent as respects one's own beliefs, *Watkins v. United States*, 354 U.S. 178, 196-199, is protected by the First and the Fifth. The First Amendment grants the privacy of first-class mail, *United States v. Van Leeuwen*, 397 U.S. 249, 253. All of these aspects of the right of privacy are "rights retained by the people" in the meaning of the Ninth Amendment.

Second is freedom of choice in the basic decisions of one's life respecting marriage, divorce, procreation, contraception, and the education and upbringing of children.

These rights, unlike those protected by the First Amendment, are subject to some control by the police-power. Thus the Fourth Amendment speaks only of "unreasonable searches and seizures" and of "probable cause." These rights are "fundamental" and we have

---

[3] The California abortion statute, held unconstitutional in the *Belous* case, made it a crime to perform or help perform an abortion "unless the same is necessary to preserve [the mother's] life." 71 Cal. 2d, at 959.

held that in order to support legislative action the statute must be narrowly and precisely drawn and that a "compelling state interest" must be shown in support of the limitation. *E.g., Kramer v. Union Free School Dist.*, 395 U.S. 621 (1969); *Shapiro v. Thompson*, 394 U.S. 618 (1969); *Carrington v. Rash*, 380 U.S. 89 (1965); *Sherbert v. Verner*, 374 U.S. 398 (1963); *NAACP v. Alabama ex rel. Patterson.*

The liberty to marry a person of one's own choosing, *Loving v. Virginia*, 388 U.S. 1; the right of procreation, *Skinner v. Oklahoma*, 316 U.S. 535; the liberty to direct the education of one's children, *Pierce v. Society of Sisters*, 268 U.S. 510, and the privacy of the marital relation, *Griswold v. Connecticut, supra*, are in this category.[4] Only last Term in *Eisenstadt v. Baird*, 405 U.S. 438, another contraceptive case, we expanded the concept of *Griswold* by saying:

> It is true that in Griswold the right of privacy in question inhered in the marital relationship. Yet the marital couple is not an independent entity with a mind and heart of its own, but an association of two individuals each with a separate intellectual and emotional makeup. If the right of privacy means anything, it is the right of the *individual*, married or single, to be free from un-

---

[4] My Brother STEWART, writing in the present cases, says that our decision in *Griswold* reintroduced substantive due process that had been rejected in *Ferguson v. Skrupa*, 372 U. S. 726. *Skrupa* involved legislation governing a business enterprise; and the Court in that case, as had Mr. Justice Holmes on earlier occasions, rejected the idea that "liberty" within the meaning of the Due Process Clause of the Fourteenth Amendment was a vessel to be filled with one's personal choices of values, whether drawn from the *laissez faire* school, from the socialistic school, or from the technocrats. *Griswold* involved legislation touching on the marital relation and involving the conviction of a licensed physician for giving married people information concerning contraception. There is nothing specific in the Bill of Rights that covers that item. Nor is there anything in the Bill of Rights that in terms protects the right of association or the privacy in one's association. Yet we found those rights in the periphery of the First Amendment. *NAACP v. Alabama*, 357 U. S. 449, 462. Other peripheral rights are the right to educate one's children as one chooses, *Pierce v. Society of Sisters*, 268 U. S. 510, and the right to study the German language, *Meyer v. Nebraska*, 262 U. S. 390. These decisions, with all respect, have nothing to do with substantive due process. One may think they are not peripheral rights to other rights that are expressed in the Bill of Rights. But that is not enough to bring into play the protection of substantive due process.

There are of course those who have believed that the reach of due process in the Fourteenth Amendment included all of the Bill of Rights but went further. Such was the view of Mr. Justice Murphy and Mr. Justice Rutledge. See *Adamson v. California*, 332 U. S. 46, 123, 124 (dissenting). Perhaps they were right; but it is a bridge that neither I nor those who joined the Court opinion in *Griswold* crossed.

warranted government intrusion into matters so fundamentally affecting a person as the decision whether to bear or beget a child.

This right of privacy was called by Mr. Justice Brandeis the right "to be let alone." *Olmstead v. United States*, 277 U.S. 438, 478. That right includes the privilege of an individual to plan his own affairs, for, "outside of areas of plainly harmful conduct, every American is left to shape his own life as he thinks best, do what he pleases, go where he pleases." *Kent v. Dulles*, 357 U.S. 116, 126.

Third is the freedom to care for one's health and person, freedom from bodily restraint or compulsion, freedom to walk, stroll, or loaf.

These rights, though fundamental, are likewise subject to regulation on a showing of "compelling state interest." We stated in *Papachristou v. City of Jacksonville*, 405 U.S. 156, 164, that walking, strolling, and wandering "are historically part of the amenities of life as we have known them." As stated in *Jacobson v. Massachusetts*, 197 U.S. 11, 29:

> There is, of course, a sphere within which the individual may assert the supremacy of his own will and rightfully dispute the authority of any human government, especially of any free government existing under a written constitution, to interfere with the exercise of that will.

In *Union Pac. Ry. Co. v. Botsford*, 141 U.S. 250, 252, the Court said,

> The inviolability of the person is as much invaded by a compulsory stripping and exposure as by a blow.

In *Terry v. Ohio*, 392 U.S. 1, 8-9, the Court in speaking of the Fourth Amendment stated

> This inestimable right of personal security belongs as much to the citizen on the streets of our cities as to the Governor closeted in his study to dispose of his secret affairs.

Katz v. United States, 389 U.S. 347, 350, emphasizes that the Fourth Amendment

> "protects individual privacy against certain kinds of governmental intrusion."

In *Meyer v. Nebraska*, 262 U.S. 390, 399, the Court said:

> Without doubt, it [liberty] denotes not merely freedom from bodily restraint but also the right of the individual to contract, to

engage in any of the common occupations of life, to acquire useful knowledge, to marry, establish a home and bring up children, to worship God according to the dictates of his own conscience, and generally to enjoy those privileges long recognized at common law as essential to the orderly pursuit of happiness by free men.

The Georgia statute is at war with the clear message of these cases — that a woman is free to make the basic decision whether to bear an unwanted child. Elaborate argument is hardly necessary to demonstrate that childbirth may deprive a woman of her preferred life style and force upon her a radically different and undesired future. For example, rejected applicants under the Georgia statute are required to endure the discomforts of pregnancy; to incur the pain, higher mortality rate, and aftereffects of childbirth; to abandon educational plans; to sustain loss of income; to forgo the satisfactions of careers; to tax further mental and physical health in providing childcare; and, in some cases, to bear the lifelong stigma of unwed motherhood, a badge which may haunt, if not deter, later legitimate family relationships.

Such a holding is, however, only the beginning of the problem. The State has interests to protect. Vaccinations to prevent epidemics are one example, as *Jacobson* holds. The Court held that compulsory sterilization of imbeciles afflicted with hereditary forms of insanity or imbecility is another. *Buck v. Bell*, 274 U.S. 200. Abortion affects another. While childbirth endangers the lives of some women, voluntary abortion at any time and place regardless of medical standards would impinge on a rightful concern of society. The woman's health is part of that concern; as is the life of the fetus after quickening. These concerns justify the State in treating the procedure as a medical one.

One difficulty is that this statute as construed and applied apparently does not give full sweep to the "psychological as well as physical well-being" of women patients which saved the concept "health" from being void for vagueness in *United States v. Vuitch*, *supra*, at 72. But apart from that, Georgia's enactment has a constitutional infirmity because, as stated by the District Court, it "limits the number of reasons for which an abortion may be sought." I agree with the holding of the District Court, "This the State may not do, because such action unduly restricts a decision sheltered by the Constitutional right to privacy." 319 F. Supp., at 1056.

The vicissitudes of life produce pregnancies which may be unwanted, or which may impair "health" in the broad *Vuitch* sense of the term, or which may imperil the life of the mother, or which in the full setting of the case may create such suffering, dislocations, misery, or tragedy as to make an early abortion the only civilized step to take. These hardships may be properly embraced in the "health" factor of the mother as appraised by a person of insight. Or they may be part of a broader medical judgment based on what is "appropriate" in a given case, though perhaps not "necessary" in a strict sense.

The "liberty" of the mother, though rooted as it is in the Constitution, may be qualified by the State for the reasons we have stated. But where fundamental personal rights and liberties are involved, the corrective legislation must be "narrowly drawn to prevent the supposed evil," *Cantwell v. Connecticut*, 310 U.S. 296, 307, and not be dealt with in an "unlimited and indiscriminate" manner. *Shelton v. Tucker*, 364 U.S. 479, 490. And see *Talley v. California*, 362 U.S. 60. Unless regulatory measures are so confined and are addressed to the specific areas of compelling legislative concern, the police power would become the great leveller of constitutional rights and liberties.

There is no doubt that the State may require abortions to be performed by qualified medical personnel. The legitimate objective of preserving the mother's health clearly supports such laws. Their impact upon the woman's privacy is minimal. But the Georgia statute outlaws virtually all such operations — even in the earliest stages of pregnancy. In light of modern medical evidence suggesting that an early abortion is safer healthwise than childbirth itself,[5] it cannot be seriously urged that so comprehensive a ban is aimed at protecting the woman's health. Rather, this expansive pro-

---

[5] Many studies show that it is safer for a woman to have a medically induced abortion than to bear a child. In the first 11 months of operation of the New York abortion law, the mortality rate associated with such operations was six per 100,000 operations. Abortion Mortality, 20 Morbidity and Mortality 208, 209 (1971) (U. S. Department of Health, Education, and Welfare, Public Health Service). On the other hand, the maternal mortality rate associated with childbirths other than abortions was 18 per 100,000 live births. Tietze, Mortality with Contraception and Induced Abortion, 45 Studies in Family Planning 6 (1969). See also C. Tietze & H. Lehfeldt, Legal Abortion in Eastern Europe 175 J. A. M. A. 1149, 1152 (1961); V. Kolblova, Legal Abortion in Czechoslovakia, 196; J. A. M. A. 371 (1966); Mehland, Combating Illegal Abortion in the Socialist Countries of Europe, 13 World Med. J. 84 (1966).

scription of all abortions along the temporal spectrum can rest only on a public goal of preserving both embryonic and fetal life.

The present statute has struck the balance between the woman and the State's interests wholly in favor of the latter. I am not prepared to hold that a State may equate, as Georgia has done, all phases of maturation preceding birth. We held in *Griswold* that the States may not preclude spouses from attempting to avoid the joinder of sperm and egg. If this is true, it is difficult to perceive any overriding public necessity which might attach precisely at the moment of conception. As Mr. Justice Clark has said:[6]

> To say that life is present at conception is to give recognition to the potential, rather than the actual. The unfertilized egg has life, and if fertilized, it takes on human proportions. But the law deals in reality, not obscurity — the known rather than the unknown. When sperm meets egg, life may eventually form, but quite often it does not. The law does not deal in speculation. The phenomenon of life takes time to develop, and until it is actually present, it cannot be destroyed. Its interruption prior to formation would hardly be homicide, and as we have seen, society does not regard it as such. The rites of Baptism are not performed and death certificates are not required when a miscarriage occurs. No prosecutor has ever returned a murder indictment charging the taking of the life of a fetus.[7] This would not be the case if the fetus constituted human life.

In summary, the enactment is overbroad. It is not closely correlated to the aim of preserving pre-natal life. In fact, it permits its destruction in several cases, including pregnancies resulting from sex acts in which unmarried females are below the statutory age of consent. At the same time, however, the measure broadly proscribes aborting other pregnancies which may cause severe mental disorders. Additionally, the statute is overbroad because it equates the value of embryonic life immediately after conception with the worth of life immediately before birth.

---

[6] Religion, Morality and Abortion: A Constitutional Appraisal, 2 Loy. U. (L. A.) L. Rev. 1, 10 (1969).

[7] In *Keeler v. Superior Court*, 2 Cal. 3d 619, 470 P. 2d 617, the California Supreme Court held in 1970 that the California murder statute did not cover the killing of an unborn fetus, even though the fetus be "viable" and that it was beyond judicial power to extend the statute to the killing of an unborn. It held that the child must be "born alive before a charge of homicide can be sustained." 2 Cal. 3d, at 639.

III

Under the Georgia Act the mother's physician is not the sole judge as to whether the abortion should be performed. Two other licensed physicians must concur in his judgment.[8] Moreover, the abortion must be performed in a licensed hospital;[9] and the abortion must be approved in advance by a committee of the medical staff of that hospital.[10]

Physicians, who speak to us in *Doe* through an *amicus* brief, complain of the Georgia Act's interference with their practice of their profession.

The right of privacy has no more conspicuous place than in the physician-patient relationship, unless it be in the priest-penitent relation.

It is one thing for a patient to agree that her physician may consult with another physician about her case. It is quite a different matter for the State compulsorily to impose on that physician-patient relationship another layer or, as in this case, still a third layer of physicians. The right of privacy — the right to care for one's health and person and to seek out a physician of one's own choice protected by the Fourteenth Amendment — becomes only a matter of theory not a reality, when a multiple physician approval system is mandated by the State.

The State licenses a physician. If he is derelict or faithless, the procedures available to punish him or to deprive him of his license are well known. He is entitled to procedural due process before professional disciplinary sanctions may be imposed. See *In re Ruffalo*, 390 U.S. 544. Crucial here, however, is state-imposed control over the medical decision whether pregnancy should be interrupted. The good-faith decision of the patient's chosen physician is overridden and the final decision passed on to others in whose selection the patient has no part. This is a total destruction of the right of privacy between physician and patient and the intimacy of relation which that entails.

---

[8] See § 26-1202 (b) (3).

[9] See § 26-1202 (b) (4).

[10] Section 26-1202 (b) (5).

The right to seek advice on one's health and the right to place his reliance on the physician of his choice are basic to Fourteenth Amendment values. We deal with fundamental rights and liberties, which, as already noted, can be contained or controlled only by discretely drawn legislation that preserves the "liberty" and regulates only those phases of the problem of compelling legislative concern. The imposition by the State of group controls over the physician-patient relation is not made on any medical procedure apart from abortion, no matter how dangerous the medical step may be. The oversight imposed on the physician and patient in abortion cases denies them their "liberty," *viz.*, their right of privacy, without any compelling, discernible state interest.

Georgia has constitutional warrant in treating abortion as a medical problem. To protect the woman's right of privacy, however, the control must be through the physician of her choice and the standards set for his performance.

The protection of the fetus when it has acquired life is a legitimate concern of the State. Georgia's law makes no rational, discernible decision on that score.[11] For under the Act the developmental stage of the fetus is irrelevant when pregnancy is the result of rape or when the fetus will very likely be born with a permanent defect or when a continuation of the pregnancy will endanger the life of the mother or permanently injure her health. When life is present is a question we do not try to resolve. While basically a question for medical experts, as stated by Mr. Justice Clark,[12] it is, of course, caught up in matters of religion and morality.

In short, I agree with the Court that endangering the life of the woman or seriously and permanently injuring her health are standards too narrow for the right of privacy that are at stake.

I also agree that the superstructure of medical supervision which Georgia has erected violates the patient's right of privacy inherent in her choice of her own physician.

---

[11] See Rochat, Tyler, and Schoenbucher, An Epidemiological Analysis of Abortion in Georgia, 61 Am. J. of Public Health 541 (1971).

[12] Religion, Morality and Abortion: A Constitutional Appraisal, 2 Loy. U. (L. A.) L. Rev. 1, 10 (1969).

MR. JUSTICE WHITE, with whom
MR. JUSTICE REHNQUIST joins, dissenting.

At the heart of the controversy in these cases are those recurring pregnancies that pose no danger whatsoever to the life or health of the mother but are nevertheless unwanted for any one or more of a variety of reasons — convenience, family planning, economics, dislike of children, the embarrassment of illegitimacy, etc. The common claim before us is that for any one of such reasons, or for no reason at all, and without asserting or claiming any threat to life or health, any woman is entitled to an abortion at her request if she is able to find a medical advisor willing to undertake the procedure.

The Court for the most part sustains this position: During the period prior to the time the fetus becomes viable, the Constitution of the United States values the convenience, whim or caprice of the putative mother more than the life or potential life of the fetus; the Constitution, therefore, guarantees the right to an abortion as against any state law or policy seeking to protect the fetus from an abortion not prompted by more compelling reasons of the mother.

With all due respect, I dissent. I find nothing in the language or history of the Constitution to support the Court's judgment. The Court simply fashions and announces a new constitutional right for pregnant mothers and, with scarcely any reason or authority for its action, invests that right with sufficient substance to override most existing state abortion statutes. The upshot is that the people and the legislatures of the 50 States are constitutionally disentitled to weigh the relative importance of the continued existence and development of the fetus on the one hand against a spectrum of possible impacts on the mother on the other hand. As an exercise of raw judicial power, the Court perhaps has authority to do what it does today; but in my view its judgment is an improvident and extravagant exercise of the power of judicial review which the Constitution extends to this Court.

The Court apparently values the convenience of the pregnant mother more than the continued existence and development of the life or potential life which she carries. Whether or not I might agree with that marshalling of values, I can in no event join the Court's judgment because I find no constitutional warrant for imposing such an order of priorities on the people and legislatures of the States.

In a sensitive area such as this, involving as it does issues over which reasonable men may easily and heatedly differ, I cannot accept the Court's exercise of its clear power of choice by interposing a constitutional barrier to state efforts to protect human life and by investing mothers and doctors with the constitutionally protected right to exterminate it. This issue, for the most part, should be left with the people and to the political processes the people have devised to govern their affairs.

It is my view, therefore, that the Texas statute is not constitutionally infirm because it denies abortions to those who seek to serve only their convenience rather than to protect their life or health. Nor is this plaintiff, who claims no threat to her mental or physical health, entitled to assert the possible rights of those women whose pregnancy assertedly implicates their health. This, together with *United States v. Vuitch*, 402 U.S. 62 (1971), dictates reversal of the judgment of the District Court.

Likewise, because Georgia may constitutionally forbid abortions to putative mothers who, like the plaintiff in this case, do not fall within the reach of § 26-1202(a) of its criminal code, I have no occasion, and the District Court had none, to consider the constitutionality of the procedural requirements of the Georgia statute as applied to those pregnancies posing substantial hazards to either life or health. I would reverse the judgment of the District Court in the Georgia case.

No. 70-40

MR. JUSTICE REHNQUIST, dissenting.

The holding in *Roe v. Wade*, *ante*, that state abortion laws can withstand constitutional scrutiny only if the States can demonstrate a compelling state interest apparently compels the Court's close scrutiny of the various provisions in Georgia's abortion statute. Since, as indicated by my dissent in *Wade*, I view the compelling state interest standard as an inappropriate measure of the constitutionality of state abortion laws, I respectfully dissent from the majority's holding.

LIST OF
CONTRIBUTORS

Daniel Callahan
Philosopher with the Institute of Society, Ethics and the Life Sciences

Congressman Robert F. Drinan, S.J.
Fourth District of Massachusetts

Stephen Fleck, M.D.
Professor of Psychiatry at the Yale University School of Medicine

B. James George, Jr.
Professor of Law at Wayne State University Law School and the Director of the Center for the Administration of Criminal Justice

Alan F. Guttmacher, M.D.
Professor Emeritus of Obstetrics and Gynecology at the Mount Sinai Medical School and the National President of Planned Parenthood-World Population

Robert E. Hall, M.D.
Professor of Obstetrics and Gynecology at the College of Physicians and Surgeons of Columbia University

Rabbi Dr. Immanuel Jakobovits
Chief Rabbi of the British Empire

M. Neil Macintyre
Professor of Anatomy at the Case Western Reserve School of Medicine

Gerald A. Messerman
Practicing lawyer in Cleveland, Ohio

Kenneth R. Niswander, M.D.
Professor of Obstetrics and Gynecology and Chairman of the Department at the School of Medicine at the University of California, Davis

Harriet F. Pilpel
Practicing attorney in New York City

Richard A. Schwartz, M.D.
Practicing psychiatrist on the staff of the Cleveland Clinic

Ruth J. Zuckerman
Assistant Professor of Law at Rutgers Law School